Contexts of Adult Education
Canadian Perspectives

Contexts of Adult Education

Canadian Perspectives

Edited by:

Tara J. Fenwick
University of Alberta

Tom Nesbit
Simon Fraser University

Bruce Spencer
Athabasca University

THOMPSON EDUCATIONAL PUBLISHING, INC.
Toronto

Information on how to obtain copies of this book is available at:

Website: http://www.thompsonbooks.com
E-mail: publisher@thompsonbooks.com
Telephone: (416) 766–2763
Fax: (416) 766–0398

Library and Archives Canada Cataloguing in Publication

Contexts of adult education : Canadian perspectives /
edited by Tara Fenwick, Tom Nesbit, Bruce Spencer.

Includes bibliographical references and index.
ISBN-13: 978-1-55077-160-2
ISBN-10: 1-55077-160-4

1. Adult education—Canada. I. Fenwick, Tara J.
II. Spencer, Bruce III. Nesbit, Tom, 1948-

LC5254.C663 2006   374'.971   C2006-902137-6

Cover design: Margaret Anderson and Tibor Choleva.

Every reasonable effort has been made to acquire permission for
copyrighted materials used in this book and to acknowledge such
permissions accurately. Any errors or omissions called to the publisher's
attention will be corrected in future printings. We acknowledge the
support of the Government of Canada through the Book Publishing
Industry Development Program for our publishing activities.

Printed in Canada. 1 2 3 4 5 6   09 08 07 06

Table of Contents

Contributors	7
Acknowledgments	11
Introduction by Tom Nesbit	13

PART 1. CONTEXTS IN TRANSITION

1. Intimations of a Just Learning Society: From the United Farmers of Alberta to Henson's Provincial Plan in Nova Scotia — 24
Michael R. Welton

2. Histories of Aboriginal Adult Education in Canada — 36
Wendy E. Burton and Gwen Point

3. Building Black Identity and Community — 49
Jennifer Kelly

4. Women and Adult Education in Canadian Society — 58
Nancy Taber and Patricia A. Gouthro

5. Adult Citizenship Education: An Overview of the Field — 68
Daniel Schugurensky

6. Cross-Cultural Teaching and Research in Adult Education — 81
Susan M. Brigham and Patricia A. Gouthro

PART 2. PHILOSOPHICAL AND CRITICAL CONTEXTS

7. Challenging Social Philosophobia — 92
Elizabeth A. Lange

8. Postfoundationalism in Adult Education — 105
Leona M. English

9. The Critical Legacy: Adult Education Against the Claims of Capital — 118
Michael Collins

10. Critical Adult Education: Engaging the Social in Theory and Practice — 128
André P. Grace

11. Frameworks for Synthesis of the Field of Adult Learning Theory — 140
Peter Sawchuk

12. A Way of Seeing: Transformation for a New Century — 153
Sue M. Scott

PART 3. CONTEXTS OF WORK AND ECONOMY

13. Human Capital and the Knowledge Economy — 164
Paul Bouchard

14. The Political Economy of Adult Learning in Canada — 173
Kjell Rubenson and Judith Walker

15. Work, Learning, and Adult Education in Canada — 187
Tara J. Fenwick

16. Adult Education in the Changing Context of Immigration:
New Challenges in a New Era   198
Shibao Guo

17. Labour Education   208
Bruce Spencer and Jeffery Taylor

18. Adult Education and Health: Will Words Get in the Way?   218
Donna M. Chovanec and Karen M. Foss
Critical Health Literacy in Action at the Community Level

PART 4. CONTEXTS OF COMMUNITY AND SOCIAL MOVEMENTS

19. Social Movement Learning: Theorizing a Canadian Tradition   230
Budd L. Hall

20. Popular Education and Canadian Engagements with Social
Movement Praxis in the South   239
Dip Kapoor

21. Environmental Adult Education in Canada   250
Darlene E. Clover

22. Towards Celebration through Education: Queer Canadian Adult
Education   260
John P. Egan and Anthony J. Flavell

23. Mothers as Popular Educators: Love Lives in Social Action   270
Dorothy A. Lander

24. Adult Education and the Arts   281
Shauna Butterwick and Jane Dawson

PART 5. CONTEXTS OF PRACTICE

25. Training of Adult Educators in Quebec   292
Mohamed Hrimech and Nicole A. Tremblay

26. Not Waving but Drowning: Canadian University Extension for
Social Change Revisited   298
Denis J. Haughey

27. Distance Education Online: A Forum for Adult Education?   307
Dianne Conrad and Bruce Spencer

28. Coming to Terms with Prior Learning Assessment   316
Geoff Peruniak and Rick Powell

29. Towards a Canadian Research Culture in Adult Literacy Learning   326
Maurice Taylor and Adrian Blunt

30. What Does It Mean to Be a "Professional"? The Challenges of
Professionalization for Adult Literacy and Basic Education   336
B. Allan Quigley

31. Adult Education Without Borders   347
Shahrzad Mojab

Subject Index   357
Name Index   363

Contributors

- **Adrian Blunt** retired in 2005 as Professor of Adult and Continuing Education at the University of Saskatchewan. Today he is an Adjunct Professor of Adult Education at the University of Victoria and actively working on adult literacy and food security projects.

- **Paul Bouchard** is Associate Professor of Adult Education at Concordia University, Montreal. His published works are in the areas of autonomous adult learning, education policy and education for development. His interests have led him to work at various international sites.

- **Susan M. Brigham** is an Assistant Professor in Graduate Studies in Lifelong Learning, Mount Saint Vincent University, Nova Scotia. Her main research centers on issues of adult learning and education, particularly with regard to women's learning and educational experiences in Canadian and international contexts.

- **Wendy E. Burton** is a faculty member in Adult Education, University College of the Fraser Valley. Her teaching interests are in diversity, Aboriginal adult education, education for social change, and educational technologies. Her discipline is feminist philosophy, especially epistemology and ethics.

- **Shauna Butterwick** is an Associate Professor in the Department of Educational Studies, University of British Columbia, and she specializes in adult education. Her research interests include women's learning, policy analysis, access to adult basic education, life-skills programs, learning in social movements, and arts-based inquiry.

- **Donna M. Chovanec** is an Assistant Professor in Educational Policy Studies, University of Alberta. She has experience as a social worker, adult educator and researcher in health and social services. Her research interests include learning in social movements and women who use substances.

- **Darlene E. Clover** is an Assistant Professor in the Faculty of Education, Leadership Studies, University of Victoria, British Columbia. Her current and recent research and activism focuses on socio-environmental adult education, community and cultural leadership, and women's collective arts/crafts practices.

- **Michael Collins** is a Professor of Adult and Continuing Education at the University of Saskatchewan. A former Chair of the Adult Education Research Commission (AERC), he has experience as an adult educator and schoolteacher in the UK, Canada and the US.

- **Dianne Conrad** is the Director of the Centre for Learning Accreditation at Athabasca University. Her research focuses on the relationship of community to online learning and on online learning as a social and educational force.

- **Jane Dawson** is an Associate Professor of Adult Education, St. Francis Xavier University. Her areas of research interest include qualitative research and arts-based inquiry, reflective practice, the poetics and politics of lifelong learning, and the critical pedagogy of work.

- **John P. Egan** is a Research Fellow at the University of British Columbia. His research has included queer adult education, HIV/AIDS prevention, and health discourses

- **Leona M. English** is an Associate Professor of Adult Education, St. Francis Xavier University, Antigonish, Nova Scotia. She is co-author of *Spirituality of Adult Education and Training* and editor of the *International Encyclopedia of Adult Education*.

- **Tara J. Fenwick** is an Associate Professor of Adult Education in the Department of Educational Studies, University of Alberta. Her research focuses on learning through work, with particular interest in changing conditions, identities, and knowledge politics in workplace education and learning.

- **Anthony J. Flavell** is an adult educator and instructional designer. He works for a non-governmental organization offering employment skills and supported education services in Vancouver, Canada.

- **Karen M. Foss** is a nurse practitioner with experience in patient and staff education. She is currently a doctoral candidate in Educational Policy Studies, University of Alberta. Her main research interests are well-being and learning in the workplace.

- **Patricia Gouthro** is an Associate Professor in Graduate Studies in Lifelong Learning, Mount Saint Vincent University, Nova Scotia. Her research interests include critical feminist theory, cross-cultural teaching, and women's learning experiences.

- **André P. Grace** is an Associate Professor in Educational Policy Studies, University of Alberta. His research and practice in inclusive education focus particularly on sexual-minority differences. He is also interested in the construction of lifelong learning as a critical social practice.

- **Shibao Guo** is an Assistant Professor in the Faculty of Education, University of Calgary. His areas of interest include adult education and community development, citizenship and immigration, multicultural and antiracist education, and comparative and international education.

- **Budd L. Hall** is the Dean, Faculty of Education, University of Victoria. His scholarly interests include social movement learning, community-based participatory research, adult education and globalization, poetry, learning, and social action.

- **Denis J. Haughey** is an Adjunct Professor in Educational Policy Studies, University of Alberta. He is interested in leadership and administration in universities. He has extensive University Extension experience and has practiced and taught adult and higher education at the universities of Victoria, Alberta, and Athabasca.

- **Mohamed Hrimech** is an Associate Professor of Adult Education at the Université de Montréal in the Départment de psychopédagogie et d'andragogie. His main research topic concerns learning strategies of self-directed adult learners.

- **Dip Kapoor** is an Assistant Professor, International Education and Foundations, McGill University, and volunteer international project officer for HELP, an Edmonton-based NGO. His research and teaching interests include education and development, popular education and social movements, and global/development education.

- **Jennifer Kelly** is an Associate Professor in Educational Policy Studies, University of Alberta. She is author of *Under the Gaze: Learning to Be Black in White Society* and *Borrowed Identities* and is an activist within Edmonton's African Canadian community.

- **Dorothy A. Lander** is Associate Professor of Adult Education at St. Francis Xavier University, Antigonish, Nova Scotia. She teaches a graduate program delivered through distance education. Her research focuses on women as educators and learners in social movements.

- **Elizabeth A. Lange** is an Assistant Professor of Sociology at Concordia University College, Edmonton, Alberta. Her primary research interests are the sociology of adult education, transformative learning, and sustainability education. She has 25 years of experience as an educator and facilitator in community settings.

- **Shahrzad Mojab** is the Director of Women and Gender Studies Institute, University of Toronto. Her research includes critical and feminist pedagogy; immigrant women and skilling; and women, state, globalization, and citizenship. Her most recent co-edited book is *Violence in the Name of Honour* (with Nahla Abdo).

- **Tom Nesbit** is the Director of the Centre for Integrated and Credit Studies and Associate Dean of Continuing Studies, Simon Fraser University, Vancouver, British Columbia. His publications include *Class Concerns: Adult Education and Social Class*.

- **Geoff Peruniak** is an Associate Professor in Psychology and coordinator of a career development program at Athabasca University, Alberta. He has been an innovator in prior learning assessment for over 20 years.

- **Gwen Point** is currently a Doctoral Candidate in Education with research interests in Stó:l First Nation Education. She is an Instructor with the School of Social Work and Human Services and with the History Department at the University College of the Fraser Valley.

- **Rick Powell** has conducted institutional research at the Open University (UK), at the Lesotho Distance Teaching Centre, and for the past 20 years at Athabasca University, Alberta. His research interests include dropout in distance education and prior learning assessment.

- **B. Allan Quigley** is a Professor, St. Francis Xavier University, Antigonish, Nova Scotia. His main research interests are adult literacy, including the history of literacy, health literacy, professional development, literacy research-in-practice, and issues of learner attrition in literacy.

- **Kjell Rubenson** is a Professor in the Department of Educational Studies and Co-director of the Centre for Policy Studies in Higher Education and Training, University of British Columbia. His recent work has focused on the formation and outcomes of adult education in a comparative perspective.

- **Peter Sawchuk** teaches in Sociology and Equity Studies in Education and is cross-appointed to Industrial Relations at the University of Toronto. His research interests include Marxist activity theory; sociology of learning, work, and technology; and labour movement development.

- **Daniel Schugurensky** is an Associate Professor, Adult Education and Community Development, Ontario Institute for Studies in Education, University of Toronto (OISE/UT). His research interests encompass community development, popular education, citizenship learning, participatory democracy, and comparative education from a political economy approach.

- **Sue M. Scott** is a retired Professor in the Adult Education program at the University of Alberta. She co-edited *Learning for Life* with B. Spencer and A. Thomas. Her research of the interplay of the personal and social continues in the Edmonton non-formal adult education context.

- **Bruce Spencer** is a Professor at the Centre for Work and Community Studies, Athabasca University, Alberta. He is the author of *The Purposes of Adult Education* and the editor of the collections *Learning for Life* (with S. Scott and A. Thomas) and *Unions and Learning in a Global Economy*.

- **Nancy Taber** is an Assistant Professor in Graduate Studies in Lifelong Learning, Mount Saint Vincent University, Nova Scotia. Her research interests include feminist antimilitarist theory, gender socialization, and women, work, and learning.

- **Jeffery Taylor** is a Professor and coordinator of labour studies, Centre for Work and Community Studies, Athabasca University, Alberta. His publications include *Fashioning Farmers: Ideology, Agricultural Knowledge, and the Manitoba Farm Movement, 1890–1925*; and *Union Learning: Canadian Labour Education in the Twentieth Century*.

- **Maurice Taylor** is a Professor in the Faculty of Education, University of Ottawa, where he teaches and supervises graduate students in adult education. His main research interests lie in the areas of adult literacy learning, adult development, and workplace education.

- **Nicole A. Tremblay** is Professor Emeritus in adult education at the Université de Montréal, Départment de psychopédagogie et d'andragogie. In 2003 she published a book about self-directed learning: *L'autoformation pour apprendre autrement*.

- **Judith Walker** is a doctoral student in the Department of Educational Studies, University of British Columbia. Her doctoral work focuses on the impact of globalization on adult education practice.

- **Michael R. Welton** retired from Mount St. Vincent University in 2003 to live in the Comox Valley on Vancouver Island. He now teaches courses in Educational Studies at Athabasca University. His most recent book is *Designing the Just Learning Society: A Critical Inquiry*.

Acknowledgments

Compiling a book of readings such as this is a collective endeavour. We would like to thank our adult education colleagues across Canada who placed their trust in us and provided thoughtful advice and suggestions about topics and themes. We would also like to acknowledge their scholarly organization—the Canadian Association for the Study of Adult Education/l'Association Canadienne pour l'Étude de l'Éducation des Adultes [CASAE/ACÉÉA]—which had the good sense to hold a twenty-fifth anniversary at just the right time to provide the impetus for us to complete the work in a timely fashion.

Our respective universities—Athabasca University, Simon Fraser University and the University of Alberta—provided support in a variety of financial, logistical and technological ways. We wish to thank them and our colleagues for their tolerance as we sometimes borrowed time and energy from our routine university duties. We have also relied upon several people for editorial and design assistance and would especially like to acknowledge the stellar work of Lee Ellis, Linda Pasmore and Margaret Anderson. Thanks to them, the book is both more attractive and more comprehensible.

Finally, we wish to acknowledge our publisher, Keith Thompson, for his continued promotion of Canadian adult education literature. Our field is all the stronger for his efforts.

Introduction

Tom Nesbit

During the 2003 conference of the Canadian Association for the Study of Adult Education/l'Association Canadienne pour l'Étude de l'Éducation des Adultes (CASAE/ACÉÉA), two of us (Tara Fenwick and Tom Nesbit) fell into a conversation about the rapid changes in Canadian adult education and how difficult it was for our students to simultaneously gain a perspective on the breadth of our field, its historical development, and the pace at which it was changing. Despite the recent plethora of general introductions to the policies and practices of our field, we felt that none fully acknowledged the contribution of Canadian adult educators or Canada's unique participation in the international practice of adult education. During our conversation, we speculated about possibly updating *Learning for Life: Canadian Readings in Adult Education*, the excellent book co-edited by Sue Scott, Bruce Spencer, and Alan Thomas, which was sponsored by CASAE/ACÉÉA and published in 1998. In our view, producing a second edition of the book would allow us to document the emerging trends and issues that mark our field, showcase recent Canadian scholarship, and further delineate the distinct Canadian approach to adult education that is increasingly recognizable at the various international and North American conferences we attend. For example, at the joint AERC/ CASAE conference held at the University of Victoria in 2004, one of our American colleagues was overheard saying, "I don't know what it is with these Canadians; they're all so critical."

As CASAE/ACÉÉA celebrates its 25th anniversary in 2006, we thought that producing such a work in time for that year's conference would be a fitting tribute to our professional organization. We suggested this to the annual meeting of the Canadian Professors of Adult Education in 2004 and were met with an enthusiastic response. Ironically, and serendipitously, at that same meeting, Bruce Spencer reported that Keith Thompson, the publisher of *Learning for Life*, had approached him about reprinting the original edition. In no time at all, the three of us had agreed to take on the task of producing a second edition, keeping some of the original chapters, updating others, and commissioning new chapters for areas and concerns that we thought missing or underacknowledged.

Aware that our responsibilities as editors included representing the diversity of opinions about and approaches within adult education, we undertook some initial consultations. During the latter part of 2004, we polled the CASAE/ACÉÉA professoriate for their opinions of *Learning for Life* and asked them which chapters they and their students found most useful and interesting; which they would like to see kept, adapted, or abandoned; and which other areas they would like to see included in any second edition. We also solicited the opinions of the authors in *Learning for Life*, members of the CASAE/ACÉÉA email network, and others involved in the practice of Canadian adult education. These consultations produced an outline list of some 40-plus chapters, expressions of interest from 50 prospective authors, and a clear set of issues and themes that our academic and professional colleagues across Canada would like to see addressed in a second edition. Although gratified at the quantity and eagerness of the responses, we clearly had many more than would fit in the space that the publisher had allotted. So, after several discussions, we undertook to produce, not a second edition, but a separate and distinct book, one that would be distinct from, but still could be read in tandem with, *Learning for Life* and its companion texts. We then met several times at the University of Alberta and countless times over email to narrow down our list, discuss potential authors, and develop a coherent structure.

The authors we subsequently chose are all experienced Canadian adult education academics and practitioners. Given Canada's geographic and cultural diversity, we deliberately sought authors from each region of the country and attempted to balance both gender and background—a task that proved easier than it first seemed. In the end, all authors were chosen for their expertise, commitment, and capacity to provide a unique perspective. Most work in, or are affiliated with, Canadian universities where they research and teach courses about various aspects of adult education. We also deliberately sought authors across a range of experience: Some are our field's most respected and senior intellectuals, others more emergent researchers and scholars. We feel that our decision to produce a distinct book has been confirmed by our selection of authors: Of those in this book 11 also contributed to *Learning for Life* and 27 are new.

As will be clear, the sections and chapters that we have chosen seem to cover every conceivable significant area of Canadian adult education practice. Yet, in line with the advice we were given, we also sought to include chapters on such topics as Canada's involvement in the international practice of adult education, a summary of recent Canadian adult education research, and its thematic and methodological approaches. However, practical difficulties and author availability prevented their completion in time for publication. Also, our initial survey of responses to *Learning for Life* suggested that we should provide both an index of terms and names and a glossary that describes some key terms in greater detail. Readers will note that we have included the indexes, but not the glossary. It would be easy to claim that we were merely constrained by space. Although that is true, we were also aware that one of our colleagues, Leona English (2005), was simultaneously producing her comprehensive *International Encyclopedia of Adult Education*—a resource with which we would neither want nor hope to compete. We refer all readers to it for its masterful discussion of most major adult education concepts.

Finally, 18 months after our first discussions, we were able to contract with prospective authors and begin the long process of soliciting, drafting, and editing chapters. You are holding the result.

The Broad Context of Canadian Adult Education

We do not place ourselves among those who bemoan the current marginalization and declining relevance of adult education. Instead, we find it both vigorous and central, in Canada at least. Our views are based partly on personal experience, but also on a couple of recent and more systematic reports. First, a team from the Organisation of Economic Cooperation and Development (OECD) conducted a survey of adult learning in Canada in 2001. As their report (OECD, 2002) makes clear, almost 30 percent of Canadian adults participate in some form of education. The OECD review team was also impressed by many of the programs they visited. As they put it:

> Canada has many programs to be proud of, and many models in adult education that could provide inspiration both to other providers within Canada and to other countries. The sheer size of the country, the variations among provinces, and presence of both provincial and federal initiatives means that the country has a vast amount of experimentation and innovation. (p. 8)

This finding is also supported in the 2004 report of the Canadian delegation to the midterm review of the Fifth International Conference on Adult Education (CONFINTEA V; Canadian Commission for UNESCO, 2004), which documents Canada's rich tradition of adult education and learning—even though, as the commission acknowledged, this tradition is more frequently recognized by other nations than it is here at home.

Both the OECD (2002) and the Canadian Commission for UNESCO (2004) noted some aspects of Canada that made studying its provision of adult education particularly challenging. As the OECD reported:

> While much of the population is concentrated in cities along the southern border, considerable numbers of people live in relatively sparsely populated northern areas, making the provision of services difficult and making it hard to understand what services are available in far-flung regions of the country. The country has an enormous cultural diversity, with different ethnic and historical backgrounds among First Nations, Métis, French, Anglo-Saxon, and other immigrant populations from all over the world adding to the variety of values and perspectives. (p. 4)

The OECD and the Canadian Commission for UNESCO also identified three special problems in studying adult education in Canada: The uncertain relationship between the concepts of lifelong learning and adult education; a lack of clarity about what steps should be taken once the need for lifelong learning has been accepted; and the wide variety of forms that Canadian adult education can take. The latter two points are taken up later by chapters in the book, but we would like to briefly address the concern with terminology.

In Canada, as in other industrialized countries, lifelong learning is rapidly becoming a social and institutional reality. Concepts and terms such as *information society, knowledge-based economy, learning societies,* and *learning communities* feature prominently in educational and governmental policy discourses, and the importance and relevance of learning at every stage of human development is now becoming widely recognized. Also, it is commonly understood that K–12 education can only lay the ground for the learning and relearning that has to take place throughout people's lifetimes. In particular, educational sectors and institutions that have previously tended to marginalize adult and other so-called "nontraditional" learners are increasingly expected to provide a range of opportunities for lifelong learners.

The concern for developing lifelong learning is also acknowledged by Canadian governments. For example, the January 2001 Speech from the Throne (Government of Canada, 2002) recognized that building a skilled workforce requires a national effort:

> Countries that succeed in the 21st Century will be those with citizens who are creative, adaptable, and skilled. By providing opportunities for all Canadians to learn and to develop their skills and abilities, we can achieve our commitment to economic growth and prosperity and demonstrate our social values of inclusion and equality. (p. xx)

In recent government reports, the Advisory Committee for Online Learning (2001), Human Resources Development Canada (2002), and Industry Canada (2002) detailed the skills and learning challenges that Canada faces while simultaneously reinforcing the call for all Canadians to have access to post-secondary educational opportunities. Such reports acknowledge the broad needs of adult learners while linking those to a concern for a continuous system of learning development to support Canada's economic growth and improve the quality of life for those who live here. Repeatedly, the reports identify the positive contribution that adult education and lifelong learning can make to the development of an educated citizenry which will, in turn, benefit individuals, their communities, and Canada's national interests. One of Canada's greatest assets is the educational abilities of its residents, and improving them is a major governmental aspiration.

Adult education and lifelong learning are often regarded as ambiguous, contested, and overlapping concepts. Without wanting to delve too far into the nuances of terminology or our scepticism towards recent governmental approaches, we continue to prefer *adult education* and therefore use it in our title. For us, *lifelong learning,* although underscoring that people can and do learn throughout their lives, is too limiting. In general it is individually focused, acontextual, and adopted a little too readily by those who believe that education entails adherence to, rather than challenge of, social orthodoxies. In contrast, *adult education* is the more straightforward and inclusive term. It is commonly understood by the general public and, despite our separate interests, still serves to describe our work. We use the term broadly to cover all the approaches, processes, and activities having to do with the education of and learning by adults and the broad set of beliefs, aims, and strategies centred around the tenet that learning opportunities should be accessible to all, regardless of age and status. Such a term also underscores that in a rapidly changing world education should not be an isolated and singular phenomenon: Learning continues into and throughout one's adulthood and should be supported by a variety of educational activities. Finally, such a term also suggests that, because all adults' lives differ, learning and education are highly context specific. So, for us, adult education—broadly defined, diffuse, and multilocational—best describes the professional and practitioner commitment to Canada's long-term educational and societal development.

Why Contexts?

How then to make sense of and place order upon such a complex endeavour as the practice of adult education in Canada? To provide an overall structure to the book, we have adopted the notion of *contexts*. This allows us, organizationally at least, to encompass the three main and enduring traditions of Canadian adult education:

- a set of unyielding social purposes, informed by passion and outrage and rooted in a concern for the less-privileged;
- a systematic and sustained philosophical and critical analysis that develops the abilities to connect immediate, individual experiences with underlying societal structures; and
- a keen attention to the specific sites, locations, and practices where such purposes and analyses are made real in the lives of Canadians.

For us, the practice of adult education in Canada is not the manifestation of a set of abstract concepts, but one part of a broader and vital mission for "really useful knowledge" that helps create a more equitable world at individual, family, community, and societal levels.

We opted, therefore, somewhat arbitrarily, for an arrangement of five different *contexts* that we see as affecting the contemporary developments of Canadian adult education. These include transitional and historical contexts that shape current practice, the philosophical and critical contexts that underpin them, the socio-economic contexts by which they are informed, the community and social movements contexts in which they are located, and the contexts of practice that they reveal. Within each specific context, we have selected half a dozen chapters that exemplify and clarify its diversity and richness. Taken together, the chapters focus on several different levels: the theoretical, the socio-political, the institutional and organizational, the practical and applied, the interpersonal, the internal, and the psychological. Our goal has been to provide a broad and critically informed overview of Canadian adult education while also highlighting many of the current and emerging trends and issues. However, admittedly, our framework is partial, and structurally as well as conceptually driven. The approaches and practices of Canadian adult educators are certainly so interconnected that the links between individual chapters are manifold and the ideas of one clearly overlap with several others. Also, most chapters are both theoretically and practically informed and thus could quite easily be placed into one or more sections. However, in that we wished to ensure that the sections would be roughly equivalent in length, we arrived at the current structure. We beg the authors' and reader's indulgence for our idiosyncratic selection.

Which Contexts?

By way of introduction to the first section, Contexts in Transition, Michael Welton questions whether the current fashion for seeing learning as a response to social problems and concerns is at all new. For him, Canadian adult educators have always drawn upon a range of spiritual, moral, and intellectual resources to tackle contemporary issues. In reviewing several significant moments in Canadian adult education history, he shows how our forebears consciously sought to help people—especially the less-advantaged—to build a more stable, safe, and just society. The written history of Canadian adult education has tended to accentuate the activities of White men. The next three chapters focus on the significant contributions of groups whose participation is not as great nor as recognized. First, Canada was home to a great many people before it was colonized by White settlers. With that in mind, Wendy Burton and Gwen Point describe the history of First Nations and other Aboriginal peoples and their approaches to education. They document the paternalistic and often malevolent attempts by successive governments to assimilate Aboriginal peoples into Western culture, but they also detail the more recent reassertion of self-governance and reliance upon Aboriginal traditions, cultures, and ways of learning. Second, Jennifer Kelly examines how adult education has helped build Black community and identity using the notion of "communities of practice" and her experiences of adult education in Edmonton. Third, Nancy Tabor and Patricia Gouthro focus on the role of women in adult education. They argue that paying attention to women's experiences and viewpoints broadens the focus of traditional adult education research, theory, and practice. Also, by introducing a feminist analysis, they raise important questions about power, privilege, and inclusivity. Next, Daniel Schugurensky provides an overview of citizenship education for adults. He outlines the main rationales for and orientations of this growing area of adult education and presents some highlights of recent activities in Canada and abroad. Finally, Susan Brigham and Patricia Gouthro reveal how much adult education takes place in cross-cultural settings. They explore many of the issues that those who teach and research in such settings need to consider: technology, curriculum, assessment, positionality, subjectivity, and ethics. As they claim, in all of these areas respect for diversity and openness to alternative knowledge can enrich the learning opportunities for all involved.

The second section considers the philosophical and critical contexts of adult education. In our opinion, too few adult educators are encouraged to reflect on the *why* of their work or examine the theories that underpin their practice. In this way they can become fearful of philosophy or reluctant to philosophize. Challenging such "philosophobia" is the focus of Elizabeth Lange's chapter. In providing a brief overview of the dominant philosophical approaches in adult education, she encourages readers to develop a working philosophy of their own. Next, Leona English explores some of the more recent philosophical approaches: postmodernism, post-structuralism, and postcolonialism. Her chapter is designed to help readers think more carefully about such issues as power, identity, the subject, and discourse and how these issues relate to and play out in adult education. The next two chapters take this perspective a stage further. First, Michael Collins insists that adult educators develop a politically and critically engaged pedagogy. For him, such an approach is essential to challenge the neoliberal approaches to education that are so prevalent in Canada and abroad. Second, André Grace discusses critical theory and its educational complements, critical pedagogy and critical adult education. He outlines the history of these concepts and examines their role in legitimating and sanctioning particular educational approaches and activities. He concludes by considering how engagement in cultural action for social transforma-tion can better publicize alternative knowledge, drawing upon his experi-ences as coordinator of a group of young adults concerned with issues of sexual identity. The final two chapters in this section focus more specifi-cally on how philosophical and critical perspectives influence theories of and approaches to learning. First, Peter Sawchuk attempts to provide a framework for the synthesis of several recent learning theories. He iden-tifies a unique Canadian perspective in this work that involves interna-tionalism and limited insularity, a democratic impulse, and what he calls a "middle power" orientation that attempts to bridge the gap between the more individually and socially focused approaches to conceptualizing learning. Finally, Sue Scott adopts a more practical focus. She takes one of the more prominent features of recent theorizing about adult learning—the concept of transformation—and explores its relevance to change at both personal and social levels.

The third section examines the broad socio-economic context of Canadian adult education and the specific situations of work, health, and immigration. First, Paul Bouchard explains how human capital theory occupies the frontier between economics and learning. He explores the basis of human capital theory in how it helps explain the broad links between economics and social responsibility, the various relationships between such issues and work and employment, and, ultimately, their implications for adult educators. Next, Kjell Rubenson and Judith Walker examine how the recent political and economic paradigm of neoliberalism has transformed the conditions for and the practice of adult education in Canada. They argue that although federal government discourse promotes lifelong learning to meet the social needs of all Canadians, in reality, government policies on education and training are still based on raising individual competitiveness and human capital. The remaining chapters in this section examine how these ideas play out in specific contexts. First, Tara Fenwick examines the rapidly developing area of workplace learning. Acknowledging that workplaces are a significant site of adult learning, she provides a comprehensive summary of current approaches and themes and discusses their implications for practice and research. As author Shibao Guo claims, Canada is a country of immigrants: Almost a quarter of our adult population was born outside the country. This creates both massive challenges and opportunities for the practice of adult education, and Guo surveys the range of current approaches. He also questions several of the predominant practices, couching his critique in ideas concerning the legitimation of knowledge and the politics of difference. Next, Bruce Spencer and Jeff Taylor examine labour education. As they explain, the education and training provided by unions and other labour organizations is one of the most significant forms of adult education, yet it is not always acknowledged as such by adult educators. Spencer and Taylor review its historical development and current approaches and show how its predominantly collective goals and methods encourage social purpose adult education to challenge neoliberal orthodoxies. Finally, Donna Chovanec and Karen Foss explore the close links between education and health. They focus on the concept and approaches of health literacy and show how the common policies and practices of health education tend to be individually focused and deal with the results of health problems rather than the underlying structural conditions that give rise to them.

In the fourth section we explore the adult education that takes place in and around social movements and community groups and organisations. Budd Hall provides a clear conceptual introduction for readers to better examine such topics. For him, social movements derive much of their power from the learning and knowledge creation that they generate, although this is not always clearly recognized or made explicit. Drawing upon his deep knowledge of various Canadian and worldwide social movements, Hall provides a compelling case for further examining the educational aspects of social movement activity. Dip Kapoor's chapter also concerns the educational aspects of social movements—but focuses more closely on the role of popular education. He describes several coalitions between Canadian non-governmental organizations and Indigenous/ peasant groups in the South and reiterates the importance of such coalitions for countering hegemonic assumptions and practices. The rest of the chapters in this section concentrate on specific social movements. First, Darlene Clover explores those concerned with environmental and ecological issues. Adopting a critical perspective, she examines many of the root causes of current environmental concerns and situates them firmly as consequences of capitalist approaches to the natural world. She suggests that increasing our ecological knowledge and identity through education is essential for creating a more sustainable world. Next, John Egan and Anthony Flavell document the growing awareness of queer issues in Canadian society and within adult education. They offer a typology of the emergent themes and issues in this area and document educational attempts to challenge homophobia, heterosexism, and heteronormativity. For another author, Dorothy Lander, the popular educational aspects of many social movements are animated by a compassionate approach to life and learning that is frequently provided by women. Basing her chapter on three women popular educators, she focuses on their roles as leaders and educators and explores how the ideas and relationships of "compassionate love" can be seen as a major motivating force in their work and lives. Social movements and community groups often promote and represent their activities and concerns through various forms of artistic and cultural expressions. In the final chapter of this section, Shauna Butterwick and Jane Dawson explore the place of the arts in adult education. They describe a variety of well- and lesser-known examples from across Canada and show how movements and practices that engage the heart, mind, spirit, and body can engender a more holistic approach to learning and inquiry.

Our fifth and final section concerns the broad contexts of adult education practice. Two of these relate to the training of adult educators and recent developments in Quebec, a region about which English-speaking adult educators are relatively uninformed. Mohammed Hrimech and Nicole Tremblay examine how adult educators are trained in that province. They show the evolution of such training in universities and professional centres, consider the role of professional associations, discuss various approaches to professionalization and official accreditation, and conclude with some thoughts on various themes and emerging challenges. Denis Haughey also considers the role of universities, but focuses more specifically on their extension and outreach activities—a historically important aspect of Canadian adult education. Detailing how such practices traditionally have emphasized education for social change, he decries current approaches for the weight they place on skills development and economic advancement. He argues, in essence, that current approaches threaten to make university extension programs one more instrument of neoliberal social policy. Next, Diane Conrad and Bruce Spencer examine the growth in distance education and online learning in adult education. Documenting the movement away from a narrow focus on efficient "content delivery" towards modes marked by an increasing degree of learner control and flexibility, interactive communication, and group-oriented processes, they show how such changes contribute to a more socially relevant adult education practice. Next, Geoff Peruniak and Rick Powell address a recent phenomenon in the practice of adult education in formal settings—the rise of prior learning assessment (PLA). They examine the common definitions of PLA, discuss the major forces that shape it, and explore the perspectives of academic institutions and adult learners towards it. The final two chapters in this section deal with adult literacy and adult basic education—two of the most vital and significant areas of Canadian adult education. Maurice Taylor and Adrian Blunt provide an account of recent attempts to expand and strengthen adult literacy research capacity. They highlight the main factors that influence literacy research in Canada, the UK, and the US; describe current trends in Canadian literacy research; and discuss some factors likely to influence developments in this area. Finally, Allan Quigley surveys recent trends in adult literacy and adult basic education, concentrating on the expectations being placed on practitioners for increased accountability, certification, and professionalization. Rejecting an approach based on such external deficit criteria, he argues that the field is better advanced by a focus on developing the strengths of existing practices, beliefs, skills, and knowledge.

By way of a conclusion, our final chapter reflects on the state of adult education in Canada on the occasion of the 25th anniversary of CASAE/ ACÉÉA. We are delighted that the current co-president, Shahrzad Mojab, has provided such a summary. Her chapter reviews the key themes and ideas raised in the previous 30 chapters and places them in the contexts of the worldwide movements for adult education and democratic social change.

Tom Nesbit, *on behalf of the Editors*

January 2006

References

Advisory Committee for Online Learning. (2001). *The e-learning e-volution in colleges and universities: A pan-Canadian challenge*. Ottawa, ON: Industry Canada.

Canadian Commission for UNESCO. (2004). *Report of the Canadian delegation on the mid-term review of the Fifth International Conference on Adult Education (CONFINTEA V)*. Ottawa, ON: Author.

English, L. M. (Ed.). (2005). *International encyclopedia of adult education*. New York: Palgrave Macmillan.

Government of Canada. (2002). *Speech from the Throne to open the 2nd session of the Thirty-Seventh Parliament of Canada*. Retrieved January 6, 2006, from http://www.pco-bcp.gc.ca/sft-ddt/ vnav/06_2_e.htm

Human Resources Development Canada. (2002). *Knowledge matters: Skills and learning for Canadians*. Ottawa, ON: Author.

Industry Canada. (2002). *Achieving excellence: Investing in people, knowledge, and opportunity*. Ottawa, ON: Author.

Organisation of Economic Cooperation and Development. (2002). *Thematic review on adult learning: Canada*. Paris: Author.

Scott, S. M., Spencer, B., and Thomas, A. M. (Eds.). (1998). *Learning for life: Canadian readings in adult education*. Toronto, ON: Thompson Educational.

Part 1

CONTEXTS IN TRANSITION

1

Intimations of a Just Learning Society: From the United Farmers of Alberta to Henson's Provincial Plan in Nova Scotia

Michael R. Welton

Today the discourse of the learning society, the learning economy, the learning organization, and lifelong learning permeates discussions in North America, Europe, and other parts of the globe. According to some educational visionaries and policy gurus, we have arrived in the Learning Age, and this is all very good and shiny and new. But it is deeply misleading for contemporary policy makers and educators to imagine that thinking about the relationship between adult learning and the domains of work, civil society, state, and person, or the relationship between adult learning and the great challenges posed by the age, is peculiar to our Information Age. For the purposes of this chapter, I want to examine how Canadian adult educators responded to the multiple crises of their society in the agonizing period from 1900 to the end of World War II. Faced with the disintegration of the optimistic culture of Europe, and the utter failure of reason or conservative traditionalism to stem the tide of evil that swept over Europe like the plague, Canadian adult educators struggled into the depths of their spiritual, moral, and intellectual resources to learn in the face of catastrophe.

Refusing to abandon the ideal of enlightenment and empowerment—perhaps hoping against hope—Canadian adult educators opted to try to create the social and pedagogical forms to develop human potential. In a world ruined by madness, greed, and delusion, adult educators could not rely on the elite of the world to organize even a minimally just world, let alone imagine that ordinary people had the mental capacity and imagination to master their life situations. The elite had been discredited, their right to rule as shattered as the men in the mud-soaked and rat-infested trenches of World War I. The pre-eminent social movements of the early twentieth century—labour, cooperative, farm, women—created learning infrastructures to counter the desolation of mediocre common schools and nothing much for adult learners. This vision of a just learning society was embodied primarily in the creative innovations of men and women in the various movements. But they also wrote about their visions and experiences and enactments. Indeed, the writings of the movement activists are the first texts that we, as Canadian adult educators, have at our disposal. However, one has to dig in the old newspapers and journals of the day to find them. Shortly after World War I ended, our first publicly accessible texts appeared: Grant's (1919) seminal essay "The Education of the Working-man," Tompkins' (1921) self-published pamphlet, *Knowledge for the People*, and Fitzpatrick's (1923) *The University in Overalls*. Moses Coady's (1939) *Masters of Their Own Destiny* appeared at the Antigonish Movement's height, the Special Committee on Education for Reconstruction's (1943) "Report of the Proceedings of a Special Program Committee of the Canadian Association for Adult Education," Thomson's (1944) "Adult Education Theory and Policy," and Henson's (1946) "Provincial Support of Adult Education in Nova Scotia: A Report by Guy Henson." These plain texts offer us several signposts on the road to building the just learning society.

Masters of Their Own Destiny: Metaphor for the Times

Masters of Their Own Destiny (Coady, 1939), our much-beloved and cele-brated text, reflected the personal journey of Moses Coady, who suffered a heart attack while assembling it. It also reflected, I believe, the collective journeys of many ordinary Canadians on farms, at sea, and in factories and households who were becoming enlightened about the causes of their suffering and were learning how to gain power and act to change their life situations in the early twentieth century. On the prairies the literature of the agrarian protest movements such as the United Farmers of Alberta (UFA) and the Saskatchewan Grain Growers Association (SGGA) was replete with statements stressing the need to build an educative democracy. Farm men and women learned democracy by actively participating in meetings where they could learn to speak and act confidently. The farm local was a key educative form. But the movement culture was also sustained as an oppositional learning site through lectures, study clubs, speakers' networks, farm newspapers, and the annual convention. Through these social learning processes, individuals combined their intelligence. The early twentieth century agrarian movements enacted a form of a just learning society. For its part, the University of Saskatchewan Extension Department oriented itself primarily to enhancing the productive process on the farms, using dialogical methods brilliantly. Its counterpart in Alberta, equally brilliant, carried cultural vibrancy into the farm communities.

The early twentieth century also saw an explosion of learning amongst women on farms and in urban centres. Women created a host of voluntary associations, from women's institutes to peace organizations. They began to challenge their consignment to the domestic sphere. Women were no longer natural-born housekeepers. Although women did use *housekeeper* or *homemaker* as a metaphor for fundamental community-building and community-sustaining activities, they were not willing to be second-class citizens. In Violet McNaughton's (as cited in Steer, 1992) powerful words, women had a right to make a living, live a life, and express themselves. Immensely energetic, these visionary women poured out an endless stream of writings in prairie newspapers and fought for women's rights to learn to master their own destinies (see also Taylor, 2000). Women's learning crystallized around their personal suffering (lack of help in the household, overwork, poor medical care) and their struggle for recognition as human beings equal to men.

Industrial workers, as Coady (1939) and many early to mid-twentieth century adult educators knew only too well, faced daunting challenges from ruthless bosses, from the coal mines of Vancouver Island to the pits of Cape Breton. They had to face the likes of coal baron James Dunsmuir, who appeared before a federal royal commission in 1903 and told the commissioners that he objected to all unions. When asked, "Did it ever occur to you that wealth carried some corresponding obligations with it—the possession of large riches and lands?" he replied, "No sir, from my standpoint, it doesn't" (as cited in Stonebanks, 2004, p. 31). The miners who battled Dunsmuir and his ilk in the early twentieth century knew that they had been unfairly treated, that there had been a failure to enforce the proper precautions for safety in the mines, and that the government and the coal mines were bonded in sympathy.

Workers wanted a just industrial learning society. Socialist parties organized a wide variety of study clubs and public meetings. Ginger Goodwin (as cited in Stonebanks, 2004), the famed Vancouver Island miner, union organizer, and socialist adult educator wrote in July 1916:

> As the condition of the workers becomes more unbearable, the call for education and knowledge must of necessity increase, that the galling chains of wage slavery, with their accompanying evil effects of misery and want, insanity and crime, may give place to a society where slavery is no more, and happiness and joy, peace and plenty, be at the disposal. (p. 66)

The liberal-minded Workers Education Association (WEA) made inroads in Toronto in 1917, precipitating a spirited, contentious debate—both within the WEA and without—regarding just how autonomous workers' education ought to be. University elites wanted to guide the workers' instruction. They worried that, left to their own mischievous devices, the working class would embrace "dangerous knowledge" (Welton, 1991, p. 24) and that their longing to be masters of their own destiny would upset existing capitalist ownership of property.

In the aftermath of the terrible First World War, which dealt a fatal blow to Western delusions of progress and civilization, several important texts appeared. In his famous text *Knowledge for the People*, Father Jimmy Tompkins (1921) postulated that the First World War had unleashed a deep longing on the part of the common people of the world for "more Knowledge, better intellectual training, and better organized effort in their various callings" (p. 1). Adult education methods and techniques had been mobilized brilliantly for the war effort, so why couldn't this energy be harnessed to a giant project of awakening the common man? Tompkins agitated incessantly to awaken slumbering Nova Scotians. Nobody believed more deeply than this febrile priest that ordinary people could learn, and enact this transforming consciousness into social forms that would facilitate human development. Two years later in the text *The University in Overalls*, Alfred Fitzpatrick (1923) cried out against both the state's and civil society's neglect of the bunkhouse men who were living in squalor and degradation. Both Tompkins and Fitzpatrick preached a social gospel of redemption through adult education. And both men feared greatly that the horrors of the First World War and the appalling working conditions for most men and women in its aftermath would lead many to embrace false ideologies such as communism or socialism. Tompkins and Fitzpatrick were unique reformers, however, who placed adult learning in the centre of the struggle to create a more just world. Sharing this sentiment, E. A. Corbett (1929) penned one of our first texts on adult education for presentation at the Thirteenth National Conference of Canadian Universities at the University of Ottawa. Corbett believed profoundly "that the only solution of the immediate economic and social problems of rural life is by way of organization and education of the people" (p. 57). He found much evidence in the vibrant life of farms and institutions such as the Wheat Pool.

When Coady's (1939) *Masters of Their Own Destiny* appeared at the end of the depression and the beginning of World War II, his imagination had absorbed the awakening consciousness of ordinary Canadians from coast to coast. *Masters of our own destiny* was, indeed, the watchword of the times. Although I have wrestled with this man's life and thought and have been one of his relentless critics (Welton, 2001, 2003), Coady still stands out as a formidable opponent of the soul- and body-destroying power of the capitalist mode of production. He actually dared to believe that ordinary, sometimes illiterate, people had the capacity to run their own enterprises. They really could acquire the personal knowledge, skill, and sensibility to solve the social and technical problems facing them in their everyday business activities. Although history has not been very kind to the Antigonish cooperative project, it continues to shine as a beacon to the possibility of life being different, more just, and continues to inspire Catholic social activists who work with the Coady International Institute. But the big dream of cooperatives gradually eroding capitalism's grip on the mentality and outlook of Maritimers failed, as did the alternative projects of a humane socialist revolution. Oblivious to our best intentions, history presses onward, throwing up new challenges for our time, tossing dust on some of our old initiatives. Coady's passionate belief that only an unfettered imagination could release energy to burst the dams that prevent us from realizing our human potential is worth a coveted place in our traveller's kitbag.

Report of the Proceedings of a Special Programme Committee of the Canadian Association for Adult Education (CAAE), 1943

In the early war years, E. A. Corbett, the director of the CAAE, believed that unless the ruling Liberal party's postwar plans had the support of informed and vigorous public opinion, the masses of Canadians could easily be manipulated with the powerful economic interests emerging in the driver's seat. The CAAE hoped to guide the process of public enlightenment toward a more just social order. The CAAE's Council chose Watson Thomson to direct the Special Committee on Education for Reconstruction. This committee deliberated at MacDonald College in Quebec from December 27 to January 2, 1943, and Watson Thomson, Dr. W. H. Brittain of MacDonald College, and Robert T. Mackenzie of UBC's Extension Department compiled a report of the proceedings (Special Committee on Education for Reconstruction, 1943). The resulting report is one of the most important documents in CAAE history and set the tone and direction for the London conference in May 1943 that launched the Citizens' Forum. This report was written when the outcome of World War II was not yet certain, and the adult education intellectuals believed that the collective experience of the war contained significant learning potential. They also believed that a just learning society requires a "foundation in public opinion and the public will" (p. 5). At this epochal moment in twentieth century history, these intellectuals believed profoundly in the concept of public, or deliberative, space. A better world did not just happen. It had to be created and sustained by vigorous learning processes characterized by a "critical examination of the social processes by which those popular aspirations for a better world might be fulfilled" (p. 4).

The report (Special Committee on Education for Reconstruction, 1943) opened by setting the "context of the problem" (p. 3). The authors identified the fundamental problem as building

> a more dynamic popular conception of the war effort, both in terms of what we are fighting against and above all in terms of the new world which can emerge from the war if there is an enlightened and effective national will to that end. (p. 3)

It was not a question of mobilizing "adult education" to help Canadians adapt to a taken-for-granted postwar reality. Rather, they believed that citizens had to engage one another in a deliberative learning process to actively shape the emergent world. They thought that the war was teaching "men in the interests of survival, if for no higher motive, to cooperate together and to utilize their resources efficiently for an agreed social purpose" (p. 5). These collective, experiential war-learning processes of Canadian men and women, they intuited, gave them a cultural hook for the "immense and urgent educational task" of creating a people's peace and laying the foundation for a "permanent United Nations cooperation" and bridging the "gulf between the democracies and the Soviet Union" (p. 6). Designing a just learning society had to realistically face the "facts of the existing situation with all its inexorable limitations as well as its hopeful opportunities" (p. 6).

The committee then followed contextual observations with the articulation of "some fundamental principles" (Special Committee on Education for Reconstruction, 1943, p. 7; a shortened version would be adopted as the CAAE Manifesto in 1943). Never was the term *democracy* in greater need of redefinition and revitalization than it was at that time in contemporary Canada. The committee contended that people believed that narrow controlling interests lay behind the "façade of democratic procedure" (p. 16). The great ideals of political equality were almost meaningless in the face of the oligarchic control of Canadian life. Thus, the meaning of democracy ought to be thoroughly examined: Its economic meaning now had to be placed at the forefront. And the role of "community planning and 'collective action from below'" (p. 17) as a counter-balancing force to minimize the danger of bureaucratic control had to be carefully scrutinized. The authors articulated what late twentieth century political theorists have labelled "associative democracy." Paul Hirst (1997) stated that associationalism may be

> loosely defined as a normative theory of society the central claim of which is that human welfare and liberty are both best served when as many of the affairs of society as possible are managed by voluntary and democratically self-governing associations. Associationalism gives priority to freedom in its scale of values, but it contends that such freedom can only be pursued effectively if individuals join with their fellows. It is opposed to both state collectivism and pure free-market individualism as principles of social organization. (p. 38)

This vision of democracy had affinities with the guild socialism of G. H. Cole and others. Watson Thomson (1944) was, perhaps, the first Canadian public intellectual to articulate these ideas in Canada in the late 1930s and 1940s. He also attempted to create the learning infrastructure for an associative democracy in various provincial and national arenas (Alberta, Manitoba, Saskatchewan, and Canada) in less than ideal conditions.

The Special Committee on Education for Reconstruction (1943) gave considerable attention to the "Canadian scene." Here they thought that they had to identify some of the "major problems with which any Canadian reconstructionist educational programme must concern itself" (p. 12). The interpretive procedures were, first, to identify the major problem, then to offer an assessment, which was followed by the specification of tasks. For example, after identifying and assessing the "inadequacy of Canadian planning" (p. 14) as a major problem, the committee claimed that the task ensuing from this assessment was to

> focus attention on the planning philosophy which is implicit in much of our war organization and on the planning techniques which have evolved, and to show what will be required if they are to become the instruments of the achievement of a creative democratic society. (p. 15)

If Canada were to commit itself to building a stable and just world, it was imperative to understand clearly what the major groups in Canada thought about postwar reconstruction—French-Canadians, labourers, farmers, businesses, armed services, and women. Each group was examined to understand its problems (which needed solving) and its potential to create the just learning society. In the final section of the report, the committee set out its recommendations for a CAAE reconstuctionist educational program. Any such program that remained aloof from the "urgent necessities of the moment" (p. 27) was foredoomed to failure. The CAAE, as a federated organization within civil society, sought to mobilize Canadians to examine their future in the light of fundamental ethical principles.

"Adult Education Theory and Policy" (1944)

In October 1944 the Saskatchewan CCF under Tommy Douglas's leadership swept the Liberal machine out of office, winning 47 of 52 seats. Douglas wanted not only to introduce legislation on health, collective bargaining, and education, as he had promised, but also to use a campaign of grassroots radical adult education—a massive campaign of study-action throughout the province—to begin the building of a humane socialist society. Watson Thomson (1944), who arrived with his family in October from Manitoba to direct the new Division of Adult Education (the first in Canada), thought he saw exciting vistas ahead. Woodrow Lloyd, the Minister of Education, imagined that a new Division of Adult Education should clarify the thinking of Saskatchewan citizens so that desirable social and economic concepts could prevail and provide adult education with immediate and tangible aims (cooperative farming, credit unions, health-improvement facilities, community centres, and leisure-time activities). Thomson's coherent vision of a just learning society is particularly remarkable.

Thomson (1944) moved quickly to establish government policy for adult education in Saskatchewan. His brief, "Adult Education Theory and Policy," outlined what he thought was the only possible attitude to adult education for a democratic socialist government to adopt. It was of the "utmost importance" (p. 1) that members of the Saskatchewan government understand the educational theory and principles of the new Adult Education Division, both in itself and in relation to their own social philosophy. Education was not impartial and socially neutral. In Saskatchewan, an adult education that would conform with the principles of the "social" theory had two primary concrete tasks: to support the people with relevant knowledge in their movement towards the new objectives for which the way has been opened up, whether they be cooperative farms, larger school units, or new public-health projects; and to awaken the people to a sense of the "central issues of the world crisis," still unresolved, so that there would be a clear way ahead for modern society. Thomson informed the cabinet that a socially minded education had to discover where a sense of social purpose was breaking through towards liberatory social change. Then that activation had to be fostered in every possible way and fed the material for its creative job of reshaping the environment. In the fall of 1944, Thomson wagered that a significant number of Saskatchewanites had opted to move towards a more participatory and self-reliant society. He saw his task as catalytic: helping people to clarify their goals and achieve their ends through critical dialogue.

The knowledge that the Adult Education Division wanted to convey was not knowledge for its own sake, but rather for the sake of change nearer to the heart's desire of ordinary, decent people everywhere. Average people, Thomson (1944) believed, did not want to study the history of medicine in the abstract. But when they began to ask why they could not have a decent hospital in their own district and to get together with their neighbours to figure out some way of getting one, they were ready to learn some history of medicine as well as some social and economic history of western Canada. Aware that the trend in agriculture was towards increasingly mechanized, capital-intensive, large-scale units, Thomson urged farmers to bring their isolated farms together into single cooperative communities. He was convinced that the people could take the raw material of a prairie village and create a new pattern worked out by ordinary people from below. But one could not do that without study and cooperative action. "No study without consequent action. No action without previous study" (Welton, 1987, p. 156): This would be the banner of the division's study-action program.

The visionaries in the Division of Adult Education envisaged nothing less than a comprehensive adult education program for social progress through which 500,000 men and women of the province would be encouraged to become active citizens and fully rounded personalities. Under the direction of William Harding, aided by district supervisors, the department began to proceed systematically to establish starting points and growing points. A starting point, as Harding conceived it, consisted of one individual with an interest in a particular topic, a growing point of four individuals interested in a common problem or issue. When 10 units cohered around a common theme, a study group was created. Three central issues were clear to Thomson and Harding. First, they understood that the Saskatchewan government had to demonstrate to the farmers, workers, and plain people that a democratic socialist government could effect tangible material improvements. Second, they knew that the mass of people must be mobilized and activated as rapidly as possible. Only by participating in the processes of democratic deliberation and social change would people realize that "socialism is democracy extended" and that the bogey of "socialism as mere bureaucracy and regimentation" is ludicrous. Third, Thomson and Harding believed that the "political consciousness" of the mass of people must be so deepened that the foundations of prairie radicalism became unshakable (Thomson, 1945, n.p.).

The first task was one of legislation and administration, the second and third involved the consideration of matters in which adult education could play an important role. Study-action had been designed to meet the second need—mobilizing and activating the people at the grassroots level. It was essential, the study-action strategists contended, to begin with a broad approach to "communities as communities" (Thomson, 1945, n.p.) and to serve them in some appreciable way regarding their expressed needs. Study-action, citizens' conferences, and the Lighted School all aimed at serving communities in an "above-party spirit" (n.p.). It was also educationally sound, they thought, to attempt to lead study-action groups from local and immediate concerns to the affairs of the province, nation, and, eventually, the world. As one did so, the issues discussed would inevitably take on a more "political" character, and groups would look to the Division of Adult Education for guidance. That guidance could then be given on the basis of confidence earned through non-partisan services in the community-centred interests. Developing this political consciousness, though the most crucial task as far as the progressive movement was concerned, was also the most difficult.

Henson's Provincial Plan (1945/1946)

Guy Henson had cut his teeth as an adult educator in Halifax in the 1930s, setting up a chapter of the WEA and fostering Antigonish Movement style credit unions in urban Halifax and Dartmouth. Returning from war service with the Canadian Legion Educational Service in Europe in the fall of 1945, Henson was asked to create a new Division of Adult Education. He spent many months collecting data on the discipline of adult education and other initiatives worldwide as part of his own learning process. His 1946 report *Provincial Support for Adult Education in Nova Scotia* became the guide for the work of the division and, in itself, can claim an important place in the intellectual history of Canadian adult education. Like his counterpart in Saskatchewan, Henson thought that the postwar changes in society were creating the possibility of an educative society. When he took on the task of setting up the new division in 1945, he viewed adult education as closely connected to his vision of associative democracy, which was that the very life of democracy depends on the self-worth of the populace, intelligent and critical-thinking individuals who would wrestle with controversial issues of the day and collectively organize and develop their communities. In the postwar world of Nova Scotia, Henson believed that adult education could play an axial role in revitalizing society and democracy.

Henson (1946) organized his famous report into three sections: "The Goals of Adult Education," "A Constructive Approach," and "Proposals for Action." It was plainly written, but brilliantly formulated, and Henson acknowledged that formal schooling did not turn out the "finished product" and that "work activity" and the associative life of civil society had a deep "educational effect for the adult" (p. 9). "The newspaper, magazine and book, the radio, the film, the church, the political parties, occupational associations, social and fraternal groups form," he observed, "a complex of agencies which have the main part in transmitting knowledge and opinions to grown-up people" (p. 9). Recognizing that adult learning was occurring in the domain of civil society, Henson asked, "To what extent can the educational movement as such be strengthened so that an increasing body of people will turn to it for knowledge without bias, for skills efficiently taught, for attitudes towards life, and for the inspiration of the arts" (p. 9). He knew that education was an intervention in pre-existing learning domains (work, state, civil society) and that the learning process within these domains was not necessarily as deep, broad, or critical as it could be. Henson believed that the socialization of youth had left them with fragments of knowledge primarily oriented to their own pleasure and profit. Adult education would not be "realistic" (p. 10) and would not

> fulfil its task unless it [was] geared to the vital needs of life in these times and in Nova Scotia: unless it plays its full part in enabling people to use their intelligence, their skill and their finest qualities for economic and social progress, and for achieving a richer and happier life. (p. 10)

Like the formulators of the special report (Special Committee on Education for Reconstruction, 1943) and the study-action plan of action, Henson (1946) did not focus primarily on the needs of the individual. Rather, his imagination drew the circle around the system and the lifeworld. Addressing the system domains of economy and polity, Henson argued that Nova Scotia's

> economic circumstances call for more all-round intelligence and vocational skill on the part of the average citizen; for more alertness as to scientific progress, government policies, and business organization, and as to what is going on elsewhere in our markets and in competitive producing areas. (p. 11)

This simple formulation anticipated the "learning economy" and "learning society" discourse of the late twentieth/twenty-first informational age. Turning to civil society, Henson insisted that "all the agencies of daily life which disseminate information, ideas and opinions, or teach skills, or give inspiration enter into the general framework of adult education" (p. 19). This included "institutions and activities" (p. 19) normally thought of as education, as well as the press, radio, film (public spheres), churches, political organizations, trade unions, social clubs, and enlightened conversation groups (voluntary associational learning sites within the learning domain of civil society). Henson's argument, still pertinent today, was that "educational planning" had to "concentrate on multiplying the means and the efficiency of continuing self-education of leaders and the average citizen" (p. 20). Education then, within this holistic learning society frame, was an intentional intervention into preconstituted learning domains whose purpose was to foster a more just and self-conscious learning process. Henson was well aware that both the system and lifeworld domains contained mis-educative tendencies and that the actually existing functioning domains excluded some and rewarded others (he was particularly concerned about the oppression and exclusion of Black Nova Scotians from the circle of the learning society).

Henson (1946) gave considerable attention to the policy dimension of his provincial plan. He firmly believed that governments must "concentrate on multiplying the means and the efficiency of continuing self-education of leaders and of the average citizen" (p. 20). This tenet is fundamental to the vision of associative democracy and far removed from contemporary Canadian political visions. Henson believed that "democratic people want the means of self-education and help in making the best use of them. The task of educational leadership is to supply those means and that help, and to stimulate the individual and the group to realize their practical possibilities" (p. 23). Thus, civil society was the appropriate unit for continued education. Henson provided strenuous arguments for government interest in and provision for the continued education of young people who reach the age of citizenship and for men and women of all ages to have the best means of thinking and informing themselves about public affairs. In a sense, Henson's strong emphasis on the public sphere and active citizenship is a message almost forgotten by today's politicians. Henson grappled with the question of how, and to what extent, government could stimulate and support the post-school learning activities of individuals, local groups, communities, and voluntary bodies of wide scope. This question is more pertinent than ever.

The opening decades of the twentieth century are rich with experiment and initiative for Canadian adult educators who follow in their wake and must invent projects that speak to the crises and possibilities of our time. One has to admit, I think, that the containers (or forms) that we invent to express our learning are usually marked by time. But three fundamental themes are worth carrying with us into the future. First, people's learning capacities have to be consciously mobilized for continuous enlightenment and action. Second, the commitment to associative democracy, evident faintly in most of our adult education practice and brightly in the work of Henson (1946) and Thomson (1944), is pertinent to our building a just learning society. Third, Coady's (1939) insight that there would be no democracy without democratic workplaces needs to be configured for our time of runaway global capital.

References

Coady, M. (1939). *Masters of their own destiny.* New York: Harper and Row.

Corbett, E. A. (1929, May). Adult education. Paper presented at the Thirteenth National Conference of Canadian Universities, Ottawa, ON.

Fitzpatrick, A. (1923). *The university in overalls.* Toronto, ON: Frontier College.

Grant, W. L. (1919). The education of the workingman. *Queen's Quarterly,* 159–168.

Henson, G. (1946). *Provincial support of adult education in Nova Scotia: A report by Guy Henson.* Halifax, NS: King's Printer.

Hirst, P. (1997). *From statism to pluralism.* London, UK: UCL Press.

Special Committee on Education for Reconstruction. (1943). *Report of the proceedings of a Special Program Committee of the Canadian Association for Adult Education.* Toronto, ON: Author.

Steer, S. (1992). Violet McNaughton and the struggle for the cooperative society. In M. Welton (Ed.), *Educating for a brighter new day: Women's organizations as learning sites* (pp. 139–159). Halifax, NS: Dalhousie University, School of Education.

Stonebanks, R. (2004). *Fighting for dignity: The Ginger Goodwin story.* St. John's, NL: Canadian Committee on Labour History.

Taylor, G. (2000). Let us co-operate. In B. Fairbairn, I. MacPherson, and N. Russell (Eds.), *Canadian co-operatives in the year 2000: Memory, mutual aid, and the millennium* (pp. 57-78). Saskatoon, SK: Centre for the Study of Co-operatives.

Thomson, W. (1944). *Adult education theory and policy.* Brief submitted to Saskatchewan government.

Thomson, W. (1945). *Adult education in Saskatchewan: The next three years.* C. 11 and 29 June. William M. Harding Papers [in the author's possession].

Tompkins, J. (1921). *Knowledge for the people.* Antigonish, NS: St. Francis Xavier University.

Welton, M. (1987). Mobilizing the people for socialism: The politics of adult education in Saskatchewan, 1944–45. In M. Welton (Ed.), *Knowledge for the people: The struggle for adult learning in English-speaking Canada, 1828–1973* (pp. 151–167). Toronto: OISE Press.

Welton, M. (1991). Dangerous knowledge: Canadian workers' education in the decades of discord. *Studies in the Education of Adults, 23*(1), 24–40.

Welton, M. (2001). *Little Mosie from the Margaree: A biography of Moses Michael Coady.* Toronto, ON: Thompson Educational.

Welton, M. (2003). De-coding Coady: Masters of their own destiny under critical scrutiny. *Studies in Continuing Education, 25*(1), 75–93.

2

Histories of Aboriginal Adult Education in Canada

Wendy Burton and Gwen Point

This chapter relates the histories of Aboriginal adult education in what is now called Canada. The chronological narrative is divided into three sections: adult education before colonization, during colonization, and after 1952. Aboriginal, used synonymously with the term First Nations, is accepted by the Assembly of First Nations to refer to all persons for whom the Government of Canada has a fiduciary responsibility under the *Indian Act* (Department of Indian Affairs [DIA], 1876b), which includes all persons who are First Nations, Métis, and Inuit. The omnibus term Aboriginal is the currently accepted political term; unanimous acceptance of any term is unlikely. In the Canadian context the term does not denote an homogenous group whose educational needs and aspirations are homogenous. In 2005 in Canada, Aboriginal adult education includes literacy education, Aboriginal language education, academic upgrading, life skills, career preparation, parenting courses, trades training, drug and alcohol awareness and support groups, community development skills, and post-secondary entrance preparation.

"My Grandmother, She Was Here When the World Was Made"

The most generally held anthropological theory, based on observable data, that *Homo sapiens sapiens* came from Asia via the Bering Strait, was first proposed by Jesuit José de Acosta (c 1539-1600 in *Historia Natural y Moral de las Indias*, published in 1590. (Dickason, 2002, p. 4)

This "Bering-Strait land bridge" theory, proposed by Jesuits, whose publication *Jesuit Relations* laid out much of the map of education, conversion, and 'civilization' of Aboriginal peoples in North America (Thwaites, 2005; Welton, 2005), is controversial, and many Aboriginal people are deeply offended by its implications therefore that "we" are all immigrants on these continents. Many stories of Aboriginal peoples proclaim "I have been here since the world began" (Ray, 1996), and few stories exist of a migration that would evoke the trek across the Bering Strait.

From what is known of traditional methods of education in Aboriginal communities, lifelong learning is a familiar, ancient construct. Evidence of the cultivation of plants such as corn and tobacco; tools such as atlatls and harpoons; transport technologies such as canoes and sleds; technological innovations such as weirs; prepared hides, pelts, and plant fibres; and food preservation such as smoking, drying, and rendering indicate the presence of complex education processes, many of which would have been adult education. The technical expertise required of the Tsimshian, Haida, and Nootka to build seagoing dugout canoes with carved prows, custom-built totems and door poles, and ceremonial masks, trading tokens, and tribal insignias arose from the guild model of master, journeyman, and apprentice. Constructing a pound, executing a surround, and preserving huckleberries for travel and trade require the transmission of knowledge from one generation to the next, through young adults and adults as well as children.

Any human community capable of such technologies and the resource management to create these "original affluent societies" (Ray, 1996, p. 20) possesses educational systems. These educational systems were incorporated into daily lives under the rubric of Indigenous education: look, listen, learn. Beyond this, no uniform system of socialization, instruction, and vocational training existed across tribal affiliations because such education was context specific. Most communities, however, did recognize different education modes to distinguish child and adult education. At puberty, instruction usually became more formal and exacting. Although the civilizations of Aboriginal peoples are diverse, similarities are noted to do with the education of adults: the absence of institutional approaches; the powerful imperative to avoid imposing one's will on another individual; behaviour shaping by positive example in the home and communal dwellings; provision of guidance towards desired forms of behaviour through games and amusement; and stories to draw out the lessons in daytime activities and to transfer other forms of knowledge—ethical, theological, historical, ecological, and political. Storytelling is an essential feature of the lifelong learning of adult members of Aboriginal communities. Furthermore, ceremonies play an essential role in imparting lessons and the further education of specialists. Vocational skills are learned through games, copying expert behaviour and mentoring, and "first" observances—first food, first game, first garment.

The heterogeneous nature of the human universe of Canada includes Inuit fishers and sealers of the Arctic north, sedentary agriculturalists such as Huron and Iroquois, woodlands hunter-gatherers such as the Cree and the Dene, and west-coast fishing and trading peoples such as the Kwagiulth and Stolo. At the end of the fifteenth century, estimates indicate that 150,000 to 200,000 Aboriginal peoples occupied the pacific slope, 100,000 to 150,000 occupied the eastern Great Lakes and St Lawrence valley, 50,000 to 100,000 occupied the grassland-parkland areas of the Western Interior, and fewer than 100,000 lived elsewhere (Ray, 1996, p. 21).

Colonization

After the arrival of Europeans, Aboriginal adult education became the histories of documents (colonial documents), stories (post-contact stories), and federal and provincial government legislation. What is acknowledged readily is that colonial explorers, traders, and settlers learned from the

Aboriginal peoples they met. Missionaries undertook educational services to adults as well as children, teaching Aboriginal peoples to read English or French as a mode of transmitting religious education. Aboriginal leaders learned to read and write from those who learned such skills from missionaries and traders; teaching each other this new skill was an essential element of Aboriginal survival and adaptation.

Perhaps the earliest evidence of explicitly adult education occurred in 1620 when the Recollets sent Pastedechouan, a Montagnais boy, to France for five years, with the expectation that he would assume leadership in his community and lead his people to Christianity and acculturation. This attempt was a failure, and the Jesuits

> had to take him in and employ him as a language teacher in Quebec City. But by this time, Pastedechouan could not find comfort in either culture. He became an alcoholic and starved to death in the forests north of the city. (Ray, p. 62)

Further efforts included sending "a few Native girls overseas for training, to prepare them either for marriage to French settlers or for a religious vocation" (p. 62). Adult education of Aboriginal adults became a struggle between the belief of missionaries and governors that the best way to "civilize" Aboriginal peoples of Canada was to assimilate them into the emerging societies of traders, soldiers, and settlers and the belief that the best way to protect Aboriginal peoples was to set them apart from their traditional ways of life and carefully control their integration into the cultures of the colonizers. This assimilate-segregate-integrate dilemma persists and is reflected in the government documents and practices of the colonizing societies.

An early example is the Sillery reserve near Quebec City. In 1634, with the backing of Noel Brulart de Sillery, the Jesuits created an intentional community of Montagnais hunters and Algonquin people beside French farmers.

> [The Jesuits] thought the settlers could teach the displaced Native people how to farm while the priests kept a close eye on their spiritual development. The experiment at Sillery was not encouraging. The Algonquin hated their new sedentary life and were unable to feed themselves from their fields. Colonial and missionary authorities concluded . . . that each group picked up only the worst aspects of the other's culture. Consequently, the authorities decided that reserves should isolate and protect Native people from the evils of settler society so that the priests and Native catechists could teach them the arts of civilization before integrating them into French society. (Ray, 1996, pp. 62–63)

These early attempts at adult education occurred simultaneously with the development of a system of schooling for immigrants, and "as Western society grew and developed with a system of schooling to meet their own demands, values, language, and beliefs, this type of development did not happen with the First Peoples of this land" (Poonwassie, 2001, p. 156).

The British parliament passed legislation in 1670 that placed Indian relations in the hands of colonial Governors "to consider how the Indians and slaves may be best instructed and invited to the Christian religion" (Leslie and Maguire, 1978, p. 3). This legislation and its explicit intention informed all educational contacts with Aboriginal adults: Education was conversion.

The Royal Proclamation of 1763 placed the care and control—and presumably education—of Aboriginal peoples of what was to become Canada with British colonial governors. Children of immigrants to Canada who were not English were required to submit to the structure of public education in Canada that emerged in the 1800s. The first adult educators of Aboriginal adults were missionaries and Indian agents, and the first lessons had to do with Christianity, agriculture, and land management. From the outset, criticism of the education offered or forced on Aboriginal people, especially children, was frequent and often from those who were the reluctant consumers of such education (Haig-Brown, 1990, p. 231).

> It was after 1815 that the British adopted the policy of civilizing the Indian as an integral part of their relationship with the Indians. The policy evolved slowly, as a result of much propaganda in Britain and North America about the need to develop the Indian. Much of the propaganda in North America was made by Protestant sects which were in the throes of Evangelical and Revivalist movements stressing the need to Christianize all men. (Tobias, 1983, p. 40)

Draper (1998) noted that in 1816 the first *Common School Act* was passed in Upper Canada and that "adults also were allowed to learn reading, writing and arithmetic" (p. 44), presumably in English or French. Were Aboriginal adult learners included?

Adult education as a concept was not formally practiced in Canada until the 1830s with the establishment of the Mechanics' Institute and the Danish folkschools. The students of these adult education enterprises were immigrants; Aboriginal adults were often precluded from the activities to which such education enterprises were attached.

In 1836 Lieutenant Governor Bond Head reported that "an Attempt to make Farmers of the Red Men has been generally speaking a complete failure" (Leslie and Maguire, 1978, p. 15), and he recommended that Indian people be moved away from any contact with White settlers, for their own protection. One notable exception to this policy appears to be the development of an integrated community in the Red River Settlement, where Aboriginal peoples lived, worked, married, and raised children alongside White settlers and—inevitably—Métis, mixed-blood, and half-breed English, a social experiment that thrived until it met a resounding defeat in 1885.

In 1841 Lord Sydenham lamented to Russell that

> the attempt to combine a system of pupilage with the settlement of these people in civilized parts of the country, leads only to embarrassment to the Government, expense to the Crown, a waste of resources of the province, and injury to the Indians themselves. . . . He does not become a good settler, he does not become an agriculturalist or a mechanic. (Leslie and Maguire, 1978, p. 17)

These were, apparently, the two vocational choices for Aboriginal adult learners in the 1840s as they became less able to pursue a self-supporting hunter-gatherer existence in the face of advancing settlements. Two conflicting forces outside Aboriginal communities contested which approach would be most effective: to integrate Aboriginal peoples in "civilized" White society to learn "proper behaviour and social graces" or to isolate Aboriginals on reserves where the resident Indian agent, school teacher, and missionary could prepare Indians for enfranchisement. Reverend James Coleman, for example, advised the Bagot Commission, "It is necessary the Indian youth should be prevented [from] becoming hunters or fishers, and this can be alone done by locating the village where there are no facilities for either" (p. 18).

In 1844 the Bagot Commissioners recommended, among many articles related to land tenure, that

> upon a Report from an Officer of the Department that an Indian is qualified by education, knowledge of the arts and customs of civilized life and habits of industry and prudence, to protect his own interests, and to maintain himself as an independent member of the general community, the Government shall be prepared to grant him a Patent for the Land in his actual cultivation or occupation. (Leslie and Maguire, 1978, p. 20)

Education was confined to introducing Aboriginal adults to Christianity, educating them in the ways of "society," and training them to undertake "the management of property, with the outlay of money, and . . . offices . . . such as rangers, pathmasters, and other offices, for ordinary township purposes" (p. 22). The Commissioners stipulated that "the Indian be employed . . . in the erection of buildings" (p. 22).

In 1856 the Aborigines' Protection Society addressed Henry Labouchere, Secretary of State for the Colonies, advocating for fairer land and resource distribution for the Aboriginal populations and advised:

> The duty, now generally recognised as incumbent on every landed proprietor, to promote the education and improvement of the people on his estate, must be equally so on those who are *de facto*, if not *de jure*, proprietors of estates larger than the civilized part of Europe [and reminding Labouchere that as a result of the industry of the natives of the territories under the government of the Hudson's-Bay Company, it is estimated that 20,000,000 sterling has been added to the wealth of this country. (p. 8)

In spite of, or perhaps because of, the largely unsuccessful attempts by Catholic orders to education Indian children, Protestant missionaries focused on the provision of day schools similar in form and curriculum to those available to the poor of Britain. Until 1850 young Indians attended the local White schools, as a result of individuals and local bands requesting schools, and many young Indians became educated in the schools of the dominant society without losing contact with their own culture. There is evidence that Aboriginal adults took advantage of the presence of schooling for their children to learn to read, write, and calculate in English or French and that "kitchen-table schools" were commonplace as Aboriginal adults sought informal means to learn the increasingly valuable skills of reading, writing, and arithmetic in English or French.

Most legislation between 1850 and 1867 had to do with defining what was meant by *Indian* and protecting land, including the land occupied by Indians, although these legislations can be read for their implicit connection to the provision of education. For example, in 1857 the *Act for the Gradual Civilization of the Indian Tribes in the Canadas* was proclaimed. This *Act's* purpose was to facilitate the acquisition of property for Aboriginal peoples through enfranchisement that could be achieved only through education:

> Any such Indian of the male sex, and not under twenty-one years of age, is able to speak, read and write either the english or the french language readily and well, and is sufficiently advanced in the elementary branches of education and is of good moral character and free from debt. (Leslie and Maguire, 1978, p. 27)

Commissioners could recommend that any male Indian between 21 and 40, even those not able to read and write, "if they shall find him able to speak readily either the English or the French language, of sober and industrious habits, free from debt and sufficiently intelligent to be capable of managing his own affairs" (p. 27), be put on three years' probation and then be enfranchised. Clearly, education of adults (or at least males between 21 and 40) would be expected to play a role in this enfranchisement. In fact, however, only one Indian was ever known to have been enfranchised under the terms of this Act. The intention of the Act was to "wean the Indians from perpetual dependence upon the Crown," and such experiments were by 1858 declared "practically a failure" (p. 29). The explicit intention of these policies was to "civilize" and "assimilate" Indians and bring about the swift end of the Indian Department. Many of the policies merged land management with the "civilization" of the Aboriginal occupants of those lands through adult education.

The *Civilization and Enfranchisement Act* of 1859 was a consolidation of previous legislation that focused on regulations of liquor sales to Indians, land management, and road construction and maintenance through Indian land; it was largely silent on the "civilization" aspect of the *Civilization and Enfranchisement Act*, with the exception that schools as well as roads were constructed.

The new Dominion rapidly expanded, first through the acquisition of Rupert's Land and the Northwest Territories, and then through the entry into Confederation of Manitoba and British Columbia. As a consequence, the Indian population within the boundaries of Canada increased in just four years from about 23,000 to over 100,000, or from 0.7 percent to 2.5 percent of the population. Demands for assimilation of the Aboriginal population grew, with education being perceived as "the primary vehicle in the civilization and advancement of the Indian race" (Department of Indian Affairs [DIA], 1876a, p. 6). Treaty agreements frequently included clauses that promised schools as soon as bands settled permanently on their reserved land. Formal schooling had been voluntary before Confederation; thereafter, provincial governments took an increasing role in the provision of facilities to ensure that all children, including Aboriginal children, whatever their socio-economic status, received a basic education.

The *Enfranchisement Act* of 1869 was intended to free Indians from their state of wardship by effecting gradual assimilation as Indians demonstrated that they could manage the "ordinary affairs of the whiteman" (Leslie and Maguire, 1978, p. 53). The *Manitoba Act* of 1870 set aside 1,400,000 acres of ungranted lands for Manitoba's half-breed population.

In 1871, soon after joining Confederation, the British Columbia government encouraged agriculture education, which was always explicitly adult education, by passing laws to support agricultural education and societies. Directed at settlers, it is unlikely that these education efforts were made available to Aboriginal adults. Night school classes in public schools in larger urban centres were common in British Columbia, Alberta, Manitoba, Quebec, and Ontario before 1900; but once again it is unknown whether or how many Aboriginal adults were able to access this education. Furthermore, with the establishment of Farmers' Institutes in 1896 and Women's Institutes in 1909, both charters remained silent on the admission or exclusion of Aboriginal adults.

The 1876 *Indian Act* (DIA, 1876b) created a framework that has persisted, declaring the legal status of the Indians of Canada that of minors, with the government as their guardians. This stance overshadows all educational enterprises from that time forward, particularly in light of commonly held definitions of adult education as the intentional, self-directed actions of autonomous agents. The *Indian Act* of 1876 is almost completely silent on education for Aboriginal peoples, except for the continued expectation that enfranchisement would come as a result of acculturation.

The amendments to the *Indian Act* (DIA, 1876b) from 1879 to 1884 were intended to move forward Prime Minister Macdonald's policy to advance the Indians of the Northwest through establishment of model farms and industrial schools to teach agriculture and mechanical trades. It was, apparently, "difficult to recruit capable instructors who had Indian interests in mind" (Leslie and Maguire, 1978, p. 71). Notwithstanding this difficulty, proposed establishment of residential, agricultural, and industrial schools in the Territories deepened debate over the best way to facilitate rapid acculturation of all Canadian Indians.

In 1884, therefore, the *Indian Advancement Act* sought to transform tribal authorities into a system of self-government, including framing laws "as to what denomination the teacher of the school established on the reserve shall belong to" (Leslie and Maguire, 1978, p. 79) and granting enfranchisement to any Indian who held a university degree. In 1884 the *Indian Act* (DIA, 1876b) was amended to endorse the views of British Columbia agents and clergymen who were opposed to the celebration of the "Potlach" festival. Anyone found guilty of participating in either the potlach or the tawanawa dance faced two to six months' imprisonment. Thus winter ceremonials were banned, as were tribal dances and all related regalia, including masks and drums. This law was extended across Canada and banned sun dances, naming ceremonies, public gatherings to discuss treaties, funeral ceremonies, and all Aboriginal spiritual observances that were not Christian.

In 1894 amendments to the *Indian Act* (DIA, 1876b) were intended to improve educational facilities for Canadian Indians, and an independent School Branch was established. School attendance of Indian children became compulsory, and industrial or boarding schools were established. Thus the era of residential schools for Aboriginal children had begun. In 1879 the federal government evaluated the American policy of segregated Indian residential schools. The Davin Report recommended residential schools and further recommended that they be operated by missionaries, who had already demonstrated their commitment to "civilizing" Canada's Indians (Davin, 1879). The DIA approved the establishment of large industrial residential schools located away from reserves. The scope of this chapter precludes an adequate discussion of residential schools, except to say that they were the deliberate outcome of intentional education policies over more than 75 years, and the consequences are still manifest in Aboriginal adult education (Miller, 1996).

The formal education of Aboriginal adults was still restricted to agriculture and husbandry, land management, and home maintenance. At the turn of the past century, industrial education was introduced into the Canadian education system, private training schools were established, and large companies such as BC Electric and Alberta Telephone Company began technical education. Aboriginal adults who were not enfranchised were excluded from all of these opportunities. The 1920 amendments to the *Indian Act* (DIA, 1876b) were intended to change the clauses on education. The Deputy Superintendent-General Duncan Campbell Scott's intention was "to get rid of the Indian problem" through changes to Indian education and advancement "until there is not a single Indian in Canada that has not been absorbed into the body politic and there is no Indian question, and no Indian Department" (Leslie and Maguire, 1978, p. 114). These changes generally related to schooling of children between 7 and 15 years of age. Explicit mention of education for those older than 15 is infrequent.

In 1931 the Native Brotherhood of British Columbia formed at a December meeting at Port Simpson, with delegates from Masset, Hartley Bay, Kitkatla, Port Essington, and Metlakatla. Organizations such as this formed across Canada, intended to advance political actions and to educate each other about the provisions of the *Indian Act* (DIA, 1876b), the provincial regulations governing public meetings and tribal ceremonies, justice matters, and land and resource management—that is, adult education.

The hearings of 1946–1948 that led to the *Revised Indian Act* of 1951 (DIA and Northern Development, 1951) heard a multitude of voices, not all speaking as one, on issues of land management, enfranchisement, and the transfer of education from federal to provincial control. John Calihoo, President of the Indian Association of Alberta, "urged a number of changes in education, including provision for vocational training, adult education and special courses to enable Indians to take positions in the Indian Affairs Branch" (Leslie and Maguire, 1978, p. 136). Chief Yellowfly, for unaffiliated Indians of Alberta, "questioned the value of teaching a non-Indian curriculum in Indian schools, and of teaching the same curriculum throughout the country where needs of various bands were quite different" (p. 137). The Native Brotherhood of British Columbia's Reverend Peter Kelly in 1947 recommended "that Indian education be nondenominational and that the present system be altered to provide greater opportunities for Indians to attend high school and university" (p. 139). Diamond Jenness recommended increasing "the educational facilities of the migratory northern Indians" (p. 141).

In 1951 the first Indian Friendship Centre was registered as a Society in Toronto, followed by the second in Vancouver in 1952 and the third in Winnipeg in 1959. The Friendship Centre movement began in the mid-1940s for Aboriginal adults who were not living on reserves, and this movement was explicitly based on principles of adult education.

The *Revised Indian Act* of 1951 made it possible for the federal government to make financial arrangements with provincial and territorial authorities for the education of Indian children in public and private schools with non-Aboriginals students. This transfer of authority doubled the number of those who completed education past Grade 6 to almost 20 percent. The provisions prohibiting potlatches and other tribal festivals were repealed, and ceremonies continue to be the site of transmission of culture, knowledge, and values. That this knowledge survived is a testament to subversive strategies such as those described by Bob George, who remembered his brothers travelling through British Columbia as musicians who, in between songs, instructed their audience on the traditions of the longhouse.

Indian Control of Indian Education

The grassroots activism of the 1960s resulted in community development programs such as leadership training and consciousness raising, which led to the development of Indian rights organizations such as the National Indian Brotherhood—which coincided with Hawthorn's (1966-1967) survey. The Liberal government, led by Pierre Trudeau, came to power on the promise of a "just society," and the White Paper of June 1969 articulated what such a society would mean for Aboriginal peoples of Canada. The dynamic tension between cultural survival and assimilation into the mainstream Canadian society culminated in the crisis generated by the intentions of this White Paper.

The Cultural/Educational Centres Program was established in 1971. This program provides financial assistance to Aboriginal tribal/district councils, Inuit communities, and Aboriginal/Inuit non-profit corporations to promote Aboriginal, Métis, and Inuit culture and heritage through programs and services developed at the community level. This is accomplished through the funding of established centres. Indian Friendship Centres received core funding, and the number increased from 26 in the mid-1960s to 120 in 2000 (History of the Friendship Centre Movement, 2005).

The manifesto *Indian Control of Indian Education* (National Indian Brotherhood, 1972) is "a statement of the philosophy, goals, principles, and directions which must form the foundation of any school program for Indian children" (p. 1). The parental and community responsibilities inherent in this document require the continuing education of the adults who will assume those responsibilities. The document includes a section on adult education and basic training and skills development (p. 12).

With the declaration of Indian control of Indian education came a policy change that resulted in individual bands and tribal councils organizing and often running educational programs for adults. The DIA directed funds to educational programs for Aboriginal adults that focused on adult basic education and technical training. As a consequence, many community colleges and school boards contracted to offer adult basic education on reserves. In the mid-1970s adult basic education classes were often taught by non-Aboriginal adult educators hired by committees made up of representatives of local tribal authorities and school board or college administrators. Programs designed explicitly to increase access to teaching, law, medicine, and forestry were developed. Often based on the "training-day" model, Aboriginal adults were expected to attend from 9:00 a.m. to 3:00 p.m. every weekday. Students were not allowed to be late, and attendance was mandatory. Customary absences for community events such as funerals were forbidden (Millard, 1983).

Indian-controlled, band-run adult basic education continued to develop in centres on reserves. Both adult basic education and life skills training frequently occurred simultaneously, because the ability of Aboriginal adults to maintain attendance/learning in such classes was often compromised by perceived life skills inadequacies. Private Aboriginal-owned and -operated education societies were developed. Because the *Indian Act* limits the application of the Act to Indians between the ages of 7 and 17 who ordinarily reside on a reserve, the province has had responsibility for post-secondary education through legislation, and adult basic education is frequently offered by colleges and private institutions, as well as local school boards.

In the late 1980s, in response to evidence that Aboriginal learners were severely underrepresented in the post-secondary system in British Columbia, a Provincial Advisory Committee on Post-Secondary Education for Native Learners was formed to develop a report for the Ministry of Advanced Education, Training, and Technology. This committee produced the Aboriginal Post-Secondary Education and Training Policy Framework, which recommended that the Ministry of Advanced Education, Training, and Technology work with individual institutions to restructure the adult basic education curriculum and delivery methods to incorporate skills development and on-the-job training opportunities to meet local demand, provide funding for transition programs in Aboriginal and non-Aboriginal institutions, respond to the urgent need for community-based literacy programs, and provide resources to develop new curriculum and evaluate existing curricula. Similar initiatives have occurred across Canada.

The Aboriginal adult education enterprise from the mid-1980s has focused on the provision of education that is relevant and culturally appropriate, takes into account learning styles of Aboriginal adults, and is explicitly intended to assist Aboriginal adults to access post-secondary education and training. As the consequences of the residential school became evident, and as survivors began to offer testimony, efforts were redoubled to produce Aboriginal educators for the burgeoning adult education clientele. Returning to learning as an adult learner characterized most Aboriginal adult education programs and their learners.

In the early 1990s Aboriginal adult education was offered in communities, Aboriginal-controlled educational institutions, public post-secondary institutions, and tribal associations with educational departments, and through affiliations between Aboriginal and non-Aboriginal organizations. The Royal Commission on Aboriginal Peoples came to the same conclusions reached through the numerous commissions and hearings throughout the previous 200 years: that public education had failed Aboriginal peoples.

Decentralization toward community control of education is taking place throughout the country, supported by federal policies such as the Aboriginal Human Resources Development Strategy, a five-year, $1.6 billion initiative that came into effect in April 1999; the Department of Indian and Northern Affairs University College Entrance Preparation Program; and the Indian Studies Support Program (ISSP), delivered by First Nations or their administering organizations, with funding as of 2002–2003 that totalled $298 million. The number of students supported increased from about 3,600 in 1977–1978 to approximately 27,500 in 1999–2000 (Indian and Northern Affairs Canada, 2005).

Aboriginal adult education exists in many post-secondary institutions and school-board centres on and off reserves across Canada. Some of these institutions are controlled by Aboriginal boards of governors, offer Aboriginal content and methods, and are funded through federal and provincial initiatives. Most provinces and territories in Canada have provincially administered programs funded by federal dollars. Life-skills, job-readiness, and career-preparation programs are offered through band- or tribal-affiliated education departments. The participation rate for Aboriginal adults in post-secondary education is significantly less than that for any other identifiable group in Canada, and the high school completion rate of Aboriginal youth is 43 percent, which indicates ongoing pressure to provide adult education that is responsive to communities. The federal government initiative *Full Aboriginal Participation in Life-Long Learning* is the latest phase in the histories of Aboriginal adult education. In British Columbia in January 2004 the Indigenous Adult and Higher Learning Association was established, whose purpose is to promote quality education for Aboriginal learners partly through developing and implementing culturally appropriate and meaningful education programs, and similar associations have appeared in other provinces and territories.

As James Draper (1998), among others, has pointed out, Aboriginal peoples of Canada have a past without documents before 1450, including those related to the history of Aboriginal adult education. This does not mean an undocumented past, however. Oral history is now recognized as a valid mode of learning our histories. This past without documents reoccurs in the period beginning in 1971, because much of the grassroots, community-level adult education programming has not been archived. One logical outcome of such a beginning is a chronology of Aboriginal adult education, now underway as a joint project between the University College of the Fraser Valley and the Sto lo Nation.

What emerges from a review of the histories of Aboriginal adult education in Canada is this: Throughout the last 300 years of government policies and legislation, conflicting forces outside Aboriginal communities have tussled about which approach would be most effective to educate the Aboriginal adult, confounding the most commonly held belief about adult education—that it arises from within the learner and the learner's community.

References

Aborigines' Protection Society. (1856). *Canada West and the Hudson's-Bay Company: A political and humane question of vital importance to the honour of Great Britain, to the prosperity of Canada, and to the existence of the Native Tribes; being an Address to the Right Honorable Henry Labouchere.* London: William Tweedie.

Davin, N. (1879). *Report on industrial schools for Indians and Half-breeds.* Ottawa, ON: Queen's Printer.

Department of Indian Affairs. (1876a). *Annual report.* Ottawa, ON: Queen's Printer.

Department of Indian Affairs. (1876b). *The Indian Act.* Ottawa, ON: Government of Canada.

Department of Indian Affairs and Northern Development. (1951). *Revised Indian Act.* Ottawa, ON: Government of Canada.

Dickason, O. (2002). *Canada's First Nations: A history of founding peoples from earliest times* (3rd ed.). Don Mills, ON: Oxford University Press.

Draper, J. (1998). Introduction to the Canadian chronology. *Canadian Journal for Studies in Adult Education/RCÉÉA, 12*(2), 33–43.

Haig-Brown, C. (1990). Border work. *Canadian Literature, 124–125,* 229–241.

Hawthorn, H. (Ed.). (1966–1967). *A survey of the contemporary Indians of Canada.* Ottawa, ON: Indian Affairs.

History of the Friendship Centre Movement. (2005). Retrieved November 18, 2005, from http://www.mifcs.bc.ca/movement.html

Indian and Northern Affairs Canada. (2005). *Post-secondary education programs, 2005.* Retrieved November 18, 2005, from http://www.ainc-inac.gc.ca/ps/edu/ense_e.html

Leslie, J., and Maguire, R. (1978). *The historical development of the Indian Act.* Ottawa, ON: Indian and Northern Affairs.

MacLean, H. (1973). *A review of Indian education in North America* (rev. ed.). Toronto, ON: Ontario Teachers' Federation.

Millard, E. (1983). *Indian adult education: A northern perspective.* Whitehorse, YT: Yukon College Press.

Miller, J. (1996). *Shingwauk's vision: A history of Native residential schools.* Toronto, ON: University of Toronto Press.

National Indian Brotherhood. (1972). *Indian control of Indian education.* Ottawa ON: Author.

Poonwassie, D. (2001). Parental involvement as adult education: A microstrategy for change. In K. Binda and S. Calliou (Eds.), *Aboriginal education in Canada: A study in decolonization* (pp. 155–165). Mississauga, ON: Canadian Educators' Press.

Ray, A. (1996). *I have lived here since the world began.* Toronto, ON: Lester.

Thwaites, R. (2005). *The "Jesuit Relations" and allied documents: Travels and explorations of the Jesuit missionaries in North America (1610–1791).* Retrieved April 29, 2005, from http://puffin.creighton.edu/jesuit/relations/ (Original work published 1896–1901)

Tobias, J. (1983). Protection, civilization, assimilation: An outline history of Canada's Indian policy. In I. Getty & A. Lussier (Eds.), *As long as the sun shines and water flows: A reader in Canadian Native studies* (pp. 39–55). Vancouver, BC: University of British Columbia Press.

Welton, M. (2005). Cunning pedagogics: The encounter between the Jesuit missionaries and Amerindians in 17th-century New France. *Adult Education Quarterly, 55*(2), 101–115.

3
Building Black Identity and Community

Jennifer Kelly

The purpose of this chapter is to examine Black experience in Canada, to look at how adult education can build Black community, and to identify and look reflexively at the concept of community in relation to my own practices. In the present day we still continue to use the concept of community and derivatives such as communities of practice as if they are agreed upon, unproblematic terms that have implications for working in communities. This chapter will draw upon my experience of working in the Black/African Canadian community in Edmonton, a small community that is defined by heterogeneity rather than homogeneity and is both in and of the wider Edmonton community. How does such an actuality affect our ability to work with the concept of community that so often assumes homogeneity?

I will begin by examining disciplinary perspectives on the concept of community before moving to an account of the history of African Canadian community in Alberta. Next I will recount the problems associated with building community and identity within such a heterogeneous Black population using the example of a public adult education initiative, the Living History Group. The chapter concludes with a brief review of this group as a "community of practice."

Perspectives on Community

The chapter draws on an interdisciplinary approach that encompasses a critical cultural studies framework and sociological theory. Cultural studies had their origins in adult education, in the extramural/Workers' Educational Association (WEA) courses offered by the likes of Raymond Williams, Edward Thompson, and Richard Hoggart (see, for example, McIlroy and Westwood, 1993; Steele 1997). Cultural studies approach an understanding of people's lives by accepting Williams' caveat that "culture is ordinary" and by examining the everyday lives lived in the context of the political and social events as they are experienced and acted upon by individuals and social groups in society. In particular, this chapter draws on the works of Paul Gilroy (1993), Stuart Hall (1990), Rinaldo Walcott (1997), Zygmunt Bauman (2001), and Joan Scott (1992). Many of these writers have been influenced by poststructuralist orientations and conceptual understandings of community. For example, Bauman indicated that the use of "community" as homogeneous has brought charges of essentialism; this is a charge familiar to feminists and political activists alike, who are often regarded by anti-essentialists as responsible for the growth of identity politics at the expense of class or broader community politics. Yet at times there is a necessity to act politically on issues of concern to those who might self-identify as Black. Abandoning such a political project might stymie the ability to fight for social justice for African Canadians.

Theories of identity formation such as those espoused by Gilroy and Hall indicate that Black identities are fluid and not static. In translating this understanding to the area of communities, we can perhaps begin to view communities as generated; or as Benedict Anderson (1983) would argue, "imagined" rather than static, waiting to be found, imagined through and constructed by symbols. Similarly, we need to bear in mind Joan Scott's (1992) caution about taking the identities of those under discussion as self-evident. Without such problematization, what results is an ahistorical conception of what it means to be an African Canadian. Therefore we need to attend to the historical processes and the ways in which individuals are constituted through experiences.

It may be useful at this point to relate an actual example of a community formation that took place in Alberta generally and Edmonton specifically. The history of African Canadian communities within Edmonton (and Canada) highlights how African Canadian communities have been imagined and constituted.

The History of African Canadian Community in Alberta

If we examine the cultural and economic formation of Alberta as a province at the turn of the twentieth century, we find that from 1907 to 1912 various strategies were employed by the immigration authorities to discourage Blacks from moving to the Canadian west from Oklahoma and other parts of the US. Alberta was foremost among the western provinces that fought to stem the flow of Black immigrants. Official organizations in Edmonton, such as the Board of Trade and the Imperial Order Daughters of the Empire, gathered petitions of protest to send to Ottawa. The basis for their disquiet was racism and a belief that Blacks were unable to live peacefully together with Whites. The dominant Anglo-Celtic groups viewed Blacks as biologically inferior and incapable of assimilating (for references to this section see Kelly, 1998; 2004; for an overview see Winks, 1971).

Analysis of archival documents such as newspapers, government documents, magazines, and minutes of political meetings during this period of immigration reveals differing and competing racial discourses that intersect with regional, gendered, and political allegiances. The most consistent discourses drew on biological determinism and social Darwinism to construct Anglo-Celtics as biologically different from and superior to Blacks and other ethnic groups. Through these racialized discourses, the dominant White group constructed Blacks as antithetical to the budding capitalist environs that dominant groups in Canada wanted to cultivate. Blacks were posited as opposite to the thriving, hardy, and self-reliant northern Europeans. According to Cooke's 1911 *Maclean's* article (cited in Kelly, 1998), they were perceived as "lacking," initiative with a "sense of humour and predisposition to a life of ease [that] render[s] [their] presence undesirable" (p. 42). For Black women, stereotypes were gendered and racialized; there was concern about the ability of such "unsuitable" bodies to produce future potential citizens who did not conform to conceptions of the "ultimate Canadian" bred of the "best stock that could be found in the world" (p. 42).

Such discursive practices played out through existing regionalized, classed, and gendered discourses. Chinese, Hindu, and Black immigrants were contrasted to the preferred group who consisted of northern Europeans who were considered easily assimilated, of hardier stock, and likely to thrive in Canada's northern climate. Many feared a Black invasion that would result in a "Black Alberta" and blamed the eastern-based Liberal government for being out of touch with western sentiments. Women were no less tainted with racism, and the Anglophile women's organization, the Imperial Order Daughters of the Empire, claimed that Black men were a sexual threat to White women. This argument illustrates the ways in which subjectivities often operate at the intersections of social categories.

Those Black immigrants who made it into Alberta between 1907 and 1911 formed the core of the early Black settlers. The Black pioneers settled primarily in four isolated rural communities: Junkins (now Wildwood), Keystone (now Breton), Campsie (near Barrhead), and Amber Valley (20 miles from Athabasca). Populated by groups who had fled persecution in Oklahoma, Amber Valley was the longest surviving of these Black communities. It had its own baseball team, its own school, and its own church—a self-contained community. Of all immigrants who took out homesteads from 1905 to 1930, almost half failed: In many cases Black immigrant communities lacked infrastructural development, were isolated on marginal lands, and faced racial discrimination. Many of the settlers returned to the United States, particularly after some middle and western states repealed "Jim Crow" laws. The rest resettled in Calgary or Edmonton and their surrounding communities, leaving only a few settlers on the pioneer homesteads. This group of pioneer families and their descendants remained the dominant Black group in the province until the second wave arrived.

For town dwellers who had to interact with Whites on an ongoing basis, racism and discrimination were much more of an everyday occurrence. However, political responses were still required. The Coloured Protective Association was formed in the early 1900s in Calgary to resist White racism. In the 1920s, organizations such as the Universal Negro Improvement Association were also active in the community, as was the Alberta Negro Colonisation and Settlement Society. Testament to community activity during the 1920s and 1930s is seen in the regular *Edmonton Bulletin* column entitled "Our Negro Citizens." The cultural/social occasions advertised and commented on were often organized through members of the Shiloh Baptist Church.

In the late-1950s, the Brotherhood of Sleeping Car Porters, active in organizing the all-Black CPR sleeping-car porters, translated their fight for human rights beyond their workplace into other areas of employment and housing. Along with groups such as the Alberta Association for the Advancement of Coloured People, their fight for human rights in Calgary resulted in Blacks' being able to access public sector employment. These cultural/social groups provided a means of getting together and expressing common concerns, a process that enabled the development of Black identity formation and group consciousness—a form of adult and community education. Such groups encouraged a collective identity formation and enabled the recognition that although they came from differing class and cultural backgrounds, they had commonalities with regard to racism. As part of identity formation, a group comes to identify itself by differentiating itself from others. Organized initially through churches, these groups allowed peoples of African descent to assert a degree of social agency not readily available in the wider, White-dominated society. Within these organizations, women played a vital role in developing a sense of community. During the 1920s and 1930s the majority of women of African descent were directed towards servile roles as domestics, children's nurses, or servants. In an interview that I conducted for the Edmonton-based Alberta Labour History Institute in 2001, Gwen Hooks, a descendant of these early pioneers who was born and grew up in Alberta, spoke about opportunities for employment in the 1940s:

> Housework was about all there was at that time, [whereas men] . . . usually had jobs shining shoes; that's about all they could get. Then eventually they got to be porters; but shining shoes [was mainly what was available]. I wanted more, and I decided I wasn't scrubbing any more floors unless they were my own.

Within Black communities there was a sharing of experience and mutual support. Little has been documented about adult education within these communities, but undoubtedly people would meet at church and other social gatherings and discuss the issues of the day and plan community events. There is no reason to suppose that they were not influenced by Farm Forum radio and the travelling movie shows (from the University of Alberta Extension Department) in the same way that other rural communities were. They would also have access to news of other Black communities in such places as Halifax, Montreal, Vancouver, and the US that was carried coast to coast by the sleeping-car porters on the railways, news that would filter through from the mainline stations in Calgary and Edmonton. Black news-sheets, music, and ideas would ride the rails. The formation of the African Canadian communities reflected similar and earlier formations of African Canadian communities in other provinces (Mathieu, 2001).

It is noteworthy that such early Black organizations were also important in challenging mainstream White society's response to citizens of African descent. As with such organizations today, issues arose, such as how best to respond to living within a White-dominated society: communalist or integrationist? Historian James Walker (1980) argued that, as a compromise between the position of communalist and integrationist, Blacks set up True Band societies. The purpose of these societies is indicated clearly in Walker's description of the operation of the first such society formed at Amherstberg, Ontario, in 1854:

> Band members subscribed a membership fee which was used to establish an emergency relief fund. Black parents were urged to send their children to school regularly, and to insist on equal access to educational facilities. When blacks had an argument among themselves they were encouraged to bring them before the Band for settlement rather than airing them in public and thus contributing to an image of a squabbling disunited black community. Blacks were further encouraged to disperse throughout the province, to prevent discrimination by reducing black concentration in any one area. (p. 118)

Analysis of the aims of this society, although they challenged some aspects of racialization, nonetheless reflects a process of adult education related to surviving within a White-dominated society.

With the relaxation and opening up of the immigration laws in 1962 and again in 1967, the Alberta Black population was increased with immigrants from Caribbean countries such as Jamaica, Trinidad, Guyana, and Barbados. These revisions of the *Immigration Act* that finally took place were prompted not by any major desire by government and immigration authorities to further develop a "racially" pluralist society, but rather primarily by economic expediency. This group of immigrants was diverse in terms of geographic origins and occupational skills, many being technicians, tradesman of all kinds, clerical workers, and teachers (who were able to emigrate from the Caribbean directly into jobs as teachers, usually in rural areas). Retired teachers such as those in the Mico Old Students Association (the Mico Old Students are retired teachers who attended Mico Teacher Training College in Jamaica and still meet in Edmonton) can still recall such early immigration and teaching experiences in rural areas of Alberta or on First Nations reserves.

These workers from the Caribbean were later joined by students from the Caribbean and countries in Africa who would graduate from the University of Alberta and go on to enter a wide spectrum of professions. In the 1980s and 1990s, these groups of diasporan Blacks were joined by others from African countries who were fleeing war or trying to make a better life for themselves and their children. Approximately 2 percent of the population in both Edmonton and Calgary are Black, with the majority of those born outside Canada coming from African or Caribbean countries.

This latest period of immigration was also marked by renewed political self-organization. Cultural groups such as the National Black Coalition of Canada and the Council of Black Organizations (now the Council of Canadians of African and Caribbean Heritage), as well as the Jamaica Association of Northern Alberta, the Nigerian Association, and so on, provided a link with their homeland for many new immigrants as well as a forum for challenging the racialized state of Canadian society.

Ironically, the influx of the newer immigrants from the Caribbean and the continent served to subsume the early African Canadian pioneers. Because of the numerical dominance of this new wave and the lack of knowledge of an earlier Black presence in Alberta, there was initially little formal attempt to be inclusive and build the community. Blacks from the Caribbean were often regarded as representing the universal in terms of Black groups. Although highlighting the historical enables us to tease out some of the similarities in experiences among various African Canadian communities (primarily associated with learning to be Black in a White society), it is also worth being cautious with regard to history. Canadian theorist Rinaldo Walcott (1997) argued that "historical experience is a potent ingredient in desires for community cannot be understated because it is what often complicates discussions and leads to assumptions concerning communities of the same" (p. 226).

Building Community

For those cultural workers who are active in communities, it is imperative that one recognize heterogeneity of experiences within a community as well as heterogeneity in terms of social categories (class, gender, sexualities). Such an understanding makes problematic the notion of "working with the community" and ideas about "communities of practice"; it highlights community as something that has to be worked *at* rather than something that is ready to be worked *on*. The issue of voice also becomes problematic with such an understanding: It raises the question of who can speak on behalf of a "community." What does it mean to have community consensus? Such recognition of plurality also highlights that conflict within a community is not necessarily negative and constraining, but can be used to enable social change.

Further, if adult educators were to adopt Hall's postulation that Black identity is a political identity, how would that affect the ways in which we approach community building? Might such an adoption allow for recognition that outside of a political project it is possible to differ? In other words, that Black identity can be used strategically so that one need not fear essentialism. Here we can draw on the work of Kataya Azoulay (1997), who contended:

> Strategic essentialism does not preclude alliance between different social groups; nor does it presume that communities are bounded, fixed or that 'race' is an essence shared by all members of a given group. Instead these discursive invented 'space[s]' take the beingness of black as experiential sources which can be drawn on without apology. (p. 102)

Such an adoption would undermine the discussions of authenticity that have at times plagued racialized communities such as those of African Canadians. Although asserting an individual and collective identity has

been important and empowering historically, recognizing a common experience has also led to a political stress on "authentic subjective experience,"
which forecloses alternative conceptions of consciousness. It would call
for a plurality of identities to be recognized within the political category
of Black. Representations of Blackness would also enable a break with the
ideas of a Black community that is aligned with one way of acting and
thinking. A Black community is not consistently unified and static; it is
heterogeneous.

Living History Group (LHG)

If a community is heterogeneous, then how is it possible to undertake
any community education and activity? The Living History Group, formed
under the umbrella of Edmonton's Council of Canadians of African and
Caribbean Heritage, is a concrete example of working within a Black
community and trying to connect with differing understandings of
Blackness in the wider community.

In February 1998 Susan Ruttan (as cited in Kelly, 1998) wrote an editorial
in the *Edmonton Journal*. The article, although thought provoking, nonetheless insinuated that a celebration of Black History Month in Canada,
and especially in Edmonton, was basically a poor imitation of US-based
experiences. As a neophyte researcher, I was somewhat incensed with this
naïve claim, especially because I had spent a significant period of time in
the university library the previous summer reading the history of early
pioneers of African descent. What had I been reading about if not Albertan
Black history? What were those experiences of the struggles and triumphs
of these early African Canadian settlers? Were their experiences not significant? Were their experiences not rooted in Canada? Were they a lesser
form of US Black experience? On the other hand, was Ruttan's dismissive
comment of any concern to me since I had no familial ties to that early
settlement of African Canadians? Was I guilty of assuming that there was
a biological essentialism that linked my experiences with theirs? Or should
I not note bell hooks' (1992) warning, "I cannot assume a shared politics
with all black people based upon skin color or common experience" (p.
68)?

My response to Ruttan's (1998) article was to phone a friend, a long-
time resident of Canada who saw himself as a pan-African activist with
roots in the Caribbean. Our agreed strategy was that such misconception
about the place of African Canadians in Alberta's history was misplaced
at best and needed to be re-represented through a political strategy. We
therefore decided on a collective strategy: We called together various
peoples of African descent from within the city and booked a room in the
Faculty of Education, where we gathered to discuss our response to the
article and strategies that might be useful. We wrote the usual letters to
the media to contest the misinformation in the article, and a few people
decided to meet again to organize an event that would highlight the contributions of early African Canadians to Canadian society both in Alberta and

beyond. Although the members of our group had a strong connection to the Caribbean, we set out to explore the possibilities of including all of the diverse experiences of Edmontonians of African descent.

What connects our group is our knowledge and experiences (whether through the legacy of slavery or the economic and political ravages of colonialism) and the ways in which we have been marginalized and excluded from power within a dominant White society. To be treated as the "outsider" or "other," as the non-Albertan/Canadian "under the gaze" of dominant White society, is a common experience for peoples of African descent (and other visible minorities) that denies Canada's multicultural/multi-ethnic history. To combat this, we set about organizing a number of educational events that would challenge the "outsider" view of African Canadians. The events were designed to educate Black and White Edmontonians about Canada's Black history. We hoped that these educational offerings would help to build identity and community and go beyond the "dance, diet, and dress" approach of Heritage Days and Cari-West festivals. Although both events are useful and enjoyable, they do not speak consistently to the history of early settlers in Alberta or to ongoing social struggles of the Black community.

Our group soon recognized that we were engaged in issues of knowledge production and dissemination. We were trying to produce counter-hegemonic narratives that, although they did not necessarily displace the existing hegemonic understandings, could at least show the complex nature of the situation. In an attempt to educate all citizens, we organized subsequent events to draw on a heterogeneous group of wider Edmontonians, not just those of African descent. In practical terms we did this by organizing public lectures and presentations combined with television, radio, and newspaper interviews and articles. We linked our efforts to those of other groups by pushing broader understandings of African Canadian history and community and providing resources and support for educational and social initiatives that address current community problems and Black identity.

In addition, LHG recognized that "our" history is not created in a vacuum, but rather is constructed through interactions with the wider White-dominated communities. Thus, for example, arranging public speaking engagements and media events for Stanley Grizzle, rail union activist (member of the Brotherhood of Sleeping Car Porters), intersected with the interests of the labour movement; and those arranged for writer Olive Senior intersected with the literary-arts community in Edmonton. These and other educational events drew audiences from the wider Edmonton population. Work with the Alberta Labour History Institute has helped to profile the contributions of Albertans of African descent that would otherwise have been overlooked.

Community of Practice?

Etienne Wenger's (1998) concept of *communities of practice* is useful in indicating the temporary nature of alliances and how a community of interest needs shared practice to become a community *in* action. Communities of practice also move through various stages of development that are characterized by different levels of interaction among members and different kinds of activities. It can be argued that our LHG is an example as a joint enterprise that is continually renegotiated and has produced a shared repertoire of communal resources; it is a social entity and has capacity. Although Wenger's conception is interesting as an initial starting point for evaluating LHG, it needs to be problematized to recognize heterogeneity within communities and to include the political within understandings of community. Thus, what is underway with LHG is a community of practice that enables knowledge production and generation to take account of external socio-political contexts and draw on communal resources cognizant of Gilroy's conception of culture as more about "routes" than "roots." Such an understanding of community recognizes the various ways in which culture is syncretic rather than absolute and that the form and longevity of such a community cannot be determined beforehand.

References

Anderson, B. (1983). *Imagined communities: Reflections on the origins and spread of nationalism.* London: Verso

Azoulay, K. (1997). Experience, empathy, essentialism. *Cultural Studies, 11*(1), 89–110.

Bauman, Z. (2001). *Community: Seeking safety in an insecure world.* Cambridge: Polity Press.

Gilroy, P. (1993). *The Black Atlantic.* Cambridge, MA: Harvard University Press.

Hall, S. (1990). Cultural identity and Diaspora. In J. Rutherford (Ed.), *Identity, community, culture, and difference* (pp. 222–237). London: Lawrence and Wishart.

hooks, b. (1992). *Black looks.* Toronto, ON: Between the Lines.

Kelly, J. (1998). *Under the gaze: Learning to be Black in White society.* Halifax, NS: Fernwood Press.

Kelly, J. (2004). *Borrowed identities.* New York: Peter Lang.

Mathieu, S.-J. (2001). North of the colour line: Sleeping car porters and the battle against Jim Crow on Canadian rails, 1880–1920. *Labour/Le Travail, 47,* 9–41.

McIlroy, J., and Westwood, S. (Eds.) (1993). *Border country: Raymond Williams in adult education.* Leicester, UK: National Institute of Adult Continuing Education.

Scott, J. (1992). Experience. In J. Butler and J. Scott (Eds.), *Feminists theorize the political* (pp. 22–40). New York: Routledge.

Steele, T. (1997). *The emergence of cultural studies: Adult education, cultural politics, and the 'English' question.* London: Lawrence and Wishart.

Walcott, R. (1997). *Black like who?* Toronto, ON: Insomniac Press.

Walker, J. (1980). *A history of Blacks in Canada.* Ottawa, ON: Supply and Services.

Wenger, E. (1998). *Communities of practice: Learning, meaning, and identity.* New York: Cambridge University Press.

Winks, R. (1971). *The Blacks in Canada.* New Haven: Yale University Press.

4

Women and Adult Education in Canadian Society

Nancy Taber and Patricia A. Gouthro

Women have been actively involved in the field of adult education, but the significance and value of their unique contributions has frequently been overlooked or devalued (Burstow, 1994; Butterwick, 1998; Gouthro, 2005). In this chapter, we argue that paying attention to women's experiences in adult education broadens the focus of traditional adult education research, theory, and practice. By focusing on women's issues and bringing in a feminist analysis, important questions are raised around power, privilege, and inclusivity. Attending to these concerns opens possibilities for the development of new theoretical perspectives and research projects. An emphasis on women's contributions, viewpoints, and experiences creates opportunities to develop more inclusive educational policies and practices that will enable women to engage in a range of different lifelong learning contexts in meaningful and constructive ways.

Research on Women in Canada

Feminists have routinely noted that what is determined as great literature, what we see as art, and what parts of human history are recorded and studied to form the basis for what we deem to be relevant curriculum focus primarily on male contributions and experiences. The definition of *great* (think Alexander) has generally been created by and for men. As a consequence, most women are educated in a system that reinforces predominantly masculine achievements. Hayes (2000b) maintains that this "hidden curriculum" consists of "implicit messages" such as the "value placed on certain kinds of knowledge" (p. 25). Burstow (1994) argues that "general Canadian adult education histories provide raving accounts of individual 'great men,' for example, Coady, Corbett and Kidd" (p. 4). She continues, "We do not find such accounts of women. Educational movements by women, including the feminist movement, are not counted as adult education" (p. 4). One of the goals of feminist scholarship is to conduct research into women's experiences, to explore the absences of women's voices and stories, and to uncover contributions that women have made but have generally not been studied, such as the feminist movement itself (Rebick, 2005), women's contributions to environmentalist organizations (Clover, 1995), or women in the Antigonish Movement (Butterwick, 1998).

Frequently, feminist educators encounter resistance from students and colleagues in accepting their teaching and research. This is not just because their work challenges the status quo and existing power relations that frequently serve to privilege men over women, but also because there is a pervasive belief that women have already attained equality, so feminism is no longer needed. As Smith (2005) notes:

> It is hard to recall just how radical the experience of the women's movement was at its inception for those who had lived and thought within the masculine regime against which the movement struggled. For us, the struggle was as much within ourselves, with what we knew how to do and think and feel, as with that regime as an enemy outside us. (p. 7)

Despite the many successes of the women's movement, academic research provides important empirical evidence that challenges the assumption that women have attained full social, political, and economic equality. Educators need to question their own assumptions around power, privilege, and positionality and to consider how they can create more equitable and inclusive learning environments for their students.

Quantitative Research

Although many feminist researchers have tended to use qualitative methodology in their research, quantitative research has also provided important empirical evidence that women have not attained full social and economic equality in Canadian society. Statistical data can summarize inequities in wages and reveal the significant percentages of women who are victimized through sexual harassment (Fenwick, 2004). There are gender inequities in representation of women at higher levels of government, business, religious, and educational institutions. Women are still concentrated in traditional jobs, have fewer learning opportunities in the workforce, and, on average, earn less than men (Fenwick, 2004). Research indicates that, whereas women may be attending universities in equal or slightly higher numbers at the undergraduate level, their participation is still low in non-traditional fields such as engineering, and women's participation in academe falls off at the doctoral levels (Gouthro, 2005; Stalker and Prentice, 1998).

Statistical research has shown that many inequities between men and women still exist in Canadian society. For example, the number of hours spent on unpaid work such as child care and domestic labour is still much higher for women than for men overall (Fenwick, 2004; Gouthro, 2005). These figures have important implications for understanding women's participation in lifelong learning contexts and provide substantive data to justify policy initiatives and advocate for social change. As Gouthro points out in her analysis of lifelong learning and the homeplace, this raises central questions around the values that determine what types of work and learning will be rewarded. In looking at the marginalized position of women in the labour force, Fenwick asks, "Why should life and learning be governed by the market? Who and what is served by notions of continuous learning-for-earning? . . . Who is marginalized and who is privileged by ideals of individualism and self-reliance?" (p. 182).

Qualitative Research

Qualitative research has provided essential insights into the reasons behind women's continued lagging progress in attaining full social, economic, and educational equality in Canadian society. Narrative, auto-ethnography, and life-history approaches reveal the complex factors that articulate women's experiences in living and learning. For example, Taber (in press) uses an auto-ethnographical approach to reflect on her experience in the Canadian military, arguing that women are often penalized for not fitting the perceived image of an ideal (male) worker. Although she was an insider as a member of the military, being a woman also placed her in the status of an outsider. The hidden curriculum of her training and socialization into the military taught her how to be a woman in this context, which entailed walking a fine line between masculinity and femininity. This line became more difficult to navigate when she became a mother. Taber found that some of her male co-workers questioned the commitment of mothers to the military because caring labour in the homeplace did not mesh with their masculine definition of work and commitment to the workplace.

Similarly, in *The Illusion of Inclusion*, Stalker and Prentice (1998) detail different Canadian women's stories and their frequently poignant experiences in academe. We read about the struggles of a poor woman caught between middle-class values and expectations within an academic world that fails to acknowledge the lack of resources to which poor women have access; the concerns of many women graduate students over conflicting goals of attaining academic success and desiring adequate time to raise children; and the fear in which many women live of sexual violence and the precautions that they take during their studies to avoid victimization.

Drawing on women's stories is an important method in feminist research. Hayes (2000c) terms this *voice*, which can refer to talk, identity, and/or power. These three meanings are interrelated: Talking can help women to share their stories and begin to see how their experiences connect to structural, societal issues, leading to a changing sense of identity (or, from a poststructural perspective, identities). Voice can challenge power relations, such as when Taber (in press) uses narrative to link her experiences to societal relations to challenge the power structures of a gendered institution (the Canadian military). "For women, a goal of learning can be to acquire individual and collective power through the expression and validation of their interests, needs, and experiences" (Hayes, 2000c, p. 108).

Qualitative research strategies, including interviews, ethnography, narratives, focus groups, and life histories, provide a rich source of data for educators as they work to make sense of women's learning experiences. These methodologies enable researchers to explore the complex and interconnected variables that affect women's decisions on whether or not to continue with education, their participation in paid and unpaid labour, and the connections between different aspects of their lives. Women's stories reveal the frequently subtle but pervasive influence of *patriarchy* (the hierarchical privileging of men and masculine perspectives that creates a system of dominance over women).

Evolving *discourses* (strands of debates and conversations) of feminist theories are essential in uncovering the ways in which a predominant masculine world view reinforces power structures that frequently undermine and devalue women's contributions and experiences. Smith (2005) notes that "as women learned in the women's movement, there are experiences that a discourse will not speak" (p. 18). In naming their experience, language developed to render visible experiences of women that were previously often hidden, such as domestic abuse, date rape, and sexual harassment. Until these experiences are named, these issues cannot be addressed and underlying power structures cannot be challenged.

Feminist Adult Education Theories

At a seminar recently, a senior (male) academic asked a rhetorical question about feminism: "Can a feminist be against gun control?" and continued quickly with other thoughts, as if he had made a non sequitur. The answer to his question is, "Why not?" Women do not form an undifferentiated mass; neither do feminists. Therefore, we will pluralize the word *feminisms* to acknowledge the diverse strands of thought within this field.

Feminist *epistemology* (philosophical theory of knowledge) addresses the way that knowledge has been constructed. Historically, formalized knowledge has been created primarily by men. Abstract knowledge has often been privileged over lived, bodily experiences (Smith, 2005). As Flannery and Hayes (2000) note, "The significance of gender has been given little attention in adult learning theory, and yet women and men are products of social and cultural beliefs about what it means to be a gendered being" (p. 3). The development of feminist epistemologies raises concerns around how knowledge is constructed, recorded, and evaluated, taking into consideration gender difference in experience and understanding.

Feminist standpoint epistemology is both a theoretical and a practical investigative approach to constructing knowledge that validates women's experiences at the same time as it critiques existing social, economic, and political structures. Smith (2005) argues that "it is a method of inquiry that works from the actualities of people's everyday lives and experience to discover the social as it extends beyond experience" (p. 10). The standpoint of the individual who creates knowledge is important because the positionality of the researcher is connected to power relations of different social groups. Black feminist scholars such as Collins (1996) have drawn upon standpoint theory to assess the experiences of Black women in the larger society. People who are in more marginalized positions of power, such as women of colour, may have a more privileged perspective from which to construct certain kinds of knowledge. The experience of being a

Black woman can provide insights into the frequently subtle and insidious ways that patriarchy and racism are woven into the social fabric of everyday life.

Feminist Waves

Over time, feminist theory has evolved through different "waves," as reflected in both the larger feminist movement and the literature in adult education. These waves are not distinctly separated; their edges are blurred and overlapping. During the first wave, the emphasis was on attaining basic equality and recognition as citizens through the women's suffrage movement. During the 1960s and 1970s, the second wave of feminism emerged as a collective movement in which women began to advocate for women's issues. This period gave rise to an understanding "that what appeared to be the private individual situation of women was linked to larger social, cultural, economic and political structures and power relations" (Butterwick, 1998, p. 112). Women came together in conscious-ness-raising groups to learn from their own experiences by sharing stories, recognizing common themes, and developing strategies for change. Some successes of this movement were reflected in policy shifts that included recognition of domestic violence and the development of shelters for abused women; legal changes that provided easier access to divorce, contracep-tion, and abortion; legislation for equal pay; and increasing support for women to enter non-traditional careers such as engineering, carpentry, and medicine.

Even within the context of liberation, however, some groups of women have felt that feminism itself can be oppressive and can result in deep conflict (Rebick, 2005). Despite the collective emphasis on shared goals, a number of divisions still emerged within the feminist movement. For example, minority women, including lesbians, poor women, women of colour, and women with disabilities, argue that the feminist movement has been dominated by White, heterosexual, middle-class women and that their experiences, needs, and understandings of the world are often marginalized in this context. Collins (1996) argues that the word *feminism* has often come to mean White women's perspectives and explores the use of the terms *womanism* and *Black feminism* to better represent the chal-lenges that Black women face. Although she is an advocate of the impor-tance of a collective Black voice, she recognizes the difficulty of grouping all Black women into one category, which ignores other issues such as class and sexuality.

Although many second-wave feminists are still actively working to negotiate social change, the third wave of feminism emerged in the 1990s as a broader and more fragmented movement in which women address a wide array of issues from a feminist lens. In this stage of feminism, women recognize, and frequently celebrate, the diversity, contradictions, and differences that characterize women's experiences.

In the last couple of decades, a more global emphasis has emerged in feminism. For instance, Clover (1995) examines the effects of globalization as they relate to environmentalism, sexism, racism, and social justice. English (2005) explores post-colonialism, binaries, and religion in her research on global women adult educators. With the evolution of technologies such as the Internet, there are also opportunities for diverse learner groups, such as Aboriginal women, to connect and share common experiences and concerns (Martinez and Turcotte, 2003).

Feminisms

Today there are many feminisms. Although decrying the need for labels, Tong (1998) believes that they are useful and that "feminism is not a monolithic ideology, that all feminists do not think alike, and that, like all other time-honored modes of thinking, feminist thought has a past as well as a present and a future" (p. 1). She suggests eight categories to organize feminist thought, including liberal, radical, Marxist and socialist, psychoanalytic and gender, existentialist, postmodern, multicultural and global feminism, and ecofeminism. We will discuss five of these different strands below.

Liberal feminism suggests that women can benefit from working within existing institutions to achieve women's equality before the law and in the workplace. *Radical feminism* challenges the "root" (the origin of *radical* is L. *radix*, 'root') cause of women's oppression, which is *patriarchy*. Radical feminists argue that societal institutions have been created primarily by men for male purposes and that women cannot gain equality without changing institutional, patriarchal structures in society.

Marxist-feminists connect capitalism with patriarchy and focus upon the distribution of material wealth and class-based inequities. "Under capitalism as it exists today, women experience patriarchy as unequal wages for equal work, sexual harassment on the job, uncompensated domestic work, and the pernicious dynamics of the public-private split" (Tong, 1998, p. 123). For instance, Mojab and Gorman (2003) take up the debate on learning organizations to argue that "the failure of many organizations to offer more than a small fraction of their workforce broader opportunities for upskilling and reskilling renders the rhetoric about the learning organization concept empty of meaning and purpose" (p. 233). Typically, full-time workers in management with already significant educational qualifications are the ones who are offered further training and development opportunities, and these workers are more likely to be men.

Postmodern feminism builds on French feminists (Cixious, Irigaray, and Kristeva) and is based on the belief that "women are not unitary selves, essences to be defined and then ossified" (Tong, 1998, p. 7). According to poststructural thought, there is no universal theory, nor is there one concrete reality. A common criticism of poststructuralism is that "the concern with language and thought as representations of experience can also become excessively abstract and theoretical, and this can make it difficult to draw concrete implications for women's everyday lives and learning" (Flannery and Hayes, 2000, p. 15). Nonetheless, it is useful to "conceptualize gender as a system of social relations that are continually renegotiated, both at the level of daily interactions and at the level of the broader social structures" (p. 15).

Ecofeminism is based on the belief that all oppression is linked (including our oppression of nature); therefore, to eliminate women's oppression, we must eliminate all oppression. Clover (1995) uses the term *feminist environmental pedagogy* to explain that "the women's movement has raised its voice to condemn these visions of women and nature and fight against injustices and inequalities, working in support of peace, social change and a new relationship with the environment" (p. 250).

There are also different types of feminisms that are not included in Tong's (1998) work. For instance, Gouthro's (2005) work is informed by *critical feminism*. Drawing upon critical Habermasian theory, Gouthro adds a feminist critique to examine the structural factors that have marginalized the concerns of women learners by broadening the debates on lifelong learning to take the homeplace into consideration. She argues that the homeplace is not viewed as a learning site because of its apparent disconnection from the marketplace. Unpaid labour, including child care, is not viewed as work that requires skills or learning. "By broadening the lens through which lifelong learning experiences are assessed to consider the homeplace as an important learning site, the underlying values reflected in our society and in our educational systems will be challenged" (p. 16).

As the above demonstrates, there are many tensions within feminist adult education theories. These tensions have been central to the development of feminist thought, resulting in a rich field from which to develop our work and inform our practice.

Implications for Practice

Without putting the interests of women, as varied as they may be, to the forefront, the interests of men frequently become what is perceived as the standard, neutral focus of education. However, even when research focuses on women in adult education, this literature is not necessarily feminist, nor does it necessarily examine the power relations and structural constraints that impact on women's learning.

> For the most part, then, researchers have failed to look at issues of sexism in the power relationships involved in learning, and they have neglected to conduct wider social, economic, and political analyses of the constraints under which the process of learning actually takes place for women. (Flannery and Hayes, 2000, pp. 18–19)

Much of the adult education literature on women has focused on the contention that women learn in different ways than men do, through connection, collaboration, and sharing rather than individualism, competition, and debate (Hayes, 2000a). However, in studying *women* as a category of learners, there is a concern that educators may not attend to the diversity that exists within this group. Even the notion of *woman* is problematic because it can be argued that gender is a socially rather than biologically constructed variable. In addition, there are debates within feminism around the concept of *essentialism* (that women are essentially, biologically different from men) because this concept may lead to the argument that women can never be the same as (and therefore equal to) men.

> One danger is that such work can lead to assertions that certain attributes or qualities of women's learning are innate, fixed, and uniform across situations ("essential" attributes of women) rather than integrally connected to a particular set of situational, social, and historical circumstances, and thus changeable as those circumstances change. (Hayes, 2000a, p. 218)

Essentialism may perpetuate a binary or oppositional approach to understanding gender whereby certain characteristics are defined as masculine and therefore superior to those that are considered to be feminine (e.g., abstract/concrete, independent/collaborative). Women learners, understood in this context, would be more likely to be perceived as being deficient or in need of remedial assistance.

Many feminists would argue that the need to recognize the unique concerns of women learners stems from the belief that women are not innately different from men, but are socialized in different ways, with different expectations placed upon them. These differences pervade our society and are a result of complex, structural interactions. Feminist pedagogy then provides a means with which to challenge women's place in society through the classroom. It is about more than women learning differently from men. Tisdell (2000) states that feminist pedagogy centres on curricula

> by, about, and for women as learners, and that are intended to increase women's status and opportunity in society. In addition, feminist educators try to conduct learning activities that encourage connection and relationship, and that take affective as well as rational and cognitive modes of learning into account. (p. 156)

Stalker and Prentice (1998) discuss the constraints that women face in higher education as students and as faculty. They contend that women are marginalized in misogynist academic institutions, where they are frequently devalued, harassed, and excluded. Part of the difficulty of addressing these issues stems from the fact that men often fail to see how the overabundance of male faculty, their approaches in class, and the content they choose often exclude women: "If they were to acknowledge the discriminatory effects of apparently neutral practices, then basic assumptions that men as a group take for granted would be challenged and the privileges that also accrue to men as a group would be undermined" (p. 26). It may be in the best interests of men in academe to fail to understand how their everyday, unconscious practices affect women in their classrooms and in wider society, because otherwise they might have to change their research and teaching practices (Burstow, 1994).

Educators must recognize that the teaching and learning relationship is not a neutral, apolitical enterprise. Each of us brings certain assumptions, beliefs, and ideas into our teaching contexts around what constitutes "good" pedagogical practice and what the characteristics are of "committed" and "successful" learners. In starting to unpack these assumptions, we may find that we have certain gendered or prejudiced values. For instance, we may think that evidence of good participation is indicated when a student speaks up, but we do not value as much someone who is a thoughtful listener. Being attentive to learning dynamics, such as who is encouraged to speak, what types of behaviour are rewarded, and what kinds of learning are valued, are important factors for educators to reflect upon in their teaching practice. This focus encourages educators to attend to the diverse needs of all learners. Although feminist pedagogy is concerned with "increasing women's choices and status in society" (Burstow, 1994, p. 167), it should also be an approach to learning that is beneficial for women *and* men.

Additional Reading

For additional background reading on feminism, we suggest the following texts:

Alcoff, L. and Potter, E. (Eds.). (1993). *Feminist epistemologies.* New York: Routledge, Chapman and Hall.

Belenky, M., Clinchy, B., Goldberger, N., and Tarule, J. (1997). *Women's ways of knowing: The development of self, voice, and mind.* (10th anniversary ed.). New York: Basic Books.

Gilligan, C. (1993). *In a different voice: Psychological theory and women's development.* Cambridge, MA: Harvard University Press.

Hart, M. U. (1992). *Working and educating for life: Feminist and international perspectives.* London: Routledge.

References

Burstow, B. (1994). Problematizing adult education: A feminist perspective. *The Canadian Journal for the Study of Adult Education, 8*(1), 1–14.

Butterwick, S. (1998). Lest we forget: Uncovering women's leadership in adult education. In G. Selman, M. Selman, M. Cooke, and P. Dampier (Eds.), *The foundations of adult education in Canada* (2nd ed., pp. 103–116). Toronto: Thompson Educational.

Clover, D. (1995). Gender transformations learning and environmental action. *Gender and Education, 7*(3), 243–258.

Collins, P. H. (1996). What's in a name? Womanism, Black feminism, and beyond. *Black Scholar (Black World Foundation), 26*(1), 9–17.

English, L. M. (2005). Third-space practitioners: Women educating for justice in the global south. *Adult Education Quarterly, 55*(2), 85–100.

Fenwick, T. (2004). What happens to the girls? Gender, work, and learning in Canada's 'new economy.' *Gender & Education, 16*(2), 169–185.

Flannery, D. and Hayes, E. (2000). Women's learning: A kaleidoscope. In E. Hayes and D. Flannery (Eds.), *Women as learners: The significance of gender in learning* (pp. 1–22). San Francisco: Jossey-Bass.

Gouthro, P. (2005). A critical feminist analysis of the homeplace as learning site: Expanding the discourse of lifelong learning to include adult women learners. *International Journal of Lifelong Education, 24*(1), 5–19.

Hayes, E. (2000a). Creating knowledge about women's learning. In E. Hayes and D. Flannery (Eds.), *Women as learners: The significance of gender in learning* (pp. 217–246). San Francisco: Jossey-Bass.

Hayes, E. (2000b). Social contexts. In E. Hayes and D. Flannery (Eds.), *Women as learners: The significance of gender in learning* (pp. 23–52). San Francisco: Jossey-Bass.

Hayes, E. (2000c). Voice. In E. Hayes and D. Flannery (Eds.), *Women as learners: The significance of gender in learning* (pp. 79–110). San Francisco: Jossey-Bass.

Martinez, A. and Turcotte, E. (2003). The rise of Aboriginal women's global connectivity on the World Wide Web. In A. Martinez and M. Stuart (Eds.), *Out of the ivory tower: Feminist research for social change* (pp. 270–293). Toronto, ON: Sumach Press.

Mojab, S. and Gorman, R. (2003). Women and consciousness in the "learning organization": Emancipation or exploitation. *Adult Education Quarterly, 53*(4), 228–241.

Rebick, J. (2005). Ten thousand roses: The making of a feminist revolution. Toronto, ON: Penguin Canada.

Smith, D. (2005). *Institutional ethnography: A sociology for people.* Lanham, MD: AltaMira Press.

Stalker, J. and Prentice, S. (1998). Introduction. In J. Stalker and S. Prentice (Eds.), *The illusion of inclusion: Women in post-secondary education* (pp. 12–34). Halifax, NS: Fernwood.

Taber, N. (in press). Learning how to be a woman in the Canadian Forces/Unlearning it through feminism: An autoethnography of my learning journey. *Studies in Continuing Education.*

Tisdell, E. J. (2000). Feminist pedagogies. In E. Hayes and D. Flannery (Eds.), *Women as learners: The significance of gender in adult learning* (pp. 155–184). San Francisco: Jossey-Bass.

Tong, R. (1998). *Feminist thought: A more comprehensive introduction* (2nd ed.). Boulder, CO: Westview Press.

5

Adult Citizenship Education: An Overview of the Field

Daniel Schugurensky

This chapter provides an overview of adult citizenship education and is organized into five sections. The first presents a conceptual discussion on citizenship. The second outlines the main rationales and orientations of adult citizenship education programs. The third presents some highlights of adult citizenship education in Canada. The fourth section describes the current international agenda for adult citizenship education, and the last provides some conclusions and recommendations.

Citizenship

If citizenship education is about education for citizenship, it is pertinent to start with a few words on the concept of citizenship itself, a multi-layered term that includes at least four dimensions: status, identity, civic virtues, and agency. The most common understanding of citizenship is *status*, to the extent that often citizenship is equated with nationality or with a passport. Marshall (1950/1992), in an influential work, defined *citizenship* as "a status bestowed on those who are full members of a community" and noted that "all who possess the status are equal with respect to the rights and duties with which the status is endowed" (p. 103). The community of citizens is often the nation-state,[1] and rights and duties are codified in constitutions and related laws. All citizens of a nation are supposed to enjoy the same rights, but in every country there are structures and dynamics of inclusion and exclusion. For instance, in most countries women were not allowed to vote until the first half of the twentieth century, in others Blacks were legally segregated until the second half of that century, and today same-sex couples can marry in only three countries. Hence, it is pertinent to distinguish between ideal and real citizenship and between formal and substantive democracy. In short, formal equality is meaningless if it is contradicted by economic, social, political, and cultural inequalities. Particularly dramatic is the situation of nine million stateless who have no citizenship status in any state, and of the poorest members of society who may have little opportunity to exercise their civil, political, and social rights.

Citizenship as *identity* refers to issues of belonging and meaning. Whereas status is about being a full member of a community, identity is about feeling like a member of that community. The distinction between status and identity is prominent in multi-ethnic, multilingual, multicultural, and multireligious states, and particularly in nation-states that are multination states. In these cases identity is rooted in factors such as a common history, language, religion, values, traditions, and culture, which seldom coincide with the artificial territory of a nation-state. In the same vein, diasporic communities may hold a legal citizenship status in two or more nation-states but feel allegiance to only one of them. The difference between citizenship as status and citizenship as identity is also clear in nation-states built through conquest and colonization, usually by displacing, dominating, assimilating, or eliminating the original inhabitants. Finally, another example of a mismatch between status and identity can be observed among people with internationalist inclinations who are legally citizens of their nation-states but define themselves as citizens of the world, even if "planetary citizenship" is not yet a legal condition.

Citizenship as *civic virtues* alludes to the values, attitudes, and behaviours that are expected of "good citizens." However, there is disagreement on the traits of the good citizen. The abstract notion of the good citizen may evoke different images, from Mother Jones to Mother Theresa, from Moses Coady to Emily Murphy. For some people a good citizen is patriotic, obedient, diligent, and religious. Others emphasize compassion, respect, tolerance, solidarity, and individual responsibility. Yet others relate civic virtues to political engagement, community participation, knowledge of social reality, critical thinking, and interest for the common good.

Citizenship as *agency* invokes the idea of citizens as social actors. Agency refers to the state of being in action or exerting power. The exercise of citizenship, individual or collective, does not occur in a vacuum, but in concrete social structures mediated by power relations. The notion of agency, then, recognizes that social action occurs in a context marked by a constant interplay of domination and autonomy. It also calls our attention to the intensity and type of citizen action. In relation to intensity, although it is possible to talk in general terms about "passive" and "active" citizenship, in reality these should be understood as end points of a continuum rather than as dichotomous categories. In relation to the types of citizen action, Westheimer and Kahne (2004) identified three conceptions of the good citizen: responsible, participatory, and justice oriented. Responsible citizens are expected to avoid littering, pick up litter made by others, give blood, recycle, volunteer, pay taxes, exercise, stay out of debt, and the like. Participatory citizens are expected to take active part in the civic affairs and social life of the community, and assume leading roles in neighbourhood associations, school councils, or political parties. Justice-oriented citizens are expected to be able to critically analyze structures of inequality, consider collective strategies to challenge injustice, and, whenever possible, address root causes of social problems. The first two models promote citizens' actions that develop character and service through charity and volunteerism, whereas the social justice orientation encourages critical understandings of unequal social structures and engagement in political struggles to build a more democratic and just society.

Citizenship Education: Main Orientations

Citizenship education includes a wide range of political and pedagogical approaches, goals, and practices. Like other educational fields, citizenship education has conservative and progressive orientations. Citizenship education can be used as a tool for maintaining the status quo, but also for empowering individuals and groups to struggle for emancipatory change. Although citizenship education practices are situated somewhere along a continuum between these two orientations, they tend to gravitate towards one or the other. Citizenship education programs tend to address simultaneously the four dimensions of citizenship discussed above, but frequently they put an emphasis on one of them.

Programs focusing on citizenship as status often emphasize formal membership to a political community, usually a nation-state. They concentrate on facts about national history and geography, government institutions, and the law. In many countries these programs tend to instill uncritical patriotism among learners, naturalize social relations, and exalt national heroes. Frequently, these programs conflate formal and real membership, as well as political and economic democracy, as if they were one and the same. They usually promote the "official history" of a nation's development, reporting it from the winners' perspective and excluding compromising parts (Strong-Boag, 2002). In the margins, however, are critical programs that encourage historical revisionism and contrast the official perspective with the views of peoples who suffered conquest or discrimination. These programs also question taken-for-granted rules of inclusion and exclusion, interpret the law in the context of social dynamics of power and struggles, and promote substantive rather than formal status by pursuing the fulfillment of civil, political, social, and cultural rights.

Programs that emphasize citizenship as identity tend to stress nation building and the assimilation of minority groups into the dominant groups. Often this has meant the mainstreaming and "malestreaming" of curriculum content and elevating the hegemonic language, religion, and culture to the pedestal of civilization. In many countries the metaphor of the *melting pot* is used to justify educational policies of forced assimilation (e.g., residential schools for Indigenous peoples). Other programs, however, promote the development of diversified curricula and multicultural and intercultural education. Whereas multicultural education usually consists of knowing about other groups that coexist in the same territory, intercultural education promotes mutual recognition and equitable relations. Whereas multicultural education tends to take a superficial and uncritical approach (focusing on the 3Fs of folklore, food, and festivities and the 3Ds of dance, dress, and diet), intercultural education aims at encouraging deeper analyses and interactions and challenges discrimination and advancing social justice. Intercultural education tries to address the difficult balance between fostering equality while respecting difference and is often inspired by related approaches such as critical multiculturalism and antiracist education (Kanpol and McLaren, 1995; Sabariego, 2002). Other citizenship education programs strive to develop a planetary consciousness and an identity as world citizens. These programs are usually known as *global education* and are often connected to peace and environmental education.

Programs that emphasize the development of civic virtues tend to emphasize certain values and dispositions. These range from national allegiance to international solidarity, from religious indoctrination to agnostic pluralism, from obedience to autonomy, from compliance to critical reflection, and from supremacist values to beliefs in equity, fraternity, and justice. In each context the particular selection of values promoted by a particular program will depend on a variety of social, institutional, and personal factors. In Canada there is a long tradition of adult education programs that focus on the development of social-justice oriented values and dispositions.

Two main approaches tend to prevail in the pedagogy of values and beliefs: *character education* and *values clarification*. Character education programs tend to instil a set of values and dispositions through exhortations and inducements. In theory, these programs claim to teach respect, responsibility, and autonomy; but in practice, they typically tend to use a pedagogy of indoctrination that fosters blind patriotism, uncritical obedience to authority, industriousness, faith in the establishment, and the like (Kohn, 1997). Values clarification programs aim at helping learners develop their own values by examining ethical dilemmas and different perspectives. In this approach there is no right or wrong set of values: Any value is valid as long as it is a personal value. Hence, this approach proposes to examine values in a valueless vacuum. Thus it can easily fall into an extreme moral relativism in which all values are acceptable, even if they are based on racist, sexist, or homophobic attitudes (Howe and Covell, 2005).

Between these two approaches, several models exist. One of them is the cognitive development approach (Kohlberg, 1985), which argues that educators should be allowed to promote certain values, but a democratic structure is needed to limit their power to indoctrinate students. This proposal complemented the progressive education idea that an effective way to learn democratic values is to practice democracy in a democratic community (Dewey, 1916). Theoretically, there should be few limits to the scope of discussions that take place in those democratic communities. In practice, educators tend to avoid open discussions about controversial topics among participants. Many curriculum developers and instructors fear conflict and hence tend to implement a "safe curriculum" that reduces the possibility of risk (Osborne, 2004). Others, however, believe that the best way to nurture civic virtues is to welcome hard questions and to encourage participants "not to get along." This implies recognition of the plurality of viewpoints among participants and facilitation of a respectful dialogue among them (Hughes and Sears, 2004; McLaughlin, 2004).

Finally, programs that focus on citizenship as agency tend to promote the development of an active, engaged, and committed citizenry. Instead of conceiving of learners only as economic producers and consumers, these programs also conceive of them as active citizens who can become, as Moses Coady (1939) once noted, "masters of their own destiny." This means a citizenship education that goes beyond the segmented model of education for leadership and for followership, in which the elite are groomed to rule and the masses are trained to follow orders. An education for active citizenship thus aims at nurturing citizens as political subjects. This means that, among other things, they are informed about the issues of the day, have a critical understanding of those issues, and are ready to propose alternatives and influence decisions when needed through individual and collective action. An education for active citizenship also aims at nurturing community development initiatives that foster self-reliance, empowerment, grassroots democracy, and social transformation. This tradition of citizenship education for social action is closely related to popular education, a movement with roots in Latin America that has been particularly vibrant in Quebec.

Adult Citizenship Education in Canada

Historically, most adult citizenship education programs in Canada have been oriented towards assimilation. The first European settlers used education to "civilize" indigenous peoples. This meant an attack on their self-government structures and culture and the imposition of a different language, religion, identity, and set of values. This process of cultural assimilation was not complemented with a process of equalization of citizenship rights, but rather with institutionalized domination and colonialism. Later, this assimilation model was used with immigrants. By the beginning of the twentieth century the emphasis was placed on nation building, and the *good citizen* was constructed upon that premise. Fitzpatrick's (1919) *Handbook for New Canadians* used at that time, for instance, proclaimed that the good citizen loves God, the Empire, and Canada. Likewise, a civics book of the same period called for an "ardent loyalty" to the Empire, as "this imperial feeling will help us in our national affairs, for it will enable us to be sympathetic with our fellow citizens throughout the Dominion" (Jenkins, 1919, p. 166). At that time, civic education explicitly promoted religion, which was portrayed as "the most important cause" that a citizen should support and as "the only force strong enough to resist those tendencies which, if unchecked, will bring on rapid national decay and ruin" (p. 170).

As immigration flows continued, most adult citizenship education programs consisted of education and language training for immigrants.[2] This included the efforts of voluntary organizations such as Frontier College (founded by Fitzpatrick in 1899) and official programs of the federal government, first through the Citizenship Branch (created in 1947) and later through Citizenship and Immigration Canada. By and large, these programs focused on naturalization and assimilation. One of the first documents of the Citizenship Branch stated that the purpose of immigrant education was to convert the immigrant into a Canadian through their learning English or French; acquiring knowledge about Canadian history, geography, and government; and becoming acquainted with Canadian habits, customs, and institutions (see Joshee, 1996, p. 117). During the second half of the twentieth century, education for newcomers continued to focus on language training and citizenship. In these programs, language training has been often tied to labour market participation, and citizenship was understood only as legal status (Derwing, Jamieson, and Munro, 1998; McKay, 1993).

Today the situation is not very different. Despite the noble aims of enabling immigrants to become full participants in Canadian society, these programs still focus on language acquisition for labour market integration and on the memorization of facts to pass a multiple-choice test to obtain naturalization. The main textbook used in these programs is *A Look at Canada* (Citizenship and Immigration Canada, 2004), which consists of basic information on Canadian history, geography, governmental institutions, and citizenship rights and responsibilities. The textbook is clearly written and informative, but it presents a history of Canada devoid of conflict and controversy. For instance, the relationship between European colonizers and Aboriginal peoples is portrayed as symmetrical and fair:

> The British and Canadian governments made many agreements, or treaties, with the Aboriginal peoples between 1701 and 1923. These treaties granted the Aboriginal peoples certain rights and benefits in exchange for giving up their title to the land. Each treaty is unique and is seen as a solemn promise. (Citizenship and Immigration Canada, 2005, p. 15)

Compare this official description with the account provided in another textbook:

> Indians were forced off their lands and onto small reserves. For many years, Native people have been unhappy with the way the Europeans treated them. . . . Losing people to disease and losing land to the Europeans were not the only problems faced by Native people. Native people's values are very different from European values. The ideas of cooperation, sharing, and respect for the land are important for the Native peoples. Europeans value individual achievement and private ownership. (Cameron and Derwing, 1996, p. 27)

A Look at Canada (Citizenship and Immigration Canada, 2005) probably succeeds in providing basic factual information about Canada that can easily be memorized to pass the naturalization test, but falls short of nurturing a critical and engaged citizenship. In terms of critical citizenship, the text does not present different viewpoints for analysis and discussion, does not address controversial topics, and does not raise questions to ponder. In terms of engagement, it is interesting to note that the textbook states that all Canadian citizens have the responsibility to vote, help others, protect the heritage and the environment, express opinions freely while respecting the rights and freedoms of others, and eliminate discrimination and injustice. However, the textbook says little about past or current instances of discrimination and injustice or about ways to eliminate them, besides the generic advice of volunteering, helping neighbours, joining a community group, or becoming a candidate in an election.

In contrast, in the social-action tradition of Canadian adult education, citizenship building has been about the development of collective agency for community empowerment and social transformation. Probably the most inspirational initiative in this regard is the Antigonish Movement, which began in 1928 and achieved remarkable economic, social, and cultural changes among poor workers in a depressed region of Canada through cooperative principles and strategies.[3] Moses Coady (1939), one of the coordinators of this project, understood the powerful impact of adult education in successfully creating and running cooperative economic institutions: "When people's economic power and control increase, they can create instruments that will enable them to have a voice and to play a more effective part in building the new democratic society" (p. 134).

The top-down government programs and the community-oriented adult education programs also involved innovative and exciting partnerships between them. One of them was the Citizens' Forum, a joint project of the Canadian Association for Adult Education (CAAE) and the Canadian Broadcasting Corporation (CBC) that started in 1943 and continued for two decades on national television. The Citizens' Forum was the continuation and expansion of a more focused project (the National Farm Radio Forum) and consisted of a weekly broadcast that examined a controversial topic from different perspectives. After the broadcast, local groups deliberated about the topic, assisted by a printed discussion guide produced by adult educator Isabel Wilson. Although the Citizens' Forum probably nurtured a more critical and enlightened citizenry, there is no evidence that it contributed to increases in citizen engagement.[4] Among other innovative Canadian initiatives on adult citizenship education were the Women's Institutes (1897), the Joint Planning Commission (1947), and the Challenge for Change (1967) experiment on Fogo Island, Newfoundland.

In the last three decades of the twentieth century, in a context marked by an attack on the welfare state and redistributive policies and the ascendance of corporate welfare and neoliberal economics, the connections between adult education, social citizenship, and democracy were weakened (Welton 1995).[5] In the first half of the century there were significant adult education programs oriented towards social justice through community organization, grassroots mobilization, and economic cooperation, but today adult education is concerned primarily with job training.

Today, however, citizenship education is attracting again the interest of progressive adult educators. One area with interesting potential for citizenship learning is participatory democracy, a model of governance based on citizens' deliberation and decision making. Participatory democracy has some potential to address the democratic deficit, which is evident, among other symptoms, in the low public confidence in professional politicians. A 2003 Ipsos-Reid poll showed that national politicians rank at the bottom of public trust (below car salespeople),[6] and a 2005 Environics Research poll found that 75 percent of Canadians do not count on politicians' electoral promises. Participatory democracy cannot replace representative democracy, but it can make a contribution to addressing some of its short-comings. As Carole Pateman (1970) noted, a virtuous circle exists between participatory democracy and citizenship learning. The more citizens participate, the more they learn; and the more they learn, the higher the quality of the democratic process. Although most of this learning is informal and incidental, adult education can make significant contributions to deepening and strengthening such learning. Current Canadian experiments of participatory democracy include the Citizens' Assembly on Electoral Reform (British Columbia) and the participatory budgets carried out in Toronto Community Housing and in the municipality of Guelph.

An International Agenda for Adult Citizenship Education

At the last International Conference on Adult Education, held in 1997 in Hamburg, Germany, more than 1,500 delegates from over 130 countries met to analyze the situation of the field and to formulate guidelines for policy and action. This conference, which since 1949 has taken place every 12 years or so, provides the framework for adult education activities and programs worldwide.[7] The 1997 conference produced two key policy statements: the Hamburg Declaration on Adult Learning and the Agenda for the Future. The Declaration makes an explicit call for a kind of citizenship education that promotes democracy, peace, justice, tolerance, dialogue, mutual recognition, and negotiation to replace the culture of violence that pervades homes, local communities, nations, and relations among countries.

The Agenda for the Future makes a great number of commitments that have been organized around 10 themes. The first theme, "adult learning and democracy," is based on the premise that the challenges of the twenty-first century

> require the creativity and competence of citizens of all ages in alleviating poverty, consolidating democratic processes, strengthening and protecting human rights, promoting a culture of peace, encouraging active citizenship, strengthening the role of civil society, ensuring gender equality and equity, enhancing the empowerment of women, recognizing cultural diversity (including the use of language, and promoting justice and equality for minorities and indigenous peoples) and a new partnership between state and civil society. (UNESCO, 1997, p. 36)

To reinforce democracy, notes the Agenda, it is essential to strengthen learning environments, encourage citizen participation, and create contexts where a culture of equity and peace can take root. In order to achieve these goals, adult educators are asked to make four commitments: to create greater community participation; to raise awareness about prejudice and discrimination; to encourage greater recognition, participation, and accountability of non-governmental organizations and local community groups; and to promote a culture of peace, intercultural dialogue, and human rights (UNESCO, 1997, p. 36).

Regarding the first commitment, educators are called to promote active citizenship and improve participatory democracy to create learning communities and to encourage and develop leadership capabilities among adults (especially women). In relation to the second commitment, adult educators are asked to ensure the elimination of discrimination at all educational levels and to uphold the legitimate right of people to self-determination, to enjoy their own cultures, and to use their own languages. We are also called to develop programs that address gender relations and human sexuality in all their dimensions; to ensure equitable representation of women, indigenous and nomadic peoples, and minorities in decision-making processes and provision; and to support the publication of local and indigenous learning materials (UNESCO, 1997, p. 37).

For the third commitment, the Hamburg Agenda asks adult educators to recognize the role that non-governmental organizations and community groups play in promoting awareness raising, empowerment, democracy, peace, and development; in providing educational opportunities for adults in all sectors; in reaching the most needy; and in contributing to an active civil society. In relation to the last commitment, we should enable citizens to approach conflicts in an empathic, non-violent, and creative manner through peace education, peace journalism, and peace culture. We are also called to strengthen the educational dimensions of human rights activities in formal and non-formal adult learning provisions at community, national, regional, and global levels (UNESCO, 1997, p. 37).

These four commitments include a broad, ambitious, and inclusive agenda for adult citizenship education theory, research, and practice. The Canadian adult education community has the right and the duty to take up some or all of these commitments, adapt them to the Canadian context whenever necessary, and add new commitments if appropriate.

Summary and Conclusions: Towards an Integrated Program

Citizenship is closely connected with democracy, and democracy is inseparable from issues of equality, participation, and self-governance. An integrated citizenship education project should build on the Hamburg Agenda and on the best traditions of Canadian adult education and must address the four dimensions of citizenship discussed in this chapter: status, identity, civic virtues, and agency. The first relates to issues of membership; the second to issues of feelings of belonging; the third to values, dispositions, and behaviours; and the last to issues of engagement and political efficacy. What follows is an outline of this proposal.[8]

Status: Inclusive Citizenship

Inclusive citizenship is fundamental in a time of growing inequalities among and within countries.

Generally, adult education programs do not serve the most vulnerable and excluded groups, but rather those who are more likely to succeed in further education or in the labour market (a sort of "train the best and forget the rest" approach). In terms of status, millions of people are not yet full citizens and are economically, politically, and socially disadvantaged. A program aimed at inclusive citizenship should address issues of inclusion and exclusion in curriculum content, pedagogical relations, and social dynamics. Hence, it must address issues of human rights, social justice, equality of opportunity, economic democracy, and redistributive social policies.

Identity: Pluralistic Citizenship

Pluralistic citizenship has to do with respect for difference and identity. This does not mean forgetting about equality. To paraphrase Sousa Santos (2003, p. 154), whereas inclusive citizenship implies the right to equality when difference leads to injustice, pluralistic citizenship implies the right to diversity when equality results in homogenization. An adult education for pluralistic citizenship acknowledges that democratic politics must allow for particularities and differences but at the same time must encourage common actions for collective benefit. This "unity in diversity" approach nurtures cross-cultural dialogue and mutual respect (particularly in heterogeneous societies such as Canada) while it fosters joint struggles based on solidarity principles. Moreover, a pluralistic citizenship approach celebrates diversity from a cosmopolitan rather than a parochial viewpoint, and hence it aims at the fulfillment of the universal declaration of human rights and related legislation.

Civic Virtues: Critical and Caring Citizenship

Critical and caring citizens are the subjects of any emancipatory educational project, of sustainable communities, and of vibrant democratic societies. Critical citizens are willing and able to raise important questions and problems in a clear way, to gather and assess relevant information, to think open-mindedly, to communicate without resorting to (or being persuaded by) arguments based on authority or tradition, and to arrive at logical conclusions. Hence, critical citizens do not take the status quo for granted; they use the power of reason and evidence to pursue the truth, consider other viewpoints, are tolerant, and are not afraid to challenge their own assumptions and perspectives. Indeed, they understand that their perspectives are shaped by the social context in which they were socialized. In addition to being autonomous and reflexive thinkers, critical citizens are also aware of power structures, the dynamics of domination, and the subtleties of hegemony building;[9] are unlikely to be manipulated by mass media; and are prepared to propose strategies for progressive social change.

Caring citizens are compassionate human beings who are concerned with the suffering of others, are empathic listeners, and are upset with unfair situations. They accept personal responsibility for improving societal well-being and translate such responsibility into concrete commitment. The compassion and empathy of caring citizens is not limited to people living in their local communities or even to living in their countries. Their allegiance is to humanity and does not recognize national borders. Moreover, caring citizens are concerned not only about fellow humans, but also about all other living species. Caring citizens are guided by principles of solidarity, are inclined to put the common good before their own self-interest, feel indignation in the presence of injustice, and have a broad environmental and planetary consciousness.

Agency: Active Citizenship

Last but not least, citizenship education should promote confidence in the individual and collective capacity to influence change, particularly among the most excluded and oppressed members of society. This political efficacy is not gained only through self-reflection, but also—and mainly—through political struggles and small incremental victories. Although empowerment has become a cliché concept, it is important to recognize that adult education has a role in activating and increasing the political agency of adult learners. Active citizenship is the antidote to democratic deficit and the increasing gap between professional politicians and the people. In the end, only active citizens can make governments accountable and generate meaningful social change.

In closing, I believe that an integrated adult citizenship education program must address simultaneously issues of status, identity, civic virtues, and agency. This can be pursued through a variety of pedagogical/political strategies that adapt and reinvent the contributions of twentieth century adult education (especially the popular education tradition) to the realities of the twenty-first century. A particular challenge of adult education is to help to build democratic communities in which citizens are motivated, empowered, and prepared to participate in decisions that concern the good of all (Herman, 1996). Democratic spaces (that is, spaces of collective deliberation and decision making such as initiatives of participatory democracy) are some of the best schools for citizenship learning and civic engagement. At the same time, more informed, critical, and engaged citizens improve the quality of democratic processes. In this regard, adult education can play an important role in improving the conditions for learning, increasing the sharing of this learning, and equalizing opportunities for learning and meaningful participation.

References

Cameron, J. and Derwing, T. (1996). *Being Canadian: Language for citizenship*. Scarborough, ON: Prentice Hall.

Citizenship and Immigration Canada. (2004). *A look at Canada*. Ottawa, ON: Minister of Public Works and Government Services Canada.

Citizenship and Immigration Canada. (2005). *A look at Canada*. Ottawa, ON: Author.

Coady, M. (1939). *Masters of their own destiny*. New York: Harper and Row.

Derwing, T., Jamieson, K., and Munro, M. (1998). Citizenship education for adult immigrants: Changes over the last ten years. The *Alberta Journal of Educational Research, 19*, 383–396.

Dewey, J. (1916). *Democracy and education: An introduction to the philosophy of education*. New York: Free Press.

Draper, J. (Ed.). (1971). *Citizen participation: Canada*. Toronto, ON: New Press.

Fitzpatrick, A. (1919). *Handbook for new Canadians*. Toronto, ON: Ryerson Press.

Herman, L. (1996). Personal empowerment. In T. Becker and R. Couto (Eds.), *Teaching democracy by being democratic* (pp. 53–74). London: Praeger.

Howe, B. and Covell, K. (2005). *Empowering children: Children's rights education as a pathway to citizenship*. Toronto, ON: University of Toronto Press.

Hughes, A. and Sears, A. (2004). Situated learning and anchored instruction as vehicles for social education. In A. Sears and I. Wright (Eds.), *Challenges and prospects for Canadian social studies* (pp. 259–273). Vancouver, BC: Pacific Educational Press.

Jenkins, R. S. (1919). *Canadian civics* (Alberta ed.). Toronto, ON: Copp, Clark.

Johnston, R. (1999). Adult learning for citizenship: Towards a reconstruction of the social purpose tradition. *International Journal of Lifelong Education, 18*(3), 175–190.

Joshee, R. (1996). The federal government and citizenship education for newcomers. *Canadian and International Education, 25*(2), 108–127.

Kanpol, B. and McLaren, P. (Eds.). (1995). *Critical multiculturalism: Uncommon voices in a common struggle*. Westport, CT: Bergin & Garvey.

Kohlberg, L. (1985). The just community approach to moral education in theory and in practice. In R. Mosher (Ed.), *Moral education: A first generation of research and development* (pp. 20–57). New York: Praeger.

Kohn, A. (1997). How not to teach values: A critical look at character education. *Phi Delta Kappan, 78*(6), 429–437.

Marshall, T. H. (1992). Citizenship and social class. In T. H. Marshall and T. Bottomore (Eds.), *Citizenship and social class* (pp. 1–51). London: Pluto Press. (Original work published 1950)

McKay, S. (1993). *Agendas for second language literacy*. Cambridge: Cambridge University Press.

McLaughlin, D. (2004). Cultivating habits of democracy: Asking the hard questions. *Education Canada, 45*(1), 33–35.

Osborne, K. (2004). Political education and citizenship. *Education Canada, 45*(1), 13–16.

Pateman, C. (1970). *Participation and democratic theory*. New York: Cambridge University Press.

Sabariego, M. (2002). *La educación intercultural ante los retos del siglo XXI*. Bilbao: Declée de Brower.

Schugurensky, D. (2001). The enlightenment-engagement dilemma and the development of the active citizen: Lessons from the Citizens' Forum and the Participatory Budget. *Proceedings of the 20th anniversary conference of the Canadian Association for Studies in Adult Education*. Toronto, ON: Canadian Association for Studies in Adult Education.

Sousa Santos, B. (2003). *La caída del Angelus Novus. Ensayos para una nueva teoría social y una nueva práctica política*. Bogotá: Universidad Nacional de Colombia and Anthropos.

Selman, G. (1998). The imaginative training for citizenship. In S. Scott, B. Spencer, and A. Thomas (Eds.), *Learning for life: Canadian readings in adult education* (pp. 24–34). Toronto, ON: Thompson Educational.

Selman, G., Selman, M., Cooke, M., and Dampier, P. (1998). *The foundations of adult education in Canada.* Toronto, ON: Thompson Educational.

Strong-Boag, V. (2002). Who counts? Late nineteenth- and early twentieth-century struggles about gender, race, and class in Canada. In Y. Hebert (Ed.), *Citizenship in transformation in Canada* (pp. 37–56). Toronto, ON: University of Toronto Press.

United Nations Educational, Scientific, and Cultural Organization Institute for Education. (1997). *Final report: Fifth International Conference on Adult Education.* Hamburg, Germany: UNESCO Institute for Education.

Welton, M. (1995). The bitter politics of Canadian adult education. *Journal of World Education, 25*(3), 17–31.

Welton, M. (1998). Educating for a deliberative democracy. In S. Scott, B. Spencer, and A. Thomas (Eds.), *Learning for life: Canadian readings in adult education* (pp. 365–372). Toronto, ON: Thompson Educational.

Westheimer, J. and Khane, J. (2004). What kind of citizen? The politics of education for democracy. In K. Mundel and D. Schugurensky (Eds.), *Lifelong citizenship learning: Participatory democracy and social change* (pp. 67–90). Toronto, ON: Ontario Institute for Studies in Education/University of Toronto Transformative Learning Centre.

Endnotes

[1] However, today it is also possible to be a citizen of a supranational political entity (e.g., the European Community). The issue of global, cosmopolitan, or planetary citizenship is still more an ideal than a reality, but the international legislation is paving the way for universal human rights.

[2] Because citizenship is a federal jurisdiction and education is a provincial one, in the area of immigrant education (which includes citizenship and language training), the specific responsibilities of each level are not always clear. For an analysis of these tensions, see Joshee (1996).

[3] For further details on the Antigonish Movement, see Selman (1998); Selman, Selman, Cooke, and Dampier (1998); and Welton (1998 and in this volume). A related initiative in the US was the Highlander Centre, founded in 1932.

[4] For a discussion on the enlightenment-engagement relationship in citizenship education in relation to the Citizens' forum, see Schugurensky (2001).

[5] Canadian adult education literature on citizen participation also weakened. One of the few publications during that period was Draper (1971).

[6] The most trusted professionals are pharmacists (91%), doctors (85%), and airline pilots (81%). At the bottom of the scale are car salespeople (10%) and national politicians (9%).

[7] The five adult education conferences were Elsinore (1949), Montreal (1960), Tokyo (1972), Paris (1985), and Hamburg (1997). The main difference between Hamburg and the previous conferences was that non-governmental organizations were allowed to participate alongside official national delegations.

[8] This proposal builds on the work of Johnston (1999).

[9] *Hegemony building* refers to the process by which dominant groups persuade the majority of the people that the status quo is "natural" and promotes the common good. Through hegemony, the dominant discourse is accepted as common sense (Gramsci, 1978).

6

Cross-Cultural Teaching and Research in Adult Education

Susan M. Brigham and Patricia A. Gouthro

Although adult educators' work lives vary considerably, all of us are challenged to develop more comprehensive and inclusive means of addressing cross-cultural issues in both our teaching and research as a consequence of globalization. Both of us have taught and conducted research in cross-cultural and international settings. Susan has done research in the Philippines and Hong Kong with migrant women and school teachers, in Nepal with preschool teachers, and in Aboriginal communities in Western Canada with youth; she has taught in Ireland, Kuwait, Jamaica, and a Canadian Aboriginal community. Patricia has done research in Jamaica with graduate students and adult educators. In this chapter, we explore some of the issues that educators who are teaching and researching in cross-cultural contexts need to take up. In teaching, these include considerations around technology, curriculum, and assessment; whereas in research some concerns include positionality, subjectivity, and ethics. In both teaching and research we argue that it is important to understand knowledge as something that is mutually constructed, shared, and negotiated, rather than as a commodity that can be packaged, consumed, or exported. We draw upon research that may be helpful for those who are learning their way into understanding some of the challenges of working in cross-cultural contexts, and we also reflect on our own experiences as educators and researchers.

Cross-Cultural Teaching

Canadian adult educators are increasingly expected and obligated to attend to diversity in their various teaching contexts, which requires consideration of both practical and ethical concerns. There are growing numbers of foreign students attending Canadian universities, and immigration is creating an increasingly diverse Canadian population. International initiatives lead to partnerships between educational institutions in different countries and increasing numbers of "off-shore" programs offered by tertiary educational institutions across Canada.

In this section, we address some challenges for educators in teaching cross culturally, including the interrelated considerations around technology (with regards to delivery and supports for students and faculty), curriculum design and content, and assessment. In addition, we critically assess the influence of the marketplace in commodifying education and discuss our own approach towards delivering an international program in Jamaica.

Technology

Educational opportunities for rural students, including those in Aboriginal communities, as well as offshore teaching are often provided through *distance education* (DE, for example, online teaching), which raises concerns stemming from bringing together, "in an unfamiliar environment, students and educators whose experience of teaching and learning education stems from very different cultural traditions" (Ziguras, 2001, p. 8). DE can create more equitably available educational opportunities for many learners, including learners with disabilities, women, and geographically remote residents; and it has great potential for knowledge transfer, bringing marginalized voices into public spaces, and thereby contributing to the generation of knowledge and creating awareness between people on a global scale (Goulding and Spacey, 2002). Yet, it can also pose exclusionary concerns for marginalized populations. A problem with delivering programs in cross-cultural contexts occurs when there is a reliance on prepackaged course notes and learning modules and technologies such as the Internet (which may be difficult to access) because these may not acknowledge or be attentive to issues of diversity.

Educators who teach by distance must consider the ways in which technology is culturally specific. For example, with reference to Australian Aboriginal adult learners, Henderson (1996) notes:

> Mental models, thinking processes, and teaching-learning strategies used by teachers and learners when interacting with electronic databases, interactive multimedia and the worldwide web. . . . For instance, questioning and justifying the validity of statements and analysis are endemic to academic discourse but are generally unacceptable in Australian Indigenous current-traditional ways of learning and teaching. (p. 102)

Although it is assumed that high enrolments in DE may lower costs to students, the pursuit of large student enrolments to achieve economies of scale may result in a decreased ability to address individual learners' needs. The largest costs for DE programs arise predominantly from program planning, providing administrative and technical assistance to learners, and using technology to promote interactions between learners. It is tempting to cut costs in these areas, which further reduces the ability of adult educators to address individual learners' needs. Once packaged courses are developed, it is expensive and time consuming to change them. Scown (2004) contends that "on-line teaching is emerging as a repetitive activity of didactic and linear transmission controlled by instructional technologists and their corporate managers who speak the language of systems capabilities, cost effectiveness, and time efficiency" (p. 205). He warns, "The sameness in method, content, and evaluation detracts from productive adult learning" (p. 205) and "reinforce[s] threats to the sustainability of diversity" (p. 205).

On this point Reinke and James (2003) caution that DE may result in treating the adult learner as an "abstract learner with no situated identity, [which can] lead to mistaken assumptions" (p. 231). This warning reminds us that in DE courses students may choose not to reveal aspects of themselves that may otherwise be readily evident in a face-to-face situation, such as their race, class, gender, able-bodiedness, and so on. Although this relative anonymity may provide a sense of freedom (e.g., it may reduce judgments, preconceptions, and stereotyping about classmates and teachers based on their "visible" features), it may also result in a one-dimensional understanding of one another (where learners and educators "remain virtual and disembodied" [Scown, 2004, p. 211]). Moreover, learners are still judged on their writing style, language usage, and content. In this potentially one-dimensional context it is more difficult for educators to ensure that students' individual needs are addressed holistically.

Curriculum

Curriculum in cross-cultural contexts frequently exemplifies how our epistemological beliefs (our understanding of how knowledge is created and shared) have evolved and reflect values from dominant cultures. For instance, in examining the ways in which webs of knowledge in education, science, and technology have emerged over the last few decades, Schott (2001) points out that the United States, and, to a lesser extent, Japan, have steadfastly assumed a central (or core) position in the production and distribution of knowledge, whereas many other countries have occupied a more peripheral, marginalized position. He explains:

> Education, science, and technology are coupled to the economy within each nation with positive effects that in a wealthy nation form an upward spiral but, relatively in a poor society, form a downward spiral, thus exacerbating the inequality in the world in knowledge and wealth. (p. 1751)

In the current global context, relationships between core countries and peripheral countries are reinforced though inequities in knowledge production and distribution.

Teaching cross culturally requires adult educators to problematize how knowledge emerges and is valued in academic and community contexts. For instance, in an article written jointly by an American professor and graduate students, Fordjor et al. (2003) compare traditional Ghanaian and Western philosophies in adult education. Western philosophies tend to emphasize individualism, whereas Ghanaian education has "been moulded by the community on socialization of man [sic] for the benefit of the larger society" (p. 190). Most Ghanaian adult education is informal or nonformal rather than institutionalized through formal programs, which is more often the case in Western contexts. There is also a holistic, spiritual emphasis that is not as commonly emphasized in Western cultures.

Some theories of adult education studied in formal adult education programs have emerged from a tradition that primarily reflects Western,

White, middle-class, male culture (Graveline, 2000; Nah, 1999). For example, the concepts of *andragogy* (teaching adults) and self-directed learning assume that "mature adults" prefer to learn in more individualized contexts. In her qualitative research on Korean women leaders in male-dominated professions, Nah argues that

> the spirit implied in self directed learning theory as it is practised in North America, does not seem to fully fit the learning processes of women in leadership positions in Korea. Among many feasible reasons for the unsuitability of self directed learning theory for Korean women's learning processes are contextual differences between the learners upon whom the theory was based and the Korean women who prioritised collectivity to individuality and interdependence to independence and autonomy. Self directed learning theory needs to reflect learners' contextual differences to represent adult learners' learning characteristic sensibility. (p. 19)

The learning theories, concepts, and methodologies that are often understood as "good practices" in Western cultures, may not be appropriate in other cultural contexts.

Assessment

MacKinnon and Manathunga (2003) argue that educators need to critically reflect upon their own cultural assumptions around assessment. Educators should consider whether their curriculum and forms of evaluation need to be modified to take into consideration different cultural backgrounds. They also have to be clear and explicit about expectations for students' work instead of implicitly assuming shared cultural understandings of curriculum and assessment practices.

To provide more inclusive assessment practices in cross-cultural contexts, educators may explore alternative forms of evaluation. For example, Graveline (2000) demonstrates that circles, ceremony, stories, and experience can be used as pedagogy in Aboriginal and non-Aboriginal contexts (p. 286). Presentation of academic work could take the form of poetry, narrative or non-written formats that incorporate deep reflection on one's life and learning experiences.

Influence of the Marketplace

Education is increasingly influenced by the globalized marketplace. While international educational initiatives may be linked with social justice concerns around diversity, inclusion and multiculturalism, they frequently garner support because of potential financial benefits. The reduction of government support for universities has led to more active recruitment of foreign students as well as the export of university programs abroad.

Educational programs are increasingly being marketed as valuable commodities. Adult educators who teach in cross-cultural contexts are enmeshed in circumstances that are frequently complex and difficult to understand. In universities, where there is pressure to demonstrate a return on investment, cost effectiveness, accountability, and economies of scale, DE, revenue from foreign student fees, and "off-shore" programs are a means of raising revenues in a competitive marketplace. This raises ethical concerns for both educators and administrators with regard to the potential for exploiting people in developing countries and regions who are already financially disadvantaged. Often there are no clear-cut answers. Although taking a degree offered by a foreign institution may be expensive, it provides students with access to learning opportunities that may not be supported by their own country's educational system. In addition, students are not required to leave their employment or their families. At the same time, the high tuition rates may place an unreasonable burden on some students, and educational institutions may not attend as carefully as they must to the concerns that we have outlined regarding providing a high-quality program that is sensitive to cultural differences and local contexts.

A Jamaican Example

Many of the concerns we discuss here are issues that we have had to (and continue to) address in designing, reconceptualizing, and developing our graduate education program, Studies in Lifelong Learning, because approximately one-third of our students are located in Jamaica. Seven years ago we began teaching in Jamaica by offering a single workshop at the start of each course, providing prepackaged course notes, and relying on teleconferencing, and the Internet for delivery. Many of our students did not have regular access to the Internet, and Internet costs were quite high as they were charged on a per-minute basis. The Jamaican telephone company did not have a bridging system (a teleconference bridge connects the "ports" from which students would call in and costs over $200,000). This meant that there were continual breaks in the phone connection to distant sites within Jamaica during teleconferenced classes, and there was often poor sound quality in the connection to Canada. Both of these problems hampered participation in class lectures and discussions. The resultant poor interactions between learners and between learners and teachers led us to revise our pedagogical approach to involve more face-to-face interaction with the students.

Now, for each course, twice each semester, faculty members fly down to Kingston, Jamaica, where we deliver two-day intensive workshops. Additionally, in some instances, Jamaican instructors are hired to teach in our program. We found that on-site workshops are only marginally more expensive, and they improve the quality of the teaching experience dramatically. Some course readings are sent down in advance, and communication before and in between workshops is conducted via email, telephone, and sometimes supplemented by WebCT (an Internet course program).

Initially, because of limited academic resources in Jamaica, we packaged most of our students' readings. This forced faculty to make assumptions about the appropriateness of the readings for students whom we had not yet met. It was also disadvantageous for students because an important part of graduate work is being able to research information in areas of one's own interest. In recent years, new library resource databases such as EBSCO (an online journal–article database) have opened up research possibilities for distance students in distant areas so that they can access academic research from around the globe.

From the beginning, our program has been connected with the Jamaican Council for Adult Education (JACAE) and the Jamaican Association for the Movement for Advancement of Literacy (JAMAL). Working with these organizations has been an important means of connecting with grassroots educators and learners in Jamaica.

In our own teaching, although we bring certain expertise that is valued as educators, we believe that our understanding of how adult education can be advanced in Jamaica must be directly informed by the localized context. Instead of viewing knowledge as a readily transferable commodity (packaged with a Canadian label), we approach our teaching as a process of negotiating meaning. We are obligated to research and learn more about Caribbean history, leaders, culture, and literature. Students are encouraged to research local resources, to carry out their practicums (by volunteering in a "hands-on" educational project) in their own communities, and to tailor their final projects (a large final paper) on topics that are relevant to their own educational experiences. We recognize that there are still inequities in that most of the research that we use for our courses is published in the Western world and most of our instructors are Canadians, and we are continually working with our Jamaican colleagues, students, and community members towards creating a program and a curriculum that are contextually sensitive and meaningful.

The devaluation of Jamaican currency and the high cost of international student fees have created financial burdens for many of our students. While other universities teaching in Jamaica frequently rent expensive hotel space for their courses, to keep our costs (and therefore student fees) as low as possible, we deliver our classes at the JAMAL site in Kingston. In recognizing difficulties with access and high Internet fees, we have minimized the technological costs of delivery. In addition, we are committed to ensuring that our Jamaican students receive a graduate education degree that is equivalent to the quality of the degree that is offered in Canada.

Cross-Cultural Research

Sparks (2002) notes, "Conducting cross cultural research is not new. From a political perspective, what is new is the growing acknowledgment of the perils of crossing cultures unconsciously" (p. 116). In this section we examine some of the issues of positionality, subjectivity, and ethics in cross-cultural research and the implications for researchers.

Positionality

When researchers engage in cross-cultural research, they need to be conscious of their own positionality (this refers to the advantages that some people have over others in a society because of particular characteristics, such as their race, social class, gender, or sexual orientation, that situate them in a more powerful position). Sparks (2002) argues that,

> at the least, researchers have a responsibility to use their power to uncover the voices of difference, subjugated knowledges, won at the front lines through experience and present those voices, perceptions, and everyday realities that rub against the grain or challenge the pattern of knowability. (p. 123)

Researchers working in cross-cultural contexts need to be critically reflective of both the methodologies that they use in their work and in their interpretations of research. There is a potential, and, historically, there is the reality, that Westernized scholarship has often reinforced inequities in power and privilege. Martin and Glesne (2002) point out that "native peoples throughout the world have for some time linked research to colonialism and imperialism" (p. 207). All too frequently researchers have observed and studied other cultures from a Eurocentric perspective that has led to misunderstanding and misrepresentation of indigenous values, knowledge, and cultural practices. Understanding other cultures frequently requires an empathetic leap that requires a conscientious willingness to set aside preconceived judgments and the automatic assumption that all people think or comprehend the world in the same way.

Subjectivity

Researcher subjectivity is inevitable in any research. Although value-free interpretation is impossible, it is important that the researcher clarify preconceptions, values, and interpretations about the problem being studied to reduce effects such as clouding and misunderstanding on subsequent interpretations. Alvesson and Sköldberg (2000) assert that emotion is a vital element throughout the research process because it plays a part in persons' thinking, attitudes on certain research issues, and specific observations. Being attentive to emotions and learning to listen carefully and empathetically to others in order to gain insights into their perspectives are important aspects of being a reflexive researcher. For instance, in their work in the Oaxaca region of Mexico, Martin and Glesne (2002) have struggled with the (assumed) simple notion of the concept of autonomy. Initially, they read the ambitions of young Mexicans who wanted to find employment as indicative of the influence of the Western marketplace and an individualized desire to be financially successful. However, upon further reflection they realized that these ambitions were linked with concerns of remaining in the community, rather than migrating, and being contributing members who would benefit the community as a whole. In trying to understand how within a Mexican culture autonomy is valued more as a communal than an individualistic concept, Martin and Glesne are provided with insights into their own location and positionality as researchers:

> Thinking about communal autonomy highlights the local forms of dependence that the researcher experiences in undertaking any kind of research in a cross-cultural setting and how frequently we are indebted to the graciousness of our hosts. In this way, the *mythic* individual autonomy of the researcher is undermined. Communal autonomy also forces us to recognize that, as researchers, we are embedded in local communities (in particular, universities and funding agencies). (p. 214)

Instead of automatically privileging Western beliefs, this shift in perspective challenges the researchers to think a little more deeply about their own research practices and relationships with the people in their study.

Ethics

Cross-cultural research raises a number of ethical questions that are not always clear cut. As Martin and Glesne (2002) note, researchers from other cultures are being permitted into communities to participate, observe, and learn. This involves power relationships that cannot be ignored because the researcher has the responsibility of representing other people's actions and perceptions to a larger audience. To do this, researchers strive for acceptance and hope for hospitality and openness. It is important, therefore, that representation (e.g., of "truth" and of participants' "voices") be as accurate as possible and that the community and the participants benefit so that the research does not become another venue for Western exploitation.

The insider/outsider debate in field research has recently been identified as one of the more important areas in cross-cultural research. The *insider* researcher is someone whose group membership (e.g., based on such factors as gender, race, class, sexual orientation, or culture) gives him or her special insight (i.e., intuitive sensitivity, empathy, and understanding) into the group being researched, which informs his or her research. The *outsider* researcher has a different, less intimate knowledge of the group being researched prior to his or her entry into the group, which results in a different production of knowledge from that of the insider.

Shah (2004) maintains that if a researcher has "outside-culture" status, not only will physical and social access to the research participants be hindered, but understanding across cultures will also be hampered because of factors such as language difference, non-verbal misinterpretations, preconceptions and stereotypes, and high anxiety. In his conclusion Shah reluctantly acknowledges important critiques of the insider-researcher advantage; namely, that research participants may not wish to disclose certain information with an insider and that familiarity may dull criticality. Shah suggests that researchers should "knowingly be aware of the nature of the context, place her/himself in the context and be explicit about limitations" (p. 569), possibly by taking cultural awareness training and working in cross-cultural research teams.

Merriam et al. (2001) contribute to this discussion by emphasizing the complexity of the researcher's insider/outsider status within and between cultures and recognize factors such as positionalities and power dynamics that have a bearing on knowledge construction and representation in the research process. In their reflections on the individual research that they have conducted in several cultural contexts, they highlight power dynamics not only as something that requires awareness, but also as something to be negotiated between researcher and participants. For instance, in their research they have found that researchers from minority cultures might be perceived as both insiders and outsiders by themselves and by their participants. Although the researchers might share the same racial or cultural background, which would make them insiders, they might simultaneously be perceived as being outsiders because they practice different religions, have different skin tones, or come from different social classes.

In assessing these differing views, we argue that in cross-cultural contexts not only will the researcher experience moments of being both insider and outsider, but also these positions are relative to the cultural values and norms of both the researcher and the participants. It is best to understand these relationships as fluid rather than rigidly defined. Part of the complexity of engaging in cross-cultural research is acknowledging these different tensions and assumptions that shape the relationships between researchers and participants.

Implications for Researchers

Nah (1999) reminds us that

> involving broader ranges of adults in studies is not aimed at establishing a grand theory that fits all adults. Instead, it is intended to guard researchers against making a cursory grand theory, which is insensitive to dynamics that the subjects may bring to their research. (p. 25)

Research in cross-cultural contexts provides us with understanding, knowledge, and insights into the lives of people who have different experiences, backgrounds, and perspectives. This type of knowledge often cannot be neatly compressed into tidy tables or figures. Rather, it is a means of helping us to better understand the complexity of human experience and our potentiality for growth and learning. We have found our experiences in teaching and conducting research cross culturally to be rich with opportunities for our own learning, but it is also very complicated work that requires reflexivity by the researcher.

Although Westernized theories can provide us with some knowledge and insight that might be helpful in different cultural contexts, theories frequently contain particular biases that screen out significant insights unless the researcher is willing and able to become attuned to cultural differences. Cross-cultural research challenges researchers to critically reflect upon taken-for-granted preconceptions, to be sensitive to issues around positionality and subjectivity, and to carefully consider the ethical dimensions and implications of their work.

Conclusion

In one brief chapter we can only hope to introduce readers to some of the concerns and challenges that are involved in teaching and researching in cross-cultural contexts. Although working in cross-cultural contexts raises many complex issues that are not easily resolved, teaching and researching in ways that are respectful of diversity and open to alternative frameworks for knowledge can provide rich and deeply meaningful opportunities for learning for both students and educators.

References

Alvesson, M. and Sköldberg, K. (2000). *Reflexive methodology: New vistas for qualitative research*. London: Sage.

Fordjor, P. K., Kotoh, A. M., Kpeli, K. K., Kwamefio, A., Mensa, Q. B., Owusu, E., et al. (2003). A review of the traditional Ghanaian and Western philosophies of adult education. *International Journal of Lifelong Learning, 22*(2), 182–199.

Goulding, A. and Spacey, R. (2002, August). *Women and the information society: Barriers and participation*. Paper presented at the 68th IFLA Council and general conference, Loughborough, UK.

Graveline, F. J. (2000). Lived experiences of an Aboriginal feminist transforming the curriculum. In C. James (Ed.), *Experiencing difference* (pp. 283–293). Halifax, NS: Fernwood.

Henderson, L. (1996). Instructional design of interactive multimedia: A cultural critique. *Educational Technology Research and Development, 44*(4), 85–104.

MacKinnon, D. and Manathunga, C. (2003). Going global with assessment: What to do when the dominant culture's literacy drives assessment. *Higher Education Research and Development, 22*(2), 133–144.

Martin, P. M. and Glesne, C. (2002). From the global village to the pluriverse? 'Other' ethics for cross-cultural qualitative research. *Ethics, Place, and Environment, 5*(3), 205–221.

Merriam, S. B., Johnson-Bailey, J., Lee, M. Y., Kee, Y, Ntseane, G. and Muhamad, M. (2001). Power and positionality: Negotiating insider/outsider status within and across cultures. *International Journal of Lifelong Learning, 20*(5), 405–416.

Nah, Y. (1999). Can a self-directed learner be independent, autonomous and interdependent? Implications for practice. *Adult Learning, 11*(1), 18–19, 25.

Reinke, L. and James, P. (2003). Learning reflectively: Technological mediation and indigenous cultures. In P. Kell, S. Shore, and M. Singh (Eds.), *Adult education @ 21st century* (pp. 221–236). New York: Peter Lang.

Schott, T. (2001). Global webs of knowledge. *American Behavioral Scientist, 44*(10), 1740–1751.

Scown, A. (2004). On-line supplementation of adult education: A change in pedagogy and a pedagogy of change. In P. Kell, S. Shore, and M. Singh (Eds.), *Adult education @ 21st century* (pp. 203–219). New York: Peter Lang.

Shah, S. (2004). The researcher/interviewer in intercultural context: A social intruder! *British Educational Research Journal, 30*(4), 551–575.

Sparks, B. (2002). Epistemological and methodological considerations of doing cross-cultural research in adult education. *International Journal of Lifelong Education, 21*(2), 115–129.

Ziguras, C. (2001). Educational technology in transnational higher education in South East Asia: The cultural politics of flexible learning. *Educational Technology and Society, 4*(4), 8–18.

Part 2

PHILOSOPHICAL AND CRITICAL CONTEXTS

7

Challenging Social Philosophobia

Elizabeth A. Lange

An education that fails to consider the fundamental questions of human existence—the questions about the meaning of life and the nature of truth, goodness, beauty, and justice, with which philosophy is concerned—is a very inadequate type of education. (Harold Titus; as cited in Knight, 1989, p. v)

The mere word philosophy conjures up images of draped Ancient Greeks or esoteric scholars behind ivy-covered, stone university walls. Given this, students of adult education expect that philosophy will be dry, abstract, and irrelevant; or they experience *philosophobia*—the fear of philosophy. Yet most individuals already carry an internal philosophy that is comprised of their often unarticulated ideas about human existence. To challenge philosophobia is to create a reflective space where adult educators can think meaningfully and analytically about their pre-existing ideas within the context of the larger questions of human existence. As part of the responsibility of adult educators to themselves and their learners, it is vital that they relate these perennial questions and existing systems of ideas to how we live our lives and how we engage in learning and education. Moreover, challenging social philosophobia is overcoming ahistoricism, depoliticization, democratic malaise, cynicism toward social ideals, and current societal preoccupations with the utilitarian, technicist, or "how" aspects of education. It is shifting toward the purpose or "why" of education, subsequently deepening our knowledge of why we do what we do and perhaps why we want to change what we do. Although there is often a sense of impatience with theory in favour of practical techniques, techniques will constitute directionless motion and remain at a superficial, even ineffectual level until the purpose of education and its relationship to life and society are considered. In sum, this chapter contends that learning ought to involve dialogue on what it is to live well, what a good society is, and how each epoch creates its own dynamic of a dominant and counter-vailing ethos as well as conflicting material practices.

Although adult educators can initiate a critically reflective practice through any number of entry points; one of the most foundational and insightful is exploring one's practice through the philosophies of adult education. This chapter will provide a brief overview of the discipline of philosophy, some schools of educational philosophy, and the dominant philosophical orientations in adult education. Beyond developing such an introductory familiarity with the philosophy of adult education, the goal of this chapter is to challenge adult educators to develop a working philosophy of adult education. A person's philosophy is the sum of his or her fundamental beliefs and convictions (Lucas, 1970). In this sense, all people carry a philosophy or "mental map" that enables them to understand their social context (Paterson, 1988). This mental map comes from a standardized belief package that evolves over time through values and teachings from one's family, life experiences, and the larger pervasive cultural ideology that suggests what is inevitable, "normal," and expected. Implicit in this mental map created through the intersection of context and biography are philosophical premises of which adult educators should be aware and critical as part of reflective thinking and reasoned inquiry. To develop a working philosophy is to devise a conscious set of beliefs about adults and adult education that serve as a guide for action.

This appeal to use rationality and critical consciousness in adult education emanates from the heritage of the European Enlightenment, succinctly expressed by Immanuel Kant (1784/1983), who defined *enlightenment* as

> man's [*sic*] emergence from his self-imposed immaturity. *Immaturity* is the inability to use one's understanding without guidance from another. This immaturity is *self-imposed* when its cause lies not in lack of understanding, but in lack of resolve and courage to use it without guidance from another. Sapere Aude! "Have courage to use your own understanding!"—that is the motto of enlightenment. (p. 41)

When we leave our belief package at a habitual level rather than making it conscious, Kant (1784/1983) suggested that guardians are then required to tell citizens what to think and how to do things, usually through rules and formulas. If the freedom to think and make self-chosen decisions is not taken seriously, educators may hold ideas that are indiscriminately eclectic and inconsistent in values. Another educational implication may be that educators merely reproduce how they were taught or how they learn best, irrespective of the learners' needs. Perhaps stated goals and actual practices are contradictory and confusing to learners. Educators can often sway with the changing ideas in their field, if the ideas are not critically evaluated for their soundness and merit. Paterson (1988; as cited in Elias and Merriam, 1995), a British analytical educational philosopher, suggested that educators need to broaden their mental maps and explore a wide range of ideas and belief systems to enhance their principles and best reach their learners. Most important, developing a working philosophy is a moral/ethical process in which educators identify what they value most, what knowledge is most important, and towards which social vision they are working. As Plato (as cited in Edwards, 2004) originally suggested, you cannot explain why you are doing what you are doing until you have formulated a clear, articulate, discussible system of ideas and principles that can stand up to cross-examination.

The Academic Discipline of Philosophy

Etymologically, the word *philosophy* (*philo*, "love of"; and *sophia*, "wisdom") literally means "the love of wisdom" (Knight, 1989, p. 4). A more extensive definition from the *Oxford English Dictionary* (Simpson, 2005) is "the love, study, or pursuit of wisdom, or of knowledge of things and their causes, whether theoretical or practical" (p. 672). The earliest written records of philosophy are the treatises of the Ancient Greeks from which the academic discipline of philosophy—or rather, "the gentle art of systematic thought"—developed. Philosophy is organized into three primary areas: metaphysics (the study of questions concerning the nature of reality), epistemology (the study of the nature of truth and knowledge and how they are attained), and axiology (the study of questions of value). Metaphysics is divided into several sub-areas: cosmology (the study of theories about the origin, nature, and development of the universe as an orderly system), theology (the study of conceptions of and about God), anthropology (the study of humankind), and ontology (the study of the nature of existence and what it means for anything to "be"; Knight, 1989). Axiology also has two sub-areas: ethics (the study of moral values and conduct) and aesthetics (the search for principles governing the creation and appreciation of beauty and art). Thus, philosophy has sought to answer such questions as, What is ultimately real? Is there a purpose toward which the universe is tending? Can reality be known? Is knowledge subjective or objective? How do we know? Are people born good, evil, or morally neutral? What is life, and why am I here? What is a good life for all people? How ought we to live together? These questions clearly relate to the process and content of the educational endeavour.

Philosophic Schools in Education

Beginning with Socrates and Plato in Ancient Greece, a class of individuals developed who understood themselves as dedicated to scholarship[1] and teaching. The first fully developed philosophy of education was Plato's *Republic*, followed by those of other philosophers and social theorists who directly addressed education over the last 2,500 years, including Augustine, Aquinas, Locke, Rousseau, Kant, Spencer, Mill, Wollstonecraft, Montessori, Addams, and Dewey. There are six general approaches to the philosophy of education,[2] but this chapter is taking the schools of thought approach primarily, while drawing secondarily from the social foundations approach (Lucas, 1970). Generally, this approach introduces the philosophers who share common presuppositions and affinity regarding certain perennial questions and, thus, who can be grouped into "schools" of thought. However, it must be clear that this classification system is just a conceptual tool for introducing adult educators to the field. Adult educators are encouraged to explore original writings and additional references to understand the arbitrariness of categorization and engage the complexity and diversity within and between these systems of ideas.

From classical philosophy the schools of thought are idealism, realism, and neoscholasticism. From modern philosophy the schools of thought are pragmatism and existentialism. Contemporary theories of educational philosophy include progressivism, perennialism, essentialism, reconstructionism, behaviourism, anarchism, and constructivism. In contrast, the analytic movement in philosophy was a reaction against the traditional aims and methods in philosophy and asserted that the core issues are not issues of reality, truth, and value, but rather issues of language and meaning (Knight, 1989). Lack of clarity and imprecision in using terminology such as *education*, prescriptions that are ambiguous (e.g., andragogy), and emotive slogans (e.g., "Adults desire to be autonomous and self-directed"), as well as the confusion between educational means and ends (e.g., transformative learning), can all confound the adult education enterprise. Together, these synoptic and analytic approaches within philosophy can assist adult educators in studying the concepts that structure their thinking as well as in excavating their foundational beliefs.

Overview of Philosophical Orientations

The philosophy of adult education, relatively undeveloped, has established its own set of theories that draw from these schools, but more closely relate to the ideas of influential adult educators and the development of practices in the field (Elias and Merriam, 1995). Thus, this chapter will extrapolate the liberal, progressive, behaviourist, humanist, radical, and postmodern orientations for their stated purpose, historical development, and key assumptions about the nature of society, human nature, learning, learners, and content; as well as offer a critique of each approach.

The Liberal Orientation

The liberal philosophy traces its roots back to the Greek philosophers Socrates, Plato, and Aristotle and contends that logic and rational discussion would lead to truth. Socrates taught students to question all assumptions and the existing order of things in the search for wisdom and a virtuous life. The most important goal was to liberate the innate powers of the human mind and acquire wisdom. A group of rivals known as the Sophists advocated and practiced a kind of vocational education for male members of the elite ruling class (the only group who received any formal education) that consisted of training in the skills of oratory and debating. Aristotle distinguished between these two wisdoms—practical (applying knowledge to daily problems) and theoretical (contemplation of the deepest principles and truths). Liberal education first flourished in Catholic-sponsored schools, in some royal courts, and later in the universities and reached an apogee in the eighteenth century Enlightenment. At this time, advocates of liberal political philosophy made such comments as Diderot's "Man will not be free until the last king is strangled with the entrails of the last priest." The ascendancy of liberal political philosophy inspired two important rebellions against existing social orders—the American and French revolutions. These, in turn, have largely shaped the modern "liberal democratic" states of Western nations.

The liberal philosophy is based on the maxim that "knowledge sets you free." Therefore, the task of educators is to fully develop the rational and moral powers of learners. A strong intellectual education includes the systematic study of a subject area that finally leads to a synthesized understanding. Liberal education promotes conceptual and moral education and fosters virtues such as justice, fortitude, temperance, and prudence. Modern liberal education is decidedly non-vocational, but now often includes a greater emphasis on natural and social sciences. At universities, faculties of arts generally offer a liberal-arts education that, ideally, is the introduction to the greatest thought or "canon" of the Western cultural tradition, including history, literature, fine art, and philosophy. Teachers' authority typically comes from their command of the subject matter and includes lecture, large amounts of reading, debate, and well-crafted argumentative papers.

The liberal philosophy is critiqued for its assumptions that the ultimate questions and truths of existence are universal across culture and history. These universal values have been said to be those of White, Western, upper-class men, particularly in the interests of the ruling elite, ignoring other social interests. Having reshaped part of the world in its own image, liberal political philosophy now tends toward the conservation rather than revolution of the existing social order. In this vein, Paterson (1988; as cited in Elias and Merriam, 1995) insisted that education should not be used as an instrument for a specific social vision, however desirable. "The commitment of education is always and necessarily to the truth, wherever it may lead" (p. 198). The liberal philosophy assumes that rational thought is the highest form of thought and discounts emotional, spiritual, and other intelligences. Finally, the expert authority and knowledge of teachers are privileged over those of learners.

The Progressive Orientation

The progressive philosophy in education is closely related to the nineteenth century political movement, both of which were strongly influenced by Charles Darwin's theory of evolution, whereby humankind and society are understood as constantly progressing toward a better society. The striking advances in all of the physical sciences and in technology in the nineteenth century fed the notion that societies could also improve and find efficient methods of dealing with the issues of social disruption that arose from the rapid urbanization and industrialization.

In contrast with liberal education, progressive education stresses the authority of science, the use of the experimental method, and problem solving. This approach was derived from philosophical pragmatism, in which ideas have no value unless they are proven useful through application. At this time education was viewed as the most powerful means of advancing societies, and this fuelled the drive for universal public education. Training teachers with the most up-to-date scientific education as well as with high ideals of social reform was considered necessary to help ameliorate social ills, train workers for national economic needs and leaders for national state needs, and socialize new immigrants. If individuals learned to use the scientific method and its problem-solving format, people's daily lives would be improved, and they would have the capacity to solve their own problems autonomously. It is not surprising that progressive educators designed university extension programs, technology institutes, and degrees such as in home economics.

Many of the principles of progressive education came from Rousseau, who believed that natural human curiosity should be tapped in the learning process. Humans were neither good nor bad, but born with unlimited potential for growth in a nurturing environment. As children interact naturally with their environment, they learn. Therefore, play and experimentation are important parts of learning. "We teach children, not subjects" became the rallying cry of progressivist teachers who designed activity-centred classroom "projects." For adults, when they are given the freedom to pursue their own interests following their natural curiosity within a supportive environment, it is expected that their knowledge, understanding, and enjoyment will also flourish, so that motivation is no longer an issue. In North America the momentum behind progressivist education was the extensive writings of American philosopher and educator John Dewey. He believed that scientific and social literacy were necessary components of a strong democracy of thoughtful, responsible citizens. As Elias and Merriam (1995) proposed, progressivism has had a greater impact upon adult education in North America than any other single school of thought.

However, progressive education in the K–12 system came under intense criticism mid-century. Much of this criticism was directed against the anti-intellectualism and excesses of "activity-centred" education. In Canada perhaps the most scathing denunciation of progressive education was in Hilda Neatby's (1953) book *So Little for the Mind.* Conservative traditionalists disliked the lack of a clear role for the teacher, believing that experimentation and innate interests would not lead to the great ideas, discipline of the mind, or the necessary virtues. Later, critiques grew out of the unquestioning use of science that has created significant social and ethical issues. Others, particularly those in the "Two-Thirds World," critiqued the notions of "progress" and "development" and well-meaning professionals who try to reengineer their societies to mimic the Western model. Radical educators critiqued the inattention to political and economic power relations that shape how scientific and national development are pursued. Simply advocating for social change without attention to who benefits is the naïve belief that "all change is progress." These criticisms, coupled with a "back-to-the-basics" movement after the launch of Sputnik in 1957, led to the virtual disappearance of the term *progressive education.* Nevertheless, these ideas live on in other philosophies.

The Behaviourist Orientation

Behavioural psychology developed in the early twentieth century as an attempt to apply the natural science methods of observation and experimentation to the study of human beings. Behaviourism was concerned with observable and measurable behaviour only, because the "mind" could be neither observed nor proven. The various ways in which an observable stimulus and response were linked was the object of carefully controlled experiments, usually with animals. By the middle of the twentieth century, behaviourism dominated university departments of psychology in North America, although it never enjoyed this degree of success elsewhere. Early behaviourists included Pavlov, Watson, and Thorndike. However, by the late 1940s B. F. Skinner, given his popular writing ability and his school of radical behaviourism, became *the* behaviourist until his death in the 1980s.

The key concept behind behaviourism is classical conditioning, based on the assumptions that humans try to avoid pain and pursue pleasure and that behaviour is determined by its consequences. Human behaviour can be controlled by the stimulus given and by the rewards/reinforcement received for certain responses. Positive behaviours can be elicited by receiving something of value, and negative behaviours can be extinguished by punishing or removing something of value. If learners are rewarded immediately, frequently, and in an obvious manner, the behaviour will "stick." The task is to design experiences that produce the desired behaviours. The deeper assumption is that freedom is an illusion; humans are the product of their physical and social conditioning. The task is not to free humans from control, but to change the kinds of controls to which they are exposed and create a better society where suffering is minimized and survival is maximized.

Although Skinner claimed that behaviourism was applicable to all types of education, this philosophy achieved its greatest success in vocational and technical training, particularly in skills training, where learning is observable and measurable. The ideal in behaviourist adult education is behavioural objectives set by the teacher, with the content arranged in a sequential manner. Students learn at their own pace, and the teacher responds immediately to the behaviours or competencies that he or she wishes to reinforce. As students master each stage of learning, it is hoped that they will internalize the reinforcement so that they no longer need external rewards. Behaviourism has been very popular in business and industry training, where, as employees meet the behavioural objectives, perks such as trips, consumer items, or salary increases are tied to desired on-the-job behaviours.

Inner behaviourism or cognitive psychology replaced outer behaviourism as the dominant school of psychology in North America. Cognitive psychology originated in the 1950s and 1960s when many scholars realized that behaviourist theory, largely based on experiments with animals, was unable to account for higher level human functions such as language and reasoning. Theories soon developed that focused on what happens between the two observable events of the stimulus and the response, particularly models of how the mind processes, stores, and recalls information. Cognitivists have described the need for "meaning structures" or patterns in the brain that organize and anchor any new incoming information. Cognitivist research has focused on how learners perceive sources of information and their techniques for enhancing memory storage. It has advocated strategies for presenting information in a logical fashion and giving learners ample opportunity to process this information, and memory-skill activities.

Humanists have critiqued outer behaviourism for its manipulative quality in which power is lodged outside the person so that the freedom to choose and the dignity to make personal judgments are lost. Generally, learning is not the ultimate goal; this theory is used to motivate learners to achieve goals that are not primarily in their own interests, particularly outside the workplace—usually company goals such as productivity, efficiency, and profit. For these reasons humanist and radical educators have contended that behaviourism lacks an ethical basis. Many educators have also demonstrated that learning is a complex phenomenon that cannot be limited to what is observable and measurable. No paper-and-pencil or skills test can fully measure what has been learned. Learning is holistic and includes emotional, intuitive, physical, spiritual, and social aspects.

The critique of cognitivist behaviourism is twofold: It considers the mind as only a large computer processor, which is reductionist; or even if it considers the values and humanity of learners, it restricts itself to mental mechanics. With both forms of behaviourism, there is an assumption that learners have a deficit that needs to be fixed, that they must accommodate to their environment rather than change it, and that learners will always be controlled by something or someone, rather than freely being able to determine their own paths.

The Humanist Orientation

In contrast to behaviourism, the humanist philosophy holds that the freedom, dignity, and autonomy of humans are sacred. Humanism flowered as a movement in the Italian Renaissance (from the 1200s to the 1400s), from whence the term *humanism* originates. Against a church tradition that saw humans as inherently sinful, humanism focused on the inherent human potential for good. Humanism surged during the Enlightenment in the eighteenth century when faith in human intellect and reason reigned. Modern humanism erupted as a protest against the Industrial Revolution and the reduction of human creativity and potential to mechanism—regarding people and the universe as machines.

In humanism people create their own *being* by becoming conscious of their existence and finding their own life meanings. There is no fundamental purpose for existence other than what people determine for themselves. Reality, then, is as you perceive it, not what exists outside of you. Given that humans have an inherent ethical sense, it is expected that they will want to create a better world and strive for the highest good. The highest state for humans is self-actualization or responsible selfhood, in which a person exhibits the characteristics of realism, acceptance, appreciation, contemplation, empathy, intimacy, and ethics. In sum, humans are free and not determined by external forces (behaviourism) or internal urges (Freudianism), but are free to exercise their human choices within the constraints of heredity, personal history, and environment.

Humanist psychology, as explicated by Maslow and Rogers, now largely informs "person-centred" and "caring" educational approaches. Two major principles frame humanist education. First, a humanist educator seeks to develop the full potential for the self-actualization of every person. Second, the relationship between the teacher and learner is central. Student-centred teaching is founded on respect and the idea that a teacher only facilitates, not dictates, learning. Surrounded by loving relationships, humans will grow and rise to their potential. Motivation is seen as generated from within, particularly from a strong self-concept, which compels teachers to focus on the self-esteem of learners. Competition is discouraged because it negatively affects a supportive environment for learning. Learning proceeds best when learners state a need and have a readiness to know, so that they take responsibility for their learning. Experiential learning is part of the humanist philosophy, in which a learner's existing knowledge, values, and emotions are the starting place for the curriculum. Real learning takes place when learners discover knowledge for themselves and assimilate it into pre-existing experience. Evaluation is best done by students themselves. Humanist teachers are responsive and empathetic, have positive beliefs about people, and are self-actualized in order to assist others in their self-actualization process.

Humanism has been critiqued for its optimism about human nature and its individualistic focus. It assumes that there are no constraints to human action—that whatever can be envisioned can be enacted. This does not account for external barriers such as the power relations that drive economic and political systems, conflict, and competition; or internal barriers such as resistance to growth and the strength of habituated behaviour. Humanists are also considered unrealistic about the ability to meet individual needs in a classroom environment with a large number of learners. Finally, they assume that individuals will embrace their personal and social responsibilities and not acknowledge the darker side of human behaviour, as explored by Freud.

The Radical/Critical Orientation

Building on the humanist tradition, the radical orientation suggests that true humanization develops only when people understand how they are situated in society (their classed, raced, or gendered positions) and how their thoughts and behaviours are shaped by the position they hold and how society regards them. Through a powerful analysis of society, individuals can learn to critique inequality in society and recognize their human agency for creating personal and social transformation *within* these historical constraints.

The *raison d'être* of this orientation is to challenge injustice and lack of freedom and promote social change toward societies that are safe, just, peaceful, ecologically sustainable, and fully democratic. Radical philosophy maintains that people are essentially good but that society is flawed, and it elicits lesser human qualities through an economic system premised on self-interest and greed, a political system that allows power to be concentrated in the hands of a few, and a social system that considers only some people as "normal." Thus, the radical[3] school asserts that the basic structures of society need to be transformed, particularly by those marginalized from power—such as the global poor, working class, women, minority groups, immigrant groups, the gay and lesbian community, and the differently abled. Through a process of empowerment, marginalized peoples can collectively uncover the power relations and hegemonic ideologies that disguise the true nature of social relations that prevent them from fulfilling their aspirations.

The radical/critical philosophy considers all education to be political. Freire (1970) was especially critical of schooling that is a banking form of education in which teachers "deposit" their knowledge into the "empty" students, who withdraw the deposits on exams. He contended that this is a form of indoctrination that promotes individual passivity and authoritarian societies. Rather, he advocated for an education focused on liberation, where participants interrogate their daily reality, learn to carry out an "ideology critique," and discuss strategies for social action, which thus constitutes a process of liberation where people are set free to be critical and creative producers of self and society (Allman and Wallis, 1990). This approach suggests that fundamental social change occurs through the struggles for power between dominant and marginalized groups; however, Freire cautioned, "Precisely because education is not the lever for the transformation of society, we are in danger of despair and of cynicism if we limit our struggle to the classroom. . . . Nevertheless transformation is an educational event" (Shor and Freire, 1987, p. 129).

Although this philosophy tries to balance the optimism of humanism and although it is sophisticated in its understanding of society and social forces, it can still be too optimistic that people are inherently inclined toward the common good, over and above their self-interests. This philosophy can often be dualistic in thought and manipulative in practice when educators assume that they can empower or transform others (Ellsworth, 1992). Furthermore, the power disparity between educators and learners must be problematized, especially if the educators are from more powerful social groups.

Postmodernism

In response to Kant's (1983) essay on the Enlightenment, Michel Foucault (1984) suggested that Enlightenment was an attitude, not a period in history, and that the role of scholarship today is to "proceed with the analysis of ourselves as beings who are historically determined, to a certain extent, by the Enlightenment" (p. 43). He saw this ethos as a limit-attitude located peculiarly within the development of European societies (pp. 43–45):

> We have to move beyond the outside-inside alternative; we have to be at the frontiers. Criticism indeed consists of analyzing and reflecting upon limits. . . . The point, in brief, is to transform the critique conducted in the form of necessary limitation into a practical critique that takes the form of a possible transgression. (p. 45)

Therefore, postmodernism is about *not* being able to determine truth, about the ambiguity of knowledge, about the limits of thinking imposed from within a certain historical period, and about the multiplicity of experience in the world. At the risk of generalizing, postmodernism became an attitude of "unmaking": It deconstructs all the knowledge from the modern period through a "critique of critique."

Postmodern thought developed in response to the crisis of the postmodern condition. Suspicious of all preceding meanings and values, it was clear that the world seemed to be drifting; science was humbled by its inability to know the universe or the nature of reality. Religion and philosophy were dismissed by their lack of rationality or empirical proof. The preceding metanarratives—such as conservatism, liberalism, and Marxism—were called into question because they could no longer explain the diverse experiences across classes, cultures, nations, genders, and histories. No one metanarrative or research method could reveal "the truth" or provide "universal knowledge and values." The Enlightenment goals of freedom, justice, and emancipation themselves became suspect.

Adult educator Derek Briton (1996) proposed three variants of postmodernism that need to be distinguished: reaction, resistance, and engagement. The postmodernism of reaction is fundamentally neoconservative and aims to maintain the existing power structure while teaching the traditional virtues of obedience, social order, self-discipline, and responsibility. The postmodernism of resistance attempts to resist the deepest levels of oppression. Therefore, the feminist movement often embraces this postmodernism as a way to affirm that the male experience cannot be generalized to women, that women have many different experiences among them that cannot be boiled down into neat packages that may be oppressive. The postmodernism of engagement tries to move beyond theories based on resistance or prescribing "the right thing to do" by assisting people in ethical thinking. It tries to maintain the emancipatory intent of the Enlightenment goals while recognizing multiplicity and contingency.

There are many criticisms of postmodernism: that it is too fragmented to guide action and too relativistic. Most often, postmodernisms lack any firm ground for knowledge making, propose an extreme relativization of moral ground, and vigorously oppose any attempt to formulate a new integrated world view. They can at once be nihilist in their despair or self-critical to the point of compulsive fragmentation and incoherent diversity. The postmodernism of resistance is the deconstruction of tradition, which questions any grand narratives that continue relations of dominance, to the point of questioning reason itself.

Conclusion

In each of these philosophies it may be difficult to identify one with the most resonance. Charles Taylor (1991) commented that this is one aspect of the malaise of modernity: the loss of a coherent, unified, moral and ethical horizon. Modern freedom was predicated on breaking loose from old moral horizons so that people had the right to decide for themselves their own convictions: the ways in which they would live their lives, what they believe is a good society, and, for our purposes, how to best engage learners. Now that the autonomous individual is tasked with finding his or her own meaning, this can lead to a dynamic of "individualism, . . . centring on the self, . . . shutting out, or even [being unaware], of the greater issues or concerns that transcend the self, be they religious, political, historical" (p. 14). Many social theorists have warned that individualism can mean the loss of social ideals, passion, and democratic public debate and risk increased political oppression and passive acceptance of corporatist or other agendas (Saul, 1995). Others have suggested that people take the easier route to self-definition through market commodities (possessive individualism), self-absorption and dependency on psychological experts (expressive individualism), or unquestioning participation in religious orthodoxies (Bellah, Madsen, Sullivan, Swidler, and Tipton, 1985). The challenge to adult educators in overcoming philosophobia is to systematically ponder one's predilections honestly and critically in terms of the described beliefs about human nature, society, and education to develop a unique working philosophy. Then, as exemplars of conscious and critical adults, they can in turn create educational spaces where citizens/learners can discuss the nature of their mental maps, their daily pattern of thoughts and practices, contending social visions, and the dominant trends in the field of adult education in terms of this larger philosophical dialogue. Adult educators today have a responsibility to consciously reflect on these prevalent philosophies and the material practices in which they are immersed and to guide more challenging, critical, and ethical visions and thoughtful practices.

References

Allman, P. and Wallis, J. (1990). Praxis: Implications for "really" radical education. *Studies in the education of adults, 22*(1), 14–30.

Bellah, R., Madsen, R., Sullivan, W., Swidler, A., and Tipton, S. (1985). *Habits of the heart: Individualism and commitment in American life.* New York: Harper & Row.

Briton, D. (1996). *The modern practice of adult education: A post-modern critique.* Albany: State University of New York.

Edwards, P. (2004). Philosophylato. In *The encyclopedia of philosophy* (Vol. 5, pp. 216–225). New York: Macmillan.

Elias, J. and Merriam, S. (1995). *Philosophical foundations of adult education.* Malabar, FL: Krieger.

Ellsworth, E. (1992). Why doesn't this feel empowering? Working through the repressive myths of critical pedagogy. In C. Luke and J. Gore (Eds.), *Feminisms and critical pedagogy* (pp. 90–119). New York: Routledge.

Foucault, M. (1984). "What is enlightenment?" In P. Rabinow (Ed.), *The Foucault reader* (C. Porter, Trans.; pp. 32–50). New York: Pantheon Books.

Freire, P. (1970). *Pedagogy of the oppressed.* New York: Seabury Press.

Kant, I. (1983). An answer to the question: What is enlightenment?" In I. Kant, *Perpetual peace and other essays on politics, history, and moral practice* (T. Humphrey, Trans.). Indianapolis, IN: Hackett. (Original work published 1784)

Knight, G. (1989). *Issues and alternatives in educational philosophy.* Berrien Springs, MI: Andrews University Press.

Lucas, C. (1970). *What is philosophy of education?* London: Macmillan.

Neatby, H. (1953). *So little for the mind.* Toronto, ON: Clarke, Irwin.

Paterson, R. W. K. (1988). Philosophy and "philosophies" of adult education. In M. Zukas (Ed.), *Papers from the transatlantic dialogue: A research exchange* (pp. 329–334). Leeds, UK: University of Leeds, School of Continuing Education.

Saul, J. R. (1995). *The unconscious civilization.* Concord, ON: Anansi Press.

Shor, I. and Freire, P. (1987). *A pedagogy for liberation: Dialogues on transforming education.* South Hadley, MA: Bergin & Garvey.

Simpson, D. P. (1977). *Cassell's Latin dictionary.* New York: Macmillan.

Simpson, J. (Ed.). (2005). *Oxford English dictionary.* Oxford, UK: Oxford University Press.

Taylor, C. (1991). *The malaise of modernity.* Concord, ON: Anansi Press.

Endnotes

[1] From *schola*, which means "school or of a school" (Simpson, 1977, p. 538).

[2] The six approaches are the great minds, the schools of thought, the problems, the didactic, the metaphilosophical, and the social foundations (Lucas, 1970).

[3] From r*adix*, which means "the root of" (Simpson, 1977, p. 500).

8

Postfoundationalism in Adult Education

Leona M. English

In this chapter the postfoundational theories of postmodernism, post-structuralism, and postcolonialism are introduced to help students and researchers think about how these theories might contribute to more fluid notions of subject, identity, power, and discourse within adult education. Insofar as is possible and from the published sources available, the chapter draws on examples of research from Canadian educators.

What Is Postfoundationalism?

Postfoundational might in some sense be equated with *anti*foundationalism, the questioning of all foundations and the sureties of modernism, which promises order, structure, cures, and unbridled progress and growth. *Postfoundational* is often used as an umbrella term to refer to an entire group of *post*-terms that include *postmodernism, poststructuralism,* and *postcolonialism* (e.g., Hemphill, 2001). Whatever the nomenclature, these areas share a resistance to universalisms and the Enlightenment's modernistic promises of order and growth.

Postfoundationalism deconstructs the grand narratives/myths of progress, rationalism, classification, and the Enlightenment's assurance that scientific progress would be the cure for all that ails us. It also disrupts the many binaries created by the modern and structural need to classify and divide; examples include mind/body; theory/practice, private/public, individual/group, literate/non-literate, and motivated/unmotivated (Hemphill, 2001, pp. 17–18). Postfoundationalism offers instead questions, uncertainty, and attention to difference. Hemphill outlined the basic themes of postfoundationalism: (a) critique of modernity and Enlightenment; (b) the decentred subject and multiple overlapping forms of marginalization and identity; (c) emphasis on and legitimation of popular culture; and (d) language, constructions, and floating signifiers, which draw attention to how the meaning in language is never static or fixed. Hemphill identified existing universalisms in adult education—self, motivation, rationality, and community—all used as if they apply to all people in all places, regardless of the different signifiers such as race, gender, class, and sexual orientation. Using these in such a generalized way furthers the modernist (and colonial) hegemony of the West.

Emphases of Postfoundationalism

Where these postfoundational approaches differ is in their respective emphases. Postcolonialism, by and large, arises from conditions of European colonization and directs itself to issues of race, diaspora, and issues of polarized geography and identity (see Battiste, 2004; Khan, 1998; Mayo, 2005). Its strong emphasis on difference is a distinguishing feature among the postfoundational theories.

Postmodernism has a broader span and speaks back to the metanarrative or universal truth, as well as to the assurances of the Enlightenment (see Briton, 1996; Plumb, 1995). Postmodernism challenges unitary selfhood (the authentic self) and points out that identity is shifting and uncertain, which makes an objective and knowable world impossible (see Clark, 1999). Poststructuralism (Dreyfus and Rabinow, 1982) is a resistance to structuralism and tends to focus on the interrelationship of knowledge, discourse, and power (see Chapman, 2003; English, 2005). Of course, these theoretical renderings of resistance to the foundational are problematic because they work to unify and solidify notions or philosophies and thereby enact the very codification of knowledge. The moment at which codification is helpful is the moment when it breaks down.

Problematizing Post

The notion of *post*, whether it is used to refer to colonialism, structuralism, feminism, Christianity, or industry, is not unproblematic. Referring specifically to postcolonialism, indigenous education scholar Battiste (2004) explained that post can be construed as signifying the end or indicating that the condition (i.e., colonialism, structuralism, modernism) has already been taken care of, when in fact post signifies an aspiration (her term) for a time to come, a hope but not yet a reality because we are not past colonialism (p. 1). Battiste was quick to note that postcolonialism (and by extension postmodernism and poststructuralism) is not only about "criticism and deconstruction" but also about "the reconstruction and transformation, operating as a form of liberation from colonial imposition" (p. 1). Despite the problematics of the term, most scholars continue to use post, but a few use *late capitalism* and *late modernity* (Bauman, 1998) to mean much the same thing as postmodern and to help them avoid the often ambiguous use of *postmodern*.

Is It a Philosophy, Theory, Approach, Lens, or Political Stance?

Part of the difficulty in classifying these theories is that they resist modernist attempts to codify and reduce the world to that which can be weighed, counted, and measured (see Hemphill, 2001). More helpful is to examine their trajectory. The first uses of postmodernism (at least by this name) may be traced to art and architecture of the 1960s and 1970s; it isn't until some time later that it came into social science discourse, and even later into adult education. Postfoundationalism, of course, owes much to early philosophical movements such as scepticism. Postfoundationalism's use in late capitalist society is distinguished by its application to science and social science. Along with being a philosophy and art movement, post-foundationalism is also a political movement (see Sim, 1999). It is a lens through which to see the world and a habit of mind that is constantly questioning, doubting, and challenging or deconstructing.

The Engagement of Canadian Adult Educators in the Theory

Although the word postmodern is ubiquitous, and indeed many Canadian adult educators will use it ambiguously as a generic descriptor for the chaotic world, a review of proceedings from annual conferences of the Canadian Association for the Study of Adult Education (CASAE) from 1990 to 2004 reveals few, if any, papers that seriously engage with these theories in a direct way. Exceptions include Plumb (2000), Briton and Plumb (1992), and Butterwick and Marker (2001). Other conference papers refer to these postfoundational areas as *trends* (Rubenson, 2000). Beyond conference papers, some significant texts in terms of length and engagement with theory include Chapman (2002, 2003), Briton (1996), Carriere (1996), English (2005, in press), and Grace (1997). The *Canadian Journal for the Study of Adult Education* has published several studies on the topic, though not by Canadians, including Brookfield (2001) and Clark (1999). Significant Canadian publications such as *Learning for Life* (Scott, Spencer, and Thomas, 1998) do not include any substantive writing on the topic. This dearth is quite significant because, according to Rubenson (2000), postmodernism, as well as critical theory and feminism, are at the forefront of social science research. Curiously though, although feminist and critical theory (especially Habermasian streams—e.g., Gouthro, 2000) have been strong in Canadian adult education writing, this is not true of postmodern studies, at least not in an overt way.

Yet cautions are many in dealing with surveys, especially of research in an interdisciplinary field such as adult education. As Plumb (2005) pointed out, postmodern sensibilities have become an integral, if unstated, part of the theory and practice of adult education. He noted that "recent feminist, antiracist, and queer theory discourses in adult education, challenge predominant notions about the nature of knowledge and learning, and draw on some of the same themes, and modes of critique as postfoun-dationalism" (n. p.). Plumb (1995) himself, although operating in other theoretical frames such as critical theory, has drawn simultaneously on postmodernism to make his case. Grace (1997) too has been heavily influ-enced by the postfoundational turn, especially in his engagement with cultural studies and queer theory.

It might be argued that any research into "difference" or binary logic (especially true of feminist research) and indeed "reflective practice" with its questioning of universal assumptions fits the "classification" of postfoun-dational and takes place precisely at that point where codification breaks down. Such borrowing, *bricolage*, *pastiche*, and mixing are emblematic of

postmodern approaches. Others such as Brookfield (2005) have accentu-
ated the common goals of postfoundationalism and critical adult education.
Yet, despite the overlap, in this chapter postfoundational approaches are
treated separately from other kinds of critical and theoretical perspectives.

Focusing in on the Specifics and Examples

The broad introduction above begs the questions, What does postfoundationalism look like? Are there any specifics? What are Canadian scholars
saying about it?

Postmodernism

I begin with postmodernism because it is the broadest of these terms
and the one that is occasionally used synonymously with at least one of
the others; namely, poststructuralism (e.g., Sim, 1999, p. ix; Tisdell, 2000,
p. 170). Postmodernism can be used to illustrate how notions of the grand
narrative (universal and unified theory) in adult education (progressive
development, education for all, self-actualization) affect our thinking,
views of practice, and main adult learning preoccupations of self-directed
learning, experiential learning, andragogy, and perspective transformation.

The first and most comprehensive Canadian, if not North American,
treatments of postmodernity within adult education came with Briton's
(1996) *The Modern Practice of Adult Education*. Briton's text enumerates all
the ways that adult education has made common cause with modernism
by engaging in the use of mechanistic techniques, focus on professional
practice, and self-absorbed individualism (e.g., andragogy, self-directed
learning). As an alternative in a postmodern age, Briton argued for a
pedagogy of engagement that is based on Havel's postmodernism of hope;
this pedagogy involves living with tensions, working for select issues that
we value, and being open to the ever-changing nature of our field (pp.
117–188). Although strong on identifying the modernist trends in adult
education—our commitment to teaching techniques, for example—Briton
stopped short of giving any specific practices or suggestions.

In a second substantive treatment of postmodernism, English and Gillen
(2000) speculated on what a postmodern adult religious education would
look like. Citing considerable disenchantment with the surety of religious
institutions and their allegiance to universalism, dualism, supernaturalistic
theism, individualism, anthropomorphism, and patriarchy, they identified
a new postmodern type of religious education that encourages a continuous negotiation of the tension between the collective and the individual through constant dialogue, interchange, and symbiotic relationship.
They advocated exploration of difference, which dissolves rigid divisions
between children and adults, theory and practice, and mind and body.
Finally, they suggested critically reflective practice as a form of resistance,
a way of challenging universals/metanarratives and of speaking truth to

power. Critically reflective practice and reflexivity particularly are post-modern practices in adult education that have been around for a long time before being classified as postfoundational.

Plumb (2000) presented a third treatment of postmodernism and adult education and focused on "postmodern morality for adult educators in Nova Scotia, Canada and Kingston, Jamaica" (p. 336). Building on the work of cultural theorist Zygmunt Bauman (1998), Plumb researched two groups of five people, one from Jamaica and one from Nova Scotia. Plumb wanted to "make sense of their experiences as adult educators in postmodernity, to question the ways in which they feel their moral sensibilities are being influenced in contemporary times, and to explore with them the current potentials of adult education" (pp. 338–339). Whereas the Canadians in his study embraced social change and some of them even saw the role of adult education as to expedite change to include the marginalized, the Jamaican participants were more suspicious. Significantly, all participants were mostly undecided about the role that adult education might be able to play in cultural and social change in a postmodern world. Plumb offered the opportunity to problematize the "discourse" of postmodernity. The Jamaicans could be enacting postmodern practice and questioning/challenging the discourse without having the language at hand to do it. Plumb's research is a reminder of the pervasive influence of postmodern discourse in northern intellectual circles. One could argue, meanwhile, that popular education, which is more common in the South, is postfoundational given its commitment to opposing power and scepticism of universal assumptions.

Poststructuralism

Like other postfoundational approaches, the poststructuralist turn, which began emerging in the late 1960s, expresses a disenchantment with the sureties of modernism, and particularly with structuralism's belief that there is a base structure or analyzable system to all reality. Poststructuralism exists in many strands and forms, influenced by writers such as Lyotard (1979/1984) and Foucault (as cited in Dreyfus and Rabinow, 1982). Although Derrida's poststructuralism is perhaps more influential in cultural studies, Foucauldian poststructuralism seems to have become the most influential strand in adult education (see Carriere, 1996; Chapman, 2003; English, 2005), possibly because of its attention to the body, power, discourse, and knowledge, all of which are directly relevant to education and learning. Foucault (as cited in Dreyfus and Rabinow, 1982) gave particular attention to governmentality, or the ways in which our bodies and lives are governed by a number of technologies (techniques or practices) of power. By *government* he meant "conduct of conduct" (pp. 220–221) or the control of how we act. Rather than a sovereign power (the boss, God, the prime minister, the king), Foucauldian poststructuralism offers a far more comprehensive notion of power as exercised (used) rather than held (owned) by all people. He developed the concept of disciplinary power, which is power embedded in the complex web of relationships and discourses that surround us and which is always operating. Most telling, it was the self-discipline or the ways that we regulate ourselves that were of most interest to Foucault (sitting obediently in our seats, taking wrong directions from our boss, not talking back). Foucault used the term *subjectivity* rather than *identity* or *selfhood* to describe self-regulation.

Disciplinary power challenges the notion that educators can empower anyone, because learners and educators all hold and exercise power in different ways; that is, they use technologies or practices of power such as group work and critical personal narratives/life histories to produce effects (we tell all to strangers; we "act" cooperatively in a workgroup so that others will like us). This power is capillary and works its way through systems of human interaction and language. For example, in a reflective assignment such as recording their learning journey, students may well include extensive personal information to please the teacher. Or they may invent the stories to subvert or resist the exercise. In popular education history we have the example of women suffragettes carrying banners and marching in parades in "resistance" to the male and military symbolism (binary logic) of these acts of resistance. Resistance to a technology of power such as an academic assignment or the government's rules is integral to poststructuralism.

Foucauldian poststructuralism challenges universalisms or regimes of truth, the unwritten laws that govern or operate. For instance, within adult education there is a regime or truth that the best teaching is facilitative or participatory. Poststructuralism serves as a challenge to these universal truths (metanarratives) and troubles (challenges) the notion that all people want to learn in this way. Learners are varied in their approaches to learning, and not all people want to share their personal lives in a learning situation. Poststructuralism helps us to see how some of our *foundational* beliefs such as andragogy, self-directed learning, and perspective transformation are only partially true and partially helpful. Not all people are self-directed in all areas of their learning, not all people learn from experiences, and not all people want to be transformed; nor are they transformed by engaging in critically reflective practice. And, despite the fact that innocuous teaching practices such as team learning are good as ideas, in practice they also produce effect. The team members, whether or not it is true, conduct themselves as if they are being observed, putting themselves in a Panopticon (a jail-like situation in which they feel that they are being observed continuously). The self-discipline that this produces also produces the resistance of trying to deceive other members into thinking that they are as busy as or busier than the others are, producing "profound" ideas for the group, or smart and helpful.

A key idea in poststructuralism is that there is *resistance* to the exercises or technologies of power, such as team learning, facilitation, learning circles, and learning journals. Learners can resist, for instance, reproducing the adult educator's knowledge by creating their own, or they can resist intense questioning by leaving the room or staying silent. Learners can resist the reflexive practice of journal writing by challenging it verbally and making visible that it is problematic and confessional. These resistances can be written or verbal. Plumb (1995) and Brookfield (2001) pointed to the circle as a technology of power within adult education, because it produces the effect of self-surveillance or the controlling of speech and action because of fear of who might be watching.

Chapman (2003) did some of the most beautiful writing on pastoral power and poststructuralism. The autobiographical tale that she completed for her University of British Columbia dissertation was published in proceedings (Chapman, 2002) and in refereed journals (e.g., Chapman, 2003). Working with the idea of disciplinary power, she examined how her schooling served to regulate everything from eating to eliminating to swarming (moving from the school to the work world and the middle class). Her intention was to show that her body is controlled through practices/technologies of power that she, teachers, and others exercise that serves, to produce effects—in some cases compliance, in others self-discipline, and in still others outright resistance or rebellion. This power has produced her as a subject. In doing autobiography, she writes back to her life and in so doing raises issues of power and identity. This research resists traditional forms of qualitative research and notions of sovereign power as "power over," and replaces it with pastoral power which is seemingly more benign yet pervasive. Chapman's work in poststructuralism highlights how the body is worked upon and sometimes forgotten in learning spaces. Her work shows how poststructuralism can span adult education settings in the community and workplace.

Postcolonialism

Postcolonialism is the inherent questioning by the colonized that comes from their attempts to disrupt the effects of Eurocentrism (English, 2005). Mayo (2005) noted that many, including Freire, have resisted colonization and supported the voice of the voiceless through advocating for the rightful place of indigenous knowledges. Canadian-educated Mayo cited Said's contrapuntal readings, though not specifically called postcolonial, as samples of postcolonial work. Postcolonial writing draws attention to race, diaspora, and identity and tries, in part, to uncover the effects of the colonization; Mayo provided the example of Britain's use of adult basic education taught in English to further the Anglicization of Malta and other colonies and to expand Britain's empire. Postcolonial adult education speaks back to this by celebrating local language, indigenous knowledge, and culture and by popularizing adult learning techniques such as popular theatre, which honours local issues and involves local people.

Mayo (2005), a frequent contributor to Canadian conferences and publications, challenged the use of the term *postcolonial* to refer to any kind of marginality in any place, such as race, ableness, or class, and preferred instead to use it in reference to those places that were colonized by

Europeans (usually thought of as Asia, Africa, and the Caribbean). Yet this is not always the way that postcolonialism is employed (e.g., English, 2005). Ontario-based Khan (1998) pointed out that postcolonial can also refer to people who are not in the colonial context but in the West. In *Muslim Women*, she reported on a study of Muslim women from Asia who lived in the diaspora, explored who they are as Muslims in the Canadian reality, and probed in depth issues regarding their hybridized identity. Lander and Prichard (2002), representing the settler nations of Canada and New Zealand, respectively, combined postcolonial and poststructural analyses in their writing on how their professional identities as academics in adult education and management education have been ordered, constructed, and hybridized within colonial histories.

Research on postcolonialism within adult education generally is fairly sparse, and within Canadian circles is even more so. This may speak more to the absence of interest in areas where postcolonialism has taken hold—race, First Nations, identity—than to the lack of interest in postcolonialism itself. Or, more probable, it may speak to the strong Marxist feminist tradition in Canada, which resists much postfoundational writing on the grounds that it destabilizes identity. However, in the broader field of education, and especially in First Nations education, there is interest in postcolonialism. Battiste (2004), for instance, has worked toward using postcolonial insights in establishing the indigenous humanities (p. 1) or discovering a way to work across disciplines to link First Nations indigenous knowledge with "scholarly" ideas of knowledge, most often European, that have been used to suppress indigenous knowledge. The key educational question arising from her work is, How can curriculum, schools, teacher education, and universities be agents of postcolonial education? (see p. 5). Battiste's suggestions for postcolonial pedagogical practices are helpful. They include pragmatic cooperation, strands of connectedness among diverse life forms, the recognition that humans are interdependent with nature, sharing and cooperation, and recognition of the spiritual in education (p. 8).

English's (2005) research is another Canadian example of postcolonial notions of identity and hybridity in a study of 13 women who practice adult education in the global sphere. In that qualitative study, English explored how their identity was affected by transnationality, how they came to be involved in their work, and how they viewed the practice of adult education in diverse settings. This study dealt with postcolonialism in terms of the countries in which these women worked—almost all ex-colonies—and with how they negotiated the identity of White, Western, and feminist. English probed how their identities are in flux, a hybrid between the place of origin and the place of destination, between development goals and local goals, between an African way of thinking and a Western way of thinking, between spirituality and religion. She developed from this research the notion of a third-space practitioner who works in the in-between spaces to effect change.

Challenges of Postfoundational Approaches

Postfoundational approaches have been and continue to be suspect partly because they are strong on fluidity and critique and short on concrete ideas or suggestions for practice. Briton (1996), for instance, set out to include some concrete ideas in his book-length treatment, but even he did not go far enough. Yet our field, one with strong ties to practice, holds out hope for these ideas. If, as Brookfield (2005) noted, critical theory and postmodern ideas hold sway in adult education research conferences, why hasn't this theory had more practical influence, and why hasn't it been as well received in Canada? This is a question well worth asking. Lack of attention to practice, however, is not the only critique of postmodern approaches. As Rubenson (2000) lamented, these approaches draw attention away from discussions of the state, which he saw as essential discourse in a globalized world. He believed that even those who subscribe to critical theory are engaging with the nonstate/systemic part of the theory; namely, the lifeworld (see, e.g., Plumb, 1995). This is a significant critique and one that challenges adult education, a field that aspires to effect global change and to participate in a new world order.

Rubenson's (2000) critique is not unlike the critique that some strands of feminism offer to postmodernism, especially that branch of feminism that has attended to the structural inequities that include race, class, and gender. The argument here is that postmodernism breaks down attention to a strong sense of self (subjectivity) or structure that is so important an accomplishment of feminism. In negating a strong core or self and advancing a de-centred self, postmodernism destroys the achievements of feminism and ignores structural inequity and issues such as class that have been most problematic for women (see, e.g., DiStefano, 1990). Feminists informed by Marxism (including those popular educators influenced by Marxist writers Freire and Gramsci) react to this strong notion of postmodernism that no longer attends to the ways that patriarchy has been structured to exclude women (e.g., Mojab, 1998). They see it as a challenge to the gains made by feminists in developing solidarity and the sovereignty of experience. Postmodernism's fluidity and non-unitary subjectivity make the identification of the enemy (organizational structures, class barriers, gender inequities) much more difficult and harder to rage against.

Offering the Field of Adult Education

What then is the advantage or the draw of postfoundational approaches? There are several things they offer that we ought to take seriously. Yet, even in making these suggestions, there is irony (a fully postmodern concept) because postmodernism resists recipes, charts, tools, skills, and formulaic responses. In the spirit of contradiction, we might begin by identifying the features of our current repertoire that are postfoundational in all but name.

Critical reflection on and questioning of universals. Critical reflection on and questioning of universals, and interrogating assumptions are consistent with Foucauldian poststructuralism, which analyzes and questions power and authority. Critical reflection is also consistent with Bauman's (1998) assertion that scepticism underpins postmodern reflexivity. Canadian popular educator Shelene Razack (1993) offered examples of storytelling for social change, in which she positioned herself in the tradition of Freirean critical pedagogy, from two incidents during the summer college in human rights at the University of Ottawa. Yet she drew heavily on feminist and postcolonial writers such as Trin Minh-ha and Gayatri Spivak to advocate for "instinctual immediacy," which involves questioning "one's point of departure at every turn so that strategies (such as replacing rationality with emotions)" (p. 67) do not become codified adult education practice. Critical autobiography or self-writing (Chapman, 2003) can also be named as a poststructural adult education practice that resists the binary logic of reason/emotion, man/woman, public/private, culture/nature.

Multiplicity of voices. These postmodern approaches offer room for difference and the acceptance of a multiplicity of voice. The challenge for adult educators, especially those in a more liberal stream, is to take difference seriously and to engage with not only the like-minded, but also those in human-resource development, competency-based education, and more behaviourally oriented studies. This multiplicity ought not to replicate the tyranny of the left or right. We may want to question what Brookfield (2005) identified as the exclusionary practice of academics in accepting mostly critical theory and postfoundational papers, to the exclusion of humanistic studies; or, in the case of CASAE, of soliciting more First Nations members. If indeed we have an *Espace francophone* at our annual CASAE conferences, could we not also have a First Nations space?

Pedagogy of inclusion. This emphasizes the need for the active involvement of all citizenry and a concerted movement to resist the fixed "truth" of modernity. A pedagogy of inclusion involves the whole civil society in our conversations and our discourses. On a practical level for adult education, a pedagogy of inclusion might embrace active involvement in civil society organizations such as the International Council for Adult Education, the Canadian Network for Democratic Learning, CASAE, or community-based organizations. Engagement may be a concrete way to address Rubenson's (2000) claim that postmodern ideas avoid discourse of the state. Putting postmodern and postcolonial theory into practice involves resisting the binary logic of the lifeworld versus the state, the private versus the public, or the family versus the workplace (see, e.g., Gouthro, 2000, on the homeplace as it shapes the global marketplace, the workplace, and the higher-education classroom).

Creative responses. A postmodern approach is evolving that resists formulaic responses to teaching and educating adults. It is open to new ways of doing things. With transformative learning, for instance, we ought to avoid the lock-step approach of phases and move forward with keener eyes and wits to figure out where transformative learning occurs and what its meaning is. We can also move beyond the belief that adult education solves all ills or that it single-handedly has much to offer the world's problems. We might move beyond the lockstep models of program planning and explore more emergent possibilities for our field.

Learning possibilities. Essentialist and stereotypic readings of areas such as women's learning also need to be challenged. The separation of different categories of knowers such as women learners is no longer tenable in this postmodern age. We need to move beyond the binaries of women's and men's learning, resist the idea that women learn in different ways, and constantly be open to the possibilities of different modes of learning, whether the learner be male or female. Because identity is fluid in post-modernism, the essentialism inherent in the use of "women's learning" is problematic. We might find careful and in-depth explorations of particular women's or men's construction of identity more useful (e.g., Chapman, 2003) to see how this is enacted rather than generalizing or engaging in binaries and essentialism.

Concluding Note

Although I have made some attempt to explicate these terms and to illustrate their use with practical and research examples, there is still room for exploration. The postfoundational approach is necessarily critical in that it is questioning, shifting, and non-unitary. Although I have attempted to describe each theory, I acknowledge the fragmentary and partial nature of my effort to define or codify postfoundational work. This, however, is a modest start.

References

Battiste, M. (2004). Animating sites of postcolonial education: Indigenous knowledge and the humanities. Plenary address at the Canadian Society for Studies in Education conference. Retrieved on July 25, 2004, from www.usask.ca/ueducation/people/battistem/csse_battiste.htm

Bauman, Z. (1998). *Globalization: The human consequences.* New York: Columbia University Press.

Briton, D. (1996). The modern practice of adult education: A postmodern critique. Albany: State University of New York Press.

Briton, D. and Plumb, D. (1992). RoboEd: Re-imaging adult education. In *Proceedings of the 11th Annual Conference of the Canadian Association for the Study of Adult Education* (pp. 38–43). Saskatoon: University of Saskatchewan.

Brookfield, S. D. (2001). Unmasking power: Foucault and adult learning. *Canadian Journal for the Study of Adult Education, 15*(1), 1–23.

Brookfield, S. D. (2005). *The power of critical theory: Liberating adult learning and teaching.* San Francisco: Jossey-Bass.

Butterwick, S. and Marker, M. (2001). Postcards from the edge: Towards a tribal postcolonial view of adult education. In *Proceedings of the 20th Annual Conference of the Canadian Association for the Study of Adult Education* (pp. 31–36). Laval University, Quebec City.

Carriere, E. (1996). Tales of the Alhambra: Women's programs as harems. In *Proceedings of the Adult Education Research Conference.* University of South Florida, Tampa. Retrieved February 10, 2005, from http://www.edst.educ.ubc.ca/aerc/proceed.htm

Chapman, V.-L. (2002). Knowing one's self: Selfwriting, power and ethical practice. In J. M. Pettitt and R. P. Francis (Eds.), *Proceedings of the 43rd Annual Adult Education Research Conference.* Raleigh: North Carolina State University. Retrieved February 10, 2005, from http://www.edst.educ.ubc.ca/aerc/proceed.htm

Chapman, V.-L. (2003). On "knowing one's self': Selfwriting, power, and ethical practice: Reflections from an adult educator. *Studies in the Education of Adults, 35*(1), 35–53.

Clark, M. C. (1999). Challenging the unitary self: Adult education, feminism, and nonunitary subjectivity. *Canadian Journal for the Study of Adult Education, 13*(2) 39–48.

DiStefano, C. (1990). Dilemmas of difference: Feminism, modernity, and postmodernism. In L. J. Nicholson (Ed.), *Feminism/postmodernism* (pp. 63–82). London, UK: Routledge.

Dreyfus, H. and Rabinow, P. (1982). *Michel Foucault: Beyond structuralism and hermeneutics. With an afterword by Michel Foucault.* Chicago: University of Chicago Press.

English, L. M. (2005). Third-space practitioners: Women educating for civil society. *Adult Education Quarterly, 55*(2), 85–100.

English, L. M. (in press). Foucauldian pastoral power and feminist organizations: A research direction for adult education. *Studies in the Education of Adults.*

English, L. M., and Gillen, M. A. (2000). A postmodern approach to adult religious education. In A. L. Wilson and E. Hayes (Eds.), *Handbook of adult and continuing education* (pp. 523–538). San Francisco: Jossey-Bass.

Gouthro, P. (2000). Globalization, civil society, and the homeplace. *Convergence, 33*(1–2), 57–77.

Grace, A. P. (1997). Where critical postmodern theory meets practice: Working in the intersection of instrumental, social, and cultural education. *Studies in Continuing Education, 19*(1), 51–70.

Hemphill, D. F. (2001). Incorporating postmodernist perspectives into adult education. In V. Sheared and P. A. Sissel (Eds.), *Making space: Merging theory and practice in adult education* (pp. 15–28). Westport, CT: Bergin & Garvey.

Khan, S. (1998). *Muslim women: Creating a North American identity.* Gainesville, FL: University of Florida Press.

Lander, D. A., and Prichard, C. (2002). Life on the verandah: Colonial cartographies of professional identities. In M. Dent and S. Whitehead (Eds.), *Managing professional identities: Knowledge, performativity, and the "new" professional* (pp. 235–251). London, UK: Routledge.

Lyotard, J.-F. (1984). *The postmodern condition: A report on knowledge* (G. Bennington and B. Massumi, Trans.). Minneapolis: University of Minnesota Press. (Originally published 1979)

Mayo, P. (2005). Postcolonialism. In L. M. English (Ed.), *International encyclopedia of adult education* (pp. 489–491). New York: Palgrave Macmillan.

Mojab, S. (1998). Muslim women and Western feminists: The debate on particulars and universals. *Monthly Review, 50* (7), 19–30.

Plumb, D. (1995). Declining opportunities: Adult education, culture, and postmodernity. In M. R. Welton (Ed.), *In defense of the lifeworld: Critical perspectives on adult learning* (pp. 157–193). Albany: State University of New York Press.

Plumb, D. (2000). Postmodern morality in adult education: A cross-cultural study. In T. Sork, V.-L. Chapman, and R. St. Clair (Eds.), Proceedings of the Annual Adult Education Research Conference (pp. 336–340). Vancouver: University of British Columbia.

Plumb, D. (2005). Postcolonialism. In L. M. English (Ed.), *International encyclopedia of adult education* (pp. 491–494). New York: Palgrave Macmillan.

Razack, S. (1993). Story-telling for social change. *Gender and Education, 5*(1), 55–70.

Rubenson, K. (2000). Revisiting the map of the territory. in T. Sork, V.-L. Chapman and R. St. Clair (Eds.), Proceedings of the Annual Adult Education Research Conference (pp. 397–401). Vancouver: University of British Columbia.

Scott, S. M., Spencer, B. and Thomas A. M. (Eds.). (1998). *Learning for life: Canadian readings in adult education.* Toronto, ON: Thompson Educational.

Sim, S. (Ed.). (1999). *The Routledge critical dictionary of postmodern thought.* New York: Routledge.

Tisdell, E. J. (2000). Feminist pedagogies. In E. Hayes and D. Flannery (Eds.), *Women as learners: The significance of gender in adult learning* (pp. 155–184). San Francisco: Jossey-Bass.

9
The Critical Legacy: Adult Education Against the Claims of Capital

Michael Collins

The events of 9/11 took the wind out of the sails of the anti-globaliza-tion movement. . . . The task for revolutionary anti-capitalists today is to develop new forms of convergence that move beyond ephemeral actions and the rhetoric of "diversity." (Hurl, 2005, pp. 61–63).

This opening quotation from a Canadian activist and student of sociology that focuses on the anti-globalization movement might seem a little too edgy, but the reality and sentiments expressed are right on if critical pedagogy today, in practice and theory, is to escape what, from the standpoint of this chapter, is its current postmodern malaise.

Adult Education in Canada and the Political Dimension

In the first chapter of his book *Adult Education in Canada*, Gordon Selman (1995), former professor of adult education at the University of British Columbia and long-time adult education practitioner, commented on the difficulty of defining his chosen field of practice and research: "One of the most striking characteristics of adult education is its diversity and the fact that it is so widely dispersed throughout society, much of it in the private sector and virtually invisible to the casual observer" (p. 15). Selman's char-acterization resonates well with professors of adult education and their students who recognize in it a source of both mild frustration and challeng-ing potential when it comes to defining adult education. Subsequently, Selman (1998), as a way of tidying up our discernment of adult education, envisaged the field as encompassed by three "main clusters or groupings of adult education services" (p. 410), each as a distinctive area, though "not discreet or mutually exclusive" (p. 410) of vocational commitment: (a) a concern for "academic, credential and vocational" (p. 411) attain-ment, largely in the formal education sector; (b) the provision of organized educational activities for "personal interest and development" (p. 411); and (c) adult education for "social action and social change" (p. 411).

The kind of adult education practice and research with which this chapter is concerned might be conveniently assigned to Selman's (1998) third category, which is indicative of "active efforts to critique and change society in some way" (p. 411). More precisely, the connections made are to a historical legacy of adult education that knowingly sets its peda-gogical course, in theory and practice, *against the claims of capital* and the political, economic, and social conditions with which it undermines on a daily basis those aspirations for what Thomas Hodgskin, the early nine-teenth century English adult educator, political economist, and co-founder of the mechanics' institutes movement, described as "the education of a free people" (Collins, 1998a, p. 136). Selman (1995, 1998) wrote about the mechanics' institutes in Canada without reference to the movement's political significance for adult education. (Marx cited Hodgskin's work approvingly on a number of occasions in *Capital*.)

This pedagogical legacy, albeit frequently co-opted and disconnected from its revolutionary implications in liberal progressive and even critical discourses on adult education, is nowadays evident in educational practices that more or less invoke the work of Paulo Freire, especially as it is described in *Pedagogy of the Oppressed* (Freire, 1981). Freire's pedagogy, guided by an understanding that, in political terms, education cannot be neutral is intended to advance the interests of the majority of ordinary men and women and is shaped from the standpoint of oppressed people. In this regard, Freire referred us to the radical, politically engaged work of Frantz Fanon (1988) on *The Wretched of the Earth*.

From the position adopted in this chapter, a critically informed and politically engaged pedagogy is necessary to defend and advance the still relevant liberal-progressive and social-democratic aims of prominent Canadian adult educators (Ned Corbett, Roby Kidd, and Alan Thomas, among others) and characteristically Canadian educational initiatives (such as Frontier College, Farm Forum, the Canadian Broadcasting Corpo-ration, women's institutes, and the Antigonish movement) that have contributed significantly to shaping our conceptions about the distinctive nature of adult education in Canada. However, shorn of the insights and commitments derived from a critically informed and politically engaged pedagogy *against the claims of capital*, seemingly progressive adult education discourses now become merely accommodative of neoliberal imperatives around the marketization of education, innovation agendas in education at public expense (particularly at the university level) that favour private sector interests, and restructuring initiatives in our public institutions that are unmindful of participatory decision making.

In these circumstances, adult education practices that combine critical insights with informed political (action-oriented) intentions have become more relevant across all three "clusters or groupings" that Selman (1998) discerned as characterizing the scope of adult education. For sure, constraints militating against, as well as reasonably hopeful possibilities for creating, countervailing pedagogical strategies vary from one context to another. However, the damaging effects of prevailing neoliberal policies (including the ideological mindset they reinforce—a kind of "Wal-Mart pedagogy" around the sovereignty of consumer choice) are now as prob-lematic for the survival of a publicly funded academic and vocational credentializing enterprise in adult education as they are for adult learning for personal development and community-based adult education for social change. The challenge at this time is to design pedagogical strategies that combine critique *for* resistance with the development of appropriate alternative adult education initiatives (Collins, 2003).

W(h)ither Critical Adult Education?

This chapter is in effect an update, in light of reflections on subsequent events and their implications for practice and research, to my contributions to *Learning for Life: Canadian Readings in Adult Education* (Scott, Spencer, and Thomas, 1998): "Critical Returns: From Andragogy to Lifelong Education" and "Lifelong Education as Emancipatory Pedagogy" (Collins, 1998b, 1998c, respectively). Along with contributions from other authors whose work falls under the broad category that Selman (1998) defined as adult education "to critique and change society in some way," it is anticipated that these two chapters will remain accessible following this publication, *Contexts of Adult Education: Canadian Perspectives*. In any event, the two chapters specified here from *Learning for Life* serve as points of reference for these commentaries on critical practice and research in adult education.

It is now virtually commonplace to note how conditions flowing directly from the events of September 11, 2001 (9/11), have shaped the ideological landscape worldwide in favour of the militant neoconservative tendencies identified with the administration of George W. Bush. Reinforcing neoliberal interests in the enthronement of free-market values, cutbacks in public services, and the implementation of globalization initiatives according to World Bank and International Monetary Fund (IMF) missions, ascendant neoconservatism in the US is more overtly aggressive in the pursuit of pre-emptive reconstruction, including military intervention, on an international scale. Thus, neoconservatism, finding its expression now in the Bush administration, is even less nuanced in dealing with the concepts and strategies of power in advancing its imperialistic intents abroad and "protecting" them through tightened security on the home front. Undoubtedly, the ideological tendencies that legitimize these developments have had consequences for critically informed emancipatory pedagogy.

Although there is still space for critical discourse (we can still "talk the talk" in our academic forums), it has lost much of its cutting edge and now poses no discernible challenge to neoliberal innovation that imposes marketplace values at the expense of publicly funded education and other services funded from the public purse. However, though the "War on Terror" and other ideologically driven neoconservative incursions out of 9/11 have been relatively effective in curtailing anti-oppression initiatives (much in line with Freirean pedagogy) and the anticapitalist movement as a whole (largely organized around resistance to the globalization policies of the World Bank and IMF), it is with these anti-oppression and anticapitalist activities that a critically informed emancipatory pedagogy in adult education should connect to maintain credibility with regard to its aspirations in the area of social change. Otherwise, critical pedagogy, whether informed by Marxian and neo-Marxist theory or postmodern/poststructuralist analyses, constitutes little more than a *socialism of the academe* around which critical insights are recirculated in the absence of necessary engagement with strategies for resistance and political emancipation.

Many of us in adult education who identify with critical pedagogy are politically engaged in this way as a matter of course. The point to be emphasized here is that this aspect of our work—active engagement in the politics of change implied by our critical theory—now requires more emphasis. This is not to diminish the contributions of critical pedagogy to our understanding of the ways that unequal relationships of power, the predominance of technical rationality, and the commodification of everything we value (including, even, critical pedagogy) function in shaping our everyday experience of the world. Through critical pedagogy we gain a better sense of the consequences for teaching practice, curriculum and program development, educational policy formation, and social learning processes. Further, the discourse on critical pedagogy in adult education, especially where it is informed by Marxist and neo-Marxist thought (in the work of Jurgen Habermas, for example), provides us with reasons that we should systematically incorporate dialogue and empowering strategies—in line with the politically engaged teachings of Paulo Freire, Thomas Hodgskin, and other adult educators concerned with the pursuit of social justice against the claims of capital—into our practice. In this regard, critical pedagogy surpasses the typical rhetoric on critical thinking in education and recognizes, in a Hegelian sense, the radical potential of persisting with reasoned analysis: "This power it is not as the positive that looks away from the negative—as when we say of something, this is nothing or false, finished with it, turn away from it to something else" (Hegel, 1807/1967, p. 408). On the other hand, and while retaining an all-important understanding of the dialectical relationship between theory and practice (as *praxis*), Marx's (1888/1967) view on the matter is even more instructive for critical pedagogy at this juncture: "The philosophers have only interpreted the world in various ways; the point is to change it" (pp. 401–402).

While mindful, as was Marx (1888/1967), of the need to avoid any suggestion of mindless activism, it is reasonable for us to focus on how our interest in critical pedagogy engages us in political work beyond the classrooms and professional forums. Likely, many of us whose pedagogical orientation is informed by critical theory can respond in some measure to the question of "How do we walk the talk?" In any event, to avoid the irrelevance implied in a socialism of the academe isolated from practice, it will help if that question becomes more central to a discourse on critical pedagogy in which the politics of engagement take priority.

When we refer to pedagogy the intended focus is usually on the work of teaching—on the agency of the teacher. This emphasis differs somewhat from that of mainstream adult education's discourse on self-directed learning and draws on, by way of examples, the work of Malcolm Knowles and Allen Tough and critically oriented adult education (e.g., Welton, 1995), which is largely advanced, though not exclusively, from the standpoint of the learner and the learning process. A concern for the agency of the teacher, however, in no way diminishes the necessity for focusing on the interests of the learner. Martin Heidegger's (1968) viewpoint on the role of the teacher is particularly instructive for us in this regard:

> Teaching is more difficult than learning because what teaching calls for is this: to let learn. The real teacher, in fact, lets nothing else be learned than learning . . . [and] is ahead of his [sic] apprentices in this alone, that he has still far more to learn than they—he has to learn to let them learn. (p. 15)

In addition to connecting with the experience of their students through dialogue, adult educators whose practice is authentically informed by critical pedagogy will, according to the critical perspective adopted in this chapter, also be learning from actual engagement with anti-oppressive initiatives against those claims of capital that are detrimental to the interests of the majority of ordinary people through the elevation of marketplace imperatives that erode vital aspects of our everyday lifeworld. By initially thematizing the agency of adult educators in both defending and advancing the interests of learners and the intrinsic value of learning processes, we highlight the significance of our politically engaged work towards a more just and equal society.

Postmodern Sensibilities and the Evasion of Political Engagement

In *Learning for Life* contributors posed questions about the influence of postmodernism in adult education and argued that "the relativizing deconstructions of postmodern discourse in education does not advance the prospects for lifelong education as emancipatory pedagogy" (Collins, 1998c, p. 112). Since that time the influence of postmodern and poststructuralist tendencies in academic arenas have become more pervasive in adult education and education in general. These tendencies overlap sufficiently for them to be treated together for the necessarily abbreviated critique of this section. Ben Agger (1991) laid out a useful account of the connections and distinctions between critical theory, poststructuralism, and postmodernism. Otherwise, the position that I have taken in this chapter views postmodernism and poststructuralism as dancing to the same tune, and, as far as a critical theory and practice of adult education is concerned, the performance is virtually over.

Unfortunately, during the past few years (since 9/11) the evasive attitudes towards engagement in political initiatives that are formed by postmodern and poststructuralist orientations, whether or not they are directly invoked, are more discernible. This trend is problematic for a critical pedagogy that aims to identify both *reasons* and sensible strategies (at local, national, and international levels) for countering the effects of neoliberal initiatives as they manifest themselves within the global reach of late capitalism's developments. There is no doubt that postmodern and poststructuralist commentaries in education drawn in large measure from the work of European academics Michel Foucault, Jacques Derrida, Jacques Lacan, and Jean Baudrillard (who in turn drew on the philosophical insights of Friedrich Nietzsche, Soren Kierkegaard, and Martin Heidegger and who, curiously, have been seldom directly referenced in the papers of academic educators) are insightful. They illuminate for us the effects of unequal power relationships (including both overt and more cunning mechanisms of surveillance and control) and identify specific groups who are oppressively marginalized within society at large. Through a deliberate process of *deconstruction*, oppressive and variously wrought regulatory practices that prevail in "texts" of various kinds (regardless of the initiators' intentions), including curriculum and educational policy documents, institutional arrangements and everyday legitimated practices are revealed.

These insights are derivable and find confirmation in the wider legacy of critical theory (including Marxian and neo-Marxist praxis). And, as with this critical legacy, postmodernist/poststructuralist perceptions recognize the tendencies under late capitalism of reinforcing marketplace imperatives, the cult of efficiency (technical rationality), the erosion of lifeworld (community-oriented) interests in the face of bureaucratic encroachments, and the compelling impulse towards commodification of all that is valued. At the same time, postmodern sensibilities seemingly revel in the fragmentary, pluralistic, and relativizing discourses and practices that exemplify the workings of neoliberal ideology. The problem of relativism cannot be fudged by advocates of postmodernism and poststructuralism given their airy dismissal of the quest for establishing *rational* grounds through *reasoned* argument as the basis for theory and practice.

It is with postmodernism's antipathy towards aspirations for a more rational society (grounded in reasoned thought and action) and the identification of strategies, the success or failure of which can be assessed through the lens of critical theory, that an emancipatory pedagogy against the claims of capital takes issue. Any suggestions, which emanate easily from the relativizing tendency of postmodernist/poststructuralist discourse, that a rapprochement can be effected between a critically oriented pedagogy against the claims of capital and postmodernism need to be taken up initially from a standpoint that the tendency hinders rather than advances the prospects for emancipatory practice.

Since *Learning for Life* (Scott et al., 1998) was written, in which the chapter on emancipatory pedagogy (Collins, 1998c) opened with a quotation from Adrienne Rich (1993; as cited in Collins, 1998c), who regretted that "there is still no general collective understanding from which to move" (p. 107) and included a section that questioned the effects of postmodern tendencies that were just being adopted in adult education, further substantial criticisms of postmodernism have appeared that raise concerns about how preoccupation with the "politics of the personal" and "identity politics" affords us "no general collective understanding from which to move" (p. 107). Terry Eagleton's (2003) thought-provoking text, in line with the concerns expressed here and firmly opposed to postmodern/poststructuralist influences, merits attention from adult educators interested in critical practice and theory.

These observations are not intended to imply that educators who are drawn to postmodern discourses are not otherwise, as a matter of course, actively involved in progressive social-change initiatives for a more just society. It is just that there is a disconnection between that social activism and the postmodern sensibilities that they espouse that deliberately eschew giving recognition to agency as manifested in the leadership role of the teacher, political activist, engaged intellectual, and so on. The legitimate concern of a postmodern orientation is that the propensity to take on a leadership role and engage in strategic planning will ultimately result in non-democratic vanguardism and some form of oppression, however just the cause. Postmodernism dismisses what it regards as the grand theory quest to grasp, from a particular event or immediate circumstances, an understanding of what is at stake in relation to a totality shaped by the conditions and forces of advanced capitalism. Though postmodernism/post-structuralism is useful in illuminating the effects of educational practices and institutional arrangements, as is also the case with analyses from the larger legacy of critical theory, it is not pedagogical in the way that critical theory intends. In fact, the work of Foucault and other poststructuralists, such as Nietzsche, is antipedagogical and, in particular, against the notion of mass education. Along with the idea of leadership, pedagogy constitutes yet another discourse ("truth regime") to be subverted.

Within the discourses on critical pedagogy, postmodern and poststructural sensibilities have undermined our capacities to think and act strategically in the development of anti-oppression and anticapitalist educative initiatives. The postmodern emphasis on expression, the privileging of difference, replaces a concern for strategizing, organization, practical outcomes, and ongoing political involvement. To counter this postmodern depoliticizing tendency, it would be useful to reconfirm an understanding, in line with the pedagogical work of Paulo Freire (1981) and Antonio Gramsci (1971) as prime examples, that authentic education is inescapably political and requires leadership, especially with respect to the agency of teachers.

Upping the Ante: Politically Oriented Pedagogy

A re-awakened politically oriented pedagogy, at a time when there is a discernible, though slowly emerging, eagerness among adults of all ages to become engaged in constructive activism, calls for a view of the whole or, more precisely in Marxian terms, a conception of "totality" (Bottomore, 1983, pp. 479–481) alongside participation in local or regionally based initiatives. In this regard, the work of world-renowned activist and intellectual Subcommandante Marcos is instructive (though not necessarily "the model") for those of us concerned about the development of a politically engaged pedagogy from within the largely academicized and increasingly commodified discourse on critical theory and practice in education.

Subcommandante Marcos, about whose anti-oppression and anticapitalist activities there is a growing body of information on the Internet, is a leading voice in the Zapatista movement. Following its fight for the rights of indigenous people in the Chiapas (one of Mexico's poorest regions), the movement now represents the interests of the country's indigenous population of 10 million. Though the most visible among the Zapatista leadership, Marcos has been careful to reject the mantle of vanguardism for himself and the movement and instead has emphasized the critical importance to mass organizing of popular democratic participation.

Although the focus for Marcos and the movement still remains on the Chiapas, his activism is not just localist. Rather, it extends to an analysis of relevant connections to the totality of global developments, in particular to the global reach of neoliberalism and "New World Order" militarism. Thus, the more "progressive" news media worldwide have become interested in the localized circumstances of the Chiapas' indigenous people and in the connections to be drawn from Marcos' planned mass education initiative about conditions under advanced capitalism on the planet as a whole.

A politically oriented critical pedagogy in this vein is not intended to privilege activism over critical thought or localized events over a critical understanding of the totality of conditions within which they operate. Rather, it is a reasonable appeal, contrary to postmodern/poststructuralist attitudes, for critical pedagogy to be engaged in politics without losing sight of theoretical problems that strategizing for a more just society against the claims of capital entail.

For all of this focus on strategizing and counteracting the harmful fallout of neoliberal ideology, it is important to keep in mind the significance of the aesthetic dimension within a politically oriented emancipatory pedagogy. Our experience of music, painting, poetry, and the arts in general contains the portents of alternative ways of living, not merely in the form of escapism from the daily drudgery of alienated existence. The emancipatory potential of aesthetic experience in this engaged sense is convincingly portrayed in Ernst Bloch's (1995) magnificent three-volume study *The Principle of Hope*, which provides a sterling rationale for subsequent discourses on a pedagogy of hope. It would be a mistake to infer that the emancipatory potential of aesthetic experience necessitates that artistic endeavour be determinedly political. Marxist and other critical theorists who draw our attention to the emancipatory potential of the aesthetic will have none of that crude appropriation of the arts. At the same time, however, a politically oriented pedagogy can be properly engaged with artistic endeavours that are intended as expressions of support for a more just society.

No doubt the relevance of the aesthetic dimension for a more politically oriented pedagogical practice can serve the aspirations of adult educators interested in reinvigorating the historical connection between adult education and the arts.

On Canadian Content

Even as this chapter is being written, obituaries celebrating the lifework and remarkable global influence of the Canadian ecologist, co-founder of Greenpeace, and public educator Bob Hunter are being featured in the international press. Nostalgia aside, there is a distinctly Canadian touch to the way that Hunter and his associates pursued their commitments that are inspirational for the political project of emancipatory pedagogy. Similarly, internationally influential radical intellectuals and educators from the US, such as Noam Chomsky (by his own admission), remain quintessentially American in ways that are readily recognizable by many Canadians. In regard to this discernment about the significance of distinctive approaches, reference can be made to two pedagogically useful (in terms of globally significant social critique) film documentaries by the American Michael Moore, on the one hand (the Hollywood blockbuster director of *Fahrenheit 9/11*), and, on the other hand, by two Canadian activists (Naomi Klein and Tel Lewis, 2004) who, in their international award-winning film production of *The Take*, reported on the emergence of worker cooperatives in Argentina in the face of opposition from discredited business corporations.

By sustaining distinctive points of view and ways of practice, and without the kind of enfeebling anti-American parochialism (still encountered even among some Canadian intellectuals and activists) that emerges, understandably, from existence alongside the elephantine US, adult education in Canada provides a context from which a politically significant contribution towards a global emancipatory pedagogy might be advanced. Can a critical theory and practice of adult education in Canada, turning away from inclinations towards a postmodern socialism of the academe, take its cue from the first issue of a new Canadian periodical, *Upping the Anti: A Journal of Theory and Action* (Conway, Keefer, and Khan, 2005)? *Upping the Anti* set out its prospectus in the following terms: "In this, our first editorial, we outline the impetus for the [collective] project, and reflect upon the strengths and limitations of such concepts as anticapitalism, anti-oppression, and anti-imperialism in building new radical movements in Canada and internationally" (p. 4).

References

Agger, B. (1991). Critical theory, poststructuralism, and postmodernism: Their sociological relevance. *Annual Review of Sociology, 17*, 105–131.

Bloch, E. (1995). *The principle of hope.* Cambridge, MA: MIT Press.

Bottomore, T. (Ed.) (1983). *A dictionary of Marxist thought* (pp. 479–481). Cambridge, MT: Harvard University Press.

Collins, M. (1998a). *Critical crosscurrents in education.* Malabar, FL: Krieger.

Collins, M. (1998b). Critical returns: From andragogy to lifelong education. In S. M. Scott, B. Spencer, and A. M. Thomas (Eds.), *Learning for life: Canadian readings in adult education* (pp. 46–58). Toronto, ON: Thompson Educational.

Collins, M. (1998c). Lifelong education as emancipatory pedagogy. In S. M. Scott, B. Spencer, and A. M. Thomas (Eds.), *Learning for life: Canadian readings in adult education* (pp. 107–113). Toronto, ON: Thompson Educational.

Collins, M. (2003). The people's free university: Counteracting the innovation agenda on campus and model for lifelong learning. *Saskatchewan Notes, 2*(9), 1–4.

Conway, A., Keefer, T., and Khan, S. (Eds.). (2005). *Upping the anti: A journal of theory and action, 1*(1). Toronto, ON: Autonomy and Solidarity Network.

Eagleton, T. (2003). *After theory*. London: Allen Lane.

Fanon, F. (1988). *The wretched of the earth*. New York: Grove Press.

Freire, P. (1981). *Pedagogy of the oppressed*. New York: Continuum.

Gramsci, A. (1971). *Selections from the prison notebooks*. New York: International.

Hegel, G. (1967). The preface to the phenomenology of mind. In W. Kaufmann (Ed.), *Hegel: Reinterpretation, texts, and comments* (pp. 363–549). New York: Doubleday. (Original work published 1807)

Heidegger, M. (1968). *What is called thinking?* New York: Harper & Row.

Hurl, C. (2005). Anti-globalization and "diversity of tactics." *Upping the Anti: A Journal of Theory and Action, 1*(1), 26–32.

Klein, N. and Lewis, A. (2004). *The take*. Ottawa, ON: Canadian Broadcasting Corporation.

Marx, K. (1967). Theses on Feuerbach. In L. Easton & K. Guddat (Eds.), *Writings of the young Marx on philosophy and society* (pp. 401–402). New York: Doubleday. (Original work published 1888)

Scott, S. M., Spencer, B., and Thomas, A. M. (Eds.). (1998). *Learning for life: Canadian readings in adult education*. Toronto, ON: Thompson Educational.

Selman, G. (1995). *The foundations of adult education in Canada: Historical essays*. Toronto, ON: Thompson Educational.

Selman, G. (1998). *The foundations of adult education in Canada*. (2nd ed.). Toronto, ON: Thompson Educational.

Welton, M. (Ed.). (1995). *In defense of the lifeworld: Critical perspectives on adult learning*. Albany: State University of New York.

10

Critical Adult Education: Engaging the Social in Theory and Practice

André P. Grace

Theory is "a borderland where conversations begin, differences confront each other, hopes are initiated, and social struggles are waged" (Giroux, 1993a, p. x). When embedded in these critical perspectives, theory and practice are in dynamic equilibrium, mutually informing *praxis* (action that is informed by critical reflection on earlier action). In this chapter I explore these ideas in a discussion of critical theory and its educational complements: critical pedagogy and critical adult education. I begin by discussing the tendency to abort theory in education. I note why this often happens as students engage it and why staying with theory and struggling with it is worthwhile. Next I provide a conspectus of critical theory that outlines its history and parameters for social analysis as I consider its value and some of the challenges to its discourse. I then describe critical pedagogy and critical adult education as complementary studies in education that critique education's role in replicating the status quo by sanctioning and legitimating particular roles and actions. I conclude with a consideration of critical praxis as an engagement in cultural action for social transformation that aims to make knowledge public. I use the Out Is In project that I coordinate as an example. This project, which focuses on the social and cultural learning needs of LGBTQ (lesbian, gay, bisexual, trans-identified, and queer) young adults aged 25 and under, has been developed and implemented using arts-informed educational strategies that foster cultural action for social change.

Staying with Theory Despite the Tendency to Abort It

Some academic educators and students tend to abort theory in education when their struggles with language and meaning become too much. In the name of valuing the intellectual, perhaps they should see their abandonment as a pandering to a sterile practice that usually places doing outside the textures of context (social, cultural, historical, political, and economic), disposition (attitudes, values, and beliefs/ideologies), and relationship (hierarchies and domination arising from differences across class, gender, gender identity, sexual orientation, race, ethnicity, age, and ability). With regard to students, Stephen D. Brookfield (2005) relates in *The Power of Critical Theory* that he has consistently encountered student resistance in his own experience of teaching critically over the years. His list of elements of the critical tradition that tend to provoke this resistance includes the emphasis on Marx, the critique of capitalism the theory entails, the questioning of democracy (particularly the identification of the tyranny of the majority), the difficult language used by critical theorists, and the radical pessimism induced by constantly reading analyses that emphasize the power of dominant ideology and the way it effectively forestalls any real challenge to the system. (pp. 358–359)

Although Brookfield (2005) admits to finding "the texts of critical theory at best complex and challenging, at worst impenetrable" (p. ix), his tendency is to stay with theory and work cautiously with it. I challenge us all to do the same. Brookfield insists that there is intellectual danger in attempting to translate theory into a language that oversimplifies and thus distorts key ideas such as democracy, freedom, social justice, equity, and the ethical use of power, all of which are embodied and embedded in critical theory. He concludes, "One can sometimes be so concerned with making things accessible that the power and complexity [and thus the meaning and value] of the original analysis are lost" (p. xi). Brookfield casts such oversimplification as a neutering of the work and a diminishment of the voices of powerful critical theorists. Thus he holds that engaging primary texts and working to make meaning and sense of them through dialogic discussion is a key pedagogical element in teaching critically. To assist this process of making meaning and sense, learners can draw on comparative readings of secondary texts that involve varying degrees of language complexity, and they can employ auxiliary learning tools such as vocabulary and etymological dictionaries, sociological and philosophical dictionaries, thesauruses, and field encyclopedias (Grace, 2001).

Seeking the mutuality of theory and practice is genetic to critical educational practice (Brookfield, 2005; Freire, 1998; Giroux, 1992). Theory helps us to problematize practice and interrogate the status quo as we make the familiar unfamiliar in a process of seeing the self, culture, society, and others in a new textured light that the lens of theory offers. Brookfield contends that "theory is full of activist intent" (p. 350) and that the critical tradition "should be considered seriously as a perspective that can help . . . [educators and students] make some sense of the dilemmas, contradictions, and frustrations they experience in their work" (p. vii). For him, this requires that we engage in a politics of challenge and change to expose and research the assumptions that impact what we believe and how we behave. In essence, this is interrogating hegemony, "the process by which a grossly iniquitous society uses dominant ideology to convince people this is a normal state of affairs" (p. viii). To employ this political and pedagogical approach is to teach critically, taking method (how we teach) and focus (what we teach) into account (Brookfield, 2005).

Critical Theory: Then and Now

The Purview of Critical Theory

Critical theory emerged in Germany in 1923 with the founding of the Frankfurt School (Institute for Social Research at Frankfurt am Main). During the twentieth century it became known as a discourse that deliberates the nature and meaning of *the social* as a notion shaped amid the intricacies of context, disposition, and relationship. Critical theory has provided a framework in which to critique modernity as a historical condition bounded by systems and structures that affirm science as a powerful agent of order, progress, and predictability. This social theory has critiqued the forces of modernization that are inextricably linked to scientific, technological, and industrial progress and development. It has also critiqued culture and interrogated authority, consumerism, alienation, and their expressions in the modernization process. As critical theory emerged, its expanding discourse has provided understanding and critique of such notions as the State, ideology, civil society, social control, resistance, social movements, and social justice. Critical perspectives on ethics, transformation, praxis, and agency have been advanced; and the political ideals of modernity—democracy, freedom, and social justice—have been presented in critical discourse as ideals to be preserved and fostered rather than displaced in the rush to modernize. As a theory about moving society forward, critical theory has promoted—and indeed has itself been an engagement in—a politics of hope and possibility.

The Assault on Critical Theory and New Moves Beyond It

Theory is affected by historicity and politics, and it is always susceptible to intellectual fashion, commodification, the vagaries of translation, and the limits of language (Peters, Olssen, and Lankshear, 2003). Critical theory has certainly felt the sway of these influences. Indeed in recent decades it has been devalued in some intellectual circles as postfoundational theorists and some feminists became enamored with "post everything" as they worked to expose absences in critical theory (Peters, Lankshear, and Olssen, 2003, p. 1). For example, postmodernism has focused on what it perceives as critical theory's inattention to identity, difference, and relationships of power; poststructuralism has focused on what it perceives as critical theory's misunderstandings of subjectivity, language, and meaning; and postcolonialism had focused on situating critical theory in the realm of privileged discourse.

However, there are new moves to reclaim space and place for critical theory and critique (Peters, Olssen, and Lankshear, 2003). These moves remember the tradition of critical philosophy—a philosophy that reflexively engages a key question: What counts as knowledge? Still these moves are influenced by "post" discourses, re-articulating critical theory within a perspective that engages theory as "a *practice* [their emphasis] which resists all unitary thought to celebrate multiple potentialities" (p. 14). This re-articulation takes critical analysis beyond the exclusive domain of the Frankfurt School, and those historically and conceptually linked to it to include, for example, broadly critical versions of feminism and cultural theory as well as multiperspective discourses such as Peter McLaren's (2003) version of critical pedagogy. Taking critical theory into these dynamic and often tension-filled intersections with other theoretical discourses helps to revitalize its value as a lens for educational and larger social analyses. Utilizing critical perspectives, social analysts can reflexively take up how knowledge that is deemed to have the most worth impacts the teaching–learning interaction as an ecology that encompasses instructors, learners, and the learning environment. This process emphasizes dialogue, deliberation, and reflection on action, all of which drive praxis.

Although critical theory has indeed been a contested discourse, particularly since the 1980s, it has nonetheless made a valuable contribution to a broader social theory of life, learning, and work. For example, critical theory remains important in the current framing and practice of education as an inclusive project designed to transform historical conditions that have shaped education in the service of an exclusionary status quo (Peters, Olssen, and Lankshear, 2003). In elucidating power and interests and critiquing how value is placed on knowledge, critical theory points to the importance of theory itself and to the need for theorizing as a key element of praxis. It provides a lens to help us problematize particular socio-cultural formations, including globalization linked to privatization, which assaults the State and undermines its public responsibility; and neoliberalism, which sidelines the social by melding it with the economic. In contemporary times, critical theory can help us to understand oppression and disenfranchisement in terms of new social relationships of domination, control, and racial and ethnic profiling that are associated with particular socio-cultural formations such as global terrorism and American imperialism. It can guide us as we focus on the kind of resistance needed to counter their debilitating social effects.

The Importance of Jürgen Habermas to Adult Learning

Since the mid-1960s the intellectual work of Jürgen Habermas has been central to the continuing development of critical theory. In his theorizing, Habermas has emphasized critique, agency, and democracy as central categories in modernist discourse (Giroux, 1992). He has acknowledged and elucidated the dark side of the Enlightenment project—a politics built on power places risks on human survival—but he clearly has held on to the hope of freedom, justice, and happiness (Aronowitz, 1992; Lyon, 1994). To move the modern project forward, Habermas has developed his emerging theory of society as a theory of communicative action that uses dialogue aimed at ideal speech as an organizing construct. This theory is grounded "through the embedding of reason in *language* [his emphasis] in general, and in *communication* in particular" (Giddens, 1987, p. 227).

As Habermas (1992) has theorized it, distorted communication hampers human learning, so it is necessary to reveal "the traces of violence that deform repeated attempts at dialogue and recurrently close off the path to unconstrained communication" (p. 264). Habermas's thesis is that "*the unity of knowledge and interest proves itself in a dialectic that takes the historical traces of suppressed dialogue and reconstructs what has been suppressed* [his emphasis]" (p. 264). Although Habermas has not been sufficiently attentive to relationships of power in his theorizing (Giroux, 1992) and although, as Michael R. Welton (1995) has argued, his revision of critical theory as a human-learning theory is not unproblematic, his influence on social theorizing is profoundly significant. For example, Welton has pointed out that Habermasian theory pays crucial attention to both instrumental and moral-practical knowledge. This has created an important point for deliberation for theorists and practitioners concerned with the development of a critical theory of adult learning (Mezirow, 1991).

Situating adult education as a critical project, Jack Mezirow (1995) has viewed the field of study and practice as a site of resistance and a sphere of action against the hegemony of the system. His belief is that adult education can act as a socially integrated action context whose goal is to have all adult learners engage in communicative learning that is not constrained by the system. In agreement, Welton (1995) has argued that Habermas, by locating learning processes at the heart of his critical project, presents a critical social theory that is able to link the crises and potential of late capitalism to a theory of adult learning that releases this potential in particular times and locations. This critical theory of adult learning values communicative rationality as the enabler of free and full participation in the learning process. Habermas's notion of communicative rationality can be explained as follows.

> Barriers to free and open communication must be dismantled, with the goal in mind of an 'ideal speech situation.' In the modern period, the social system—the bureaucracy, capitalism—has increasingly encroached on the 'lifeworld'—that sphere of acting subjects trying to understand each other. Rationalization has occurred in the system at the expense of the lifeworld, so the two require recoupling. The way forward then, is through an expansion of the 'public sphere,' a process already encouraged by the growth of new social movements that resist further lifeworld colonization. (Lyon, 1994, p. 79)

Habermas has given critical educators ways to think about dialogue and communication within the politics and power dynamics of system–lifeworld interactions. His perspective, framed as the theory of communicative action, can contribute to multi-perspective theorizing by providing points for deliberation with postdiscourse understandings of language, communication, and power-knowledge.

Critical Studies in Education: Critical Pedagogy and Critical Adult Education

Collectively, critical studies in education comprise a political and democratic project that keeps social responsibility and responsiveness at the heart of pedagogical matters. These studies raise particular questions: What knowledge is of most worth? How does formal education act in the interests of dominant ideology and practices? How might critical forms of education advance *the social* as an ethical, just, and inclusive political and pedagogical project? As critical studies answer these questions, they expose how the mainstream educational enterprise sanctions and legitimates particular ways of being and acting intended to replicate the status quo. However, they also investigate how education can play a key role in political and cultural action for social transformation when the enterprise takes a critical turn (Allman, 1999). Critical studies in education began with critical pedagogy, which emerged in the 1970s to focus on the interplay of power and interests in schooling. Paulo Freire's (1972) *Pedagogy of the Oppressed* is arguably critical pedagogy's founding text. Other influential texts include Henry A. Giroux's (1983, 1992, respectively) *Theory and Resistance in Education* and *Border Crossings*; Kathleen Weiler's (1988) *Women Teaching for Change: Gender, Class, & Power*; and Peter McLaren's *Life in Schools: An Introduction to Critical Pedagogy in the Foundations of Education,* which had its fourth edition published in 2003.

Critical pedagogy complements and informs critical adult education. The latter gained a certain prominence during the 1980s as it focused on the relationship between power and interests in life, learning, and work in adulthood. Influential texts in critical adult education include Michael Collins's (1991) *Adult Education as Vocation: A Critical Role for the Adult Educator* and Michael R. Welton's (1995) *In Defense of the Lifeworld: Critical Perspectives on Adult Learning.*

Critical Pedagogy

Critical pedagogy is an educational design that gives precedence to "*how* [his emphasis] schooling has come to mean what it has" (McLaren, 2003, p. 190).

> [This design] is founded on the conviction that schooling for self and social empowerment is *ethically prior* [his emphasis] to a mastery of technical skills, which are primarily tied to the logic of the marketplace (although it should be stressed that skill development certainly plays an important role). (p. 188)

Critical pedagogy tries to make sense of the nature of schooling and the contexts, power, and interests that influence it. It positions schooling as a form of cultural politics that "always represents an introduction to, preparation for, and legitimation of particular forms of social life" (pp. 186–187). It critiques these cultural politics designed to protect exclusionary tradition and hierarchical social structures.

Critical pedagogy investigates "the political economy of schooling, the state and education, the representation of texts, and the construction of student subjectivity" (McLaren, 2003, p. 185). It draws on diverse discourses, including critical theory, "post" theories, multiculturalism, and feminist discourses, to examine how educational policy, program design, and the fortunes of education are tied to the logic of corporate capitalism and techno-scientific emphases on efficiency, productivity, and predictability. This multiperspective approach values dialectical theorizing, which is a rational search for contradictions that go against the critical grain. This theorizing is linked to praxis as a reflexive engagement with action aimed at transforming society. It situates praxis within a politics of hope and possibility that society can be more democratic, just, and inclusive.

In addition to dialectical theorizing in his articulation of a design for critical pedagogy, McLaren (2003) has identified other key features that include the central tenet that knowledge is socially constructed and politically contrived so that "its emphases and exclusions partake of a silent logic" (p. 196). This view of knowledge construction sets up one of critical pedagogy's main tasks: to situate the culture-language-knowledge-power nexus that infuses the social in schools and society as a site of struggle over the production, exchange, and distribution of knowledge. This task is inextricably linked to another. Based on the critical notion that knowledge is always linked to ideology and particular interests and relations of power, critical pedagogy is committed to exposing these linkages. This exposition requires an interrogation of how theoretical and practical knowledge constructs different students' worlds in relation to potentially conflicting world views. It demonstrates that power is an omnipresent facet of culture, language, and knowledge that has to be rendered visible in praxis for social transformation.

Critical Adult Education

Critical adult education, as a way to think about collective human interests in relation to the culture-language-knowledge-power nexus, has predominantly concerned itself with advancing social and cultural forms of education focused on life, learning, and work for adults. Since its inception as a counterforce to mainstream modern practice, critical adult education has critiqued instrumentalized forms of adult education as generally demonstrative of the commodification and tendency toward reductionism shaping the field of study and practice (Welton, 1995). This radical form of adult education has offered important analyses of field facets including individualism, scientism, technicism, and professionalism. Unfortunately, in its zeal to offer ongoing critique during the 1980s, critical adult education distanced itself from human-resource development and instrumental sectors in the field. In the process it may have contributed to its marginalization as a component of adult education. This was certainly not productive to the advancement of the field of study and practice that already had to struggle for space and place in culture, society, and the larger disciple of education (Grace, 1999, 2000). Recognizing the problem of divisiveness from within, Sherman Stanage (1994) has stressed the need to move beyond

> a present situation in which the 'fault line' of individualism and social reform is ever-deepening and ever-widening, while both parties to the fault are increasingly inundated by the fragmentizing (and more heavily funded) demands of external sources articulating the reductionistic nuts and bolts programs generated too often by technical rationality. (p. 349)

Stanage's words still ring true as contemporary forces like neoliberalism and global corporatism confront the field of study and practice and keep it largely in reactive mode (Grace, 2004, 2005).

With its focus on praxis and the importance of theorizing to a reflexive engagement with action for social transformation, critical adult education has value in shaping encompassing and discerning field practices. As it deliberates the parameters and possibilities of a more holistic practice, critical adult education is preoccupied with how the field of study and practice might become more ethical, just, and inclusive so that it can respond better to the needs and desires of adults who are mediating the demands of homeplace, learning place, and workplace. To help it reach this goal, critical adult education fosters an interdisciplinary approach to theory building and practice, drawing on perspectives from disciplines including sociology and philosophy and academic areas of study including women's studies and cultural studies.

In exploring life, learning, work, and their possibilities, critical adult education asserts that knowledge is socially and historically constructed. It emphasizes collective action and reflection in learning processes and community building. It frames dialogue, communication, conflict, and change as necessary and contributive to the mediation of life, learning, and work in a change culture of crisis and challenge (Grace, 2004, 2005). In this contemporary change culture, critical adult education needs to review its past and gauge its present and future through a reflexive analysis in which it brings its keenness for theorizing and reflection to bear on itself. It has to address Black insurgent, feminist, queer, postdiscourse, and other critiques of its past inadequate attempts to engage an encompassing social as the culture-language-knowledge-power nexus impacts it (Grace and Hill, 2004; Sheared and Sissel, 2001). In the face of the contemporary melding of the social and the economic, it is important for critical adult education to take up this critique. An expanded critical approach to adult education demands that we interrogate exclusion and how particular relationships of power impact individual dislocation, worker obsolescence, and possibilities for building communities accommodating and respecting difference. A turn to multiperspective theory is useful here, and an eclectic approach to theorizing is required. Dialogue and deliberation in critical studies in education are enhanced by drawing on diverse theoretical scaffoldings that variously take up issues of power while attending to matters of context and disposition. Collins (1991), in upholding adult education as social education, has fostered such eclecticism and raised the value of theory in his call for academic adult educators to move beyond timid armchair intellectualism to develop a theory of action to guide practice. Recognizing that theory and practice are mutually informative, he has concluded, "It is not so much a matter of trying to put theory into practice as of critically engaging with it while we try to put ourselves into practice" (p. 109).

Critical Praxis: Engaging in Cultural Action for Social Transformation to Make Knowledge Public

If adult education is a vocation as Collins (1991) has argued it should be, then one way that educators and students can live out this vocation is by being activists and cultural workers who shape adult education and public life as democratic sites where we interrogate knowledge-power and make knowledge public. This social kind of vocationalism finds expression in what Giroux (1993b) calls a *pedagogy of place* that addresses "the specificities of the experiences, problems, languages, and histories that students and communities rely upon to construct a narrative of collective identity and possible transformation" (p. 121). LGBTQ young adults and the spectral community to which they belong comprise a diverse group engaged in such critical pedagogy. Their collective action has ramifications for adult education. Queer educational ventures, activism, and cultural work help shape an ethical and transformative pedagogy of place that is more accepting and accommodating of those historically marginalized (Grace, 2001). If it committed to this pedagogy, then critical adult education could play a key role in fighting LGBTQ exclusion through strategic political engagement, which Paula Allman (1999) has argued is essential to cultural action for social transformation. However, this largely remains a future field project. Unfortunately, many queer educational ventures for social justice take place in public sites beyond adult education's field of study and practice. When it comes to making space and place for LGBTQ educators and learners, adult education, at least in its North American formation, has been demonstrably resistant to queer (Grace and Hill, 2004).

In this exclusionary scenario, LGBTQ young adults have come to rely on public pedagogy in community venues as a means to create a pedagogy of place where their roles as social change agents and cultural learner-workers can be accommodated. This pedagogy confronts the struggle to be, become, and belong as it seeks "to make clear the power, limits, partiality, and indeterminacy of the sites which inscribe and enable one's sense of place, identity, and possibilities for action" (Giroux, 1993b, p. 78). As a public pedagogy, a pedagogy of place holds that moral knowledge and cultural politics that are truly concerned with all human beings as persons and citizens cannot arbitrarily exclude LGBTQ differences to serve the interests of those subscribing to particular secular or religious ideologies. For example, in Canada *sexual orientation* has been *read into* Section 15 (1) of the *Canadian Charter of Rights and Freedoms* since 1995 when, in *Egan and*

Nesbit v. Canada, the Supreme Court of Canada (2004) unanimously agreed that sexual orientation is a protected category analogous to other personal characteristics listed there (MacDougall, 2000). The Supreme Court also confirmed equality rights for LGBTQ Canadians in the 1998 decision in *Vriend v. Alberta* (MacDougall, 2000). When these minority protections are not endorsed and upheld by any contingent of Canadians, the right of all Canadians to full citizenship is devalued as a constitutional given. In dialectical terms, when conservative factions such as the Canadian Council of Catholic Bishops or the Conservative Party of Canada historicize democracy within an exclusionary tradition that leaves LGBTQ citizens out, there is a contradiction in their purported democratic stance because they apparently do not hold that every Canadian citizen is entitled to the rights and privileges of full citizenship. If all citizens are not included and valued, then we create a hierarchy of domination that flies in the face of the *Canadian Charter of Rights and Freedoms* and its core principle that there cannot be a hierarchy of rights in Canada (Supreme Court of Canada, 2004).

These days LGBTQ young adults want to free themselves from the silence, exclusion, and symbolic and physical violence that heterosexism and homophobia provoke in education, culture, and society. They seek a transformation of historically disenfranchising cultural practices and social relations that subjugate them in life, learning, and work. Given that heterosexism and homophobia are so culturally engrained that they are residual even when some struggles for LGBTQ inclusion are won, this political and pedagogical work focused on greater accommodation and respect is taxing. It involves educational activism and cultural work to problematize LGBTQ-exclusive educational policies and practices, enhance communication in the intersection of the moral and the political, and monitor the state of the struggle, the extent of transformation, and the need for further social and cultural action (Allman, 1999; Grace, Hill, Johnson, and Lewis, 2004). This work is an engagement in critical praxis.

When LGBTQ young adults engage in praxis that is critically queer, its dynamic orientation is political, pedagogical, transgressive, and transformative. The Out Is In project that I facilitate exemplifies this praxis. The key purpose of this public pedagogical project, which is partially funded by Public Safety and Emergency Preparedness Canada's Community Mobilization Program, has been to develop and implement an arts-informed educational program that fosters recuperation, social learning, open dialogue, critical questioning, resiliency, and cultural action for social change. Because queer young adults constitute an invisible minority often underserved in many traditional adult educational services and programs, Out Is In fills a void in their learning in early adulthood. The disaffected and marginalized queer young adults who participate in this program often see limited possibilities in life, learning, and employment. Many of these individuals feel stigmatized and ashamed because of the broad and pervasive cultural negativity toward their sex, sexual, and gender differences. As a result, some act out of a sense of frustration, often exhibiting a range of socially negative behaviours that can include social withdrawal, drug and alcohol abuse, suicide ideation or attempts, and physical and/or verbal aggression. Out Is In works to counter this social exclusion and fallout. The project employs an educational model with informal and nonformal arts-informed pedagogical elements. This model engages queer and allied young adults in self- and social learning through active engagements in drama (such as Boal's Forum Theatre of the Oppressed workshops), music (song writing as exploration of the queer self and community), photography (the creation of digital photo collages in the Freirean context of exploring the word and the world), and art installations (using art to engage citizen-learners in expressive learning for social justice). Participants have been using these arts-informed initiatives to raise community consciousness about what they see as impediments to their social learning, development, and inclusion. Whatever medium they use, they make it clear that heterosexism and homophobia are pervasive in the socially conservative province of Alberta, and younger LGBTQ persons need organized educational and community supports to help them in their struggle against it.

Cultural workers in the Out Is In project have built a network of community supports to create safe spaces for queer and allied young adults to participate in socially inclusive and responsive learning activities. Helping LGBTQ young adults feel and become connected to their communities is vital in building their collective capacity and resiliency to address issues related to safety, health, and discrimination in their communities (Grace and Wells, 2004). In utilizing this model, the project participants have opportunities to counter their traditional status as fugitive learners as they explore personal and social issues that impact their everyday lives. Collectively, these opportunities provide critical learning moments and constitute cultural action for social transformation.

References

Allman, P. (1999). *Revolutionary social transformation: Democratic hopes, political possibilities, and critical education.* Westport, CT: Bergin & Garvey.

Aronowitz, S. (1992). *The politics of identity.* New York: Routledge.

Brookfield, S. D. (2005). *The power of critical theory: Liberating adult learning and teaching.* San Francisco: Jossey-Bass.

Collins, M. (1991). *Adult education as vocation: A critical role for the adult educator.* New York: Routledge.

Freire, P. (1972). *Pedagogy of the oppressed.* New York: Herder & Herder.

Freire, P. (1998). *Teachers as cultural workers: Letters to those who dare teach.* (D. Macedo, D. Koike, and A. Oliveira, Trans.). Boulder, CO: Westview Press.

Giddens, A. (1987). *Social theory and modern sociology.* Stanford, CA: Stanford University Press.

Giroux, H. A. (1983). *Theory and resistance in education.* South Hadley, MA: Bergin & Garvey.

Giroux, H. A. (1992). *Border crossings.* New York: Routledge.

Giroux, H. A. (1993a). Foreword. In W. G. Tierney (Ed.), *Building communities of difference: Higher education in the twenty-first century* (pp. ix–xii). Toronto, ON: OISE Press.

Giroux, H. A. (1993b). *Living dangerously: Multiculturalism and the politics of difference.* New York: Peter Lang.

Grace, A. P. (1999). Building a knowledge base in US academic adult education (1945-1970). *Studies in the education of adults, 31*(2), 220–236.

Grace, A. P. (2000). Canadian and US adult learning (1945-1970) and the cultural politics and place of lifelong learning. *International journal of lifelong education, 19*(2), 141–158.

Grace, A. P. (2001). Using queer cultural studies to transgress adult educational space. In V. Sheared & P. A. Sissel (Eds.), *Making space: Merging theory and practice in adult education* (pp. 257–270). Westport, CT: Bergin & Garvey.

Grace, A. P. (2004). Lifelong learning as a chameleonic concept and versatile practice: Y2K perspectives and trends. *International Journal of Lifelong Education, 23*(4), 385–405.

Grace, A. P. (2005). Lifelong learning chic in the modern practice of adult education: Historical and contemporary perspectives. *Journal of Adult and Continuing Education, 11*(1), 62–79.

Grace, A. P. and Hill, R. J. (2004). Positioning Queer in adult education: Intervening in politics and praxis in North America. *Studies in the Education of Adults, 36*(2), 167–189.

Grace, A. P., Hill, R. J., Johnson, C. W., Lewis, J. B. (2004). In other words: Queer voices/dissident subjectivities impelling social change. *International Journal of Qualitative Studies in Education, 17*(3), 301–323.

Grace, A. P. and Wells, K. (2004). Engaging sex-and-gender differences: Educational and cultural change initiatives in Alberta. In J. McNinch and M. Cronin (Eds.), *I could not speak my heart: Education and social justice for gay and lesbian youth* (pp. 289–307). Regina, SK: University of Regina, Canadian Plains Research Centre.

Habermas, J. (1992). Knowledge and human interests: A general perspective. In D. Ingram and J. Simon-Ingram (Eds.), *Critical theory: The essential readings* (pp. 255–267). New York: Paragon House.

Lyon, D. (1994). *Postmodernity*. Minneapolis, MN: University of Minnesota Press.

MacDougall, B. (2000). *Queer judgments: Homosexuality, expression, and the courts in Canada*. Toronto, ON: University of Toronto Press.

McLaren, P. (2003). *Life in schools: An introduction to critical pedagogy in the foundations of education* (4th ed.). Boston: Allyn and Bacon.

Mezirow, J. (1991). *Transformative dimensions of adult learning*. San Francisco: Jossey-Bass.

Mezirow, J. (1995). Transformation theory of adult learning. In M. R. Welton (Ed.), *In defense of the lifeworld: Critical perspectives on adult learning* (pp. 39–70). New York: State University of New York Press.

Peters, M., Lankshear, C. and Olssen, M. (Eds.). (2003). *Critical theory and the human condition: Founders and praxis*. New York: Peter Lang.

Peters, M., Olssen, M. and Lankshear, C. (Eds.). (2003). *Futures of critical theory: Dreams of difference*. Lanham, MD: Rowman & Littlefield.

Sheared, V. and Sissel, P. A. (Eds.). (2001). *Making space: Merging theory and practice in adult education*. Westport, CT: Bergin & Garvey.

Stanage, S. (1994). Adult education as ethical and moral meaning through action. *Proceedings of the 35th Annual Adult Education Research Conference* (pp. 348–353). Knoxville, TN: University of Tennessee, College of Education.

Supreme Court of Canada. (2004). *Reference re same-sex marriage (2004 SCC 79; file no.: 29866)*. Retrieved December 9, 2004, from http://www.lexum.umontreal.ca/csc-scc/en/rec/html/2004scc079.wpd.html

Weiler, K. (1988). *Women teaching for change: Gender, class, & power*. New York: Bergin & Garvey.

Welton, M. R. (1995). The critical turn in adult education theory. In M. R. Welton (Ed.), *In defense of the lifeworld: Critical perspectives on adult learning* (pp. 11–38). New York: State University of New York Press.

11

Frameworks for Synthesis of the Field of Adult Learning Theory

Peter Sawchuk

Unless the lines to the present, in the actual process of the selective tradition, are clearly and actively traced, . . . any recovery can be simply residual or marginal. It is at the vital points of connection, where a version of the past is used to ratify the present and to indicate directions for the future, that a selective tradition is at once powerful and vulnerable. Powerful because it is so skilled in making active selective connections, dismissing those it does not want as 'out of date' or 'nostalgic,' attacking those it cannot incorporate as 'unprecedented' or 'alien.' Vulnerable because the real record is effectively recoverable, and many of the alternative or opposing practical continuities are still available. Vulnerable also because the selective version of 'a living tradition' is always tied, though often in complex and hidden ways, to explicit contemporary pressures and limits. (Williams, 1977, p. 116)

In North America, general reviews of adult learning theory, some book length, have been available for a quarter of a century. In them we can find detailed examination of individual theories and theorists. Valuable as they are, however, they tend to be nominal; that is, they provide a laundry list, often categorized, but they still provide little substantive sense of the interrelations amongst traditions or their origins/inspirations in the human sciences more broadly.

In this chapter I aim to review theories of adult learning against a relatively deep historical backdrop of social science. I try to provide a means of synthesizing a diverse, multidisciplinary field of adult learning theory that has grown immensely over the past three decades. But this "field"—to the degree that we can call it this—has remarkably mobile boundaries; framing it is daunting, not simply because of this mobility, but for the more basic challenges of tracing intellectual origins that are so often left implicit. But by tracing these origins, we open up important new ground for imagining how different ideas in fact relate to one another. The opening quotation from Raymond Williams (1977) is meant to point us in this direction, but also to jar us into the political reality of our efforts. Synthesis or mapping efforts are always politically as well as intellectually challenging. All such efforts are "powerful and vulnerable." We must reconstruct and explore what Williams referred to as "the real record" and ultimately develop awareness of the complex and often hidden ways that contemporary "pressures and limits" have nudged our willingness to entertain or exclude alternatives.

To begin, I will take a moment to explore the possibility of a "Canadian accent" to research on adult education and, through it, adult learning theory. I offer a working hypothesis about what might be distinctive about our thinking and how it relates to openness and hybridity. I then review a model that helps us both to go back to first principles and to trace their contemporary expression. Later, I provide constructive criticism and put forth a key integrating concept in order to extend the model. The overall goal is to propose the possibility of enhancing dialogue amongst established scholars and novices alike. By the end, I hope, we will be in a better position to understand the breadth of adult learning theory, to better grasp the interrelations across theories, and to better imagine other models, perhaps radically different from but equally powerful to the one that I discuss below.

Hypothesizing a "Canadian Accent" in Adult Learning Theory

The focus of the *Learning for Life* (Scott, Spencer, and Thomas, 1998) collection is Canadian adult education. So, then, what can be said about a distinctive Canadian character in this area? Is there a detectable "Canadian accent" to our theoretical work? To be sure, Canada has offered more than its share of giants to the world of adult education. Among them, the field has traditionally (though not exclusively) been cast as either a social movement in its own right or, to borrow Mitchell's (as cited in Hardy, 1967) phrasing, the "force that makes a social movement move" (p. xii), a view that Cooley Verner and Ralph Spence (1953; as cited in Hardy, 1967), for example, forefronted with their emphasis on the knowledge essential for an intelligent approach to social action (p. 42). Indeed, leading Canadian adult educators have taken this "social movement" dimension seriously, as in the case of Moses Coady, Ned Corbett, and Roby Kidd; or, in terms of more contemporary scholarship, in terms of Patti Gouthro, Angela Miles, and Shauna Butterwick's work with the women's movement; Shahrzad Mojab's feminist and international solidarity work; Darlene Clover and Bud Hall's work with the environmental movement; André Grace's work with lesbian, gay, bisexual and transgendered communities; Bruce Spencer's, Nancy Jackson's, D'Arcy Martin's, and Tom Nesbit's ongoing partnerships with organized labour; and so on.

Readers should be encouraged to explore each of these authors directly. My point is, however, that although *theorizing* is embedded in all these works, it remains unevenly articulated. Thus the distinction between the writings of *adult education* and the sustained development of *adult learning theory*, which Selman and Dampier (1991) addressed with the statement, "A diligent search through the Canadian literature of the field . . . will reveal that a great deal has been said about the functions, goals and philosophy of the work, almost always as part of telling another story" (p. 294). Selman and Dampier's assessment provides a portrait of adult learning theory as identifiable along a mix of sociological and philosophical lines—function-alism, conflict theory, hermeneutics, and ethics—which largely rejects the suggestion of a distinctive Canadian character. And now, more than a decade and a half later, at least understood in these terms, one is tempted to affirm this view.

Breaking out of this classification scheme, however, I think that we may yet identify something unique to Canadian theoretical contributions past and present. If so, to my mind, it would revolve around three intertwined themes, themes that also give shape to this chapter: internationalism and limited insularity, the democratic impulse, and conditioning these first two themes, a type of view that could be described as a *middle-power* orienta-tion. These three themes play out across the field of adult learning theory in both English Canada and Quebec (though differently), for example, in the sense that the core theoretical building blocks that inspire us tend to come from elsewhere, other centres of social science and conceptual innovation, minimally Europe (e.g., cultural studies, poststructuralism, critical theory), North Europe (e.g., folk education, activity theory), the United States (e.g., pragmatism, cultural studies, critical pedagogy), and Latin America (e.g., popular education, action research). In other words, our intellectual borders are, when compared to these and most other countries, porous. This results in sometimes striking conceptual combinations, fuelled by less restrictive programmatic allegiances. Around the world a strong democratic impulse lies at the centre of much adult education work, but it may be particularly pronounced in countries such as Canada. This may be rooted in what I've called a middle-power perspective. It is dangerously easy to overgeneral-ize on this point, but simply put, a middle-power perspective refers to the overall institutional framework of society in relation to other nations, in which collective solutions, accommodation, and negotiation are seen as both necessary and legitimate. Welton's (1997) historical work gives some flesh to this assertion in his discussion of the roots of adult education in the farm, women's, workers', and cooperative movements:

> They understood adult education as part of the resistance movement to capital's maniacal drive to break into bits and create possessive individualists out of us all. They knew, to use the language of adult education in the Canadian farm movement, that "combined intelligence" enabled us to command our life-situations. Left to our individual resources, we would not be strong enough to counter those forces fracturing us. (p. 31)

If these forces were strong in the past, we might expect them to be doubly so now in the era of even larger, more powerful transnational corpora-tions and international "free-trade" zones. It is these types of impulses that encourage nuance, openness, multiple and hybrid perspectives, and thus complexity—all factors that encourage the creative development and application of new forms of adult learning theory.

In fact, the diverse origins of theory that make up the dialogues on adult learning in Canada are enormous and seldom clear-cut. Many of our leading thinkers have developed, and continue to develop, their conceptual outlooks rather than merely defending past positions to build unity approaches. Therefore, if there is a "Canadian accent" to the field, it is like the country itself: the perpetually shifting result of a contested mosaic. Whatever the status of these claims of distinction, however, what is clear is that understanding this or any other hypothesis requires a framework for synthesis that brings such mosaics of ideas clearly into view.

Adult Learning Theory as a "Tension Field"

The most compelling synthesizing frameworks go back to first principles. Echoing Raymond Williams (1977), to understand "a living tradition" (p. 116) we must actively trace "the lines to the present" (p. 116). To do this, we need to develop a means of backtracking to the basic building blocks of adult learning in terms of human development and social action.

In perhaps the most comprehensive framework for adult learning theory currently available, Illeris (2002) traced the key foundational components of human development: "All learning comprises three different dimensions—i.e., that all learning is, so to speak, stretched out between three poles and accordingly may be looked at and analyzed from three different approaches" (p. 18). Irreducibly, human learning always involves all three dimensions at the same time. These dimensions are the cognitive, the emotional, and the social, and they are mapped onto what Illeris called a *tension field*. Within this field he located theories of adult learning according to their central preoccupations and conceptual strengths (see Figure 1). Through this, the work of different authors can then be placed spatially, which allows us to imagine relations between theories that all too frequently neither refer to nor even acknowledge one another.

In going back to first principles, Illeris (2002) began his discussion with a focus on cognition rooted in the foundational works of Piaget (cf. Gruber and Vonèche, 1977). As with his discussion of each dimension, Illeris began with a foundational scholar and then moved forward to more contemporary research that, either implicitly or explicitly, expressed, pushed forward, and developed upon their views. In beginning with cognition, however, it is perhaps important first to note that as the starting point for the discussion it is positioned as the keystone of adult learning. Indeed, individual cognition is one of the most persistent, orienting principles of mainstream theory. Like all theoretical positions, this is political; it privileges a certain perspective on the individual and society, a position that is ratified in very deep ways by many of our social institutions (schooling, labour markets, the workplace, etc.). Thus, before discussing Piaget, we can note both that it may be deeply problematic were we to allow cognition to "stand in" for learning as a whole and that, nevertheless, individual cognition *does* matter. Therefore the work of Piaget and those who have very much stood on his shoulders (with or without knowing it) require attention. Thus, in turning to the cognitivists, we might say that, in theorizing adult learning, cognition has a place *and* it must be kept in its place.

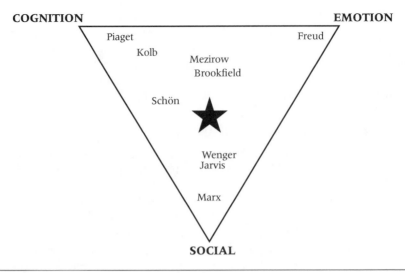

Figure 1. Illeris's (2002) tension field of learning theory.

There is little reason to believe that Piaget's core theoretical contributions are not as valid today as they were when they shook the world of psychology in the early twentieth century. His model of cognitive schemes and the patterns through which they undergo change are both instructive and, among adult learning theorists, underappreciated, possibly because of their genetic/biological emphasis and narrow association with child development. The portrait of change established by Piagetian thought can be characterized as largely conservative. Consider, for example, the key Piagetian principles of *equilibration, adaptation,* and *assimilation* through which an individual strives to maintain a steady state in his or her interactions with the surrounding world. Here we see a description of *individual change* but *social stasis* that tells us little about how society changes because of a person's (let alone persons') learning and action. Moreover, although there can be no doubt that, as a developmental approach, Piagetian learning theory treats individual psychological phenomena historically (e.g., a cognitive scheme is established and undergoes change, the primary determinant of learning outcome is prior learning, and so on), this is a narrow model of history indeed. The Piagetian concept of "transcendent learning," or rather the adaptation of the environment to meet an individual's emergent cognitive schemes, was less clearly addressed by Piaget or those rooted in this tradition, despite the fact that Piaget partially anticipated related issues in his later years (cf. Piaget and Garcia, 1989).

The degree to which core Piagetian principles of human learning are expressed in adult learning theory today, however, is striking. In tracing the lines of development from these foundational building blocks, we can see that Piaget's theory of stages is an implicit element of andragogy (Knowles, 1970), and it directly informs Kolb's (1984) experiential learning concept. Piaget's model is also inherent in Schön's (1983) "reflective practitioner" concept, and it goes a long way in informing a good deal of the various variations of the self-directed learning theory lineage as well. Illeris (2002) added that theories as diverse as Gregory Bateson's (1972) and Jack Mezirow's (1991) also fit well within the Piagetian/Kolbian tradition. But it is the movement beyond Piaget's preoccupation with formal logic, accomplished by these later researchers, that is amongst the necessary changes for developing a critical conception of cognitive development (cf. Kincheloe and Steinberg, 1993).

Illeris (2002) also believed that learning is *libidinal*, that it moves from cognitive psychology (i.e., dealing with learning content such as skill and knowledge) on the one hand, to the psychology of personality (i.e., dealing with motivations, affect, attitudes, and desires) on the other; just as cognition matters, so too does emotional development shape adult learning. As he did in his discussion of cognition, Illeris returned to first principles with the work of Freud. For Freud and Freudians in the field of psychology, development is related to the theoretical discovery of the unconscious and the fundamental and innate expression of the pleasure and reality principles, which results in a gradual expansion of the powerful, symbolic framework that eventually stabilizes as internal images, fantasies, desires, fears, and the orienting motivations that establish personality. As Illeris noted, "Cognitive learning is always affectively 'obsessed': there are always emotional tones or imprints attached to the knowledge being developed. . . . *These provide the psychological energy for learning*" (pp. 73–74; emphasis added). Undoubtedly, the framework serves as a foundation for filling important gaps for a comprehensive understanding of the learning theory. However, to date, the tendencies in adult learning theory around the emotional dimension appear to have been all or nothing: Either the dimension is central to analysis and virtually occludes all other dimensions of human development, or it is entirely ignored. It is important to note that the psychodynamic dimension inherently includes social-historical contexts of development vis-à-vis the many unconscious, culturally specific forms of substitution, sublimation, repression, and so on. And just as important, these features of human learning can be characterized as deeply *conflictual*, quite distinct from the "conservatism" of the Piagetian lineage. There is conflict within individuals (those inherent in id/ego relations, for example), conflict between individuals whose drives lead to a brutal clashing of opposing interests, and the fact that, when left unresolved, such conflicts funnel psychic energies central to the learning enterprise into an array of both positive *and* negative forms of learning practice.

In the realm of adult learning theory specifically, there has been a range of Canadian and international writings that have noted what we might call a "desire gap": the absence of engagement with the emotional/affective dimension of adult learning. Fenwick (2000) summarized the possibilities inherent in critical recognition of this dimension nicely:

> [It] views learning as interference of conscious thought by the unconscious and the uncanny psychic conflicts that result. Our desires and resistances for different objects, which we experience as matters of love and hate, attach our internal world to the external social world. Our daily, disturbing inside-outside encounters are carried on at subtle levels, and we draw on many strategies to ignore them. But when we truly attend these encounters, we enter the profound conflicts, which are learning. The general learning process is crafting the self through everyday strategies of coping with and coming to understand what is suggested in these conflicts. (p. 251)

Extending the thinking here, if analysts of adult learning hope to deeply engage with instances of what have been called "non-learning," "mis-learning," and any other otherwise unintentional outcomes of educational programs (see Illeris, 2002, for a summary), self-directed project or informal learning experience here would be an important element to consider. As Foley (2001, pp. 98–117) explained (see also Foley and Sawchuk, 2005), we see that one of the key psychodynamic processes that shape learning is what is known as defence mechanisms. Freud's daughter Anna (A. Freud, 1942) is credited with one of the original explanations of the phenom-enon: repression, regression, projection, isolation, blocking, phobia, distor-tion, and so on. And Foley, in his analysis of adult learning in organiza-tions, focused on the distortion mechanisms specifically that operate, on the one hand, to relieve anxieties associated with unresolved conflict; but in so doing, on the other hand, necessarily distort reality—that is, fantasize individuals (or groups), and then behave as if this fantasy is real. The explanation of the many possibilities of analyzing how the cognitive and psychodynamic dimensions of learning mutually inform and interact is a key accomplishment of Fenwick (2000) and others. What remains to be considered, according to Illeris's (2002) tension field model, however, is the question of the analytic treatment of context, its character, and its role in the adult learning enterprise. Can even the most developed theory of learning as cognitive/psychodynamic processes provide an account of indi-vidual and collective action *in situ*?

According to Illeris (2002), the lead-off man for discussions of the social dimension is Karl Marx, whose theory of societal change is said to be foundational. There was no discussion of Marx per se, however. Instead, Illeris turned to German social theorist Oskar Negt (associated with the Frankfurt School) and focused on experience and communication. Here social interaction is analyzed with reference to public spheres, which refer to the many overlapping systems of communication through which adults become informed and develop according to distinctive social standpoints. It is thus comprised of a system of domination and power that produces distortions of experience and communication.

Given my initial discussion of the value of social action, and the social movement perspective that has infused adult education in Canada, Illeris's

(2002) analysis might have comfortably included theoretical contributions by the many Canadian researchers mentioned earlier. In this regard, perhaps the most significant contemporary debate in adult education in terms of the social dimension has emerged as a response to Mezirow's (1991) "perspective transformation" theory. As Mezirow's work rose to prominence in the early 1990s, authors concerned about sustaining the social models of adult learning and adult education seemed to rise in number to re-emphasize this dimension: In these can be found some of the most coherent reassertions of the importance of the social dimensions currently available. In this regard, some refer to Mezirow directly and others not, but in seeking to respond to the individualizing biases of adult learning theory, Canadian researchers have in various ways emphasized the social dimension: Spencer (1998), who framed learning in relation to various social purposes (economic justice, diversity, social change); Collins (1998) who has sought to "counter the homogenizing effects of the andragogical model" (p. 47); Miles (1996), who researched adult education and the feminist movement; Alan Thomas (1991), who analyzed the role of adult learning in democratic institution building; and others.

Mediation as a Missing Link in the Tension Field of Adult Learning Theory

As I noted at the start, my aim in this chapter is not to provide a detailed account of specific adult learning theories, but rather to provide a framework for synthesis; in fact, a synthesis that might work in conjunction with other reviews. Illeris's (2002) work is important but still leaves something to be desired from the perspective of a "Canadian accent." The tension field model provides a substantive rather than nominal structure in that it is rooted in a real mix of living human capacities, yet there remains the issue of articulation. Is there a conceptual element missing from Illeris's work that would help us to further understand how the cognitive, emotional, and social poles relate to each other? In this section I propose an answer to this question, with an emphasis on addressing both the symbolic *and* the material conditions that ultimately lie beneath each of the three dimensions. For this we turn to what is known as socio-cultural analysis, a key sub-school of which is cultural historical activity theory (CHAT). Its most important contribution for our purposes here is the concept of *mediation*.

To best understand the concept of mediation, it is worthwhile briefly to retrace the steps of one of the leading, contemporary voices in the tradition, Yrjö Engeström (1987), and to draw on his seminal work *Learning by Expanding*. One of his goals here was to understand the symbolic and material mediation of individual and collective human practices that define the learning process. Mediation refers to an important and often grossly ignored process through which a person(s) or subject(s) interact with the world. This principle says that a subject always, without exception, interacts with the world through symbolic and/or material tools or artefacts. These artefacts can run the gamut of possibilities. An artefact could refer to the types of cognitive schema described in the cognitive traditions, it could refer to the type of libidinal structures outlined in the psychodynamic tradition, or it could refer to the types of material or institutional structures understood in the sociological tradition. What is more, all of these artefacts have a history; that is, they are the product of past experiences, past efforts, or, rather, past labours.

To fully understand the process of mediation, Engeström (1987) interrogated the most developed social scientific attempts. First, he examined the work of Charles S. Peirce, a man credited, along with Ferdinand de Saussure, as the founder of modern semiotics—the study of signs, signification, and interpretation—the forerunner to much of the literary studies research and a good deal of postmodern social theory to boot. For Engeström, although Peirce produced a detailed treatment of mediation between subject and object vis-à-vis the sign and interpretation, the process that he described was too restrictive. It dealt primarily with intentional, logical, and purely linguistic dimensions of human action. In the end, Peirce's framework was found to be limited in terms of a full account of human interaction, learning, and development.

Engeström (1987) then turned his attention to the social psychology of George Herbert Mead. Mead, along with the likes of John Dewey, established what is known today as the field of pragmatics, an increasingly influential tradition within both philosophy and social analysis that has dealt with issues of learning and education in a sustained way. Mead's approach to mediation was built on the process of meaning production, though meaning understood in a broader sense than Peirce's approach allowed. He understood the generation of meaning in terms of the formula [gesture] –> [adjustive response] –> [result], a form of mediated social action. However, similar to Peirce, Engeström found that Mead's formula provided only a limited account of the sensuous, material aspects of action.

Finally, Engeström (1987) turned to the work of Lev Vygotsky (1987) and the cultural historical or CHAT school. Vygotsky's goal was nothing less than a complete reorganization of the psychology of learning and development, with an emphasis on a dynamic (i.e., dialectical) theory of culture, materialism, and social history. In contrast to the biological-genetic roots of Piagetian and Freudian traditions (both were originally trained in the physical sciences as a biologist and a physiologist, respectively), Vygotsky's concept of mediation placed social participation as primary to the development of higher order mental functions of cognition, emotion, motivation, and self-directed behaviour. For Vygotsky, the concepts of "turning" or "interiorization" defined the process through which external social relations—in fact, whole socio-historical systems in a constant process of change—are translated into the internal mental functions, outcomes and embodied states that we associate with notions of knowledge and skill, all governed by the principles of symbolic and material mediation.

The libidinal dimensions of learning were, admittedly, underdeveloped by early researchers in this school of thought. Nevertheless, there remains open space for their inclusion along with the cognitive and social dimensions within a comprehensive framework of adult learning where the concept of mediation can serve an important integrating function. That is, individuals and collectivities constitute social and material relations vis-à-vis mediation, and these relations, in turn, mediate the development of individuals and collectivities; and human freedom and individuality are mediated through myriad symbolic as well as material artefacts, which makes it implicitly an historical process.

Filling the Gaps in the Tension Field

I argue that the concept of mediation may be the conceptual "glue" that helps to link together more coherently the three dimensions that Illeris (2002) otherwise persuasively contended define the learning process. I also argue, however, that adult education and adult learning theory in Canada have important, inherent affinities with the social dimension vis-à-vis its concern for social movements and the social dimension more broadly. Modifying Illeris's model to reflect some of these concerns, we might insert a new zone (the dashed-line box in Figure 2) that might help to represent the location within the tension field of a space that reflects the "centre of gravity" for the preoccupations of contemporary adult education and learning theory in Canada specifically. This zone, in my view, would include the CHAT tradition and the work of Vygotsky as, to date, the most developed mix of cognitive and social concerns in adult learning theory. One would also have to recognize, however, the need to address the work of Foucauldian researchers (a key gap in Illeris's work) with their model of desire, discourse, subjectivity, and disciplinary regimes as the most potent mix of emotional/social structural concerns. And finally, the zone that I have proposed would have to further develop the social dimension generally to reflect approaches to adult learning that represent a broader range of social theory (e.g., functionalist, social constructivist, feminist, antiracist, postcolonial, and strictly Marxist concerns; see Figure 2).

Within this space, classifying and positioning the work of others is a dicey business, not in the least because the work of many of our most important thinkers shifts over time with new influences—again, an expression of hybrid thinking. However, I think in the spirit of new learning and dialogue it is worth going out on a limb. In examining Figure 2, we could ask ourselves important questions that Illeris (2002) never did to reveal both the gaps that may exist within adult learning theory in Canada and the interesting interrelations between approaches. Where, for example, might the influential work of Allen Tough, the father of self-directed learning research, fit? Its individual/humanist orientation places its contributions very close to the upper-left-hand edge of our "adult education zone." Likewise, the work of Alan Thomas might be similarly

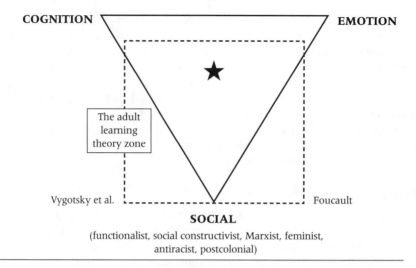

Figure 2. Adult education approach within Illeris's (2002) tension field of learning theory.

positioned. Compare this, on the other hand, with the concerns of Michael Welton, whose analyses, to my mind, place him much closer to the social pole (lower edges of our zone), though with his focus on Habermas and rational discourse also suggest a placement slightly to the left (toward the cognitive dimension) rather than the right side (emotional dimension). Tara Fenwick's work, in contrast to both of these, might be located closer to the right side of our zone because she has dealt to a significant degree with issues of desire and development. Her work might, however, be positioned slightly more to the centre of the zone in comparison to the works of Derek Briton, André Grace, and Donovan Plumb, whose conceptual orientations are perhaps closer to those of Foucault in many ways. My own work might be located to the lower-left-hand portion of the zone; the work of Shahrzad Mojab lower, but more to the centre of our zone; and so on.

Of course, this list of examples is far from exhaustive and should properly be the subject of a carefully articulated assessment (for which there is no space here). Nevertheless, I hope that it has become clear that a framework for synthesis such as Figure 2 offers a medium for dialogue and debate, a means for all of us to communicate better with one another about different theories of adult learning, by carefully laying out the rationale for differing assessments and placements.

Conclusions

In this chapter I aimed to introduce a framework for synthesis and dialogue across the diversity of contributions to adult learning theory. I attempted to get beyond nominal systems of classification that characterize many of the other reviews of adult learning theory available and to develop a framework with substantive comparative structure. Thus, I turned to the work of Illeris (2002), who began from some of the most basic building blocks of human development. In this context we covered the foundational conceptualizations in the areas of cognition, emotion, and social interaction—conceptualizations that, it is argued, live on in various forms in contemporary adult learning theory. Illeris's model, I noted, is not perfect. Several substantive gaps were added in a second modified model that includes a specific zone of adult learning theory that helps to more accurately capture a sense of the "centre of gravity" of adult education research in Canada. Crucially, I supplemented the original model with a discussion of what I feel to be a central concept for understanding across many different theories; that is, symbolic and material mediation.

Going back to first principles, interrogating the implicit assumptions and theoretical lineages of available theory is never time wasted, but rather a recipe for creative, hybrid thinking that, as I have suggested, tend to mark the "middle-power" perspectives of countries such as Canada and Northern Europe. This type of resistance to insularity, comfort with hybridity, and the embracing of internationalism is something that goes with it hand in glove. And the democratic impulse compels the Canadian researchers referenced above in their consistent articulation of social movements and themes of democratic transformation.

A general model or framework for synthesis will not be useful to those who prefer to remain bunkered in theoretical silos. But for those of us who are *still learning*, who recognize the value of new influences, and who seek to build more expansive theories of adult learning, *active dialogue*—and models that stimulate it—should always be a welcome sight.

References

Bateson, G. (1972). *Steps to an ecology of mind*. San Francisco: Chandler.

Collins, M. (1998). Critical returns: From andragogy to lifelong education. In S. Scott, B. Spencer, and A. Thomas (Eds.), *Learning for life: Canadian readings in adult education* (pp. 46–58). Toronto, ON: Thompson Educational.

Engeström, Y. (1987). *Learning by expanding: An activity-theoretical approach to developmental research*. Helsinki: Orienta-Konsultit.

Fenwick, T. (2000). Expanding conceptions of experiential learning: A review of five contemporary perspectives on cognition. *Adult Education Quarterly, 50*(4), 243–272.

Foley, G. (2001). *Strategic learning: Understanding and facilitating organizational change*. Sydney, Australia: University of Technology, Centre for Popular Education.

Foley, G. and Sawchuk, P. (2005). Social, psychodynamic, and technological dimensions of informal learning in organizations. In K. Künzel (Ed.), *International yearbook of adult education* (pp. 127–142). Cologne: Böhlau-Verlag.

Freud, A. (1942). *The ego and the mechanisms of defense*. London: Hogarth Press.

Gruber, H. E. and Vonèche, J. (Eds.). (1977). *The essential Piaget*. New York: Basic Books.

Hardy, N. (1967). *Farm, mill, and classroom: A history of tax supported adult education in South Carolina to 1960*. Columbia, SC: University of South Carolina.

Illeris, K. (2002). *The three dimensions of learning: Contemporary learning theory in the tension field between the cognitive, the emotional, and the social.* Frederiksberg, Denmark: Roskilde University Press.

Kincheloe, J. and Steinberg, S. (1993). A tentative description of post-formal thinking: The critical confrontation with cognition theory. *Harvard Educational Review, 63*(3), 296–320.

Knowles, M. (1970). *The modern practice of adult education: Andragogy versus pedagogy.* Chicago: Follett.

Kolb, D. (1984). *Experiential learning.* Englewood Cliffs, NJ: Prentice-Hall.

Mezirow, J. (1991). *Transformative dimensions of adult learning.* San Francisco: Jossey-Bass.

Miles, A. (1996). *Integrative feminisms: Building global visions, 1960s-1990s.* London: Routledge.

Piaget, J. and Garcia, R. (1989). *Psychogenesis and the history of science* (H. Feider, Trans.). New York: Columbia University Press.

Schön, D. A. (1983). *The reflective practitioner: How professionals think in action.* New York: Basic Books.

Scott, S., Spencer, B. and Thomas, A. (Eds.). (1998). *Learning for life: Canadian readings in adult education.* Toronto, ON: Thompson Educational.

Selman, G. and Dampier, P. (1991). *The foundations of adult education in Canada.* Toronto, ON: Thompson Educational.

Spencer, B. (1998). *The purposes of adult education.* Toronto, ON: Thompson Educational.

Thomas, A. (1991). *Beyond education: A new perspective on society's organization of learning.* San Francisco: Jossey-Bass.

Vygotsky, L. (1987). *The collected works of L. S. Vygotsky: Volume 1: Problems of general psychology.* New York: Plenum Press.

Welton, M. (1997). In defence of civil society: Canadian adult education in neo-conservative times. In S. Walters (Ed.), *Globalization, adult education, and training: Impacts and issues* (pp. 27–38). Leicester, UK: NIACE.

Williams, R. (1977). *Marxism and literature.* New York: Oxford University Press.

12

A Way of Seeing: Transformation for a New Century

Sue M. Scott

W hen you think of someone going through a transformation, what do you see? Do you think of an individual who has changed her hair colour and lost weight? She looks different, but has she actually transformed? Consider the word transformation. *Trans* means across, beyond, to the other side, through; and *form* means structure. *Transform* then means to change or go beyond or across structure, or "to change completely or essentially in composition or structure; a metamorphosis" (Webster's Third New International Dictionary, 1981, p. 2427). How are we as adult educators to participate in the transformation of adults?

The history of adult education includes the assumption that instructors participate in the development of adults' ongoing growth; we are to engage and catalyze adult change in progressive, positive ways. For instance, adults learn a skill that adds to their growing expertise, a kind of change, and certainly skill building is a way to grow. Another way is to help adults to learn critical thinking; what students assume thus is challenged and broadened. For change to become transformation, in the above instance, an assumption would have to change in structure from one thing to another. There are primarily two kinds of transformation prevalent today. First, transformation can include changes in adults' development; for example, changes from abstract formal reasoning to vision logic or into further spiritual developmental stages (see Wilbur, 1986). These stages are recognized structures in the life of adults, and leaving one stage does not mean that he or she cannot do it. It means that one is more engaged (and interested) in the next development stage (or structure) to guide one's life. This would be called transformation of personality championed by the analytical depth psychologists (Jung, 1954). A second kind of transformation is a perspective transformation, which would include changing several assumptions in a world view or frame of reference and is derived from a critical society theoretical paradigm. Although teachers participate in adults' ongoing personal change, the question becomes, To what extent can teachers participate in students' transformation? For this chapter I will review these two most common frameworks used to help adult learners transform at this turn into the twenty-first century, the critical social paradigm and the analytical depth paradigm. First, however, I will include a very brief history of transformation.

History of Transformation

The notion of transformation has been around a long time. Ancient Greek and Roman myths have people transforming into trees (e.g., Osiris, the consort of Isis) and gods and goddesses transforming from celestial immortals to earthly mortals (e.g., the god Eros). Aboriginal religions show in their art the transformation of fish into birds, people into wolves, figures that are half-animal and half-fish. There is a change in form from one thing to another. The church in more recent centuries has perpetuated the notion of transformation through documentation of visions and conversions, and the steady transformation of believers through a disciplined life. Biblical stories capture people's imaginations with the conversion of Saul, a Roman leader, to a Christian, after witnessing the voice of God in a blinding light (Acts 9). In more modern times, Paulo Freire (1970) reported the transformation of poor peasants in Brazil who, while learning to read and write, also shifted from a magical consciousness to a critical consciousness, what he called *conscientization*. For Freire the word *critical* was more than constant questioning; it includes an awareness of the social forces that are running our lives. Jack Mezirow (1991) sought to explicate Freire's conscientization and showed that a change in perspective constitutes a transformation. It seems that adults who undergo a substantive trigger event (death, immigration, loss of job/a child, a divorce, to name a few) and who go through dialogue in a safe and supportive social space, also go through a kind of transformative process that, when it is made conscious, is powerful and enduring. While the transformation occurs in the individual, it is mediated by social forces, is rooted in a critical analysis of those social forces, and usually involves a group of people. The people and the society around them transform into something else in a dialectical way; it looks, feels, and is different structurally to a large majority of people.

Other theorists operating from a Jungian paradigm (Boyd and Myers, 1988; Dirkx, 2001; Washburn, 1988) suggested that the transformative process must include awareness of something that is beneath the surface, that is not readily known by an individual. Whereas the critical paradigm above assumes that what is not known is an awareness of the social forces that are really running society, the analytical depth paradigm assumes that what is running society is unconscious material embedded in people who are unable or unwilling to delve into the dark, forbidden recesses of their psyches. Analytical depth theorists are interested in body work, soul work, the spirituality of a people. To transform, people have to pay attention to their dreams, their cultural mores, what they value, and what drives their behaviour. What guides society and, consequently, behaviour is in the interior soul. What transforms first in this paradigm is the individual, who then transforms society. Both a critical rational view of transformation and a critical non- or extra-rational view of transformation are important paradigms to learn for adult educators.

Both views require a consciousness that can facilitate our understanding of what is happening. Knowledge of these two paradigms can help educators view their students in various ways, looking for signs and starting points to scaffold meaning and knowledge. It requires that we see differently, on various structural levels. For instance, the way that one abstracts with words can become a perspective transformation, a rational process. What one sees on the concrete level—for instance, the bread and wine in communion—on another level represents something else. This requires symbolic thinking or seeing things as symbols that give sometimes extraordinary meaning to ordinary objects, a non-rational process. We never fully grasp the nature of a symbol. On an even deeper level of seeing, we transcend the boundaries between the self and the otherness of the world and momentarily merge with the thing seen. In a similar way, the boundaries merge between the other and the images and fantasies we feel, those that we imagine either in dream life or in semi-awake life, which is an extra-rational process. The same merging boundaries are also present between the individual and the social. So what we are witnessing as social chaos or structural change externally in society is happening internally, perhaps to the same proportion. Individuals as well as political systems and social organizations are transforming at unprecedented speed at the beginning of this century. The amount of literature, research, reports, and conferences that include or focus on transformation is ballooning. What are adult educators to do in light of this kind of huge change in form and structure? The guiding questions for us to assess whether something has transformed or is transforming include the following:

- Exactly *what* is changed, and what are the structures that change?
- What are the conditions that mediate transformation?
- How are adult educators to participate in this massive tectonic shifting of plates beneath the ocean's surface of both individuals and social systems?

I seek to answer these questions within the frameworks of the two paradigms briefly described above.

Critical Social Theory and Perspective Transformation

Within the broad philosophical framework of critical social theory (CST), the aim of education is to learn to see "the reality as it really is." For these theorists, for example, capitalism fools people into believing that consuming or acquiring material wealth is a mark of an advanced society. What our ancestors wanted was a "better" life for their children and grandchildren. They worked hard to give their children better breaks, more education, more freedom to act, and more skills (even if they had to move to another country) to spare them the hardships they endured. A critical theorist would say that the way capitalism has evolved is erroneously to assume that consumerism stands for citizenship or participation in democracy. To be a good citizen, one must be a good consumer. What about those who cannot consume because they are too poor, or not able-bodied to get to the shops? Are they bad citizens?

Critical social theorists are often more interested in the broad picture, social systems, and social arrangements; often across countries for comparison; and critically analyze issues within the various social orders. Educators would look at the curriculum of social studies in elementary education or high school. They would be interested in the way that schools are organized to allow for more freedom of expression or more democratic decision making among the staff members. They would be interested in who holds the power to make decisions and what the social hierarchy and organization is that inhibits or constrains progress. They would define progress in a particular way, not as neoliberals would as more and bigger business. There is an underlying philosophical orientation to CST that guides thinking and action.

Because the object of analysis and critique is the social arrangement of family, political, and social systems, the individual is defined as a social agent who has a sense of agency about what to do and how to act within the social or body politic. He or she could be deluded, much like the masses, and because the aim is to increase the well-being of all of the citizens of a country, the individual has to see the light, the way that society is really being run. Nothing is better than good social debate to ferret out sound policy. The individual is seen primarily as a social player in a broader matrix of society. He or she certainly has a mind, which needs to be trained/educated to think in a particular way, a critically social way.

Mezirow and Associates' (2000) theory of transformative learning is a technical theory to explain what happens in individual transformation. What changes in a cognitive/constructive notion of transformation is a meaning perspective, a habit of expectation that filters how we think, believe, and feel and how, what, when, and why we learn (Mezirow and Associates, 2000). We interpret reality through these filters and construe to what extent we will change, alter, or maintain our current perspective. We are adapting or assimilating information all the time. But in Mezirow's theory a meaning perspective is large, a world view, that includes belief systems and assumptions about such things as democracy, marriage, work, home, and family. As noted above, transforming a perspective requires a trigger event that profoundly challenges the meaning we construe to that perspective, such as a divorce, the loss of a job, the dissolution of a family, or a political upheaval (as in the sponsorship scandal).

Social theorists focus on context as a way to highlight the growing alienation of the individual from the social, or the hype of the workplace to possess the soul of the individual, or the social implications of communication technologies that deny embodied communication (Menzies, 2005). Dysfunctional social places contextualized by individuals and reported by researchers (Lange, 2001) become triggers for individuals courageous enough to step outside the rat race and listen to their bodies and spirits.

The motivation to change starts from social contexts that harm health and belief systems. According to Lange, rather than adapting or assimilating the value system of the workplace, the transformation of the individuals revolves around restoring a belief system with which they grew up and that was more conducive to creativity, health, and well-being. It meant stepping outside the norm and denying big salaries, with no time for families and friends. It took critical analysis in dialogue on what was important in one's work to change and augment a work lifestyle that was more meaningful.

In her recent dissertation, Chovanec (2004) also looked at social context as catalyst for transformation. The women in her study survived 17 years of the Pinochet atrocities in Chile, to become the impetus for his final downfall. Fuelled by memories of social connectedness and cohesion prior to Pinochet's dictatorship, the older women in Chovanec's study relentlessly pushed for social justice until the democratic process was reinstated. The younger women have yet to recover from the atrocities, the slaughtered fathers *and* absent mothers who worked for survival and social action. The structural changes within the women were mediated through the social upheaval in their environment. Chovanec found that although the women used the word *consciousness* from their Marxist training in everyday language, the lack of reflection in the praxis between action and reflection denied the ultimate lasting transformation of a society. The women were instrumental in changing the political process, however, and developed a new gender consciousness, which occurred on a national/regional level and resulted in law changes, equal rights for women, and altered relationships with men as a consequence. Thus there was a feminist transformation on a social and personal level.

My own study of the leaders in the Lincoln Alliance (Scott, 1991), a broad-based association composed of 26 organizations in the 1970s, also showed the importance of context and dialogue to make change in a city. There was clear evidence that meaning perspectives were changed. For instance, as one participant claimed, "I always thought citizen participation was important for democracy and citizenship. What I learned was that to have real power in citizen participation requires a forum for critical analysis of the issues and support" (p. 193). This particular individual went on to become a city council member. But citizen participation was no longer just sitting on a city board; it was also an informed group of citizens who debated the issues publicly. That was real democracy. What was required for the process was a critical mass of people to serve as a forum, and particular criteria for assessment, what we ought to do to advance society, to eliminate evil and suffering. In Mezirow and Associates' (2000) definition, that is transformation, and in my study it took about four to five years for the leaders interviewed to "transform" into public players with changed perspectives on everything from family life to democracy.

Personal Transformation on a Dynamic Depth Level

As the reader can see, what I am talking about here is a structural understanding of transformation. That is to say, if we are to distinguish it from mere change, there has to be a criterion for assessment. One of the current ways to view transformation is structurally. When certain structures change, there is transformation. For Mezirow and Associates (2000), the structural change involves cognitive shifts in meaning schemes and perspectives. It is possible to look at the structure of one's meaning schemes and decide not to change them; in that case there is no transformation. When one reconstructs his or her meaning schemes through a dialogical process in a relatively safe group of people, there is a change in form in one's perspective toward that world view. Democracy simply does not look the same after experiencing it, dialoguing about it, and critically analyzing it. In Mezirow and Associates' theory there is a reconstruction in the rational-ego structure, with some delving into the personal unconscious—that which we know but have not articulated or experienced fully. The personal unconscious is still within reaches of the rational; thus it is safe to say that Mezirow and Associates' theory is primarily a rational restructuring of large perspectives, frameworks, or world views.

A different paradigmatic way of thinking about transformation structurally involves acknowledging the presence of the collective unconscious, the third structure in psychic configuration. Carl Jung's (1954) discovery of the collective unconscious, which is considered vaster and more powerful than any rational-ego function, is accessed primarily through dreams and fantasies. When one pays attention to one's dreams and fantasies, associates feelings and images with time and place occurrences in life, and acts on the meaning derived from this internal dialogue, one transforms over time. A depth transformation usually begins at midlife, when the rational ego in a person has had time to develop in strength; without that ego strength one can be literally swept away from the encounters with the collective unconscious. A definitive work that illustrates this transformation process is that of Murray Stein (1998). He described the transformation as a change in form, like a worm in a cocoon that changes into a butterfly, and suggested that this often includes hormonal changes in humans, similar to a process in the evolution of a butterfly. Certainly the rational ego changes, but only after true engagement with the emotional upheaval (anger being one of the major ones)—the loneliness, the disorientation or fragmentation, and disengagement from the world—that accompanies this kind of transformation. It starts with a relationship to the images in the unconscious, then a relationship to the emotions that these images evoke. One could say that the images mediate the transformation. (In Mezirow and Associates', 2000, theory, words mediate the transformation.) A relationship with the collective unconscious, which we experience as more powerful than the rational function, requires silence, listening, meditation, time, and caring individuals. Logic and words rarely help. This is called intrapsychic dialogue, a kind of dialogue with one's own images and emotions. Journaling, painting the images, using metaphors, writing poetry, reading and relating to ancient myths, working with a wise person, and participating in body work (massage, certain exercises such as yoga) are chief ways that the collective unconscious becomes more available to us.

When futurists emphasize the feminine as one of the factors in the future, they are speaking about the archetype of the feminine, present in both men and women. Quite different from feminist, the feminine is evoked through the darkness, what Jung (1954) called the dark night of the soul. Soul is considered a person's total self in its living unity and wholeness and seems to be located in the core of the body, around the energy of the solar plexus. The spirit is often referred to as the breath of life, is derived from the word *pneuma*, meaning "breath" in Greek, and seems located in the head and above the crown. Both words are referred to in the feminine and are considered key words in describing the deep structure of the collective unconscious, sometimes called the *Dynamic Ground* (Washburn, 1988). It appears to the ego as a dark and threatening, yet compelling force. Ways to view the Dynamic Ground include the notion of archetypes (e.g., Father, Mother, Hero, Lover, Crone, Warrior, Queen, and King) or collections of energy around issues forged by these names; they have both negative and positive aspects. Another, more differentiated view of the unconscious, now being called the *dark feminine* (Baker, 1996; Woodman and Dickson, 1997), is derived from ancient myths and writings. *She* shakes things up, is not sentimental sweetness, and is typically on the periphery or the borders of consciousness. She is experienced as dissonance, out of harmony, and lives in matter and instinct. For balance to occur in personality, for projection to be turned inward (not outward), and for emotional wounds to be healed, it is essential that this inner darkness be acknowledged and related to. It provides vibrancy in life, wakes us up, and engages our desire to reunite with the missing parts of ourselves and our destinies. Work in this area helps us to recoagulate into a new form.

What is changed in analytical depth psychology is a clear pathway between the rational and the extra-rational collective unconscious. It is a structural change in the relationship between the ego and the unconscious in its dynamic flow and release of emotional awareness. In North American society many of us are "walking heads," with bodies necessary only to get the heads around. Because the Dynamic Ground is perceived to be in opposition to the ego, which has attempted to keep a lid on the Ground since the ego developed in the early years of our lives, the Dynamic Ground is undeveloped and immature. Without experience in dealing with it, it escapes under pressure as slips of the tongue, name calling, inappropriate anger, and/or volatile reactions, to name a few. This kind of transformation requires the attention that one would give to a treasured relationship. In fact, the essence of the change depends on the nature of the relationship; that is, spending time with it, making it conscious, and being willing to move *through* the fears engendered from past experiences. The conditions that mediate the transformation are the images in internal life viewed as symbols. Through interpretation and active imagination, the relationship to one's internal matter at once fascinates and guides the learner to new ways of being. This self-knowledge includes not only cognitive shifts in thinking, but also the ability to loosen ego control and allow the Ground to lead one into future endeavours. It depends on the level of attention, on the trust to go where the soul guides, and on the willingness to sustain the process. It also requires a container that is trustworthy; that is, a community of people to contain and support the emerging new personality, but also the body of a person as a container or vessel that one can trust, not just as a walking stick, but also as a whole entity of matter that contains memories, emotions, images, and thoughts in muscles, tissues, and cells.

Instructors of adults can provide the function of a wise crone/person for their students, but it does require personal work. One of the best known examples of an instructor who had done his personal work and who was not afraid of using archetypal images is Robert Boyd, at the University of Wisconsin Adult Education Department, in the 1980s. In a transformative learning class, he was working with a group of students and simply put out the word *mother* to the group, who struggled to understand what he was driving at; but he stayed silent until one young woman began to talk about her mothering. She reported that after the class she went outside and sat in her car for a long time, and hardly slept at all that night. Bob had evoked the Great Mother archetype in her by accessing her personal mother. With some help she sorted out some issues and completed her studies as a more whole person. To what extent she transformed completely is hard to say.

In my own study of the leaders in the Lincoln Alliance (Scott, 1991), non-formal learning in community action, one man, a minister in the United Methodist Church, seemed to shift from rational-ego stages of development to the more spiritual ones. This man explained that community organizing creates more disequilibrium than do classroom experiences. This man learned that he could not live out of his own resources, but only out of a spiritual base that required discipline. Otherwise, social action could not be sustained. He said:

> The only way you can hang in and continue to care is to be sustained by some spiritual resources that transcend the immediate situation, . . . and one needed to be able to believe in new possibilities where there were none before—new possibilities in yourself, in social situations, and in others—and depend on those to be there. To be able to do that is a faith stance. To be able to believe in it is not just an intellectual matter, which is probably what I had to begin with, but is a spiritual dynamic that is sustained beyond (myself) through a spiritual discipline. That was an unexpected dividend from the Alliance. (p. 110)

Summary

In adult education today we need good theories that help us to view students in the process of transformation. The two theoretical frameworks briefly highlighted above can help instructors to locate students within one or both of the frameworks. Both frameworks require that instructors do their own personal work, particularly the mytho-poetic (Dirkx, 2001) or depth framework, because transformation is truly understood only when it is experienced. I have shown *what* is changed in individuals when they intend to learn from trigger events and/or internal compelling images and messages. What changes are cognitive structures within a rational framework, and within the depth paradigm there is access, recognition, and relationship to the emotional material in the deep structure of the collective unconscious. Words mediate the changes in meaning perspectives, and images and emotions become mediators for transformation in the deep structures in the psyche.

References

Baker, C. (1996). *Reclaiming the dark feminine: The price of desire.* Tempe, AZ: New Falcon.

Boyd, R. and Myers, J. G. (1988). Transformative education. *International Journal of Lifelong Education, 7*(4). 261–284.

Chovanec, D. (2004). *Between hope and despair: Social and political learning in the women's movement in Chile.* Unpublished dissertation, University of Alberta, Edmonton.

Dirkx, J. M. (2001). The power of feeling: Emotion, imagination, and the construction of meaning in adult learning, In S. B. Merriam (Ed.), *The new update on adult learning theory* (pp. 63–72). San Francisco: Jossey-Bass.

Freire, P. (1970). *Pedagogy of the oppressed.* New York: Seabury Press.

Jung, C. (1954). *The development of personality* (R. F. C. Hull, Trans.). Princeton, NJ: Princeton University Press.

Lange, E. (2001). *Living transformation.* Unpublished dissertation, University of Alberta, Edmonton.

Menzies, H.(2005). *No time: Stress and the crisis of modern life.* Vancouver, BC: Douglas & McIntyre.

Mezirow, J. (1991). *Transformative dimensions of adult learning.* San Francisco: Jossey-Bass.

Mezirow, J. and Associates. (2000). Learning to think like an adult: Core concepts of transformation theory. In J. Mezirow and Associates (Eds.), *Learning as transformation: Critical perspectives on a theory in progress* (pp. 3–34). San Francisco: Jossey-Bass.

Scott, S. M. (1991). *Personal transformation through participation in social action: A case study of the leaders in the Lincoln Alliance.* Unpublished dissertation. University of Nebraska, Lincoln.

Stein, M. (1998) *Transformation: Emergence of the self.* College Station, TX: Texas A & M University Press.

Washburn, M. (1988). *The ego and the dynamic ground: A transpersonal theory of human development.* Albany: State University of New York Press.

Webster's third new international dictionary. (1981). Vol. III. Chicago: Encyclopedia Britannica.

Wilbur, K. (1986). The spectrum of development. In K. Wilbur, J. Engler, and D. Brown (Eds.), *Transformations of consciousness* (pp. 65–105). Boston: Shambhala.

Woodman, M. and Dickson, E. (1997). *Dancing in the flames: The dark goddess in the transformation of consciousness.* Boston: Shambhala.

Part 3

CONTEXTS OF WORK AND ECONOMY

13

Human Capital and the Knowledge Economy

Paul Bouchard

In the past few years, we have witnessed the spread of the widely shared view that so-called "developed" countries must depend increasingly on the expansion of knowledge-driven activities for their economic health and survival. This is seen as the natural result of recent advancements in information technologies and the new dominance of the third-sector (service) economy, in which competence is synonymous with productivity, and knowledge with competitive edge (Barnow and Smith, 2005). Another important factor has been the removal in recent years of many of the traditional barriers to the movement and transfer of goods and capital, which has been a central part of the process more widely referred to as the globalization of the economy. With the removal of trade barriers such as tariffs and import taxes, "poor" countries can sell their goods anywhere at a cheaper price than "rich" countries can, to such an extent that in developed economies the exploitation of natural resources, as well as many—if not most—of their manufacturing sectors, is quickly becoming irrelevant. Hence our need to develop "knowledge capital" more or less as a substitute for the loss of our other competitive capabilities on the world markets. In other words, we are shifting our dependence from the more traditional forms of natural, work, and physical capital to what we now call human capital in order to build the new "knowledge economy."

In a previous article in this series (Bouchard, 1998), I questioned some of the seemingly natural assumptions that lie hidden behind the notion of "valuable" knowledge. For instance, how do we know what types of knowledge will be useful by the time it will have taken to develop and acquire them? What are the consequences for the job market of the continuous inflation of educational requirements? What is the role of knowledge in an economy where most employment is created in low-level service jobs? In this chapter I would like to ask a few more questions, such as, What is the relationship between education, knowledge, and the economics of human capital? What is gained—and by whom—from the current discourse on the urgency to develop human capital? And, finally, how can these issues inform current educational policy?

From a theoretical perspective, human capital is situated at the frontier between economics and human learning. What does the field of political economy have to do with adult education? you may ask. As a science, economics is concerned with explaining the behaviours of local and world markets in order to better understand them and, hopefully, to assist in their smooth functioning. Adult education, on the other hand, is concerned with human learning and all those things that can influence, help, or hinder its development. Not much relationship, you say? Think again. Throughout the world, including in Canada, social and economic policy is being shaped with the explicit goal of promoting what are now called *human capital* and the *knowledge economy*. In other words, the acquisition of new knowledge—through education and learning—is now seen as the key to the meal ticket of the nation: its economy. Adult educators, who make it their business to develop, share, expand, or otherwise broker knowledge in its many forms, should also make it their business to keep an eye on issues that incorporate human learning at the heart of public policy.

Human Capital: What Is It?

Human capital is a concept that was first developed in the 1960s by Theodore Shultz (1950, 1961, 1963, 1964, 1971) and Arthur Lewis and further developed by Gary Becker throughout the 1980s and 1990s. The main idea is that although humans possess tangible financial capital such as bank accounts and stocks, they are also the repository of knowledge, skills, and qualities that can also be considered capital. Becker (1975) argued that it is a worthwhile endeavour to *invest* in human capital. As he put it, "Economists regard expenditures on education, training, medical care, and so on as investments in human capital" (p. 74).

The name itself is interesting enough. We usually refer to the human element in productive organizations as human *resources,* which distinguishes employees from other resources such as materials, machines, and infrastructure because they are useful to the organization through what they *do*, which is anything that machines or tools, on their own, cannot. Human *capital*, on the other hand, carries a symbolism of a different dimension. Whereas a *resource* is something that one transforms, uses, or exploits in order to derive some benefit, *capital* is something that one *owns*, and as such it possesses intrinsic value for individuals and for society. Just like physical capital, knowledge capital can be acquired (through education) and preserved (through continuing education) and can yield dividends in the form of productivity and, arguably, the wealth of whoever owns it. But unlike other forms of capital, human capital cannot be separated from its holder, and its value is entirely dependent on that person's capacity to apply his or her knowledge in an economically profitable enterprise.

As a macro-economic theory, human capital enables us to see how human knowledge and creativity can be elements in the production of wealth, just as other factors of economic organization can. In fact, in a world where quality is replacing price as the main factor of competition and where large-scale savings are taking second place to innovation and creativity (Favreau and Lévesque, 1996), it would seem that human capital theory is here to stay and that its influence is not about to decrease.

What is the cash "value" of human capital? Becker (1975) computed the relative earnings of persons with various educational backgrounds and came to the conclusion that "high school and college education . . . greatly raise a person's income, even after netting out direct and indirect costs of schooling" (p. 132). Among the indirect costs of schooling, Becker calculated that the time spent on learning, rather than on being gainfully employed, carries an opportunity cost even greater than the actual costs of tuition. Regardless of this fact, education remained a viable investment in Becker's calculation.

Another economic observation that tends to support the link between schooling and prosperity is the fact that when university tuition fees are raised, university enrolment does not diminish proportionately (Murphy and Welch, 1989). If education were a consumer object rather than an investment, variations in its price would be reflected in variations in its consumption, just as raising the price of apples reduces the demand for apples. On the other hand, the cost of a business investment is determined by the benefits that one anticipates from that investment rather than by its intrinsic value. This is why the cost of a downtown commercial building greatly exceeds the cost of the actual materials used to build it. It is interesting that studies have shown that as the cost of higher education rises, the income of educated professionals also rises. This greatly reinforces the perception that the cost of education is actually an "investment" very much comparable to other types of business investments, as Schultz (1963) observed. It does not elucidate, however, whether salaries go up with the cost of tuition or whether colleges and universities raise the costs of their programs to cash in on their rising job-market value.

In Canada formal statistics relating income to education show an almost one-on-one relationship between the two (Statistics Canada, 2003). The higher the degree, the higher the income, and vice versa. Overall, Becker's (1975) assertion proved itself true in many countries, over many years, and it is today accepted as a fact of economic life that higher education increases productivity and therefore income.

The Macro-Economic Value of Knowledge

But wait. There is something not so oddly naïve about accepting as proof of the direct economic benefit of education its correlation with a few market indicators such as school costs and salaries.

Whereas it is one thing to compare the relative incomes of college graduates with those of high school drop-outs and to remark that the former earn more than the latter, it is quite another matter to explain how divisions in scholastic achievement are mimicked by corresponding economic divisions found in the social strata. Indeed, there can be any number of sociologically sound explanations for this apparent symmetry, the first of which could be that our education system is an *instrument* of social stratification rather than one of its "natural" causes. One good measure of this theory would be to see what happens when too many people gain access to higher education. Would the overall prosperity of the nation increase proportionately, or, on the contrary, would the value of education diminish with diminished scarcity? This is exactly what happened during the 1970s when the "return on investment" of education dropped sharply as more young people flocked to colleges and universities than ever before. This led Freeman (1976) to call attention to the phenomenon of, as he called it, "the Overeducated American," which would perhaps be more aptly labelled "*too many* educated Americans."

Furthermore, if knowledge directly produced wealth, there would be no theoretical limit to the yields of human capital, as Schultz (1963) contended in his early works. As the world becomes more and more knowledgeable, it should also become more and more prosperous, indefinitely. That assertion leaves considerable room for doubt, for obvious reasons. It also raises an all-important question: Does education actually improve a person's economic productivity, or does it just separate low earners from high earners by acting as a selection criterion? Becker (1975) himself admitted that education could simply provide signals ("credentials") about talents and abilities rather than determine real economic potential. We might further conjecture that the credentials provided by education may correspond to much more complex means of determining social appurtenance than Becker's mere workplace "talents" or "abilities." For instance, Bourdieu (1984) convincingly argued that education is one important factor in a person's *cultural capital*, which in turn determines largely where an individual will stand on the social-economic ladder. Becker himself admitted that his measurements suffered one possible flaw: "Persons differing in education also differ in many characteristics that cause their income to differ systematically" (p. 79).

The failings of the assumption that knowledge is the source of wealth are observable also in the broader organizational context. Large corporations are increasingly dependent on their customer service to differentiate themselves from competitors who offer identical products at identical prices to the same customers. This "soft" sector can be developed only by providing additional training to employees, which is one reason that companies claim that knowledge is essential to profits. Although this may have direct consequences for the manager of a local business, it nevertheless amounts to a zero-sum game in which the same number of customers, receiving the same services, simply redistribute themselves according to some condition such as the perceived quality of customer support. In this case increasing competitive capacity, and not productivity, does nothing to further the goal of a stronger economy for all.

Finally, let's look at the proviso that human knowledge is the property of its holder. It is a well-documented fact that in developing countries, any investment beyond basic education benefits the individuals who have gained higher knowledge, but does very little for the economic or social benefit of the nation. The reason is simply that higher education either serves directly the interest of the educated or is lost to the phenomenon known as *brain drain*. In developed economies, we can assume that the "knower" is still at the centre of the equation and that the owners of marketable knowledge derive a benefit from their savvy. The problem, however, is that knowledge-based wealth, because it *replaces* production-based earnings in the new knowledge economy, does not "trickle down" as would be necessary for a complete economic cycle. Indeed, it would seem logical to assume that in the absence of a healthy manufacturing sector, a country's knowledge-based wealth will be quickly exported to second-sector-intensive developing countries in exchange for imported manufactured goods. In this perspective, we can safely surmise that the "knowledge economy" is also a "high-unemployment economy."

Another direct consequence of promoting knowledge-based economics is that by creating a policy system that values how people apply their knowledge, we are overlooking their other contributions that, in the absence of such policy, would receive more adequate support. Recognizing the value of human competence is far from a novelty in economic science, except that in its new incarnation, human labour—work—is becoming de-politicized, and *removed from the social-political sphere*. By using human knowledge (associated with *ownership*) rather than work (associated with *production*) as the new criterion for attributing value, we are in effect saying that the economy is legitimately owned by "those who know" and that economic policy should therefore be guided to meet their ends. However, in simple quantitative terms, so-called "knowledge-based industries" such as the high-tech production and communications sectors do not account for the activities, nor do they represent the interests of the majority of people in any nation in the world. They do, however, represent a force that pressures public policy to devalue entire sectors of the labour economy, thereby justifying social irresponsibility and the concentration of wealth among the few at the expense of the many. In other words, human capital and the knowledge economy, when used as ideological trappings for public policy, directly serve to further the neoliberal agenda.

Economics and Social Responsibility

From the very beginnings of theoretical economics, the notion of social responsibility emerged as one of its fundamental issues. In the late eighteenth century Thomas Robert Malthus warned us of the natural limitations of any economy, simply because of the fact that resources are never limitless. Because the ability of humans to produce children is proportionally much higher than their ability to produce food (Malthus used the expression "geometrically higher," but who could verify this?), or even to clear arable land for the production of food, economic equilibrium can be achieved only by limiting the reproductive output of humanity. This can be done either by such "natural" checks as famine, disease, and war, or more preferably by the imposition of a "moral social order" that curbs the natural desires of humans for the act of reproduction, through religion, ideology, or personal responsibility. Furthermore, as Amartya Sen (1981) reminded us, calamities such as war and disease are almost never caused by the scarcity of natural resources, just as famine is almost never caused by a lack of food. Hence, "public morality" was seen very early as a direct consequence of economic reality and as necessary to human survival as the air we breathe.

The Malthusian *physiocratic* view of economics, which places the Earth's natural resources as the ultimate source of all wealth, as well as the precepts of *mercantilism*, which advocates upholding a strong local economic protectionism for the benefit of the feudal classes and the Sovereign, were soon to be replaced by the ideas of the first liberal economist, Adam Smith, along with a very different, but equally powerful, commitment towards moral economics. In his seminal work, *An Inquiry Into the Nature and Causes of the Wealth of Nations*, Smith argued that the true source of wealth is human productivity, which can be achieved and maximized through the division of labour among the population and the multiplication of competing economic agents. Smith also argued strongly against the application of limitations on international trade such as tariffs and import taxes and predicted that the pursuit of self-interest would inevitably benefit everyone's interest. Thus, free trade would become the only balancing factor in an otherwise "liberal" economy.

In our era of globalized economics, Smith's discourse sounds strangely familiar, and indeed it is utilized freely by those who have a stake in the neoliberal agenda. What they don't tell us, however, is that, not unlike Malthus, Smith came to reckon very early that the ultimate goal of economics was to provide for the "common good" and that this could not be achieved without the application of some kind of "enlightened regulation." In other words, Adam Smith himself, the inventor of "liberal" economics, was the first to admit that we could not leave the "invisible hand" of the market entirely free lest we risk economic havoc and, above all, grave social injustice and suffering. *— need moral guidance*

One of the obvious problems of an uncontrolled economy, Smith said, would be the rise of monopolies that could neutralize the self-regulating forces of supply and demand. Therefore, various regulations are required in order to prevent the unhealthy concentration of market share in one or two companies in any given economic sector. These safeguards, although relatively simple to implement in traditional production economies, become almost impossible to apply in the knowledge economy. Indeed, the nature of highly complex or technical knowledge usually requires an equally complex form of organization in order to flourish. This is the reason that knowledge industries often require not only the intricate infrastructure of a single corporation, but also the synergy afforded by what are known as *clusters* of knowledge-based organizations. Examples of clusters would be Silicon Valley and Wall Street. These clusters have become an essential feature of the knowledge economy and are usually dependent on govern-

— clusters of knowledge based corps becoming new monopolies

ment policy and handouts. However, because of the complex nature of their organization, knowledge industries cannot be duplicated indefinitely, and this tends to limit their numbers. For this reason, many knowledge industries have transformed into what economists have called *natural monopolies*. Traditionally, natural monopolies have been public services that would be too bulky or costly to reproduce (for example, public transport services or water distribution). Today, high-tech corporations function in much the same way as natural monopolies do, their sheer bulk guaranteeing low competition from others (unless we can be fooled into believing that two telephone distributors instead of one will ensure the fair exercise of market forces!). Here we see at work one important feature of neoliberal economics: Contrary to Adam Smith's exhortations, the new agenda is not concerned with curbing the inherent defects of the market economy, which is essential to the pursuit of the common good, but rather with ensuring that those who benefit from the systemic deficiencies continue to do so freely. → widening gap b/w rich + poor → not necessarily to the benefit of the nation.

Adam Smith's publication was subtitled "A Treatise of Political Economy," which is a good reminder that there is no "economy" outside of the social-political organization of human affairs and that good economic progression cannot be separated from good political governance. Today we are faced with deciding whether to oppose economics and politics as two distinct spheres of activity or to reaffirm the fact that economics *is* politics. In short, the challenge of public policy today is to redefine the relationship between the *social* and the *economic* spheres of human activity and to shape the nation's economic activities in such a manner that they pursue nothing less than Adam Smith's "common good." This cannot be done by limiting the notion of human capital to high-tech development and international competition.

Work and Employment

In the context of citizens being assessed for their human capital, the question of social responsibility is very closely linked to the way we consider work and employment and from which point of view we do it (Favreau and Lévesque, 1996). For example, *employment* has been defined variously as (a) the productive role of a person in a profitable enterprise, (b) the exchange of a person's time and work for remuneration, and (c) the way in which much of human activity is organized in our society. The first two are economic definitions, the third a sociological one. Obviously, the notion of *work* carries both economic and social meanings, which is why, for example, labour organizations voice such outrage when decisions are made according to the one set of criteria while disregarding the other (such as when an "economically justified" plant closure is socially unjustifiable). Contrary to the precepts of human capital, the value of work and employment for people reaches far beyond the value of commercial exchange. The workplace is a locus of human interaction that touches on all spheres of society, including the way we organize our family life and run our communities. Furthermore, work confers to its members the status of active participants in the affairs of society, and indeed the social fact of being employed is ingrained in the very identity of citizenship. This is why any policy that purports to have an effect on the quality or the composition of the workplace must pursue, above all else, the goal of social inclusion rather than that of a pecking order determined by knowledge. Human capital theory in its current form promotes just that: the competition among individuals for the privileges associated with employment, using a meritocratic system based on the ownership of knowledge.

If we look at recent Organisation for Economic Cooperation and Development (OECD) and Canadian policy statements on human capital, we find that they refer almost exclusively to the globalized, competitive, for-profit, commercial sectors of the economy and that they rarely mention other areas of occupation that Statistics Canada (2003) called the *social economy*, which includes not-for-profit organizations such as cooperatives, credit unions, volunteer organizations, the education sector, and health care. According to Statistics Canada, these together accounted for 20 percent of all productive work in Canada in 2004. To put this into context, the social economy in Canada is 11 times greater in size than the automobile manufacturing sector, 4 times greater than agriculture, and 2 times greater than mining, petroleum, and gas extraction combined.

The distinction between what is *profitable* for high-tech and high-knowledge corporations and what is *beneficial* to the collective is an important one, especially in the current context of human resource policy in Canada, which tends to favour one at the expense of the other.

As adult educators we are more liable to encounter the least "knowledgeable" persons in our society, precisely those who are the most unlikely to benefit from investments in high-tech "knowledge" industries. Of course, we must acknowledge the need for some business sectors to invest in training, and therefore the need for adult educators who are knowledgeable in the areas of instructional design, program planning, and the like. But the greater majority of adults who require educational services are faced with marginalization and exclusion, *not* with falling behind on the latest machine code. We must not assume, as the knowledge-for-money theorists would have it, that social exclusion and educational deficit are synonymous or somehow related through cause and effect. We must ask instead, By what mechanisms are sections of the population marginalized, and how can adult education address, and redress, the systemic forces that get in the way of social equality? The notion that educational deficit is the reason behind social exclusion and that the cure is, naturally, more education is a value that serves the interest of the well-off and educated among us. The belief that by inculcating such mainstream values in disenfranchised populations we will somehow cure marginalization is nothing less than a falsehood.

Human capital is a macro-economic theory, which is not the same thing as a set of rules by which to organize our lives and our society. However, this is precisely what happens when we accept the premise that society must invest massively in so-called "marketable" education, and especially in technical education. This slip in logic is frequent and can be found in many forms in the current discourse that values marketable knowledge above other forms of human development. Canadian government policy, and by ricochet our colleges' and universities' programs, are heavily focused on investing in such "valuable" knowledge, as can be seen especially in Human Resources and Skills Development Canada's goals and activities (though, in all honesty, that agency also gives attention to workplace inclusion issues, but almost exclusively through the angle of training and retraining). Traditional institutions of knowledge production and dissemination—namely, colleges and universities—are also hopping on the bandwagon and shifting their priorities to so-called "economically viable" sectors of knowledge and diminishing their support for learning that is not so market driven. We are simply arguing that there is a danger that in such a climate some very real social issues will be lost in the shuffle, to the detriment of our society and its population.

References

Barnow, B. S. and Smith, C. (2005). *Job training policy in the United States*. Kalmazoo, MI: W. E. Upjohn Institute for Employment Research.

Becker, G. S. (1975). *Human capital: A theoretical and empirical analysis with special reference to education*. New York : Columbia University Press, National Bureau of Economic Research.

Bouchard, P. (1998). Training and work: Myths about human capital. In S. M. Scott, B. Spencer, and A. M. Thomas (Eds.), *Learning for life: Canadian readings in adult education* (pp. 128–139). Toronto, ON: Thompson Educational.

Bourdieu, P. (1984). *Distinction: A social critique of the judgement of taste*. Cambridge, MA: Harvard University Press.

Favreau, L. and Lévesque, B. (1996). *Développement économique communautaire: Économie sociale et intervention*. Sainte-Foy, PQ: Presses de l'Université du Québec.

Freeman, R. (1976). *The overeducated American*. New York: Academic Press.

Murphy, K. M. and Welch, F. (1989). Wage premiums for college graduates: Recent growth and possible explanations. *Educational Researcher, 18,* 17–27.

Schultz, T. W. (1950). Reflections on poverty within agriculture. *Journal of Political Economy, 43,* 1–15.

Schultz, T. W. (1961). Investment in Human Capital. *American Economic Review, 51,* 1–17.

Schultz, T. W. (1963). *The economic value of education*. New York: Columbia University Press.

Schultz, T. W. (1964). *Transforming traditional agriculture*. New Haven: Yale University Press.

Schultz, T. W. (1971). *Investment in human capital: The role of education and of research*. New York: The Free Press.

Sen, A. K. (1981). *Poverty and famines: An essay on entitlement and deprivation*. New York: Oxford University Press.

Statistics Canada. (2003). *Adult education and training survey*. Ottawa, ON: Author.

14
The Political Economy of Adult Learning in Canada

Kjell Rubenson and Judith Walker

As in the rest of the Anglo-Saxon world, neoliberalism has come to comprise the raison d'être of Canadian politics over the last two decades (Clement and Vosko, 2003). "It has narrowed the discourse of political, economic, and social debate, transforming what it means to be liberal, social democratic, or even progressive conservative by asserting itself against social entitlements, rights, and citizenship" (p. viii).

In this chapter we will examine how the new political–economic paradigm has transformed the conditions for and meaning of adult learning in Canada. Our analysis starts with a short overview of the political project of adult and lifelong learning as it is being fostered by intergovernmental bodies such as the European Union (EU), the Organisation for Economic Cooperation and Development (OECD), and the United Nations Educational, Scientific, and Cultural Organization (UNESCO). We then focus on the Canadian version of neoliberalism and conclude with an analysis of its impact on adult learning in Canada.

The Political Project of Lifelong Learning

In the 1970s, a time of concern for equality and democracy when many adult educators were informed by critical theory, adult educators lamented over the marginal status of the field. Today the situation is very different. Driven by a mainly neoliberal agenda that has promoted economic or corporate globalization, adult learning has become a central issue in national policies on education, the economy, and welfare in Canada and around the world (Government of Canada, 2002a; 2002b; EU, 2000; OECD, 1996; 2003).

Within adult leaning circles there is currently a strong resentment of what is being seen as the colonization of adult learning and its humanistic and libratory traditions by an 'economic' agenda, resulting in a drastic change in the conditions under which adult education operates (Gustavsson, 2002). The current promotion of lifelong learning, with an emphasis on adult learning, signals a deconstruction of welfare through a reconstruction of citizenship as the responsibility of an individual to an economic agenda (Bastow and Martin, 2003).

Critics of the current discourse on adult learning often invoke the ideals and goals that dominated during the first generation of lifelong learning (Rubenson, 1999). The idea of lifelong learning first appeared in the 1970s, at a time when post-World War II optimism about development, prosperity, and the ability of schooling to promote social equality was being challenged. As a result, there were calls for new paradigms to inform educational policy. In this climate and within a humanistic tradition, lifelong learning was advocated—particularly by UNESCO—as a model that would promote a better society and quality of life and allow people to adapt to as well as control change (Dave, 1976; Lengrand, 1970). The concept was one of personal development; people were encouraged to "make themselves" rather than "be made." An important issue in the analysis of the day was how a "system of lifelong learning" could reduce educational gaps in society. The humanistic generation of lifelong learning saw a strong role for civil society and was primarily promoted by the volunteer sector, and in most countries the state and the market remained largely absent from the debate (Rubenson, 1999). The idea put forward in humanistic tradition and with utopian vision was diametrically opposed to the neoliberal tide that came to sweep the Western world. Indeed, issues such as equality, democratization, and civil society, which underpinned the first wave of lifelong learning, ceased to inform the educational discourse in the coming years.

Driven by a different ideology with different goals and dreams, the second generation of lifelong learning appeared in the late 1980s. This was a period of change and uncertainty for the OECD economies. In a climate of rising unemployment, declining productivity, and increasing public deficits, "education and the economy" became a catchphrase for those dissatisfied with the status quo of education (OECD, 1989, p. 17). The OECD noted, "The key appears to be the ability of people to cope with changes and to turn them to advantages in the future" (OECD, 1986; as cited in Marginson, 1993, p. 48). The 1989 OECD report *Education and the Economy in a Changing Society* ushered in what has been labelled the second generation of human capital thinking in educational policy, replacing the original theory of the 1960s (Marginson, 1997). These ideas were quickly picked up by the political sphere but not by representatives of the field of adult learning. For example, former US Labour Secretary Robert Reich (1992) argued that in a competitive market economy those who are adaptive to the knowledge economy, as well as marketable, tend to succeed; whereas those who do not possess the necessary skills and technological know-how struggle to stay afloat. In Canada several commissions on economic development made the same connection between learning and economic prosperity, as exemplified in the upcoming section, "Adult Learning Under the Canadian Way."

In short, discussions on lifelong learning became framed within a politico-economic imperative that emphasized the importance of science and technology, as well as highly developed human capital. It is of interest to note that whereas the first generation of lifelong learning talked about education as enabling individuals to control and adapt to change, the second generation saw learning only as a mechanism for individuals to adjust to a society that was shaped without their input.

Towards the end of the 1990s, policymakers had come to the insight that although the New Economy holds the promise of increased productivity and an improved standard of living, it also introduces a new set of transitions and adjustment challenges for society, industry, and individuals. Sensing a public disgruntled with free-market capitalism and its seeming disregard for social and individual issues, political circles became increasingly aware that these challenges needed to be addressed. Increased exclusion or marginalization of large segments of the population and exacerbated socio-economic divisions were seen as a threat to global capitalism as such. The new understanding in policy circles came to affect the international discourse on lifelong learning and resulted in a softening of the economistic perspective (Field, 2003; Rubenson, 2004). This change is embedded in policy documents on lifelong learning, which are no longer exclusively concerned with human capital issues, but also include references to social purposes (see, e.g., EU, 2000; OECD, 2003).

The current third generation of lifelong learning is a "softened" economistic version that can be seen as a reflection of what has become known as the *Third Way* (Giddens, 1999), which claims to reinsert issues of social cohesion, civic participation, and democracy into politics. For Third Way governments, in particular, training and education have been identified as playing a key role in easing the transition into a knowledge economy. Giddens wrote that "education and training have become the new mantra for social democratic politicians" (p. 109), and Tony Blair himself is quoted as saying, "Education is the best economic policy we have" (Martin, 2003, p. 567).

According to critics, under Third Way governments up-skilling, training, or lifelong learning are conceived mainly in terms of generating wealth— for the individual and for the country (Newman and De Zoysa, 2001). "The emphasis on education, re-skilling, and lifelong learning are all policies concerned with enhancing the competitiveness of the British economy" (Bastow & Martin, 2003, p. 98). Indeed, although social cohesion and social justice have been a purported mission of Blair's Labour government, "equity has been tagged on to Labour's priorities rather than taking a centre stage" (Ball, 1999, p. 204).

From the perspective of implementing lifelong learning, the three generations reflect different roles for—and interrelations among—the three major institutional arrangements: state, market, and civil society (see Figure 1). According to Figure 1, the relationships among these three institutional arrangements are expected to strongly influence the conditions under which adult and lifelong learning operate and hence shape its practice.

The first generation of lifelong learning, as expressed in the UNESCO tradition, saw a strong role for civil society; whereas the second generation privileged the market, downplayed the role of the state, and almost completely neglected civil society. Thus, during the first generation NGOs

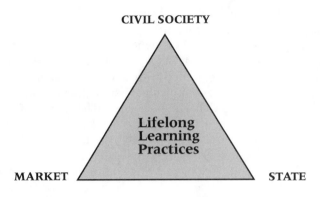

Figure 1. Institutional arrangement and lifelong learning practises.

came to play a relatively important role, but the emphasis during the second became privatization and deregulation of public education. It is important to stress that these institutional arrangements are not static but interrelated. Therefore the influence of the market on adult learning opportunities cannot be fully understood by referring to the shift from state control towards privatization and decentralization of adult education. Thus, with relevance becoming the key concept driving government policies on adult education and training during the second generation of lifelong learning, the interests of business were privileged, and the sector was given the lead role in defining what competencies and skills the public adult educational system should produce. With a recognition of market failures and growing concerns over large groups not participating fully in social and economic life, the third generation can be read as a shift in balance among the three institutional arrangements. The market still has a central role in adult learning, but the responsibilities of the individual and the state are also visible. The language is one of shared responsibilities. However, a closer reading of the text and the understanding that seems to dominate the current policy debate might lead one to be more sceptical of what looks to be a major shift in the public discourse on lifelong learning. Despite repeated references to the involvement of all three institutional arrangements, what stands out in recent policy documents is the stress placed on the responsibility of individuals for their own learning—something that is underscored time after time. The stress on individual responsibility can be seen to reflect the Third Way program and its ethos that "the precept 'no rights without responsibilities' applies to all individuals and groups" (Giddens, 2000, p. 165). Giddens continued, "Governments must maintain a regulatory role in many contexts, but as far as possible it should become a facilitator, providing resources for citizens to assume responsibility for the consequences of what they do" (p. 165).

Third Way rhetoric is not foreign to the Canadian discourse on the political economy, a topic to which we now turn.

The Canadian Political Economy

Ideological struggle over 20 years has resulted in an acceptance of a reduced role for the state and the taking for granted of free-market forces and global competitiveness as the only alternatives available to Canada (Clement and Vosko, 2003; McBride 2001). In 1995 the Canadian Assistance Plan and the *Established Program Financing Act* were replaced by the Canadian Health and Social Transfer scheme. The new federal programs came with fewer restrictions on how the provinces could spend the money, but at much reduced funding levels. The situation was made more precarious by severe provincial cuts and changes to their welfare schemes. According to McKeen and Porter (2003, p. 115), this involved privatization of many services, introduction of workfare programs within social assistance programs, and restructuring of education and health. They further concluded that inflation and productivity came to replace unemployment as the core concern. During the previous Keynesian period, which came to an end in the late 1970s, the state recognized that unemployment could be the fault of the economy and not the individual. Consequently, the state assumed some responsibility for trying to keep unemployment at a relative low level and for providing income security to those who were affected (McKeen and Porter 2003). Although some programs had restrictions on eligibility, there was greater emphasis on universality than would have been the case under the neoliberal regime. Under neoliberalism, conversely, unemployment is seen less as a market failure and more as a result of individuals' failure to invest in their human capital and/or to have the right attitude toward work. Active labour market policies and accompanying changes to the security system are promoted on the grounds that they overcome the previous system's disincentives for work.

The change in the Canadian political economy has been achieved over the last two decades through two processes, *neoliberal constitutionalism* and *disciplinary neoliberalism* (Gill, 2003). The former term refers to the legal institutionalizing of neoliberalism through supranational organizations such as the WTO or the IMF or through free-trade agreements such as NAFTA. The latter term is used to explain the internalization of neoliberal ideology that occurs within governments and individuals. Through self-governance and self-regulation, individuals come to pursue a neoliberal agenda—even though there may be no legal requirement or policy that dictates such action. Consider, for example, the message that global economic forces leave us no choice, which is stressed time after time by politicians and the business community. David O'Brian, former CEO of one of the most influential lobby groups in Canada, the Canadian Council of Chief Executives, stated, "The Global economy is at our doors. It is not a question of deciding what we want to do: it is deciding for us" (Watkins, 2003, p. 4).

The Canadian state cooperates with the market—not always because of coercion, but rather because of the neoliberal agendas and desires of the government involved (McBride, 2001). Rather than hapless recipients of neoliberalism, "governments act as the midwives of globalization" (Brodie, 1996, p. 386). Similarly, there are several accounts of how the forces of globalization have differential impacts on countries. Hall and Soskice (2001) separated the economies of OECD countries into two distinct categories: the *liberal market*, which comprises Anglo-Saxon countries, and the *coordinated market system*, which includes the Nordic countries, Germany, Belgium, and Switzerland. Anglo-Saxon countries, they argued, have been more affected by the rhetoric and reality of neoliberalism than have those nation-states within the coordinated market system.

Third Way politics commonly refers to the political philosophy of Anthony Giddens (see 1999, 2000) and the political platform of Tony Blair's New Labour. It is therefore interesting to note that when in 2000 President Bill Clinton held a summit to explore the Third Way, he insisted that then Canadian Prime Minister Jean Chrétien attend "on the grounds that the Third Way was inspired by Canada" (Coyne, 2000, p. 1). Chrétien described the *Canadian Way*, a term that is attributed to the former Prime Minister (see Coyne, 2000), as *"a balance that promotes individual freedom and economic prosperity while at the same time sharing risks and benefits* [emphasis added]" (p. 1). As former Minister of Finance and current Prime Minister Paul Martin declared in the Budget Speech of 2000 (Department of Finance Canada, 2000):

> The success we have achieved as a nation has come not only from strong growth but from an abiding commitment to strong values—caring and compassion, an insistence that there be an equitable sharing of the benefits of economic growth. (p. 5)

In *Canada's Performance 2002* the President of the Treasury Board (2002) described the Canadian Way as

> an approach marked by an accommodation of cultures, a recognition of diversity, a partnership between citizens and the state, a sharing of risks and benefits, and a positioning of government as an instrument of collective action. It is an approach centred on a goal that is common to all Canadians—improving the quality of life for all. (p. 8)

Canada's federal budgets (Department of Finance Canada, 1997, 1999, 2000, 2001, 2003, 2004, 2005a, 2005b) can also provide some insight into the social cohesion/neoliberal divide in the new nation-building venture. Table 1 shows the titles and themes of the budgets for seven years.

Table 1: Themes and Topics in the Federal Budget 1997, 1999–2001, 2003–2005

TITLES		THEMES/TOPICS					
		Accountability	Communities	Economy	Environment	International	Social
05	Delivering on commitments	Accountability	Communities	Economy	Health	Learning	
04	New agenda for achievement	Accountability	Communities	Economy			
03	Building the Canada we want	Accountability	Economy	Health care and society			
01	Securing progress in an uncertain world	Fiscal progress	Security	Investment			
00	Better finances, better lives	Tax reduction plan	More innovative economy	Improving quality of life			
99	Building today for a better tomorrow	Fiscal management	Health care	Tax relief and fairness	Federal transfers	Knowledge and innovation	
97	Building the future for Canadians	Restoring confidence in the country's finances	Investing in jobs and growth	Investing in a stronger society			

From appearances, all budgets are committed to unifying the country and fit within a Third Way framework of using language around neoliberalism and human capitalism as well as social provision/cohesion. Furthermore, it could be argued that over the seven years shown in Table 1, the language has become more geared towards social cohesion and the humanizing elements of the Third Way—especially since 2004 when community was introduced as a budget priority. In the 2005 budget the Liberals promised "a new deal for Canada's communities" (Department of Finance Canada, 2005a, p. 1). In this statement it is hard to miss the reference to the *New Deal*, a term used to refer to Roosevelt's welfare state. *International* refers to Canada's "meeting global responsibilities," and *social* entails the government's guarantee to "secur[e] social foundations" (Department of Finance Canada, 2005b, p. 1). *The environment*, a proclaimed pillar of the Third Way (Giddens, 1999), signals a commitment to "the green economy" (Department of Finance Canada, 2005b, p. 1). At the same time, although accountability and the economy have been common themes, *tax relief* no longer figures, nor do specific mentions of finance. Embedded in the 2005 budget is the notion of Canadians' commitment to each other and Canada's responsibility to others in the country and overseas; state strength is conceived as more important than GDP.

Similar to the Third Way, the Canadian Way strongly embraces the "no rights without responsibilities" (Giddens, 2000, p. 165) philosophy. However, we would argue that the Canadian Way goes beyond the Third Way, injecting a distinct Canadian flavour in an effort to revive a sense of nation allegiance. Yet the "New Canadian Nationalism" promoted by the Liberal government differs from other interpretations of Canadian nationalism. Critics have stated that the particular understanding of nation, nation building, and national identity, which were integral in the post-World War II citizenship efforts, is missing from the new version (Brodie, 2002). Although in the previously cited quotation, Chrétien (as cited in Coyne, 2000) mentioned or alluded to diversity and multiculturalism (two feature factors deemed important to Canadians in defining their identity; see Kunz, 2001) values associated with state services are absent. Brodie lamented Canada's abandonment of "the social covenant upon which the postwar social citizenship regime was built" (p. 378). Instead, Canadian values are now alleged to be most suited to a competitive marketplace; at a summit for the Business Council on National Issues, the speaker opened with a tribute to Canadian values, asserting that these values are what will triumph in a competitive world (Carroll, 2002).

As we shall try to demonstrate in the following section, just as in Blair's Third Way, skill building and adult education are considered of vital importance to the Canadian Way.

Adult Learning Under the Canadian Way

In the early 1990s the economistic paradigm started to shape the Canadian discourse on adult and lifelong learning. The federal Speech from the Throne on May 13, 1991 (Government of Canada, 1991), proclaimed, "In the dawning knowledge age, how well we live will depend on how well we learn" (p. 8). Similarly, a 1994 report from the Ontario Premier's Council on Economic Renewal (p. 2) states: "Lifelong learning, therefore, is the key link between our educational and economic strategies as the twenty-first century approaches." The connection made between learning and earning can be seen in titles such as *Lifelong Learning and the New Economy*, a report from the Ontario Premier's Council on Economic Renewal (1994) or in the 2001 Statistics Canada report on participation in adult education-cleverly titled *Learning a Living*. This language reflects the hegemonic dominance of the economic imperative in learning in today's society. The economization of lifelong learning and adult education by government can be understood as a response to the changes taking place in the economy. These changes are becoming a threat not only to capital accumulation, but also to political legitimization and social harmony.

Canada's Innovation Strategy, launched in an aim "to move Canada to the front ranks of the world's most innovative countries" (Government of Canada, 2002a, p. 2) reduces adult education to an instrument for the development of an appropriately skilled workforce. Two key documents emerged from this government strategy: *Knowledge Matters: Skills and Learning for Canadians* (Government of Canada, 2002b) and *Achieving Excellence: Investing in People, Knowledge, and Opportunity* (Government of Canada, 2002a). It is unsurprising that competitiveness, economic growth, and innovation are placed at the forefront of both documents—ideas and terms that are associated with neoliberal conceptions of education. Up-skilling is promoted as a national concern through which to increase competitiveness and productivity. Individuals are urged to undertake their civic duty and participate in lifelong learning or post-secondary education, knowing that Canada's education advantage diminishes as other countries' participation rates rise. The strategy aims to encourage the "individual entrepreneurial spirit" (Government of Canada, 2002b, p. 6), because business and entrepreneurship of individuals are the "key drivers of innovation" (p. 9). These documents do not appeal solely to self-interest, but also to a national interest. The US is often used as a comparison point. We are told that Canadian venture capital remains smaller than its American counterpart, and therefore "we must become more productive and improve at a faster rate than the US" (p. 14). There is the sense that Canadians can band together and if not beat, then challenge the US. The narrow focus on skills framed within a neoliberal ideology may help to explain why the only comparative statistics on participation in adult education presented in the two reports is the percentage of employed adults who participate in employer-sponsored job-related training.

There is a striking contradiction between the language used to introduce the Innovation Strategy (Government of Canada, 2002a) and the framing of adult education within this agenda. The first page of *Knowledge Matters* (Government of Canada, 2002b) contains a speech by Prime Minister Chrétien in which he stressed that Canada should invest not only in technology and innovation, "but also in the Canadian Way" (p. 1). In attempting to reach out to all Canadians, Chrétien proposed that we "create an environment of inclusion" and commit to putting forth an action plan "that includes all of us" (Government of Canada, 2002a, p. 2). However, in the sections on building a world-class workforce, there is little reference or appeal to social cohesion or the creation of an environment of inclusion. No attempt is made to analyze the inequalities in access to and participation in workforce training that are so glaring in all official statistics on participation in adult education (see, e.g., Statistics Canada, 2001).

The "rule of ideas" embedded in the second generation of lifelong learning, and more specifically in the Innovation Strategy (Government of Canada, 2002a), to put it in a Gramscian perspective, is translated into structures and activities as well as values, attitudes, beliefs, and morality and becomes the "common sense" of understanding adult education and adult learning. This understanding is reflected in, among other factors, how the concept of adult education has been operationalized in Statistics Canada surveys. Traditionally, surveys on participation have given equal weight to general and work-related adult education, which is reflected in the list of motivations (Rubenson, 2002). Concerns about the state of civil society in Canada are reflected in the questions, and the list of providers includes NGOs, formal educational institutions, and employers.

The Adult Education and Training Survey (AETS), first conducted in 1986 and most recently in 2003, uses a different logic (see, for example, Statistics Canada, 2001). The AETS used work and employment as the main principle for the construction of the survey. In accordance with the mandate of what was initially Employments and Immigration Canada and later became Human Resources Development Canada, non-work-related adult education has not been of primary concern, and the majority of the survey deals with adult education pursued for work- or career-related reasons. In the questions about providers, civil society-oriented adult education is addressed only under the category *Other*. Following the launch of the Innovation Strategy (Government of Canada, 2002a), with its narrow skills agenda, any reference to non-work-related adult education was completely dropped in the 2003 AETS, which severely restricted the official understanding of adult education in Canada.

Thus, it is not surprising that studies on adults' learning behaviour have confirmed an influence perhaps best characterized as "the long arm of the job," which refers to the fact that participation is increasingly shaped by labour-market conditions. As in other countries (see Bélanger and Valdivieso, 1997), this shift has radically altered the Canadian landscape of adult education since the 1970s. The increase in job-related adult education explains much of the rise in total participation rates from the late 1970s to the early 1990s. Judging from recent surveys, this trend seems to have continued. According to the 1994 International Adult Literacy Survey (OECD, 1995), 86% of Canadians who had participated in adult education mentioned that they had done so for job-related reasons, compared to only 27% who had taken a course or program for personal reasons. The findings from the 2003 Adult Life Skills and Literacy Survey (OECD, 2005) indicate that whereas the proportion of adult learners who reported job-related reasons was unchanged, the figure for personal reasons had dropped to 17% (Rubenson, Desjardins, and Yoon, in press). The data on sources of direct financial support for adult education and training in 2003 further underline the dominance of employment-related adult education. Slightly over half of the participants reported that they had received financial support from their employers, but only 8% reported direct support from government sources, and the remaining 40% relied completely on self-financing (Rubenson et al., in press).

The rhetoric of the Canadian Way may make frequent references to inclusion and equality of opportunity, but the participation data speak a different language. According to the Adult Life Skills and Literacy Survey (OECD, 2005) 26% of those with less than an upper secondary education participated in 2003 compared to 65% among those with a university education. From the perspective of basic capability equality, to use Amartya Sen's (1982) concept, it is problematic that whereas only 22% of those with the lowest level of functional literacy (level 1) participated, the rate was 69% among those with the highest level (4/5). Another disturbing finding is the reduction in government support for those who are outside of the labour market. In 1994, 44% of those outside the labour market who had participated in adult education reported that they received direct government support to study. By 2003 this figure had dropped to 20%. Instead, individuals without stable connections to the labour market have increasing difficulties in receiving adult education. Further, those in managerial jobs are much more likely to benefit from employer-supported training. In 2003, 35% of employees in high-skill service benefited from employer-sponsored education compared to only 6% of those in routine manual jobs (Sen, 1982). In short, inequalities in opportunities to receive adult education and training are shaped by a bifurcated labour market. In its review of adult learning in Canada, the OECD (2002) noted the unequal opportunities of different groups to participate in adult education and stressed the need to address the situation for marginalized groups such as Aboriginal populations, the working poor, and those with restricted literacy capacity. The reviewers reported that moving individuals from low literacy (levels 1 and 2) to level 3, which is deemed necessary to fully participate in the so-called *knowledge society*, realistically takes 12 months of full-time study under the best of conditions. However, according to their observations, very few such possibilities exist for those who really need them the most.

Concluding Comment

Both Canada's Innovation Strategy (Government of Canada, 2002a) and its federal budgets indicate that the government is interested in portraying itself as sensitive to the concerns of the Canadian citizens: Security, equality of opportunity and access, community building, and human and environmental rights have not been abandoned—at least not in discourse. These policy papers point to a desire to promote lifelong learning for a socially responsible Canada, in which the needs of all Canadians are deemed important. At the same time, though, competition and innovation are proclaimed as an integral part of the new Canadian nationalism and its skills agenda. Under this model, subsidies and protection are discouraged and eliminated because "competition not protection encourages innovation" (Government of Canada, 2002b, p. 25). The call to up-skill as a patriotic duty can be seen as in keeping more with an economic than a social democratic model. In the same way in which Robert Reich (1992) urged Americans to become symbolic analysts to ensure America's competitiveness, so too has Canada insisted that it is for the sake of the country that Canadians become "Highly Qualified People" (Government of Canada, 2002a, p. 10). We are sceptical of these efforts at nation building because the social cohesion element appears to have been "tacked on" to an economic framework; the social goal of education is more of an appendage to than a partner with the economic goals. In general, education and training are still based on raising an individual's competitiveness and human capital, as well as his or her capacity for innovation and entrepreneurship. Finally, the presented data on participation reveal a state that has abdicated its responsibilities to lifelong learning for the most vulnerable citizens. Adult learning for *all* does not seem to be the Canadian Way.

References

Ball, S. (1999). Labour, learning, and the economy: A 'policy sociology' perspective. *Cambridge Journal of Education, 29*(2), 195–206.

Bastow, S. and Martin, J. (2003). *Third Way discourse: European ideologies in the 20th century.* Edinburgh: Edinburgh University Press.

Bélanger, P. and Valdivieso, S. (Eds.). (1997). *The emergence of a learning society. Who participates in adult learning?* Oxford: Pergamon Press.

Brodie, J. (1996). New state forms, new political spaces. In R. Boyer and D. Drache (Eds.), *States against markets: The limits of globalization* (pp. 383–398). Montreal, PQ: McGill-Queen's.

Brodie, J. (2002). Citizenship and solidarity: Reflections on the 'Canadian Way.' *Citizenship Studies, 6*(4), 377–394.

Carroll, W. K. (2002). Undoing the end of history: Canada-centred reflections on the challenge of globalization. In Y. Atasoy and W. Carroll (Eds.), *Global shaping and its alternatives* (pp. 33–55). Aurora, ON: Kumarian Press.

Clement, W, and Vosko, L. (Eds.) (2003). *Changing Canada. Political economy and transformation.* Montreal, PQ: McGill-Queen's University Press.

Coyne, A. (2000, June 2). Haven't we been this way before? National Post, pp. A19–A21. Retrieved April 20, 2005, from http://andrewcoyne.com/columns/National-Post/2000/20000602.html

Dave, R. H. (Ed.). (1976). *Foundations of lifelong learning.* Oxford: Pergamon Press.

Department of Finance Canada. (1997). *Building the future for Canadians: Budget 1997.* Retrieved May 1, 2005, from http://www.fin.gc.ca/budget97/binb/bp/bp97e.pdf

Department of Finance Canada. (1999). *Budget in brief: Building today for a better tomorrow.* Retrieved May 1, 2005, from http://www.fin.gc.ca/budget99/binb/binbe.html

Department of Finance Canada. (2000). *Better finances, better lives: Budget plan 2000.* Retrieved May 1, 2005, from http://www.fin.gc.ca/budget00/pdf/bpe.pdf

Department of Finance Canada. (2001). *Securing progress in an uncertain world: Budget 2001.* Retrieved May 1, 2005, from http://www.fin.gc.ca/budget01/pdf/bpe.pdf

Department of Finance Canada. (2003). *Building the Canada we want: Budget plan 2003.* Retrieved May 1, 2005, from http://www.fin.gc.ca/budget03/pdf/bp2003e.pdf

Department of Finance Canada. (2004). *New agenda for achievement: Budget 2004.* Retrieved May 1, 2005, from http://www.fin.gc.ca/budget04/pdf/bp2004e.pdf

Department of Finance Canada. (2005a). *Delivering on commitments: Budget 2005.* Retrieved May 1, 2005, from http://www.fin.gc.ca/budget05/pdf/bp2005e.pdf

Department of Finance Canada. (2005b). *Delivering on commitments: Budget 2005 themes.* Retrieved May 1, 2005, from http://www.fin.gc.ca/budtoce/2005/budliste.htm

European Union. (2000). *A memorandum on lifelong learning.* Brussels: Author.

Field, J. (2003). Civic engagement and lifelong learning: Survey findings on social capital and attitudes towards learning. *Studies in the Education of Adults, 35*(2), 142–157.

Giddens, A. (1999). *The Third Way: The renewal of social democracy.* Cambridge, UK: Polity Press.

Giddens, A. (2000). *The Third Way and its critics.* Cambridge, UK: Polity Press.

Gill, S. (2003). *Power & resistance in the new world order.* New York: Palgrave Macmillan.

Government of Canada. (1991). *Speech from the Throne.* Ottawa, ON: Author.

Government of Canada. (2002a). *Achieving excellence: Investing in people, knowledge, and opportunity.* Retrieved April 27, 2005, from http://www.innovationstrategy.gc.ca

Government of Canada. (2002b). *Knowledge matters: Skills and learning for Canadians.* Retrieved April 27, 2005, from http://www.innovationstrategy.gc.ca

Gustavsson, B. (2002). What do we mean by lifelong learning and knowledge? *International Journal of Lifelong Education, 21*(1), 13–23.

Hall, P. A. and Soskice, D. (2001). *Varieties of capitalism: The institutional foundations of comparative advantage.* Oxford: Oxford University Press.

Kunz, J. L. (2001, November). *Social inclusion and diversity: Fries or stir-fry?* Paper presented at the conference *A New Way of Thinking? Towards a Vision of Social Inclusion,* Ottawa, ON.

Lengrand, P. (1970). *An introduction to lifelong education.* Paris: UNESCO.

Marginson, S. (1993). *Education and public policy in Australia.* Melbourne: Cambridge University Press.

Marginson, S. (1997). *Markets in education.* St. Leonards, Australia: Allen & Unwin.

Martin, I. (2003). Adult education, lifelong learning, and citizenship: Some ifs and buts. *International Journal of Lifelong Learning, 22*(6), 566–579.

McBride, S. (2001). *Paradigm shift: Globalization and the Canadian state.* Halifax, NS: Fernwood.

McKeen, W. and Porter, A. (2003). Politics and transformation: Welfare state restructuring in Canada. In W. Clement and L. Vosko (Eds.), *Changing Canada: Political economy and transformation* (pp. 109–134). Montreal, PQ: McGill-Queen's University Press.

Newman, O. and De Zoysa, R. (2001). *The promise of the Third Way: Globalization and social justice.* New York: Palgrave.

Organisation for Economic Co-operation and Development. (1989). *Education and the economy in a changing society.* Paris: Author.

Organisation for Economic Co-operation and Development. (1995). *Literacy, economy and society.* Paris: Author.

Organisation for Economic Co-operation and Development. (1996). *Lifelong learning for all.* Paris: Author.

Organisation for Economic Co-operation and Development. (2002). *Thematic review on adult learning: Canada: Country note.* Retrieved July 2, 2005, from http://www.cmec.ca/international/oecd/adult.note.pdf

Organisation for Economic Co-operation and Development. (2003). *Beyond rhetoric: Adult learning policies and practices.* Paris: Author.

Organisation for Economic Co-operation and Development. (2005). *Learning a living: First results of the Adult Literacy and Life Skills Survey.* Paris: Author.

Premiers Council on Economic Renewal. (1994). *Lifelong learning and the new economy.* Toronto, ON: Queen's Printer for Ontario.

President of the Treasury Board. (2002). *Report from the president: Canada's Performance 2002: Annual report to Parliament.* Retrieved April 25, 2005, from http://www.tbs-sct.gc.ca/report/govrev/02/dwnld/cp-rc_e.pdf

Reich, R. (1992). *The work of nations: Preparing ourselves for 21st century capitalism.* New York: Vintage.

Rubenson, K. (1999). Adult education and training: The poor cousin: An analysis of OECD reviews of national polices for education. *Scottish Journal of Adult Education, 5*(2), 5–32.

Rubenson, K. (2002). *The Adult Education and Training Survey: Measuring motivation and barriers in the AETS: A critical review.* HRDC Research paper R-02-9-2E. Ottawa, ON: Human Resources Development Canada.

Rubenson, K. (2004). Lifelong learning: A critical assessment of the political project. In P. Alheit, R. Becker-Schmidt, T. Gitz Johansen, L. Ploug, H. Salling Oleson, and K. Rubenson (Eds.). *Shaping an emerging reality: Researching lifelong learning* (pp. 28–47). Roskilde, Denmark: Roskilde University Press.

Rubenson, K., Desjardins, R. and Yoon, E.-S. (in press). *Adult learning in Canada: A comparative perspective. Results from the Adult Literacy and Life Skills Survey.* Ottawa ON: Statistics Canada.

Sen, A. (1982). *Choice, welfare, and measurement.* Cambridge, MA: MIT Press.

Statistics Canada. (2001). *A report on adult education and training in Canada: Learning a living.* Ottawa, ON: Author.

Watkins, M. (2003). Politics in the time and space of globalization. In W. Clement and L. Vosko (Eds.), *Changing Canada: Political economy and transformation* (pp. 3–24). Montreal, PQ: McGill-Queen's University Press.

15

Work, Learning, and Adult Education in Canada

Tara J. Fenwick

Workplace learning is fast becoming a central topic in fields that have little else in common. You can find its literature in journals of economics, innovation, organization science, management/ business studies, health care, and human-resource development. What is particularly distinct in adult education literature is that work studies tend to focus on the well-being and development of workers rather than on creating competitive and profitable organizations. Particularly in Canadian research and practice in the workplace, strongly rooted in our histori-cal adult education tradition of radical communitarianism, dialogue, and critical labour education, the general assumption is that workers' well-being cannot be collapsed into organizational productivity or shareholder benefit. But is it possible to foster workers' rights and improve working life through workplace learning? This chapter explores this issue and examines directions of practice with special attention to Canadian contexts.

Canadian historian Michael Welton (1995) has long promoted a vision for "developmental" workplaces, rooted in Habermasian ideals where learning is an "extension of communicative action into systemic domains" (p. 144). He holds that workplace education can foster three key objectives of critical learning: collective autonomy, self-clarity, and the capacity to defend one's rights. In a similar vein, David Livingstone and Peter Sawchuk (2004) believe that "learning should enhance working people's individual and collective agency in the social world and also in the process of repre-senting that world" (p. 28). From this perspective the purpose of workplace learning is a moral one; that is, to enable flexible, expansive, integrated persons and communities. In workplaces people should have the opportu-nity to learn to *participate* fully, meaningfully, fairly, and compassionately in existing systems and to *resist* when those systems become overcontrol-ling, harmful, or dehumanizing.

Thus workplaces are well recognized as significant developmental sites for adult learning, change, and resistance. This is perhaps the main reason that workplace learning deserves due recognition by adult educators as a distinct field of research, theory, and practice. But *workplace* misleadingly signifies a stable, unitary, and identifiable location. Work organizations are only one type of site. Work unfolds differently in home, community, or cyber sites or distributed across multiple sites. It can be paid, unpaid, or both. It can be structured through organizational, client, personal, or family relationships. That learning involving people, objects, and systems occurs in all of these configurations is generally accepted. The questions that interest most educators are, *What* is learned that is developmental (benefits the workers doing the learning and improves their conditions), and *how* can developmental learning in the workplace be enabled?

Definition and Contexts

Theoretical orientations emerging in adult education workplace learning research are wide ranging: interpretive-constructivist, participative, critical (including historical materialist, poststructural, antiracist, and some feminist theories), psychoanalytic, and systems (including enactivist, activity, and complexity theory) orientations. Notions of "useful knowledge" differ among these and affect how workplace learning is understood. For example, where innovation is valued, the study of learning may focus on disturbances, emergence of the novel, rhythms of change (episodic or continuous), and change magnitude (adaptive or generative). These learning constructs differ from those employed when "useful knowledge" is understood as preservation and diffusion of existing ideas or as interruption of tradition and resistance to naturalized practices of exploitation or inequity.

Definitions of what comprises learning or cognition also shift according to the unit of analysis. A focus on individuals might explain processes in acquiring concepts, developing expertise or practical intelligence, or transforming beliefs. A community focus might examine social learning processes, construction of cultural narratives, or forms of knowledge production and change that occur in the group. Here, *workplace learning* might signify change in consciousness or behaviour that expands human possibilities for flexible and creative action and occurs primarily in activities and contexts of work. The assumption is that learning and knowledge associated with work are practice based, embedded in material and social activity, highly contextual, fluid, and not necessarily connected with intentionality or educational initiatives.

Workplace learning as an analytic category also deserves scrutiny. Are learning processes in work so different from learning in community, classroom, or everyday life that they deserve distinction? David Beckett and Paul Hager (2002), in their postmodern study of learning and work, claim that they do. Unlike instructional or everyday contexts, workplace learning occurs in the press of "hot action" (p. 77): Decisions must be made and action taken without certainty or prior knowledge, often in contested terrain with serious consequences. In fact, the study of learning in and through work opens up alternative approaches to understanding experiential learning processes and their links to social relations, identity, and language. Finally, workplace learning as an embodied, social phenomenon challenges the academy's authority over the legitimation of knowledge. The action-based messiness and high-stakes politics of learning in work demand new explanations of adult learning that open wide our conceptual traditions.

Themes in Workplace Learning Research

Issues of workplace learning begin with contexts and pressures. Globalization has accelerated competition among corporations. As they jostle for position to meet changing consumer tastes, increasing pressure for specialization has created the need for innovation to produce endless variation in customized goods and services. At the same time, international standards have helped homogenize and instrumentalize "method" and contributed to an obsession with accountability in work. The information and communication technology revolution has transformed modes of doing business, the nature of services and products, the meaning of time in work, and the processes of learning. Flexibility is endemic to job structures, skill demands, pay, and learning. Workers are expected to accept constant change as a given, to forego expectation of stable employment and organizational loyalty, and to assume personal responsibility for adapting to organizations' changing needs for skills and labour.

At the organizational level, increasing examples of "post-Fordist workplaces" are appearing where people are inculcated into new regimes of truth: roles and textual practices of self-directed teams, centralized missions and values, and technologies associated with "learning communities." Hierarchical power structures and divisions of labour continue to exist, along with the pedagogic practices embedded in time-space arrangements of flexible work. As Canadian commentators have argued, knowledge work is not typical of most jobs, and companies are not primarily in the knowledge business, despite their claims to the contrary (Bratton, Helms Mills, Pyrch, and Sawchuk, 2004, p. 8). Indeed, the vast increase in jobs has been in part-time, low-income, and low-skilled work. Thus the workplace is highly political. Ebullient discourses of innovation and flexibility circulate among workers' everyday learning struggles, anxieties, boredom, contradictory allegiances, and knowing-in-action. Neoliberal policies induce workers to be more entrepreneurial and self-reliant individuals—to make choices and take charge of their learning—with little acknowledgment of gendered and raced work and learning conditions. Much of the "progressive," learning-orientated HR strategy evident in the latter half of the twentieth century has disappeared (p. 38). Union strength has declined steadily, even though the labour educators' call to solidarity and consciousness raising is still evident.

Among the vast issues bubbling in current workplace learning literature, four are selected for discussion here. These four, I would argue, are critical for adult educators in Canada: Their exploration in research and practice may have the greatest potential for enhancing working people's individual and collective agency in the social world.

Lifelong Learning Amidst Changing Forms of Work

In Canada the policy focus is on upgrading workers' skills. This has been prompted by the continuous changes in work structures and technology described in the preceding section, coupled with rhetoric about skilled labour shortages and skill needs for the new economy. Citing concerns for "untapped potential, . . . increasing the participation of those who have been excluded, [and ensuring] a productive economy" (HRSDC, 2005, para 5), Canada introduced a wide-ranging individualistic *Essential Skills* agenda. This initiative develops and measures nine skill areas that have been declared "essential" for all occupations. The problem with this focus on training workers' skills is threefold. First, workers' effective participation relies more on complex interplays of contextual practices, individual meanings of the activity, and organizational politics than it does on individual "skills"; besides, a skills approach is a fragmented, gendered, and inaccurate way to understand human knowledge and learning processes (Jackson, 1997). Second, as Livingstone and Associates (1999) showed in their major national study, workers are in fact overtrained and underemployed; the main problem is that organizations do not seem able or willing to provide workers with opportunities to apply the vast unrecognized skills and knowledge that they have already developed. Third, there is no empirical evidence that shows that basic skill training corresponds positively with organizational productivity or even to workers' employability. In the first instance, organizations have demonstrated that they rely on measures of eliminating workers and increasing workloads more than on worker skills to increase their competition. In the second, "excluded" workers' struggles to enter or move up in the labour marker are wrapped up with forces of racism, sexism, classism, and ableism (Cohen, 2003). Worker training that ignores gender, race, and class will not improve employability.

On this theme, Sawchuk (2003) studied the technology learning practices of workers that were integrated with everyday life and mediated by artefacts such as computer hardware and organizational settings. He presents a "working-class standpoint" that opposes even while it accepts managerial control and that often copes through subversion. Sawchuk found that for working-class people, computer technology is a "key signifier" for workers' deepest class-based desires and fears: the sense of losing control and being left behind in an inevitable techno-obsessive world, the frustrations of trying to figure out capricious computer processes, or the trials of purchasing the "right" computer on limited incomes. Yet working-class learning thrives in informal networks, what Sawchuk calls "solidaristic networks" (p. 123): where mutuality and group orientations within stable working-class communities produce knowledge in everyday computer learning. It is here that Sawchuk found an "enormous surplus" of knowledge production capacity as well as emancipatory potential for working-class people.

Critical workplace learning is often envisioned as radical transformation among workers: empowerment purposed towards workplace reform. Transformation is positioned in opposition to reproduction, where learning accommodates workers to exploitive, hierarchical structures; subjugates people; and reproduces existing (inequitable) power relations. However, this traditional dualism may be overly simplistic. In studying immigrant women garment workers who were learning ICT skills, Mirchandani, Ng, Sangha, Rawlings, and Coloma-Moya (2002) show that learning can be simultaneously reproductive and transformative. Empowerment of workers needs to be understood from different standpoints and needs to appreciate both how reproductive/transformative learnings are entwined and what workers themselves want to learn. In this vein of understanding critical workplace learning as multi-faceted and internally contradictory, Church, Shragge, Fontan, and Ng (2000) draw attention to learning in work as combining organizational learning, definition of self, and solidarity learning. Solidarity in their findings is not necessarily confined to political learning; that is, workers' engaging in social action to challenge their status. In fact, Church et al. argue that solidarity is visible when workers such as immigrant women learn to develop a collective identity and share strategies for negotiating their lives as non-English-speaking immigrants.

A promising area that is developing in workplace research examines how learning is shaped by particular written texts—such as documents, policies, record-keeping forms, or employee growth plans—in changing workplace environments For example, Lesley Farrell (2001) analysed such documents to determine how texts standardize what counts as knowledge and thus control the work practices and working relations of people employed. This sort of analysis reveals that taken-for-granted notions of learner, learning process, skill, and work activity are highly constructed and much more dynamic and interwoven than we sometimes acknowledge.

Subjectivities Developing in Work

Researchers have used life-history methods to understand connections among individuals' learning at work, knowledge development, identity, and social relations. Some have focused on professionals' shape-shifting and others on working-class, racialized, and hybrid identities and knowledge. Shauna Butterwick (2003) examined women's histories of learning and work as information technologists and found these marked by oppressive pressures to "keep up" with rapid knowledge changes, in a difficult weave of formal and informal learning (often unrecognized), gender, race, immigrant, and class locations. Stephen Billett and Margaret Somerville (2004) described masculinities produced in mining communities and subjectivities created by work in aged care institutions. They also examined explored identities that emerge in the relational dependency between the individual and social agency in work situations among hairdressers, professionals, and adult educators. In these cases, work cultures shaped particular identities, but people learned to resist and reconfigure these into more expansive subjectivities.

Questions are raised about *limitations* and *possibilities* afforded to human identity by workplace conditions, activities, and relationships and how people learn their way through these. What identity categories are considered "normal" and "deviant" or "other than normal" in a workplace? How do people "learn" coherent identities amidst the fragmentation, anxiety, and constant change of their work conditions? How do people learn to position themselves and to construct, negotiate, or resist particular subjectivities in particular workplaces? Further, psychoanalytic perspectives have helped to theorize the dynamic of desire in workplace learning. As Britzman (1998) writes, "The dreary language of excellence, expertise, and competence" (p. 42) obscures the dynamical qualities of love and hate centred in learning work and life and ignores real struggles for subjectivity that initiate internal conflicts in which learning and development erupt.

Processes of Practice-Based (Informal) Learning

Some continue to view workplace learning as fundamentally driven by reflection-on-action, in the "swamp" of uncertain, ambiguous, contradictory dilemmas of practice. Reflection during and after the "doing" supposedly transforms experience into knowledge, which can then be represented and generalized to new contexts. Critics have maintained that this emphasis on reflection is simplistic and reductionist, overemphasizes rational thought, and understates the unpredictable social tangles of everyday practice in which people develop.

Practice-based (or participative) perspectives of workplace learning are concerned instead with what kinds of learning are embedded in particular sociocultural activities, tools, and communities in which people participate. They may ask, How do particular practices emerge in particular communities of work? What subjectivities and knowledge are produced by these practices? And more to the point for practicing educators, how can practices be reconfigured to enable more expansive environments and subjectivities? Beckett and Hager (2002), for example, focus on developing know-how in the workplace, particularly through making practical judgments. Their model rests on five principles: daily work is non-routine decision making; problems must be solved efficaciously; reflection occurs in decisional action; the immediate must be addressed in judgments; and judgments are basically connative, emotional, and ethical. Stephen Billett (2001) developed a useful model of guidance (direct, indirect, and environmental) that moves workers towards fuller participation in workplace activity and hence to more comprehensive and critical knowledge as actors in their community of practice. Beckett's (2001) theory of work learning is most interested in workers' intentions. Valuable working knowledge is "anticipative action" (p. 83) in particular situations, a back-and-forth dynamic between means and ends as a worker makes judgments in the "hot action" (p. 77) of work situations. Individuals' life histories and subjectivities are not abandoned, but theorized in intersection with social patterns of participation.

Long popular in Nordic research of workplace learning, but just recently emerged in Canadian research (Sawchuk, 2003), is cultural-historical activity theory (CHAT). Here, learning is viewed as change in a community's joint action. The community's activity is shaped by its rules and cultural norms, division of labour and power, and "mediating artefacts" (language, tools, technologies) that it uses to pursue the object—a problem at which activity is directed. Learning occurs as the collective construction and resolution of tensions or contradictions that occur within this activity system. Unlike other practice-based systemic perspectives of workplace learning, Sawchuk maintains that CHAT retains its Marxist influences in its recognition of the inherent contradictions in capitalist work systems based on labour exchange and in its analysis of the historical emergence of particular practices and ideologies.

In organizational studies and increasingly in educational study in Canada, complexity theory is also gaining acceptance as a useful way to understand how activity, knowledge, and communities emerge together in the process of workplace learning. Individual interactions and meanings form part of the workplace context itself: They are interconnected systems nested within the larger systems in which they act (Davis and Sumara, 2001). As workers are influenced by symbols and actions in which they participate, they adapt and learn. As they do so, their behaviours and thus their effects upon the systems connected with them change. The focus is not on the components of experience (which other perspectives might describe in fragmented terms: person, experience, tools, and activity), but on the *relationships* that bind them together. Workplace learning is thus cast as continuous invention and exploration in complex systems.

Critics suggest that such practice-based studies of workplace learning bypass questions of politics and power relations: Who is excluded from the construction of knowledge in a community of practice, what dysfunctional or exploitive practices are perpetuated in communities of practice, and what hierarchical relations in the workplace reproduce processes of privilege and prejudice? At issue is the extent to which socio-cultural learning theories, including notions of communities of practice, complex adaptive systems, or even CHAT, suppress or enable core questions about whose interests are served by workplace learning. In adult education any discussion of work-learning processes and how to facilitate these only makes sense within, on the one hand, an overall understanding of the political economy driving the changes that erode working life and workers' rights and, on the other, a clear purpose related to workers' own needs.

Justice, Equity, and Human Rights in Workplace Learning

Although concern for workers' well-being often drives adult educators' inquiry into workplace learning, there is considerable debate about how to facilitate this in equitable, non-exploitive terms. Worker "empower-ment," once a rallying cry for transforming workplaces into democratic learning communities, has become a target of critique. Many wonder just how democratic organizations can pretend to be when they commodify workers' knowledge and colonize hearts and minds as capital resources. Joe Kincheloe (1999) shows how current organizing of work and workplace education cultivates inequality by widening the chasm between workers and management.

Case studies demonstrate that even rosy "learning organization" initia-tives are wielded for worker subjugation and control (Fenwick, 2001). The learning organization discourse of popular literature positions employees as perpetually in deficit, in danger of being "left behind." They are balanced on a precipice of risk because in a climate of continuous inno-vation and change they can never be grounded in a sense of expertise or stability, but must constantly prove their knowledge "value" to the organization's changing needs. They are urged to learn more, learn better, and learn faster—with little personal control over what is to be learned or why. Learning organization technologies of "open" dialogue, critical reflection, personal growth plans, and so on render employees' hearts and minds visible, subject to constant assessment and discipline. All of this is conducted through the rhetoric of trust, relationship, and community that usually does not acknowledge its own contradictions.

Gender issues are exacerbated in the "learning organization" agenda. Women continue to confront gendered work knowledges and training structures in organizations based on patriarchal values, male-oriented communication patterns, and family-unfriendly schedules. New learning expectations often create task and paperwork overload that individuals are expected to absorb. Women in particular are often expected to nurture the close relationships and community that organizations want, to mentor others, and to display cheerfulness (Mojab and Gorman, 2003). Yet the learning most valued and supported in organizations tends to be related to leadership development, knowledge creation, and organizational growth—in professional/managerial jobs where women continue to be underrepresented. Meanwhile, Canadian women who are new immi-grants and women of colour are overrepresented in precarious, contingent employment such as call-centre, food-service, and home-based work. Here training is almost nil, wages are too low or hours too variable to allow individuals' part-time study, and government training programs, funded for the unemployed, are off limits because they hold jobs.

Adult educators need to address individuals' access to learning oppor-tunities in work, particularly that of vulnerable workers. We need to examine forms of exclusion that circulate in the knowledge and language of a workplace community. We need to ask, What forms of knowledge and learning experiences, and whose, are most valued as "useful"? What identities are recognized and rewarded in the workplace? How do existing policies and popular ideas about work and learning reinforce social and economic inequities? Through what processes do people critically inter-rogate, interrupt, resist exclusive organizational practices, and agitate for more inclusive policies and practices?

Implications for Practice and Research

Within these issues, then, adult education focuses on analysing the nature, processes, and influences on learning that unfold through work activities in particular socio-cultural environments. Educators have experi-mented with different pedagogical practices to enable learning that avoid the limitations of conventional teacher–classroom pedagogies: guided practice, scaffolding, emancipatory action learning, storytelling, cross-functional projects, collective biographies, amplified system disturbances, and manipulated material space to encourage conversations. Critical pedagogy in work has a long history in Canadian union education (Taylor, 2001), with particular emphasis on workplace literacy and helping workers to critically analyze workplace power relations; for example, through popular education approaches.

Future research in workplace learning will be most fruitful if it continues to blend theoretical perspectives that embrace the sociology and political economy of work, cultural analyses of workplace practice, human narra-tives, and the psychology of learning and reflection. Research also is needed to generate more multi-faceted methods for observing and analyzing people's learning in practice-based activity. What questions may guide scholarly exploration focused on workplace learning in the near future? Symes and McIntyre (2000) offer the following:

1. What is the nature of working knowledge? And how does work-based learning challenge our existing theories of knowledge?
2. How is knowledge formed and learned at work?
3. How is working identity configured in the learning process?
4. What are the conditions that bring about work-based learning?
5. How adequate are our explanations of "new modes" of contem-porary work-knowledge production, such as knowledge situated in communities of practice?
6. What should be the role and practice of educators in light of these understandings of working knowledge and work-based learning?

Above all, as researchers and educators we need to be clear about our purposes and allegiances when we take up one of these questions. Perhaps somewhere a balance can be struck between employees' and employers' interests in creating the goals of workplace learning, moving towards what Kincheloe (1999) envisions as productive, sustainable environments supporting meaningful work and strong communities. Such a balance is riddled with political negotiations among diverse ideologies, languages, and values. But as Garrick (1999) suggests, "The most useful ways of theo-rizing workplace learning tolerate and recognize the productive potential of diversity and ambiguity, while at the same time enabling skill development and the creation of new knowledge" (p. 225).

References

Beckett, D. (2001). Hot action at work: Understanding 'understanding' differently. In T. Fenwick (Ed.), *Socio-cultural understandings of workplace learning* (pp. 76–87). San Francisco: Jossey-Bass.

Beckett, D. and Hager, P. (2002). *Life, work, and learning: Practice in postmodernity.* London: Routledge.

Billett, S. (2001). *Learning in the workplace: Strategies for effective practice.* Sydney, Australia: Allen & Unwin.

Billett, S. and Somerville, M. (2004). Transformations at work: Identity and learning. *Studies in Continuing Education, 26*(2), 309–326.

Bratton, J., Helms Mills, J., Pyrch, T., and Sawchuk, P. (2004). *Workplace learning: A critical introduction.* Aurora, ON: Garamond.

Britzman, D. (1998). *Lost subjects, contested objects: Towards a psychoanalytic theory of learning.* New York: State University of New York Press.

Butterwick, S. (2003). Missing in action: Women's alternate and informal IT learning. *Proceedings of the 'Changing Face of Workplace Learning Conference,' Work and Learning Network.* Edmonton: University of Alberta.

Church, K., Shragge, E., Fontan, J. M., and Ng., R. (2000). While no one is watching: "Social learning" among people who are excluded from the labour market. In P. Sawchuk (Ed.), *Researching Work and Learning conference proceedings* (pp. 241–249). Calgary: University of Calgary.

Cohen, M. G. (2003). Training the excluded for work: Access and equity for women, immigrants, First Nations, youth, and people with low income. Vancouver: University of British Columbia Press.

Davis, B. and Sumara, D. (2001). Learning communities: Understanding the workplace as a complex system. In T. Fenwick (Ed.), *Socio-cultural understandings of workplace learning* (pp. 88–97). San Francisco: Jossey-Bass.

Farrell, L. (2001). The 'new word order': Workplace education and the textual practice of economic globalisation. *Pedagogy, Culture, and Society, 9,* 59–77.

Fenwick, T. (2001). Questioning the concept of the learning organization. In C. Parrie, M. Preedy and D. Scott (Eds.), *Knowledge, power, and learning* (pp. 74–88). London: Paul Chapman/Sage.

Garrick, J. (1999). The dominant discourses of learning at work. In D. Boud and J. Garrick (Eds.), *Understanding learning at work* (pp. 216–231). New York: Routledge.

HRSDC. (2005). *Essential skills: Ten myths we shouldn't believe about essential skills.* Retrieved October 13, 2005, from http://www15.hrdc-drhc.gc.ca/english/general/Myths_e.asp

Jackson, N. (1997). Reframing the discourse of skill. In J. Kenway, K. Tregenza and P. Watkins (Eds.), *Vocational education today: Topical issues* (pp. 121–128). Geelong, Australia: Deakin University, Deakin Centre for Education and Change.

Kincheloe, J. (1999). *How do we tell the workers? The socio-economic foundations of work and vocational education.* Boulder, CO: Westview Press.

Livingstone, D. W. (1999). *The education-jobs gap: Underemployment or economic democracy.* Toronto, ON: Garamond Press.

Livingstone, D. W., & Sawchuk, P. H. (2004). *Hidden knowledge: Organized labor in the information age.* Boston: Rowan and Littlefield.

Mirchandani, K., Ng, R., Sangha, J., Rawlings, T., and Coloma-Moya, N. (2002). *Ambivalent learning: Racialized barriers to computer access for immigrant contingent workers* [Working paper, NALL Project, OISE/UT]. Unpublished manuscript.

Mojab, S. and Gorman, R. (2003). Women and consciousness in the "learning organization": Emancipation or exploitation? *Adult Education Quarterly, 53*(4), 228–241.

Sawchuk, P. H. (2003). *Adult learning and technology in working-class life.* Cambridge, UK: Cambridge University Press.

Symes, C. and McIntyre, J. (Eds). (2000). *Working knowledge: Higher education and the new vocationalism.* Buckingham: SRHE and Open University Press.

Taylor, J. (2001). *Union learning: Canadian labour education in the twentieth century.* Toronto, ON: Thompson Educational.

Welton, M. R. (1995). In defense of the lifeworld: A Habermasian approach to adult learning. In M. R. Welton (Ed.), *In defense of the lifeworld: Critical perspectives on adult learning* (pp. 127–156). New York: State University of New York Press.

16

Adult Education in the Changing Context of Immigration: New Challenges in a New Era

Shibao Guo

anada is an immigrant country. Immigration played an important role in transforming Canada into an ethno-culturally diverse and economically prosperous nation. The 2001 Census of Canada (Statistics Canada, 2003b) reveals that as of May 15, 2001, 18.4% of Canada's total population were born outside the country and that 13.4% identified themselves as visible minorities. Furthermore, according to the Ethnic Diversity Survey (Statistics Canada, 2003a), almost one quarter (23%) of Canada's total population of 22.4 million people aged 15 years and older were identified as first-generation Canadians who were born outside Canada. The latter number indicates that a large proportion of the new immigrants are adults.

The changing demographics in Canada have posed new opportunities for development as well as challenges for adult education. On the one hand, as new citizens of Canada, immigrants need educational programs to help them upgrade their language, knowledge, and skills. On the other hand, many of the recent immigrants are highly educated professionals who come with a wealth of knowledge and skills. One of the most outstanding challenges concerning new immigrants pertains to the non-recognition of immigrants' international credentials and work experience. A number of studies have revealed that many highly educated immigrants experience deskilling or decredentializing of their prior learning and work experience in Canada. In this regard adult education has been criticized for failing to build an inclusive education and accept differences as valid and valuable expressions of the human experience.

This chapter examines the politics of difference as manifested in nonrecognition of international credentials and prior work experience of immigrant professionals in Canada. It is organized into four parts. It begins with a review of contextual information pertaining to immigration in Canada. The second section examines studies pertinent to nonrecognition of international credentials and prior work experience in Canada. Third, the chapter analyzes the current debate on differences and knowledge, in particular relating to how these factors are perceived and treated by mainstream Canadian society in the process of international credential recognition. Finally, this chapter concludes that assessment and recognition of prior learning as political acts. Although certain forms of knowledge are legitimized as valid, the learning and work experience of internationally trained professionals are often treated as suspicious or inferior. This chapter draws on perspectives from critical theory and postmodernism and examines the relationship between knowledge and power.

Canada's Immigration Past and Present

Overview of Canadian Immigration Polices

Immigration has always played a central role in the nation building of receiving countries. Economic and demographic interests of the receiving nation are usually the driving force behind immigration. For example, in the nineteenth century massive immigration was used as a strategy to populate and develop Western Canada. In addition, immigration has served as a means of social and ideological control. In deciding who are the most desirable and admissible, the state sets the parameters for the social, cultural, and symbolic boundaries of the nation, as manifested in historically racist Canadian immigration policies. From the Confederation of Canada in 1867 to the 1960s, the selection of immigrants in Canada was based on racial background, with the British and Western Europeans being deemed the most "desirable" citizens, whereas Asians and Africans were considered "unassimilable" and therefore "undesirable." For example, based on superficial racial and cultural differences, the Canadian government imposed a head tax on the Chinese in 1885 to keep them out and legislated a restrictive *Chinese Immigration Act* in 1923 that virtually prohibited Chinese immigration into Canada until its repeal in 1947. After the Second World War, Canadian immigration policy continued to be "highly restrictive" despite external and internal pressures for an open-door policy (Knowles, 1997).

In the mid-1960s Canada was experiencing the greatest postwar boom in its history (Whitaker, 1991, p. 18). Skilled labour was required to help build this expansionary economy, but Europe, as the traditional source of immigrants, was not able to meet these needs because of the labour demands of its own economic recovery. Thus the Canadian government turned its recruitment efforts to traditionally restricted areas—Third World countries. In 1967 the Liberal government introduced a point system that based the selection of immigrants on their "education, skills and resources" (p. 19) rather than on their racial and religious backgrounds. According to Whitaker, this new system represented "an historic watershed" and "did establish at the level of formal principle that Canadian immigration policy is 'colour blind'" (p. 19).

Whitaker pointed out further that the point system was generally successful in reversing the pattern of immigration to Canada away from Europe and towards Asia and other Third World countries. By the mid-1970s there were more immigrants arriving from the Third World than from the developed world. The largest number came from Asia, followed by the Caribbean, Latin America, and Africa. Between 1968 and 1992, 35.7% of 3.7 million immigrants admitted came from Asia; and 58% of 1.8 million immigrants who arrived in Canada between 1991 and 2001 were also from the same region (Li, 2003; Statistics Canada, 2003b).

Immigrant selection practices since the mid-1990s have given more weight to education and skills, favouring economic immigrants over family-class immigrants and refugees. As Li (2003) noted, this new shift was based on the assumption that economic immigrants brought more human capital than family-class immigrants and refugees did, and therefore were more valuable and desirable. According to Li, economic-class immigrants made up more than half of all immigrants admitted throughout the late-1990s. Among them a considerable number are highly educated professionals, particularly scientists and engineers. In 2000, of the total 227,209 immigrants and refugees admitted, 23% (52,000 individuals) were admitted as skilled workers (Couton, 2002). Despite Canada's preference for highly skilled immigrants and despite the fact that these professionals bring significant human capital resources to the Canadian labour force, a number of studies have shown that many of these highly educated immigrant professionals experience barriers to having their international credentials and work experience recognized after they arrive in Canada (Basran and Zong, 1998; Henry, Tator, Mattis, and Rees, 2000; Krahn, Derwing, Mulder, and Wilkinson, 2000; Li, 2001; Mojab, 1999; Reitz, 2001).

International Credentials Assessment: Mapping the Process

Statistics Canada (2003b) defined *international credentials* as any formal education higher than a high school diploma, including professional or technical qualifications and any other degrees, diplomas, or certificates received outside Canada. In Canada there is no central place where immigrants can go to have their credentials evaluated. Depending on the purpose of the evaluation, immigrants may need to approach one or all of the following organizations: (a) provincial and territorial credential assessment services, (b) regulatory or professional bodies, (c) educational institutions, and (d) employers. The outcomes of the evaluation may serve one of the following purposes: general employment, studying in Canada, and professional certification or licensing in Canada.

Given the diversity of assessment and licensing bodies, no generalizations can be made regarding the national criteria for evaluating foreign qualifications. Reviewing the requirements of a number of assessment and licensing bodies in Canada, I found that the evaluation of international credentials usually considers the following criteria: level and type of learning, duration of study program, status of issuing institutions, the education system of the country concerned, and authenticity, currency, relevance, trustworthiness, and transferability of the credential. Couton (2002) maintained that immigrant professionals may encounter a number of barriers in the process of having their international credentials recognized. First, poor information on accreditation procedures is a major barrier to be faced. Second, there is no national body responsible for the evaluation of international credentials. Third, there is no agreed-upon national standard. Educational and professional standards vary by province.

The Social Construction of Immigrant

At the centre of this analysis are immigrants themselves. It is important to review what this term means to us. According to Li (2003), the notion of *immigrant* is socially constructed. He argued that it is often associated with people of non-White origin. In the context of Canada, early settlers came mainly from Europe, and only since the immigrant point system was introduced in 1967 has Canada attracted an increasing number of immigrants from Third World countries, notably those in Asia and Africa. Descendents of early European settlers, now long-time Canadians, do not think of themselves as immigrants. As Li put it, the term immigrant becomes a codified word for people of colour who come from a different racial and cultural background, who do not speak fluent English, and who work in lower position jobs. Li contended that the social construction of immigrant uses skin colour as the basis for social marking. These individuals' real and alleged differences are claimed to be incompatible with the cultural and social fabric of the "traditional" Canada, and they are therefore deemed undesirable. Immigrants are also often blamed for creating urban social problems and racial and cultural tensions in the receiving society. The social construction of immigrant places uneven expectations on immigrants to conform over time to the norms, values, and traditions of the receiving society.

A New Challenge in a New Era: Deskilling and Discounting

Wanner (2001) claimed that nonrecognition of international credentials and prior work experience is the "central immigration issue of the new century not only in Canada, but in all postindustrial societies receiving immigrants" (p. 417). In a study of 404 Indo- and Chinese-Canadian immigrant professionals in Vancouver, Basran and Zong (1998) reported that only 18.8% of their respondents worked as professionals (doctors, engineers, school/university teachers, and other professionals) after immigrating to Canada. They also discovered that the most important factor in their inaccessibility to professional occupations and the resulting downward social mobility was the nonrecognition or devaluation of their international credentials. Basran and Zong further pointed out that immigrant professionals are usually caught up in a double jeopardy. In the first place, nonrecognition of international credentials prevents them from accessing professional jobs in Canada and acquiring Canadian work experience, which subsequently makes it difficult for them to be qualified for professional jobs.

Highly educated refugees also encounter similar barriers in Canada. In a study of 525 refugees, Krahn et al. (2000) demonstrated that refugees with high educational and occupational qualifications experienced downward occupational mobility after arriving in Canada. A lack of recognition of prior learning and work experience was identified as the top contributing factor to this downward mobility. Other factors include a shortage of Canadian references and work experience, English language difficulties, and employer discrimination. Krahn et al. particularly emphasized that in the process of recognizing international credentials, professional associations often function as labour market shelter. By retaining strict control over the adjudication of international credentials, these associations restrict competition for well-paying professional jobs.

The situation for immigrant women is even worse. Many (e.g., Gannage, 1999; Ng, 1996) have argued that in the labour force, the category of *immigrant women* has served to commodify them to employers, reinforcing their class position in providing cheap, docile labour to the state under exploitive conditions that are often permeated with racism and sexism. In her research with immigrant women, Mojab (1999) found that skilled immigrant women faced deskilling in Canada. She maintained that advanced capitalism simultaneously creates and destroys jobs and requires both the skilling and deskilling of the labour force. Highly skilled immigrant women are usually seen as a potential source of manual labour. They face unemployment or are pressured into nonskilled jobs. Mojab also argued that access to the job market is not determined by education alone, but is constrained by other factors such as gender, national origin, race, and ethnicity. Finally, she pointed out that systemic racism and ethnicism affect immigrants differently. Women from advanced countries (such as the US, Australia, Britain, or New Zealand) are treated differently from those originating in the Third World countries. Only those with financial resources at their disposal can afford the Canadianization of their experience.

How does the nonrecognition of international credentials and prior work experience affect immigrants? Using data from the 1996 Canadian census micro data, both Li (2001) and Reitz (2001) found that one important impact that it has is on immigrants' earnings. Li compared the earnings for four groups: native-born Canadian degree holders, immigrant Canadian degree holders, immigrant mixed-education degree holders, and immigrant free-degree holders. He contended that immigrants' credentials carry a penalty compared to those of native-born Canadians. Meanwhile, Reitz assessed the annual immigrant earnings deficit caused by skill underutilization at $2.4 billion. According to Reitz, immigrants receive a much smaller earnings premium for their education: on average, half that of native-born Canadians. He also maintained that immigrant men and women receive about one-half to two-thirds as much benefit from work experience as the native-born of the same gender do. Another important finding from this analysis is that there are wide variations in earnings among immigrant origin groups. In general, immigrant men from origin groups outside Europe earn anywhere between 15% and 25% less than most of the European origin groups. However, origin-group earning differences for immigrant women are much less than those for men. Reitz further noted that if international education explains part of the origin-group earning differences, it means that Canadian employers treat schooling in certain countries of origin—mostly in Asia, Africa, the Caribbean, and Latin America—differently from that in other, mostly European, countries of origin. This finding reveals that the issue is more severe for immigrants with qualifications from developing countries.

Discussion: The Politics of Difference

The above discussion demonstrates that many organizations in Canadian society, including government agencies, professional associations, employers, and educational institutions, play a role in the devaluation of international credentials and prior work experience. As a consequence, immigrant individuals and families, along with Canadian society as a whole, have suffered severe impacts. Although some of the studies have suggested causes leading to the denigration of international credentials, many have failed to take us further to question the root of this issue. At this stage many critical questions still remain. We still need to find an answer to the questions, Why do such inequities occur in a democratic society such as Canada, where democratic principles are upheld and where immigrants are "welcome"? Furthermore, since numerous studies reported this issue a number of years ago, the situation has not improved much. Another question is, What prevents us from moving forward? Drawing on perspectives from critical theory and postmodernism, I offer the following observations in an attempt to provide a more in-depth understanding of this issue. The first two considerations pertain to our misperceptions of difference and knowledge; the last two relate to the way we approach the assessment and recognition of international credentials under the auspices of positivism and liberal universalism.

Misperceptions of Difference and Knowledge

First, nonrecognition of international credentials and prior work experience can be attributed to the deficit model of difference. In a multicultural society such as Canada, one of the articulations of such a society lies in its commitment to cultural pluralism. However, a number of researchers (Dei, 1996; Fleras and Elliott, 2002; Ghosh and Abdi, 2004) argued that Canada endorses pluralism only in superficial ways. In reality, we tend to prefer "pretend pluralism," which means that we "tolerate rather than embrace differences" (Fleras and Elliott, 2002, p. 2). In practice, differences have been exoticized and trivialized. Whereas minor differences may be gently affirmed in depoliticized and decontextualized forms such as food, dance, and festivities, substantive differences that tend to challenge hegemony and resist being co-opted are usually perceived by many as deficient, deviant, pathological, or otherwise divisive (Dei, 1996; Ghosh and Abdi, 2004). It seems clear that one of the hurdles that prevents us from fully recognizing immigrants' educational qualifications and professional experiences is the prevailing attitude toward difference. In fact, our negative attitudes and behaviours toward immigrants coexist with our commitments to democratic principles such as justice, equality, and fairness. Henry et al. (2000) referred to the coexistence of these two conflicting ideologies as "democratic racism" (p. 23). According to the authors, democratic racism prevents the government from making any changes in the existing social, economic, and political order and from supporting policies and practices that might ameliorate the low status of people of colour because these policies are perceived to be in conflict with and a threat to liberal democracy.

Second, knowledge is used as power to keep out the undesirable. Critical theorists and postmodern scholars (Cunningham, 2000; Foucault, 1980; McLaren, 2003) have suggested that knowledge is power; knowledge is socially constructed, culturally mediated, and historically situated; and knowledge is never neutral or objective. The nature of knowledge as social relations prompts us to ask the following questions: What counts as legitimate knowledge? How and why does knowledge get constructed the way it does? Whose knowledge is considered valuable? Whose knowledge is silenced? Is knowledge racialized? Studies have clearly shown that, whereas immigrants from Third World countries have encountered difficulties with their international credentials and work experience, those from advanced countries (such as the US, Australia, Britain, or New Zealand) have had relatively successful experiences. Therefore it can be speculated that knowledge has been racialized in Canada. As Li (2003) rightly pointed out, the term *immigrant* becomes a codified word for people of colour who come from a different racial and cultural background and who do not speak fluent English. Li further stated that the knowledge possessed by immigrants is deemed inferior because their real and alleged differences are claimed to be incompatible with the cultural and social fabric of the "traditional" Canada. It seems clear that the power relations are embedded in social relations of difference (Dei, 1996). In fact, this hierarchy of knowledge and power is rooted in Canada's ethnocentric past, where immigrants from Europe and the US were viewed as the most desirable and those from Third World countries as undesirable. Canada's commitment to the point-system immigration policy does not permit us to recruit immigrants on the basis of racial and national origins. Hence, we can argue that the devaluation and denigration of immigrants' knowledge and experience becomes the new head tax to keep "undesirables" out. It has also been used as a new strategy to maintain the subordination of immigrants and to reinforce the extant power relations in Canada.

Positivism and Liberal Universalism

Third, international credentials assessment and recognition in Canada suffer from positivistic measuring. Positivists believe that an objective world exists "out there," external to the individual (Boshier, 1994). They also believe that if something exists, it can be measured (Young and Arrigo,

1999). Studies cited here (Dei, 1996; Henry et al., 2000) have shown that this objectivist orientation has been the driving force behind the current practice in international credentials assessment and recognition. The existing scheme searches for an absolute truth regarding knowledge and experience. It adopts a set of "value-free" criteria that discount the social, political, historical, and cultural context within which such knowledge is produced. The claimed "neutral" assessment and measuring usually disguise themselves under the cloak of professional standard, quality, and excellence without questioning whose standard is put in place and whose interests it represents. Although immigrants are allowed into the country, professional standards deny them access to employment in their professions. As Krahn et al. (2000) rightly pointed out, the real purpose of implementing such standards is to restrict competition and to sustain the interests of the dominant groups.

Fourth, in assessing international credentials, positivism is juxtaposed with liberal universalism and in turn exacerbates the complexity of international credentials recognition. As Young (1995) noted, liberal universalism posits that universality transcends particularity and difference. She also maintained that universality promotes assimilation and a politics of difference makes space for multiple voices and perspectives. In applying a one-size-fits-all criterion to measure immigrants' credentials and experience, liberal universalism fails to answer the following questions: Who establishes criteria? Whose interests are represented and served by these standards? What constitutes valid prior learning? What should we do with knowledge that is valid but different? What forms of knowledge become Canadian "equivalent"? Sometimes the rejection of immigrants' qualifications may simply be seen by practitioners as an effort to reduce risk arising from ignorance of the credential in question (Reitz, 2001). It seems clear that by refusing to recognize immigrants' qualifications and experience as legitimate knowledge, liberal universalism privileges a regime of truth that perpetuates oppression and disadvantage of immigrants.

Conclusion and Implications for Adult Education

In conclusion, this chapter argues that the recognition of international credentials and prior work experience is a political act. The findings reported here reveal that many immigrant professionals in Canada have experienced devaluation and denigration of their prior learning and work experience after arriving in Canada. As a result, they have experienced significant demoralizing and disempowering downward social mobility. In the process of prior learning assessment and recognition for immigrant professionals, there is obviously a missing "R" (recognition). The lack of recognition can be attributed to a number of causes. First and foremost, our misperceptions of difference and knowledge can be blamed. The deficit model of difference leads us to believe that differences are deficiency, that the knowledge of immigrant professionals, particularly for those from

Third World countries, is incompatible and inferior, and hence that this knowledge is invalid. It appears safe to claim that knowledge has been racialized and materialized on the basis of ethnic and national origins. Furthermore, our commitment to positivism and liberal universalism exacerbates the complexity of this process. This chapter demonstrates that by applying a one-size-fits-all criterion to measure immigrants' credentials and experience, liberal universalism denies immigrants opportunities to be successful in a new society. It also reveals that professional standards and excellence have been used as a cloak to restrict competition and legitimize existing power relations. The juxtaposition of the misperceptions of difference and knowledge with positivism and liberal universalism forms a new head tax to exclude the "undesirable" and to perpetuate oppression in Canada.

Many adult educators (Cunningham, 2000; Freire, 1970; Welton, 2001) have faith in the role of adult education as an agency of social change. This chapter has shown that in the changing context of immigration, adult education has failed to respond to the changing needs of adult immigrants and failed to accept diversity and difference that recent immigrant learners bring into adult education. In light of this failure, I urge adult educators to revitalize the progressive role of adult education in bringing about democracy and social change and to work collaboratively with government organizations, professional associations, and prior learning assessment agencies to dismantle barriers by adopting an inclusive framework that fully embraces all human knowledge and experiences, no matter from which ethnic and cultural backgrounds they emerge. Otherwise, immigrants will be further alienated from becoming fully fledged citizens of the receiving society. I hope that this discussion will guide adult educators to face this new challenge in a new era.

Acknowledgment

The author wishes to thank Tara Fenwick for reading a draft of this chapter and for her valuable comments.

References

Basran, G. and Zong, L. (1998). Devaluation of foreign credentials as perceived by visible minority professional immigrants. *Canadian Ethnic Studies, 30* (3), 6–18.

Boshier, R. W. (1994). Initiating research. In R. Garrison (Ed.), *Research perspectives in adult education* (pp. 73–116). Malabar, FL: Krieger.

Couton, P. (2002). Highly skilled immigrants: Recent trends and issues. *Canadian Journal of Policy Research, 3*(2), 114–123.

Cunningham, P. (2000). The sociology of adult education. In A. Wilson and E. Hayes (Eds.), *Handbook of adult and continuing education* (pp. 573–591). San Francisco: Jossey-Bass.

Dei, G. J. S. (1996). *Anti-racism education: Theory and practice.* Halifax, NS: Fernwood.

Fleras, A. and Elliott, J. (2002). *Engaging diversity: Multiculturalism in Canada.* Toronto, ON: Nelson Thomson Learning.

Foucault, M. (1980). *Power/knowledge: Selected interviews and other writings, 1972-1977.* New York: Pantheon Books.

Freire, P. (1970). *Pedagogy of the oppressed*. New York: Continuum.

Gannage, C. (1999). The health and safety concerns of immigrant women workers in the Toronto sportswear industry. *International Journal of Health Services, 29*(2), 409–429.

Ghosh, R. and Abdi, A. A. (2004). *Education and the politics of difference: Canadian perspectives*. Toronto, ON: Canadian Scholars' Press.

Henry, F., Tator, C., Mattis, W. and Rees, T. (2000). *The colour of democracy*. Toronto, ON: Harcourt Brace.

Knowles, V. (1997). *Strangers at our gates: Canadian immigration and immigration policy, 1540-1997*. Toronto, ON: Dundurn Press.

Krahn, H., Derwing, T., Mulder, M., and Wilkinson, L. (2000). Educated and underemployed: Refugee integration into the Canadian labour market. *Journal of International Migration and Integration, 1*(1), 59–84.

Li, P. S. (2001). The market worth of immigrants' educational credentials. *Canadian Public Policy, 27*(1), 23–38.

Li, P. S. (2003). *Destination Canada: Immigration debates and issues*. Don Mills, ON: Oxford University Press.

McLaren, P. (2003). *Life in schools: An introduction to critical pedagogy in the foundations of education* (4th ed.). Boston: Pearson Education.

Mojab, S. (1999). De-skilling immigrant women. *Canadian Woman Studies, 19*(3), 123–128.

Ng, R. (1996). Homeworking: Dream realized or freedom constrained? The globalized reality of immigrant garment workers. *Canadian Woman Studies, 19*(3), 110–114.

Reitz, J. G. (2001). Immigrant skill utilization in the Canadian labour market: Implications of human capital research. *Journal of International Migration and Integration, 2*(3), 347–378.

Statistics Canada. (2003a). *Ethnic diversity survey*. Ottawa, ON: Author.

Statistics Canada. (2003b). *2001 census: Analysis series*. Ottawa, ON: Author.

Thomas, A. M. (1998). The tolerable contradictions of prior learning assessment. In S. Scott, B. Spencer, and A. M. Thomas (Eds.), *Learning for life: Canadian readings in adult education* (pp. 330–342). Toronto, ON: Thompson Educational.

Wanner, R. A. (2001). Diagnosing and preventing "brain waste" in Canada's immigrant population: A synthesis of comments on Reitz. *Journal of International Migration and Integration, 2*(3), 417–428.

Welton, M. (2001). *Little Mosie from the Margaree: A biography of Moses Michael Coady*. Toronto, ON: Thompson Educational.

Whitaker, R. (1991). *Canadian immigration policy since confederation*. Ottawa, ON: Canadian Historical Association.

Young, I. M. (1995). Polity and group difference: A critique of the ideal of universal citizenship. In R. Beiner (Ed.), *Theorizing citizenship* (pp. 175–207). Albany: State University of New York.

Young, T. R. and Arrigo, B. A. (1999). *The dictionary of critical social sciences*. Boulder, CO: Westview Press.

17
Labour Education

Bruce Spencer and Jeffery Taylor

*L*abour (or *union*) *education* refers to education and training offered by labour unions (trade unions) to their members and representatives. The extent to which this education is provided directly by unions, union federations, or another agency or educational institution for unions varies from country to country and union to union. Labour education attracts more participants than does any other form of nonvocational adult education in developed countries and is one of the most important forms of traditional (nonformal) adult education available to working people. But it is most often underreported and ignored in discussions about adult learning.

The term *union education* can be used interchangeably with *labour education* in this chapter. (Union education is sometimes reserved for courses run directly by unions, compared to labour education courses, which include some run for unions by other providers—whether or not they are directly sponsored by unions). The main purposes of labour education are to prepare and train union lay members to play an active role in the union; to educate activists and members about union policy, changes in the union environment such as new management techniques, or changes in labour law; and to develop union consciousness, to build common goals, and to share organizing and campaigning experience. Unions have a small full-time staff and therefore rely on what is essentially voluntary activity of their members to be effective at work and in society; the labour education program is thus a major contributor to building an effective volunteer force. Labour education can be described as *social purpose* adult education: It is not so much individual as collective education, less concerned with individual credentials than workplace and social change.

Unions remain the most important and popular form of worker (or working class) organization in most liberal democracies. Labour unions are regarded as "old" *social movements* (in comparison to women's, green, or antiglobalization movements, etc.), but as we look back on the past millennium, they have to be considered as a relatively recent social organization. If we set aside early forms of workers' associations, "modern" labour or trade unions, with significant membership, probably did not emerge worldwide until the 1840s; they are only approximately 160 years old.

We should also note that neoconservative and postindustrial commentators often predict the demise of labour unions, but, in fact, unions remain stubbornly present within most liberal democracies (the existence of strong independent unions should be considered a hallmark of democratic society). Union membership and union influence may have declined across Western societies (except perhaps in Nordic countries), but they have not vanished: Unions represent approximately one-third of all Canadian workers. Organization, representation, negotiation, lobbying, strikes, and other forms of union activity still occur worldwide (for a brief discussion of Canadian unions and structures see Spencer, 1998).

Most labour union members learn about the union and workplace relations while on the job (what is often referred to as *informal* or *incidental learning*)—a form of *workplace learning* that has often been ignored in the unitarist managerial literature on organizational learning. Trade unionists probably will learn more and become most active during negotiations, grievances, and disputes; but they also learn from coffee- and lunch-break discussions; union publications and communications; attendance at meetings, conferences, and conventions; and the union's educational programs. Although labour education caters to only a small number of members in any one year, it is *social* rather than *personal* education. It is designed to benefit a larger number of members because the course partic-ipants are expected to share their learning with other union members. Labour education has a social purpose—to promote and develop the union presence and purposes to advance the union collectively. Labour education can be described as essentially nonvocational, nonformal adult education with its origins in the traditions of *workers' education*, the seeds of which are more than a century old and predate modern unions.

Part of this history of workers' and union education can be explored through an examination of the uneasy relationship between unions and educational providers in Canada.

The WEA and University and College Labour Studies

The arrival in Canada of the Workers' Educational Association (WEA) in 1918 marked the beginning of systematic attempts to provide trade unionists with access to university-level education. The original WEA model, inherited from the British parent and established in Ontario during the 1920s, involved collaboration between a local association (with trade union membership) and a university to provide noncredit, inexpensive evening classes to a working-class constituency. The local association was expected to do fund raising, solicit individual memberships and union affil-iations, establish an annual or semi-annual program of courses, determine course fees, organize class venues, recruit students, and generally do whatever administrative work was required. The university collabora-tor, usually using government money granted to support the WEA, was expected to supply and reimburse tutors from among its academic staff. The tutors were chosen on the basis of their subject-matter expertise and their ability to present an objective account of their topic. In practice, however, WEA tutoring attracted academic staff with some sympathy for workers and unions. Instruction was at a university standard, including reading and written work, although the WEA model differed from the didactic university practice of the period in that association tutors were expected to divide their class time evenly between lecture and discussion. Nonetheless, the instructional model was that of the authoritative university expert dispensing knowledge to worker–students, albeit tempered by workers' perspectives in the discussion portion of the course (see Taylor, 2001, for detailed references for this section, which also borrows from Taylor, 2004).

This model worked reasonably well in larger centres such as Toronto or Vancouver for the small minority of trade unionists who were interested in and prepared for university-level courses. Increasingly during the 1930s, however, WEA activists became aware of the limitations of this method and experimented with other techniques such as study circles connected to regular radio broadcasts on labour topics in order to reach a broader constituency. Furthermore, many of the new industrial unions that developed in the late 1930s and the 1940s turned to the WEA for assistance in launching education programs. As a result, by about 1945 the WEA had a national labour education system in place that included short evening and weekend courses, study circles connected to radio broadcasts, visual education using film and filmstrips, summer schools, occasional conferences and workshops on specific topics, and the traditional evening university-level courses. An incipient form of educational progression existed in what WEA activists called their "mass education strategy" whereby a union learner could begin by participating in short courses or study circles and eventually make his or her way into university-level courses.

Unfortunately for its future health, the WEA was too successful in providing a valuable independent educational service for rank-and-file trade unionists. By the late 1940s international unions and labour centrals were developing their own internal educational capacity, and some considered the WEA to be a threat. Furthermore, there was a cold war waging in the Canadian labour movement during these years between communists and social democrats. The social democrats were in leadership positions in the main industrial unions, and they set about to purge communists and their sympathizers from positions of authority in the movement. The WEA was an autonomous and politically neutral organization that succeeded through its ability to work with all factions in the politically charged labour movement of the day. For the anticommunists, however, this principled autonomy was the same as being a communist fellow traveller. By the early 1950s, as a result, most unions ceased to work with the WEA, and it lost its central place in union educational provision.

The WEA's demise was a loss for Canadian labour education in many ways, including the link that it provided between post-secondary education and the nuts-and-bolts training in union activity that has subsequently become the province of internal union education programs. Ironically, during the 1950s and 1960s the labour movement attempted to re-establish connections with universities but met with limited success. The 1956

National University-Labour Conference on Education and Co-operation, co-sponsored by the Canadian Labour Congress (CLC) and the Canadian Association for Adult Education, was designed to lay the foundation for future cooperation. Trade unionists such as Max Swerdlow, CLC education director, were anxious to enter into strategic alliances with universities for assistance in training instructors, developing instructional materials, and defining programs of progression from one level of labour education to another. Universities, however, proved to be largely uninterested in union alliances during this period. Manitoba was an exception. Exploiting a healthy foundation of cooperation that had developed during the WEA years, trade unionists and sympathetic academics in Winnipeg launched the University-Labour Three-Year Certificate Program in 1962. Instructors who taught at a university level were drawn from the community as well as from the ranks of university faculty.

In the absence of a sustained and widespread commitment from universities to cooperate with unions after the 1956 conference, the labour movement turned inward to provide the university-level instruction that many felt was necessary to equip leaders with the skills they required to function effectively. The CLC cooperated with the Quebec-based Confederation of National Trade Unions (CNTU) to establish a Canadian labour college. After being spurned by two Ontario-based universities, the labour centrals were successful in convincing the University of Montreal and McGill University to partner with them in their venture. In 1962 the Labour College of Canada opened its doors for its first intake of students. Offering a traditional university-level social science curriculum in a seven-week program, the college was governed by a board with representatives from the four founding organizations. By the 1980s the CNTU and the two universities had cut their formal ties with the college, and it continued as a CLC organization, offering university-level courses in a six-week summer residential program supplemented by a popular distance-education course.

The general context of union-university relations changed significantly during the 1970s. The expansion of community colleges across the country, funded largely by the federal government and with a mandate to provide technical training tailored to local community needs, provided a new venue for labour education. In addition, increased funding for universities coupled with more critically minded and labour-friendly faculty in areas such as sociology, history, economics, and industrial relations provided the impetus for the development of labour studies programs in some institutions.

Niagara College in Welland, Ontario, was the first college or university in the country to establish a labour studies program, which it began in 1969. John Whitehouse, with 20 years of labour education experience with the Textile Workers Union of America, was its first director. Six years later Humber College in suburban Toronto opened its Centre for Labour Studies as a joint venture with the Labour Council of Metropolitan Toronto. The Humber centre, which concentrated on occupational health and safety training in its early years, flourished until the labour council severed its connection with the institution in the mid-1980s and partnered with George Brown College in downtown Toronto. McMaster University in Hamilton, Ontario, meanwhile, established its labour studies program in 1976 amid tensions between the program planners and the labour movement.

British Columbia colleges such as Capilano in North Vancouver and Cariboo in Kamloops and the British Columbia Institute of Technology attempted to build links to the labour movement with mixed results. Capilano and Cariboo approached the CLC with separate proposals to establish a formal collaboration with the Labour College of Canada. Both were rebuffed. Capilano did launch a labour studies program in 1976 with the participation and endorsement of the CLC. Almost immediately, however, the CLC withdrew its imprimatur because the college would not allow it to have control over the program. Simon Fraser University, however, was willing to let the labour movement determine the content and nature of its labour program, and the CLC Pacific office began working with it instead. This partnership led to other initiatives such as the Summer Institute for Union Women and a Certificate Program in Labour Leadership. The CLC did not cooperate with the Capilano program again until the late-1990s.

The most successful example of university–labour cooperation during this period was the Atlantic Region Labour Education Centre (ARLEC), launched in 1972. Governed jointly by the labour movement, the federal government, and St. Francis Xavier University, and supported by federal government funds, ARLEC provided advanced labour education at St. Francis Xavier's Antigonish, Nova Scotia, campus. Although some in the labour movement were critical of ARLEC's university and federal government links because of the conservative effect they believed that they had on the program, the centre was an important component of the labour education system in Atlantic Canada until the federal government withdrew its funding in 1997.

The irony of this period of relations between the labour movement and post-secondary educational institutions is that after decades of university aloofness, universities and colleges in the 1970s were finally signalling that they were willing and able to make their educational resources available to labour organizations and their members. But the labour movement, feeling self-sufficient as a result of a major grant to the CLC from the federal government that allowed it to establish the Labour Education and Studies Centre, believed that it could afford to rebuff the universities and colleges. Indeed, in 1977 the CLC took the extraordinary step of circulating a set of guidelines to every college and university president in the country that stipulated that college and university labour studies programs must operate under the control of the labour movement. More specifically, post-secondary programs were to be managed by a committee appointed by the relevant labour council or federation, with responsibility for all aspects of the program including instructor selection, the establishment of fees, and course content and materials. Although sympathetic post-secondary educators cautioned union officials against insisting on this degree of control and contended that, in fact, the control that they were demanding was illegal in some jurisdictions, their protests fell on deaf ears.

In retrospect, the 1970s were the glory days for university and college labour studies programs, despite the labour movement's general hostility to public-sector provision of labour education. And it is unfortunate that firmer connections could not have been made, because it might have meant that labour studies programs would be stronger today. In the past 25 years some new programs have been established and others have disappeared. Currently, many are enjoying a precarious existence.

The Capilano College program in Vancouver continues to operate, although college administrators are demanding that it become self-sufficient. And Simon Fraser University established a credit-based labour studies program to complement the noncredit labour program that it has offered for some time. Athabasca University in Alberta, meanwhile, offers a unique distance-education labour studies degree and certificate program to the entire country. Athabasca also partners with the Labour College of Canada to deliver a distance-education course. The University of Saskatchewan also provides a certificate in labour studies through its College of Commerce. At the University of Manitoba, the University-Labour Three-Year Certificate Program that began in 1962 was forced to close its doors in the mid-1990s when university administrators demanded that the program pay its own way. But the university continues to offer a labour studies degree, which started in 1979, and is developing a credit-based certificate as a replacement for the old three-year program.

The Ontario scene has changed significantly in the past couple of decades. Niagara College, the grandparent of college programs, was forced to close recently because of declining enrolments. A similar fate caused the closing of labour studies at Ottawa's Algonquin College. McMaster University continues to offer degree and certificate programs, and Laurentian University launched a new degree in 2000 with good relations with the local labour movement and a unique collaboration with Athabasca University. And York University, Brock University, and the University of Windsor operate degree programs. McMaster and York have borrowed Manitoba's model of offering student placement courses in which students earn university credits for work done in labour organizations. George Brown College continues its collaboration with the Labour Education Centre of the Labour Council of Metropolitan Toronto, in which it accredits the centre's labour studies certificate. The college is also developing its own diploma in labour studies and seeking articulation agreements with universities. Finally, Mohawk College in Hamilton recently developed a certificate in conjunction with local labour councils.

With the demise of ARLEC in 1997, when federal funding ceased, there is no local labour studies program left in Atlantic Canada. St. Francis Xavier University, which was involved in labour education from the 1930s to the 1990s, has apparently lost interest in this area of adult education. And Dalhousie University, which was involved sporadically in labour programming from the 1940s to the 1980s, is no longer in the field.

Collaborations have worked best when both parties have been clear about and comfortable with their spheres of control. Universities have never been interested in teaching *tools* courses, which unions in Canada view as their responsibility. But unions, for the most part, have been uninterested in the educational offerings of universities. They have turned to universities primarily for research assistance and collaboration. Colleges, on the other hand, have offered a combination of *tools* and *issues* courses as a reflection of their institutional mandates. Hence, trade unionists have been more wary of these arrangements unless they felt that they had sufficient control of the programs to determine or at least co-determine their content.

Labour Education Today

Core Labour Education

Most of the labour education courses provided by unions are *tools* courses (for example, shop-steward training, grievance handling, and health and safety representative courses). The next largest category is *issues* courses (for example, sexual harassment, racism, or new human-resource management strategies), which often seek to link workplace and societal issues. A third group of courses can be labelled *labour studies,* and they seek to examine the union context (for example, labour history, economics, and politics) as illustrated in the discussion on unions, the WEA, and post-secondary institutions. Note that university and college labour studies and labour relations courses and programs are available to the general public, not just union members.

Tools courses directly prepare members for active roles in the union, to become representatives of the union; tools courses are targeted at existing or potential union activists. In Canada they are largely provided directly by the unions, by labour federations, or by union centrals (such as the CLC). Many unions layer their courses to offer introductory, intermediate, and advanced courses and programs. Some of the introductory tools courses lead on to issues courses (sometimes referred to as *awareness* courses) that are specifically targeted at raising awareness and union action around the issues discussed.

Perhaps the most innovative recent example of a *labour studies* program offered to union members is the negotiated paid educational leave program developed by the Canadian Autoworkers (CAW) and now also offered by the Canadian Union of Postal Workers (these are mainly run at the

CAW family education centre at Port Elgin, Ontario). The core offering is four separate but linked one-week units targeted at all members, not just representatives and activists, and funded by an employer levy negotiated at the bargaining table (the unions retain sole control over content).

The differences between the types of labour education courses are fluid. Some courses will have elements of each type in one course; for example, an introductory course for shop stewards could have a history or political-economy component and an issues section. Where unions put their emphasis may vary depending on such factors as the type of union philosophy advocated—business unionism (accommodative/adaptive) versus organizing model (oppositional/militant). The first philosophical approach may result in more emphasis on *tools* and less on *labour studies* (see Gereluk, 2001, for examples of union provision).

Curriculum and teaching methods for these core labour education courses have been hotly contested over the years and have been linked in the assertion that labour education should adopt a *popular education* or *Freirean* approach. In its extreme form, it was argued that courses would have no specific course content, would be experientially based, and would respond to the concerns of only the participants who attended a particular course. All other educational approaches were dismissed as forms of *banking education*. Although this debate may have been beneficial in reminding labour educators of the importance of democratic participation in the classroom and in the union and the links between the two (for a recent example see Burke, Geronimo, Martin, Thomas, and Wall, 2002), it distracted attention from issues of course content. The need to address some of the key issues facing union members and discuss information that may be outside of their immediate experience needs planned course content as well as participatory methods. John McIlroy's (1990) chapters in *The Search for Enlightenment* illustrated that the emphasis on participation can mask a retreat into technical training courses denuded of content and represent a move away from the traditions of workers' education committed to establishing an understanding of political economy among labour activists. It is more common now for unions to offer a range of courses with different focuses and to incorporate participatory methods and experiential elements as appropriate. Whereas some courses are essentially experiential, others are not. Mike Newman (1993) in the *Third Contract* discussed the question of which adult educational philosophies and teaching methods are appropriate in different kinds of labour education courses and showed that a range of different educational approaches can be beneficial.

Other Labour Education

Although *tools, issues,* and *labour studies* might describe the traditional core labour education programs, the definitions do not encompass all labour education offerings. Unions are directly involved in a number of membership education programs, some of them with a basic skills or vocational purpose. In some cases, union-run literacy and second-language courses are tutored by fellow unionists and act as a bridge to link immigrant or illiterate workers to union concerns and publications. Similarly, unions are responsible for a number of worker-training programs that allow the unions to educate workers about union concerns alongside of vocational training. Some skilled and professional unions have a long history of union-sponsored vocational training and education courses. Unions, including noncraft unions, are becoming much more proactive in responding to company restructuring and deskilling and are arguing for reskilling, skills recognition, and skills profiling, as well as challenging employers to live up to their rhetoric on "pay for knowledge."

In some countries unions have developed a comprehensive and integrated education and training program (particularly in the UK); in others such programs include vocational training and educational opportunities for the unemployed that are linked to the drive to create worker-owned cooperatives (in Brazil). In other situations unions are engaging in workplace learning programs partnered with employers or other agencies (such as NGOs). Nor should we ignore educational provision for full-time officers; there has been a growing interest, particularly in Quebec and in Canada generally, in equipping full-time officers with the educational tools needed to conduct union business in a global economy (examples of a range of contemporary labour education from around the globe, including some named here, can be found in Spencer, 2002).

Conclusions

In general, union members and the unions do benefit when individuals take union courses. The courses help members to become more interested in the union, members are able to make better union decisions as a result of attending courses, and the courses give members the confidence to take on voluntary positions in the union and to challenge arbitrary management decisions. In addition, union education bolsters members' communal, social, and political activity. Labour education does support union activism (for references see Spencer, 1994).

In spite of the problems facing unions, labour education remains vibrant, with a renewed emphasis on general membership education and on education for union organizing. Labour education has also begun to challenge new management techniques, issues of globalization, and employer-defined workplace learning. It has responded to calls for international workers' solidarity, to educational challenges posed by widespread computer use and the Internet, and to calls for marrying job preservation to environmental protection. There has also been some rediscovery of the role of traditional workers' education within labour education provision that has led to a renewed focus on political economy and social analysis.

This diversity of approaches and vibrancy cannot mask the very real problems that unions and civil society in general face in this age of neoliberal economic policies, globalization, and rampant individualism; corporate power cannot be underestimated (Bakan, 2004). Labour education does, however, provide a space for social-purpose adult education—a place where workers can begin to "tool up" to contest hierarchy and authority at work and to gain insights and understandings to better agitate against international neoliberalism and advocate for the importance of the public interest. Labour education deserves the support of all adult educators.

References

Bakan, J. (2004). *The corporation: The pathological pursuit of profit and power.* Toronto, ON: Penguin Canada.

Burke, B., Geronimo, J., Martin, D, Thomas, B., and Wall, C. (2002). *Education for changing unions.* Toronto, ON: Between the Lines.

Gereluk, W. (2001). *Labour education in Canada today.* Retrieved September 28, 2005, from http://www.athabascau.ca/wcs/PLAR_Report.pdf

McIlroy, J. (1990). Part II: 1945-1988. In B. Simon (Ed.), *The search for enlightenment: The working class and adult education in the twentieth century* (pp. 173–275). London: Lawrence & Wishart.

Newman, M. (1993). *The third contract: Theory and practice in trade union training.* Sydney, Australia: Stewart Victor.

Spencer, B. (1994). Educating union Canada. *Canadian Journal for the Study of Adult Education* 8(2), 45–64. [Revised version in D. Poonwassie & A. Poonwassie (Eds.). (2001). *Fundamentals of adult education* (pp. 214–231). Toronto, ON: Thompson Educational.]

Spencer, B. (1998). Workers education for the twenty-first century. In S. Scott, B. Spencer, and A. Thomas (Eds.), *Learning for life: Canadian readings in adult education* (pp. 164–175). Toronto, ON: Thompson Educational.

Spencer, B. (Ed.). (2002). *Unions and learning in a global economy: International and comparative perspectives.* Toronto, ON: Thompson Educational.

Taylor, J. (2001). *Union learning: Canadian labour education in the twentieth century.* Toronto, ON: Thompson Educational.

Taylor, J. (2004). Linking labour studies and unions: Past lessons and future visions. *Just Labour, 4.* Retrieved September 28, 2005, from http://www.justlabour.yorku.ca/volume4/index.htm

18

Adult Education and Health: Will Words Get in the Way?

Donna M. Chovanec and Karen M. Foss

> Health is a basic human right. Investments in education are investments in health. Lifelong learning can contribute substantially to the promotion of health and the prevention of disease. Adult education offers significant opportunities to provide relevant, equitable and sustainable access to health knowledge. (United Nations Educational, Scientific, and Cultural Organization [UNESCO], 1997a, p. 5)

This statement from UNESCO affirms a fundamental relationship between adult education and health. Traditionally, health care practitioners have recognized the importance of teaching patients how to manage various health conditions and diseases, such as diabetes and cancer. As indicated in numerous health publications noteworthy for their focus on health education (e.g., *Family Practice*, *Patient Education and Counseling*), this is still the case today.

However, as concern shifted from disease management to disease prevention and health promotion in the 1980s, the significance of the link to adult education increased. For example, both health promotion and adult education are concerned with people having more control over their lives through community participation, learner involvement, and empowerment (Rootman and Ronson, 2005). Health promotion itself is largely an educational endeavour undertaken within primary health care, the level at which the basic health needs of people are met, including the equitable distribution of resources such as water, food, and education (World Health Organization, 1988). From an education perspective, adult educators recognize that health is an important concern for adult learners; the adult learning setting is appropriate for teaching and learning about health; health topics contribute to learner interest and motivation; and participatory education methods are useful for health empowerment (Rudd, Colton, and Schacht, 2000; Rudd, Zacharai, and Daube, 1998).

More recently, the relationship between health and education has been underscored by the acknowledgment that level of education is a major *determinant* of health. According to UNESCO (1997b), "It is well known that those who are most likely to suffer from ill health are not only the poorest, but also those with the lowest level of education" (p. 3). There are ample health studies that have demonstrated this link between health status and educational level in areas such as management of hypertension and underutilization of cancer-screening programs (American Medical Association [AMA], 1999; Rudd et al., 2000).

Canada has set precedence both in acknowledging the vital relationship between health and adult education and in pulling the two sectors together. This was evident in a seminal Canadian research collaboration between the Ontario Public Health Association (OPHA) and the longstanding adult literacy organization, Frontier College, in the *Literacy and Health Project* (OPHA and Frontier College, 1989). Their findings reveal that low literacy levels are associated with poor health status among Canadians. Given that 48 percent of Canadian adults have low-level literacy skills that affect their ability to both read and understand information encountered in their everyday lives (Statistics Canada, 1996), this is a significant problem.

The focus of this chapter, therefore, is on the concept of *health literacy*—the term coined to describe the contemporary view of the connection between health and education. First, we examine how health literacy is defined and implemented in the Western context. Then, drawing from both our adult education and health backgrounds, we demonstrate that the early promise of health literacy to address social inequities has been undermined by policies and practices that neglect the structural conditions that give rise to the problem. We conclude by introducing a fresh idea emerging from the literature, particularly within the broader scope of participatory adult education: *critical health literacy*. It is within this context of critical health literacy that the tenuous relationship between health and education can be solidified, such that we see the potential to push health literacy beyond the boundaries of personal responsibility towards social justice in a manner befitting adult education.

Defining Health Literacy

Definitions of health literacy tend to focus on the functional skills that individuals need to manage their health. For example, it may be defined as "a constellation of skills, including the ability to perform basic reading and numerical tasks required to function in the health care environment" (AMA, 1999, p. 553) or as the ability to "use health information and concepts to make informed choices, reduce health risks and increase quality of life" (Zarcadoolas, Pleasant, and Greer, 2005, pp. 196–197).

Such narrow definitions of health literacy have two major problems. First, the focus on reading fails to recognize that being health literate is more than simply having the ability to read text-based medical information (e.g., medication labels); it includes skills of comprehension and verbal reasoning (OPHA and Frontier College, 1989; Perrin, 1990). Second, these narrow definitions of health literacy assume that individuals are solely responsible for successful health care interactions and for complying with any ensuing medical recommendations (Greenberg, 2001; Singleton,

2003). Further, there exists an assumption that health opportunities and resources are equally distributed (Tones and Tilford, 2001).

As a result of these assumptions, policies and interventions tend to focus on lifestyle and cultural factors that blame the victim for her or his own poor health (Tones and Tilford, 2001). Despite cautions to the contrary in the earliest research (OPHA and Frontier College, 1989; Perrin, 1990), this insight seems to have been overlooked in subsequent initiatives. This short-sightedness presents an opportunity for adult education, with its voice of experience in other forms of literacy, to challenge these assumptions.

Responding to Health Literacy Concerns

Responses to the concern about health literacy fall into five broad areas: (a) raising awareness, (b) improving readability of health information, (c) assessing literacy levels, (d) enhancing access to health information, and (e) empowering individuals and communities.

Raising Awareness

When the relationship between health and literacy and the magnitude of the issue were first uncovered, raising awareness "of the nature of the relationship between literacy and health, what is being done and what individuals can do" (OPHA and Frontier College, 1989, pp. 51–52) was deemed an important goal. Nielsen-Bohlman, Panzer, and Kindig (2004) outlined numerous awareness-raising activities enacted in the ensuing years. However, still today, health literacy problems remain the "silent epidemic" (p. xiii); thus, there is still much work to be done (Gillis, Quigley, and MacIsaac, 2005).

Improving Readability

Research, especially that conducted by Parker, Baker, Williams, and Nurss (1995) and Williams et al. (1995)—in which approximately 40% of patients did not understand basic medical instructions, 26% did not understand appointment slips, 15% did not understand prescription labels, and 60% did not understand consent forms—sounded a wake-up call for health care professionals. Prompted by concerns for compliance seeking (Shohet, 2002), improved health outcomes (AMA, 1999; Shohet, 2002), cost containment (AMA, 1999), and a move toward patient self-care (Roter, Stashefsky-Margalit, and Rudd, 2001), there has been an attempt to make text-based health information more readable for more people (e.g., Nielsen Bohlman et al., 2004). However, there are numerous criticisms of this focus on readability. Particularly, it again promotes the commonly held view that poor readers are to blame for their reading problems, contrary to the adult literacy literature that articulated how adults with low literacy skills often are powerless to change their lives (Freire, 1972/2000). Further, to direct attention solely to readability for people who have lower reading skills is to misunderstand the complex ways that literacy problems and health problems are interconnected (Breen, 1993; Perrin, 1990).

Assessing Literacy Levels

Unquestionably, the written word is a major vehicle for transmitting health information. However, one difficulty with this blanket approach is that literacy level is not easily observable, partly because people may endeavour to mask their literacy problems (OPHA and Frontier College, 1989). Hence, health literacy screening is suggested based on the assumptions that it is important to identify people at risk for low reading ability and that knowing literacy levels will decrease the use of complex vocabulary (Nielsen-Bohlman et al., 2004).

However, the attraction to health literacy screening has been problematic. For example, health literacy screens such as the Rapid Estimate of Adult Literacy in Medicine (REALM) and the Test of Functional Health Literacy in Adults (TOFHLA) gather information out of context, do not accurately reflect actual daily health literacy tasks, ignore diversities in language and culture, and require training and time to administer (Greenberg, 2001; Shohet, 2002). Further, it seems unhelpful to make a distinction between low and high literate patients when evidence suggests that "reading level alone . . . does not explain the complex human skills involved in becoming a health literate citizen" (Zarcadoolas et al., 2005, p. 196). Certainly, health information should be understandable for everyone regardless of education and reading level (Breen, 1993).

Enhancing Access

Along with improving readability, enhancing access to health information also includes providing "alternate means of communication other than print" (OPHA and Frontier College, 1989, p. 40), such as supplemental verbal communication and visual materials. The Internet is suggested as an alternative means of communication, but its use as a health information forum has been criticized because of the disparity of access, especially for older adults and persons of lower socio-economic status (Benigeri and Pluye, 2003). "Equitable access [then] means adapting information to take into account other social and cultural factors—including language, gender, age, socio-economic status and cultural background" (OPHA and Frontier College, 1989, p.43).

Empowerment

Health education is viewed as a means to empower people to change the social, environmental, and economic factors that determine their health (UNESCO, 1997b). Drawing from critical adult educators such as Freire (1972/2000) and adult learning principles such as centring on people's own experiences, various sectors are developing participatory approaches to health education (e.g., Hohn, 1998). A Canadian example is adult literacy educators Norton and Campbell's (1998) empowerment approach to health education with women. These empowerment projects, even with their own inadequacies (Tones and Tilford, 2001), remain atypical in both health and adult education settings (Rudd, 2002).

A Critical Look at Health Literacy

At this point in the chapter, three key themes emerging from both health and adult educational literatures have been presented. First, groundbreaking research in primary health care has established a correlation between poor health and poor literacy. Second, this has suggested a relationship between health needs and educational needs that demands a collaborative effort between health and adult educational providers. Third, a plethora of recommendations and strategies have been advanced to address health literacy. In keeping with our commitment to move beyond the current boundaries of health literacy, we recognize a need to examine more closely the mix of responses to this issue.

Nutbeam (2000) proposed that three kinds of literacy must be addressed to achieve an adequate response to the health literacy issue:

- *Functional health literacy*: communicating factual information to improve knowledge of health risks and health services;
- *Interactive health literacy*: developing personal skills to improve personal capacity to act independently on knowledge; and
- *Critical health literacy*: supporting individual, social, and political action to improve individual and community capacity to act on various social and economic determinants of health. (p. 265)

Using Nutbeam's schema to analyze the evolution of health/education efforts demonstrates that, overwhelmingly, the health literacy response, especially in the health sector, has focused on *functional* literacy; that is, on improving the readability of print literacy coupled with an indefensible attempt to assess literacy skills. *Interactive* literacy, more evident in reports from adult educators, has been addressed to some extent by efforts to improve access to health information through varied media and educational programming. Yet, according to Rootman and Ronson (2005), we rarely evaluate the impact of these strategies and why so many have failed to make a real difference in the lives of Canadian adults.

The early researchers who investigated the correlation between health and literacy not only recognized the irrefutable relationship between poor health outcomes and poor social circumstances (e.g., poverty, housing, education), but also asserted that the response to this problem would require a commitment to action and change at the societal level. According to OPHA and Frontier College (1989) in the *Literacy and Health Project, Phase One*:

> Health inequalities such as those identified in this report, arising from illiteracy as well as from other socio-economic factors, can only be eliminated through

concerted action by all sectors of society. While health consequences of illiteracy may be medical in nature, resulting in increased mortality and morbidity, the solutions for the most part require non-medical interventions. Action is required in the development of healthy public policy, making workplaces safer, improving living conditions, ensuring the delivery of education for all, and along other fronts. . . . Any remedies which do not involve a major commitment and action across many different fronts would only involve tinkering, and are unlikely to make any major impact on existing inequities in health status. (p. 41)

The business of changing society is messy, long, and complex; and thus the well-established link between health and socio-economic circumstances identified in this early report was circumvented, and the imperative to respond at a systemic level went unheeded. Hence, the third kind of health literacy, *critical* literacy, is barely evident in the literature. Nonetheless, there has been increasing interest, especially from the margins, in tackling health literacy from a critical perspective that thus far includes cognitive, behavioural, and social action skills aimed at awareness and participation (Kerka, 2003; Nutbeam, 2000). Although these kinds of skills are reminiscent of a consciousness-raising approach, to think that they are automatically achieved by knowing how to read and write is faulty. Such perspectives do nonetheless invoke the notion of empowerment. As suggested earlier, this introduces a potentially more critical stance to the discussion on health literacy. That it has also been picked up in the official rhetoric of governments, workplaces, and other institutions, however, indicates the varied purposes for which this word is used. In practice, *empowerment* has been critiqued by many for a hidden paternalism that is, in the end, disempowering and neutralizing (e.g., Lather, 1991).

Thus, even the promising idea of critical health literacy is in danger of leaving us stranded within the Western discourse of individual responsibility for improving one's own circumstances. Although more evident in the emphasis on functional and interactive health literacy, the critical health literacy approach might also be guilty of the accusation that "issues get represented in ways that mystify power relations and often create individuals responsible for their own 'failures,' drawing attention away from structures that create unequal outcomes" (Bacchi; as cited in Herdman, 2002, p. 164). No matter how readable print materials are, no matter how easy it is to find health information, no matter how empowered the individual, a correlation between poor health and poor socio-economic circumstances will persist—and, more important, neither literacy nor the material realities of citizens will improve—because the current system is built on maintaining these divisions. Focusing on "downstream behavioural approaches" (Raphael, 2003, p. 399) does nothing to challenge the dominant ideology. As Labonte (2004) asked, "How can one 'include' people and groups into structured systems that have systematically 'excluded' them in the first place?" (p. 115).

What remains absent in the discussion on health literacy is attention to the "political economy of illness" (Tones and Tilford, 2001, p. 27)—a

Critical Health Literacy in Action at the Community Level

While recognizing and continuously combating mainstream notions about immigrants and newcomers, along with barriers to equal participation in the health care system, the Multicultural Health Brokers Cooperative demonstrates that local empowerment is possible. Grounded in the ideal of participatory action and social justice, the co-op builds on the strengths and existing knowledge of newcomers to collectively generate new knowledge and action. "Health brokers" from a variety of cultural communities in Edmonton provide a link between people in their own communities and the health care system. In perinatal health, for example, they bridge cultural and Western biomedical beliefs and practices (e.g., breastfeeding, nutrition, and herbs) by working together for safe choices.

Streetworks started in 1989 as the result of the efforts of eight city agencies, including police, public health, and addiction services, that were concerned about HIV and other health issues among injection drug users and sex trade workers. The agency provides a comprehensive range of health services to this community based on health promotion, community development, and harm-reduction approaches. Each of these approaches aims to build on the strengths of individuals who are typically viewed as weak and scorned by the mainstream and recognizes that high-risk activity is not only about individual behaviour, but also about societal problems. Recently, Streetworks has successfully pioneered a "natural helpers" program that draws on the strengths of people in the community who have a natural inclination to help their friends and family on the street. Their first project, an internationally recognized booklet on safer injecting, later led to a series of booklets about health and social survival strategies for street people.

(Information is used with permission from Yvonne Chiu from the Co-op and Marliss Taylor from Streetworks.)

recognition of power as a material construct in a fundamentally inequitable environment and of the structural changes that are needed to redress this. From this perspective, health is fundamentally related to the availability and distribution of resources. This does not mean that privileged people do not get sick; it means, as the early research indicated, that poor health (of various kinds) is disproportionately distributed among those with the fewest material resources.

How, then, can the original promise of health literacy be rescued from the current individualistic and technicist approach? According to Labonte (2004), our concern within both the health and the adult education fields should not be as much with the groups or conditions that are excluded, "but with the socio-economic rules and political powers that create excluded groups and conditions, and the social groups who benefit by this" (p. 120). Murray (2001) concurred:

> If it is to achieve its full potential of contributing to a reduction in the substantial social inequities in health, a comprehensive health and literacy action program needs to locate itself within the broader movement for social justice. As such, health and literacy action becomes part of the process of critical consciousness raising. (p. 4)

Although it is discouraging to see little evidence of critical health literacy at the national policy level, there are several examples at the grassroots level. Two examples from Edmonton are the Multicultural Health Brokers Cooperative and Streetworks (see sidebar). Rather than holding the narrow view that "health is an individual responsibility," these initiatives demonstrate that "health is a social responsibility" (Norton and Campbell, 1998, p. 5).

Conclusion

The implicit link between adult education and health gained momentum 15 years ago with the introduction of the *Literacy and Health Project* in Ontario (OPHA and Frontier College, 1989). Setting the stage for what later became known as health literacy, the 1989 report provided sobering evidence of the correlation between social conditions and health status. Our critical examination of the subsequent health and educational literature reveals a progressive weakening of the social change implications of this observation so that 15 years later the same concerns persist, as demonstrated in a recent literacy survey (Statistics Canada, 2005). It is our contention that 15 years from now we will still be facing the same issues unless fundamental inequities in the Canadian social structure are addressed. We need look no further for guidance than OPHA and Frontier College's 1989 report, which outlined an abundance of strategies that were predicated on a commitment to

- achieve literacy and health for all;
- make environments healthy and safe; and

- ensure equitable access to vital information. (p. 37)

Underlying these crucial areas of action is a fundamental belief in the kind of equality and justice for which adult educators strive and a critique of the socio-economic system that prevents them. If its radical potential is pursued, critical health literacy offers a promising approach for adult educators and health practitioners to work together for authentic societal change in the determinants of health that have linked poor literacy with poor health. Instead of getting in the way, words, coupled with social action, could be powerful tools to ensure literacy and health for all.

References

American Medical Association. (1999). Health literacy. Report of the Council on Scientific Affairs. *Journal of the American Medical Association, 281*(6), 552–557.

Benigeri, M. and Pluye, P. (2003). Shortcomings of health information on the Internet. *Health Promotion International, 18*(4), 381–386.

Breen, M. J. (1993). *Partners in practice: The literacy and health project phase two: Summary report.* Toronto, ON: Ontario Public Health Association.

Freire, P. (2000). *Pedagogy of the oppressed.* New York: Continuum. (Original work published 1972)

Gillis, D. E., Quigley, B. A., and MacIsaac, A. (2005). "If you were me, how could you make it better?" Responding to the challenge of literacy and health. *Literacies,* Spring(5), 28–31.

Greenberg, D. (2001). A critical look at health literacy. *Adult Basic Education, 11*(2), 67–79.

Herdman, E. (2002). 'Lifelong investment in health': The discursive construction of 'problems' in Hong Kong health policy. *Health Policy and Planning, 17*(2), 161–166.

Hohn, M. D. (1998). *Empowerment health education in adult literacy: A guide for public health and adult literacy practitioners, policy makers, and funders.* Literacy Leader Fellowship Reports, Vol. III (4, Part A). Washington, DC: National Institute for Literacy.

Kerka, S. (2003). *Health literacy beyond basic skills.* Columbus, OH: ERIC Clearinghouse on Adult Career and Education.

Labonte, R. (2004). Social inclusion/exclusion: Dancing the dialectic. *Health Promotion International, 19*(1), 115–121.

Lather, P. (1991). *Getting smart: Feminist research and pedagogy with/in the postmodern.* New York: Routledge.

Murray, M. (2001). Developing a health and literacy action program. In M. Murray (Ed.), *Health and literacy action conference report* (pp. 1–9). St. John's: Memorial University of Newfoundland.

Nielsen-Bohlman, L., Panzer, A. M., and Kindig, D. A. (2004). *Health literacy: A prescription to end confusion.* Washington, DC: National Academies Press.

Norton, M. and Campbell, P. (1998). *Learning for our health.* Edmonton, AB: Learning Centre Literacy Association.

Nutbeam, D. (2000). Health literacy as a public health goal: A challenge for contemporary health education and communication strategies into the 21st century. *Health Promotion International, 15*(3), 259–267.

Ontario Public Health Association & Frontier College. (1989). *Literacy and Health Project, Phase one: Making the world healthier and safer for people who can't read.* Toronto: Ontario Public Health Association, Frontier College.

Parker, R., Baker, D., Williams, M., and Nurss, J. (1995). The test of functional health literacy in adults: A new instrument for measuring patients' literacy skills. *Journal of General Internal Medicine, 10,* 537–541.

Perrin, B. (1990). *Literacy and health project phase one: Making the world healthier and safer for people who can't read: Research report.* Toronto: Ontario Public Health Association.

Raphael, D. (2003). Barriers to addressing the societal determinants of health: Public health units and poverty in Ontario, Canada. *Health Promotion International, 18,* 397–405.

Rootman, I. and Ronson, B. (2005). Literacy and health research in Canada: Where have we been and where should we go? *Canadian Journal of Public Health, 96*(Supp. 2), S62–S67.

Roter, D. L., Stashefsky-Margalit, R., and Rudd, R. E. (2001). Current perspectives on patient education in the US. *Patient Education and Counseling, 44,* 79–86.

Rudd, R. E. (2002). A maturing partnership. *Focus on Basics: Connecting Research & Practice, 5*(c), 1–10.

Rudd, R. E., Colton, T., and Schacht, R. (2000). *An overview of medical and public health literature addressing literacy issues: An annotated bibliography* (NCSALL Report No. 14). Cambridge. MA: National Center for the Study of Adult Learning and Literacy.

Rudd, R. E., Zacharai, C. and Daube, K. (1998). *Integrating health and literacy: Adult educators' experiences* (NCSALL Report No. 5). Cambridge, MA: National Center for the Study of Adult Learning and Literacy.

Shohet, L. (2002, March-April). *Health and literacy: Perspectives in 2002.* Paper presented at the Adult literacy and numeracy: Australian Research Consortium on-line forum. Available from http://www.staff.vu.edu.au/alnrc/onlineforum/AL_pap_shohet.htm

Singleton, K. (2003). *Virginia adult education health literacy toolkit.* Richmond, VA: Virginia Adult Learning Resource Center.

Statistics Canada. (1996). *Reading the future: A portrait of literacy in Canada. Highlights from the Canadian report.* Ottawa, ON: National Literacy Secretariat.

Statistics Canada. (2005). Adult literacy and life skills survey. *The Daily.* Available from http://www.statcan.ca

Tones, K. and Tilford, S. (2001). *Health promotion. Effectiveness, efficiency, and equity* (3rd ed.). Cheltenham, UK: Nelson Thornes.

United Nations Educational, Scientific, and Cultural Organization Institute for Education. (1997a). *The Hamburg declaration. The agenda for the future.* Report from the Fifth International Conference on Adult Education. Hamburg: CONFINTEA V.

United Nations Educational, Scientific, and Cultural Organization Institute for Education. (1997b). Health promotion and health education for adults. In *Adult Learning and the Challenges of the 21st Century. Booklet 6b.* Report from the Fifth International Conference on Adult Education. Hamburg: CONFINTEA V.

Williams, M., Parker, R., Baker, D., Parikh, N., Pitkin, K., Coates, W., et al. (1995). Inadequate functional health literacy among patients at two public hospitals. *Journal of the American Medical Association, 274*(21), 1677–1682.

World Health Organization. (1988). *Education for health: A manual on health education in primary health care.* Geneva: Author.

Zarcadoolas, C., Pleasant, A., and Greer, D. S. (2005). Understanding health literacy: An expanded model. *Health Promotion International, 20*(2), 195–203.

Part 4
Contexts of Community and Social Movements

19
Social Movement Learning: Theorizing a Canadian Tradition

Budd L. Hall

What is a social movement?

> It goes on one at a time,
> it starts when you care
> to act, it starts when you do
> it again after they said no,
> it starts when you say We
> and know you who you mean, and each
> day you mean one more.
> (From *The Moon is Always Female*, by Marge Piercy, 1980, p. 98)

W/e conclude by situating inclusive queer praxis as a transgressive and transformative practice-expression-reflection dynamic that opens an in-between learning space of immense possibility in culture and society. (Grace and Hill, 2004, p. 188)

Many of us working in adult education in Canada associate ourselves with that stream of adult education that has been closely aligned with some of the major social movements of the nineteenth, twentieth, and twenty-first centuries. We draw inspiration from the educational activities associated with the rise of labour organizing in Canada, with the suffragette and women's movements, with the peace movements of the many wars, with economic development in the Atlantic provinces in the mid-twentieth century, with the environmental movements, with Aboriginal struggles for self-determination, and with social justice movements of antiracism, HIV/AIDS, class privilege, diverse sexualities, dis/ability, and antiglobalization.

This chapter makes the case that it is precisely the learning and knowledge-generating capacities of social movements that account for much of the power claimed by these movements. Deepening our understanding of learning within the contexts of social movements is a contribution, however modest, to achieving a larger historic project of a world that we want.

What Is a Social Movement?

The poetic definition of Marge Piercy (1980) is, to my mind, the clearest and most easily communicated statement about how we understand a social movement. David Snow, Sarah Soule, and Hanspeter Kriesi (2004), in their introduction to *The Blackwell Companion to Social Movements*, noted that

> social movements can be thought of as *collectivities acting with some degree of orga-nization, and continuity outside of institutional or organizational channels for the purpose of challenging or defending extant authority, whether it is institutionally or culturally based, in the group, organization, society, culture or world order of which they are a part* [emphasis in original]. (p. 11)

Donatella della Porta and Mario Diani (1999) noted, in synthesizing an enormous variety of European and North American literature, that most social movement scholars share a concern with four characteristics of movements: "informal interaction networks; . . . shared beliefs and soli-darity; . . . collective action focusing on conflict; . . . use of protest" (pp. 14–15).

What Is Social Movement Learning?

Social movement learning refers to (a) learning by persons who are part of any social movement and (b) learning by persons outside of a social movement as a result of the actions taken or simply by the existence of social movements (Hall and Clover, 2005). Learning by persons who are part of a social movement often takes place in informal or incidental ways because of the stimulation and requirements of participation in a movement. When one becomes involved in a movement to counter home-lessness, statistics about how many people are homeless or the impact of living without fixed shelter are learned quickly simply through interaction with others in the movement or through the literature of the movement or the movement's opponents. What we all know as facilitators of learning is that nothing is as powerful a stimulus to learning as the necessity to teach or inform others. The organizational or communicative mandate of all social movements is a necessarily educational concern. And although much of the learning within social movements is informal or incidental in nature, organized or intentional learning also takes place as a direct result of educational activities organized within the movement itself.

The Canadian labour movement, as Jeffery Taylor (2001) illustrated in his book, *Union Learning*, is one of the oldest and strongest. It has a rich and well-documented history of social movement learning (Martin, 1995; Spencer, 1995, 2002; Taylor, 2001). The literature has described the sophisticated range of internal educational provision about the histories of unions, the functions of collective bargaining, and procedures of union-management life. It has also documented some of social unionism's educa-tional work on such topics as the nature of capitalism and the challenges of major national and global social issues. The biography of the life of Muriel Duckworth of Nova Scotia sheds light, as does some of the writing of the late David Smith, on many of the ways in which peace activists have worked to create organized space for learning (Kerans, 1996; Smith, 1994). This writing draws our attention to the reasons that peace must be struggled for and includes examples of peace education approaches that have been used with the broader public. Ron Faris (1975) has written in earlier works about the educational aspects of the New Canada Movement, a rural social movement that rose for some time in Ontario and had as its goal the creation of a "new and better Canada" (p. 17). The Antigonish Movement is perhaps the best-known and best-documented social movement in adult education history (see Lotz and Welton, 1997; and Welton, 2001, for two recent treatments). James H. Morrison (1989) documented the early moments of learning and the movements for better working conditions in the work camps of early English Canada through Frontier College.

The Impact of Social Movements on Learning in Broader Society

A most powerful form of social movement learning, and one often neglected in the literature, is the learning that takes place by persons who are not directly participating as members of a given social movement—by people outside of a given movement. Canadian men, for example, have learned much about gender and power relations as a result of the women's movements, not necessarily because we were part of the movements themselves. Our mothers, partners, daughters, and friends created a learning environment where we *learned* in experiential ways as we negotiate(d) our daily lives. The actions of social movements—be they large-scale media events such as Greenpeace and those that other environmental groups have staged, or benefit concerts for victims of HIV/AIDS, or the creation of quilts by women to protest the building of an unwanted power station on Vancouver Island (Clover, 2003)—create rich environments for learning by large numbers of the public.

Social Movement Learning Theorists

Given the extent to which Canadian adult education frames itself within a social movement or at least a social action or social change framework, one would think that social movement theorists themselves might have noticed us in developing their own theories! Such does not appear to be the case. A review of social movement theory reveals the invisibility of a discourse on learning and education. Indeed, neither the word *education* nor the word *learning* appears in the index of the encyclopedic *Blackwell Companion* (Snow et al., 2004) mentioned earlier.

In the absence of specific references to learning or education in the social movement literature, which ideas show the most promise as theoretical building blocks? Eyerman and Jamison (1991) were unique among social movement scholars in their recognition of the creative and central role of learning processes in what they called *cognitive praxis*. Their thoughts were drawn first to the attention of adult educators by John Holford (1995) and have subsequently been referred to by others who sought to theorize learning in social movements (Foley, 1999; Walters, 2005).

Eyerman and Jamison stated, "There is something fundamental missing from the sociology of social movements" (p. 45). North American social movement theory, they suggested, focuses on what movements do and how they do it and not on what their members think. Knowledge is seen to be largely outside the sociologist's areas of competence, according to Eyerman and Jamison. Their own work was informed by the writings of Habermas (1987), Cohen (1985), and Melucci (1988). They proposed that it is "through tensions between different groups and organizations over defining and acting in that conceptual space that the (temporary) identity of a social movement is formed" (p. 22). Through the notion of cognitive praxis, they emphasized the creative role of consciousness and cognition on all human action, individual and collective. They focused simultaneously on the process of articulating a movement identity (cognitive praxis), on the actors taking part in this process (movement intellectuals), and on the context of articulation (politics, cultures, and institutions). What comes out of social movement action is neither predetermined nor completely self-willed; its meaning is derived from the context in which it is carried out and the understanding that actors bring to it and/or derive from it.

Melucci (1988) presented some useful concepts for further developing theories of social movement learning. Social movements make power visible. They challenge the dominant meaning systems or symbols of contemporary everyday life. The "movements no longer operate as characters but as signs. . . . They do this in the sense that they translate their action into symbolic challenges that upset the dominant cultural codes" (p. 249). Social movements compete for ownership of specific social or political problems in the eyes of the public, "imposing their own interpretation on these" (della Porta and Diani, 1999, p. 70), and, in cases where they are successful, actually change the way that we understand knowledge and the relations of power. The Clayoquot Sound summer of protest over clear-cutting on Vancouver Island, for example, not only challenged forestry practices, but also changed our understanding of the relations of the rest of nature to human community and industrial exploitation. This changed understanding, which we *learned*, led eventually to public policy changes and legislation in British Columbia and to many innovations in areas of social forestry.

Mario Diani (1996), among others, offered the notion of "interpretive frames" (pp. 1053–1069) as another way of understanding social movements, which has value for a knowledge or learning agenda. An interpretive frame is a generalized conceptual structure that allows one to make sense of daily lived experiences and locate actions within an understanding of the world. Social movements suggest a variety of interpretive frames, alternative frames to the public in the contestation over meaning. Freire (1971), of course, referred to speaking from the perspective of marginalized peasants as *naming the world*. The various namings of the world, or interpretive frames, according to della Porta and Diani (1999), can be usefully categorized as "antisystem frames, realignment frames, inclusion frames and revitalization frames depending on their specifics" (p. 80).

The work of Michael Roth, a Canadian cognitive psychologist who works from a broad educational pallet, has a very promising body of empirically based work to examine (Lee and Roth, 2003; Roth, Hwang, Goulart, and Lee, 2005). He spoke of the articulation of individual and collective learning in what he called *free choice learning* within community social action projects. Drawing on Bakhtin, Lave, Vygotsky, and others, Roth and colleagues with whom he wrote noted that "collective learning fosters individual learning and vice versa, whereby individuals produce resources in action and as outcomes of their activities. These resources expand the action possibilities of the collective and thus constitute learning" (Boyer and Roth, 2005, p. 75).

Adult educators, not surprisingly, have been the major contributors to theorizing social movement learning. Although much of the writing has been descriptive, and has documented practices and shared stories, there is a growing body of more analytic and theoretical writing that has surfaced over the past 15 years. Mathias Finger, the Swiss adult educator and ecologist, and Jose Manuel Asun, a colleague from Spain, saw new social movements as the catalysts for personal transformation and the environment within which transformation occurs (Finger and Asun, 2001). Social movements define the future topics of adult education. Learning within social movements, according to Finger (1989), has a more powerful impact on society than does all of the learning that takes place in schools. Social movement learning is viewed within a framework of endogenous knowledge creation, not dissimilar to Eyerman and Jamison's (1991) cognitive praxis notion. Learning is seen as a people's tool (a political dimension), a democratic right (learning by all), and learning from the world (epistemological dimension). They contrasted this with exogenous knowledge transmission, which understands education (rather than learning) as a tool for maintaining the status quo, a package for all, and about the world.

Canadian adult educators have often drawn on Griff Foley (1999) of Australia because he directly addressed the informal learning that happens within social movements in his book, *Learning and Social Action*. He noted that informal learning emerges from as well as advances social action by contributing to building alternative organizational forms, by making links between the spiritual and the political, by illuminating the power of a small group of committed people, and by showing how expertise can be brought in from outside. He noted in the context of several diverse social movement settings—a Brazilian women's organization, an environmental campaign, and an African liberation movement—that learning deepens in the process of taking action. Foley wrote on the nature of learning and emancipatory struggle from an historical materialist theoretical framework: "A critique of capitalism must be at the heart of emancipatory adult education theory" (p. 138).

Shirley Walters's feminist explorations of learning and gender in the context of popular education on an international scale are particularly well known (Walters and Manicom, 1996). In the context of co-teaching a course on social movement learning with Shirley Walters, I gained some new insights on social movement learning that have since been partially reflected in a chapter (Walters, 2005, pp. 63–71) in the Nesbit (2005) collection *Class Concerns: Adult Education and Social Class.* Based on her experience within the South African anti-apartheid struggle, Walters made the case that the form of social movement learning is in part determined by the material conditions of the class structures from which the social movement activists emerge. The White South African allies of the anti-apartheid struggle were able to produce sophisticated policy briefs and research papers and to create a huge network of organizations. The forms of social movement learning within this class of activists involved workshops, retreats, and readings of theory from other parts of the world. For South African Blacks who worked, when they had jobs, in low-paying and insecure settings or lived long distances from the city centres in poor housing with poor transportation, the predominant form of social movement learning took place at the large rallies, the funerals, and the demonstrations where masses of people were able to be present. Leaflets, handbills, and speeches were the dominant forms of social movement learning.

John Holst (2002) of the United States added a substantial critique of much of the recent social movement and civil society learning theorizing and issued a call to adult educators to return to a deeper reading of Gramsci within the body of Marx's and Lenin's writings. He argued in his book *Social Movements, Civil Society, and Radical Adult Education,* similarly to Foley (1999), that there has been insufficient fidelity to socialist roots in the past several decades of social movement and civil society theorizing: "A theory and practice of revolutionary or radical adult education must explore the pedagogical nature of the most widely adopted and successful form of revolutionary organization of the twentieth century, . . . the revolutionary party" (p. 113). His work spoke less to the forms of social movement learning and more to the focus. Attention to social movements and civil society structures in the absence of clarity about the ultimate goal being the transfer of power from capital to the working people is misplaced at best, and at worst facilitates the very weakening of capitalist control over democratic practice that we seek as adult educators.

The Canadian Contributions

As noted earlier in the chapter, Canadian adult educators are making particularly valuable contributions to the international discourse of social movement learning.

Michael Welton (1993) argued that social movements are both personal and collective in form and content and saw them as "privileged sites" of transformative learning or emancipatory praxis. He pondered what adults are learning, particularly in the new movements of self-discovery or identity creation, and posed the question, "Is something of great significance for the field of adult education occurring within these sites?" (p. 154). Clearly, the answer is yes. Welton's historical writings, specifically *Knowledge for the People* (Welton, 1987), *Father Jimmy* (Lotz and Welton, 1997), and his biography on the life of Moses Coady, *Little Mosie From the Margaree* (Welton, 2001), have chronicled the educational dimensions of some of our best-known Canadian social movements. Both Father Jimmy Tompkins and Moses Coady believed in the innate abilities of ordinary people working together to transform their conditions. Their writings about education and learning within the era of the already mentioned Antigonish Movement most often focused on the role of education as a kind of tonic to awaken in people a desire to make change and to provide them with the tools to do so.

Jennifer Sumner (2005) drew our attention to the role of organic intellectuals within the organic farming movement (p. 255). Clover's (2000) conceptualization of environmental adult education in *The Nature of Transformative Learning* could easily be extended to help us to advance our theorizing of social movement learning. From a global perspective, she drew together many theoretical and practical contributions in her book *Global Perspectives in Environmental Adult Education* (Clover, 2003). Her current work explores the role of the arts in women's social movement interventions (Clover and Markle, 2003). In my chapter (Hall, 2004) in the *Global Perspectives* collection, I looked at the multiplicity of creative forms of social movement learning that were used by environmental action movements in the several countries and contexts of the case studies that we studied in the mid-1990s (pp. 169–192).

Leona English (2004) has explored *relational learning* within women's social action organizations in Nova Scotia (p. 136). Drawing on feminist humanistic relational learning theory and poststructural understandings, she suggested that women's learning within the settings she examined occurs often within contexts of conflict and differences of opinion. Donna Chovanec's (2004) study was of women in a Communist party women's organization in Chile and drew on Marx, Allman, and Youngman. The learning within the social movement with which she worked arose as a result of complex ideological and practical struggles over strategy and tactics (pp. 77–82). What this pointed out is not that women's organizations are prone to conflict and struggle, but that all social movement learning, because it is located in the heart of contestations over class, political, racial, gender, and/or other differences, exists within the climate of contestation.

Conclusions

The further examination of social movement learning is important for our continuing project of building truly transformative and inclusive adult education theory and practice. A more systematic investigation into the learning and knowledge strategies of social movements is also an important potential contribution to the scholarship of social movements themselves. It is time that the artificial boundaries that separate learning, educational, and knowledge theorists from the social movement theorists in sociology, history, political science, gender studies, postcolonial studies, or elsewhere are ruptured. The achievement of the Utopian project of a world that we want is brought closer as we learn how and why to transform existing power relations in living otherwise.

References

Boyer, L. and Roth, W.-M. (2005). Individual/collective dialectic of free-choice learning in a community-mapping project. *Environmental Education Review, 11*(3), 75–91.

Chovanec, D. (2004). Learning power from the margins: Analyzing action and reflection in a social movement. In D. Clover (Ed.), *Adult education for democracy, social justice, and a culture of peace: Proceedings of the joint international conference of AERC and CASAE* (pp. 136–141). Victoria, BC: University of Victoria.

Clover, D. (Ed.). (2003). *Global perspectives in environmental adult education.* New York: Peter Lang.

Clover, D. (Ed.). (2004). *Global perspectives in environmental adult education (Counterpoints: Studies in the postmodern theory of education).* New York: Peter Lang.

Clover, D. (with Follan, S. and Hall, B.). (2000). *The nature of learning: Environmental adult education* (2nd ed.). Toronto: Transformative Learning Centre.

Clover, D. and Markle, G. (2003). Feminist arts-based practices of popular education: Imagi-nation, counter-narrative, and action on Vancouver and Gabriola Islands. *New Zealand Journal of Adult Learning, 31*(2) 36–52.

Cohen, J. L. (1985). Strategy and identity: New theoretical paradigm and contemporary social movements. *Social Research, 52,* 663–716.

della Porta, D. and Diani, M. (1999). *Social movements: An introduction.* Oxford: Blackwell.

Diani, M. (1996). Linking mobilization frames and political opportunities: Insights from regional populism in Italy. *American Sociological Review, 61,* 1053–1069.

English, L. (2004). Feminine/feminist: A poststructural reading of relational learning in women's social action organizations. In D. Clover (Ed.), *Adult education for democracy, social justice and a culture of peace: Proceedings of the joint international conference of AERC and CASAE* (pp. 136–141). Victoria, BC: University of Victoria.

Eyerman, R. and Jamison, A. (1991). *Social movements: A cognitive approach.* University Park, PA: Pennsylvania State University Press.

Faris, R. (1975). *The passionate educators.* Toronto, ON: Peter Martin.

Finger, M. (1989). New social movements and their implications for adult education. *Adult Education Quarterly, 40*(1) 15–22.

Finger, M. and Asun, J. M. (2001). *Adult education at the crossroads: Learning our way out.* London: Zed Books.

Foley, G. (1999). *Learning in social action: A contribution to understanding informal education.* London: Zed Books.

Freire, P. (1971). *Pedagogy of the oppressed.* New York: Seabury.

Grace, A. P. and Hill, R. J. (2004). Positioning queer in adult education: Intervening in politics and praxis in North America. *Studies in Adult Education, 36*(2), 167–189.

Habermas, J. (1987). *The theory of communicative action.* Cambridge: Polity Press.

Hall, B. (2004). Towards transformative environmental adult education: Lessons from global social movements. In D. Clover (Ed.), *Global perspective in environmental adult education* (pp. 169–192). New York: Peter Lang.

Hall, B. and Clover, D. (2005). Social movement learning. In L. English (Ed.), *International encyclopedia of adult education* (737–747). London: Palgrave Macmillan.

Holford, J. (1995). Why social movements matter: Adult education theory, cognitive praxis and the creation of knowledge. *Adult Education Quarterly, 45*(2), 95–111.

Holst, J. (2002). *Social movements, civil society, and radical adult education.* Westport, CT: Bergin and Garvey.

Kerans, M. (1996). *Muriel Duckworth: A very active pacifist.* Halifax, NS: Fernwood.

Lee, S. and Roth, W.-M. (2003). Of transversals and hybrid spaces: Science in the community. *Mind, Culture, and Activity, 10,* 120–142.

Lotz, J. and Welton, M. R. (1997). *Father Jimmy: Life and times of Jimmy Tompkins.* Wreck Cove, NS: Breton Books.

Martin, D. (1995). *Thinking union: Activism and education in Canada's labour movement.* Toronto, ON: Between the Lines.

Melucci, A. (1988). Getting involved: Identity and mobilization in social movements. In B. Klandermans , H. Kriesi, and S. Tarrow (Eds,), *From structure to action* (pp. 329–348). Greenwich, CT: JAI Press.

Morrison, J. H. (1989). *Camps and classrooms: A pictorial history of Frontier College.* Toronto, ON: Frontier College.

Nesbit, T. (2005). *Class concerns: Adult education and social class.* San Francisco: Jossey Bass.

Piercy, M. (1980). *The moon is always female.* New York: Alfred A. Knopf.

Roth, M., Hwang, S. W., Goulart, M., and Lee, Y. J. (2005). *Participation, learning, and identity: Dialectical perspectives.* Berlin: Lehmanns Media.

Smith, D. (1994). *First person plural: A community development approach to social change.* Ottawa, ON: Mapleview.

Snow, D. A., Soule, S. A., and Kriesi, H. (Eds). (2004). *The Blackwell companion to social movements.* Oxford: Blackwell.

Spencer, B. (1995). Old and new social movements as learning sites: Greening labour unions and unionizing the greens. *Adult Education Quarterly, 46*(1), 31–41.

Spencer, B. (Ed.). (2002). *Unions and learning in a global economy: International and comparative perspectives.* Toronto, ON: Thompson Educational.

Sumner, J. (2005). Organic intellectuals: Lifelong learning in the organic farming movement. In S. Mojab and H. Nosheen (Eds.), *Proceedings of the 24th annual conference of CASAE* (pp. 249–255). London, ON: University of Western Ontario.

Taylor, J. (2001). *Union learning: Canadian labour education in the twentieth century.* Toronto, ON: Thompson Educational.

Walters, S. (2005). Social movements, class, and adult education. In T. Nesbitt (Ed.), *Class concerns: Adult education and social class: New directions for adult and continuing education, No. 106* (pp. 53–62). San Francisco: Jossey-Bass.

Walters, S. and Manicom, L. (1996). *Gender in popular education: Methods for empowerment.* London: Zed Books.

Welton, M. (Ed.). (1987). *Knowledge for the people: The struggle for adult learning in English-speaking Canada, 1828–1973.* Toronto, ON: OISE Press.

Welton, M. (1993). Social revolutionary learning: The new social movements as learning sites. *Adult Education Quarterly, 43*(3), 152–164.

Welton, M. (2001). Little Mosie from the Margaree: A biography of Moses Michael Coady. Toronto, ON: Thompson Educational.

20

Popular Education and Canadian Engagements with Social Movement Praxis in the South

Dip Kapoor

The postwar "national development" project of the 1950s, the current wave of neoliberal economic globalization, and the attendant socio-cultural and ecological penetration of the "postcolonial South" (Africa, Asia, Latin America/Caribbean) by transnational capital continue to be "blocked" by indigenous and peasant communities who rely on the regeneration of ecosystems for their material and cultural well-being. The political and strategic directions associated with these struggles/movements have been articulated by various coalitions between local indigenous/peasant social movements (SMs), non-governmental organizations (NGOs, or voluntary organizations working to address the socio-economic marginalization of disenfranchised social groups in the South), and transnational environmental, human rights, women's, and indigenous movements that continue to provide opportunities for indigenous assertions (Blaser, Feit, and McRae, 2004).

This chapter advances the social and political significance of Canadian connections to popular education (adult education that exposes and challenges oppressive social relations often characteristic of the indigenous/peasant experience; Freire, 1970) and NGO-SM praxis in the South by illustrating how popular education facilitates these coalitions/partnerships and their attempts to secure material/cultural autonomy. To accomplish this, I will (a) elaborate on some theoretical and practical connections between critical adult education (CAE)/popular education and NGO-SM activism, (b) discuss the use of popular education in a specific Canadian engagement with indigenous movements in eastern India, (c) provide other examples of Canadian popular education involvements in NGO-SM partnerships in the South, and (d) in conclusion, allude to the significance of participatory action research (PAR) in addressing related research agendas that pertain to popular education and NGO-SM activism/coalitional politics—an understated/understudied popular education contribution to constructing anti- and/or counter-hegemonic coalitions (Mayo, 1996). Canadian adult educators continue to remain engaged with such processes of politicization in the interests of the margins because these partnerships commit adult educators to global processes of radical democratization and a pedagogy of hope (Freire, 1994), a pedagogical engagement that returns a reinvigorated Freirean praxis to its anticolonial roots in the South.

Critical Adult/Popular Education and NGO-SM Praxis

NGO-SM activism for social change is best understood, analytically and in terms of praxis, in relation to CAE theory. Although there are several possible perspectives encapsulated within this label, the critique of capitalism (and its current mutation as neoliberal globalization) is the central unifying thematic/political project. Civil-societarian critics have championed the role of NGOs and SMs as international change agents that moderate and curb the impact/excesses of the market (Hall, 2000), as have theorists influenced by the work of Jürgen Habermas (as cited in Welton, 1995) who have alluded to the political significance of the "lifeworld" in relation to the state and the market. However, this emphasis on civil society and transnational NGO-SM praxis as the privileged site/agents for social change has been questioned by radical socialist adult educators/ perspectives (Holst, 2002; Youngman, 2000) who have pointed out that civil society is not unfettered from the capitalist political-economy. They have made the Gramscian assertion that NGOs are more likely to act in the interests of capital (for example, when state-corporate funding reduces them to global soup kitchens, using them as a means to privatize state services) and as agents of a "development hegemony" (Kamat, 2002, p. 1) that "NGOizes the SM grassroots" (p. 152) by actively working to depoliticize/tame these SMs.

The significance of these observations lies in their ability to expose hegemonic capitalist politics masquerading as populist/democratic in their rhetoric or appearance. However, the left-puritan predilection for the alleged futility of an NGO-SM activism that does not aspire to revolutionary social change (reducing such activism to a cacophony of isolated social movement potatoes in a capitalist sack) assumes too much in the name of socialism and the likely prospects thereof for indigenous and peasant communities in the South who often subscribe to cultures that contradict modernist (capitalist/reformist/socialist) conceptions of the good life. Critical indigenous scholarship in education (primarily in relation to formal education) is opening new critical-analytical space in this respect, as Grande (2004) forwarded the notion of a "red pedagogy" (p. 11) in a Northern indigenous context (which would appear to resonate with other indigenous/peasant contexts in the South); whereas Smith (1999) referred to a "local critical theory" that is context-specific and inclusive of the possibility of the role of the "outsider," provided that he or she supports an "Indigenous orientation to the issues" (p. 187). To varying degrees, all of these conceptions of "the critical" provide possible theoretical scaffolds and normative conceptions for developing popular praxis in Northern NGO-Southern indigenous/peasant partnerships/coalitions. In the following section I will demonstrate this prospect by examining specific Canadian engagements in India.

Canadian Engagements with Indigenous Social Movements in India

After a brief contextual description in this section of industrial development and its implications for Adivasis in India and the state of Orissa, I will elaborate on popular education efforts by a Canadian-/Montreal-based indigenous rights campaign (ALCAN't) that questions Canadian transnational corporation (TNC) mining interests (ALCAN of Montreal) in Orissa, followed by a similar explication of popular education initiatives used by a Canadian NGO-Adivasi social movement partnership addressing such developments in the same region in Orissa. Facts and pertinent information for these discussions have been drawn from documents and reports from the respective participant organizations (ALCAN't/South Asia Action Network and the NGO, HELP) and from related sources/reports from Mining Watch Canada, IndiaTogether, and the Indian Social Institute.

Implications of Industrial Development in India and Orissa for Adivasis

According to the recently established Ministry of Tribal Affairs, there are 698 constitutionally recognized "scheduled tribes" (for purposes of state initiatives for amelioration) in India, which accounts for 8 percent of the Indian population (some 82 million Adivasis/original dwellers). Despite various constitutional guarantees (including the Fifth Schedule, which establishes legal recognition of tribal rights over land, forests, and water in designated scheduled areas), the Indian Social Institute estimates that 85 percent of the 213 million people displaced by mines, dams, thermal power plants, industry, and wildlife sanctuaries for eco-tourism between 1950 and 1990 are tribals/Adivasis. These incursions continue to be met with Adivasi social movement activism across the country and in Orissa.

In the 1980s the east-coast state of Orissa attracted the world's attention when the media exposed large-scale starvation deaths and the selling of children in the harsh KBK districts. Despite its poverty (44 percent of the populace live below the official poverty line), Orissa is among the top 10 states to attract foreign direct investment. Beneath its forests, inhabited mostly by some 62 different Adivasi groups who number close to 8 million (24 percent of the state's population), lie 70 percent of India's bauxite deposits (the sixth largest deposit in the world), 90 percent of India's chrome ore and nickel, and 24 percent of its coal.

With the advent of national economic liberalization in 1991, TNCs can now secure 100 percent control over mining ventures. According to the Institute for Policy Studies, transnational investment in Orissa is being facilitated by loan guarantees and low-interest loans from the World Bank that are financing developments in the power sector and is building superhighways to facilitate industrialization. The Asian Development Bank is financing the expansion of the Paradeep port, and several G7 countries are financing various related projects. The biggest beneficiaries of G7 government loans and aided projects are TNCs. According to Mining

Watch Canada, there were some 172 mines in the state by 1994, and the Indian Social Institute estimated that 1.4 million people were displaced by development projects in the state between 1951 and 1990. Adivasis continue to face displacement, cultural uncertainty, and the prospect of a future divorced from ancestral lands, forest, and water—a modern political economy for which they have little training/skills, and a dominant socio-cultural attitude that is disdainful of their ways.

Canadian Mining Interests and Indigenous Movements in Orissa: ALCAN (Montreal) and the PSSP Adivasi Response

The Kashipur block of Rayagada district, Orissa, is home to one of the largest bauxite deposits in the world. A consortium of companies, collectively known as Utkal Alumina International Ltd. (UAIL), was formed in 1993 to mine bauxite and produce alumina in the region. ALCAN (Montreal, Canada) became an active partner in 1999, and the company's share in the venture increased to 45 percent after the withdrawal of Norsk Hydro and Tata Industries in 2001. Evaluated at over a billion dollars, the UAIL project comprises a bauxite mine and an alumina refinery/plant. The project will require 1,750 hectares of land for opencast mining, the plant site, a townsite, and a dumping area. It will also require a stretch of land 25 kilometres long and 50 meters wide for conveyor and corridor maintenance as the ore will be mined from plateau tops in the Baplimali hills and transported by conveyor belt to the refinery at Doraguda. Alumina will be exported (100 percent) from the Vishakapatnam port.

The major inhabitants of the area and/or owners of the land (as per the Fifth Schedule of the Indian Constitution) are Adivasis, who belong to the Kondh, Paraja, Penga, and Jhodia tribes. Tribal ownership rights are rarely recorded, and the government position is that the transfer of land has been made to the company and the tribals will have to vacate. UAIL has insisted that it has clear title to the land. Anywhere from 10,000 to 60,000 people are likely to be affected by this project. The alumina plant at Doraguda alone will affect some 2,500 people who reside in 24 villages, but UAIL has claimed that only 3 villages and 147 families will be affected and, hence, rehabilitated. Similarly, the company does not recognize that 42 villages in three *panchayats* (local administrative units) will be directly affected by the "opencast" mine at Baplimali, a site with religious significance for the Adivasis. The only mandatory Environmental Impact Assessment on the proposed UAIL mine, conducted by Engineers India Ltd., was never made public.

The main people's organized response, Prakrutik Sampad Surakshya Parishad (PSSP), was officially recognized by the Adivasis and Dalits of Kashipur in a mass meeting in February 1996. The momentum of the gradually growing movement over the years has stalled the project from an initial 2002 start to 2005. In the process, Adivasis have been killed in police firings (December, 2000, Maikanch village incident), a martyrdom that has catalyzed continued opposition to the project. The PSSP charter of demands to the government include (a) small-scale agricultural develop-ment (for example, minor irrigation facilities); (b) easy access to medical facilities using local resources and knowledge, augmented by allopathic medicine; (c) access to an education that is in harmony with the culture, traditions, and history of the Adivasis; and (d) the cancellation of treaties signed with companies and the scrapping of all mega projects in tribal Dalit-dominated areas, plus rehabilitation of those communities displaced by previous developments.

Popular Education in the Montreal-Based ALCAN't in India's Indigenous Rights Campaign: Agitating for Adivasi Rights

ALCAN't in India, a Montreal-based solidarity campaign with the Adivasis of Kashipur, supported in different capacities by a wide range of Canadian NGOs, research institutes (Mining Watch, Polaris Institute, Quebec Public Interest Research Group [QPIRG]), and independent donors, has been engaged in a public-awareness and social-action campaign over Montreal-based ALCAN's participation in this project. ALCAN't has not claimed to represent the Kashipur Adivasi movement but has acted as a solidarity campaign to engage the Canadian public in questioning ALCAN's involve-ment in the UAIL consortium and the proposed bauxite/alumina project in Orissa.

Over the years, this campaign has successfully used various popular education processes and organizational tactics to raise public awareness and translate it into public action directed at the Montreal-based mining giant. In amplifying the concerns of the Adivasis and Dalits of Kashipur, ALCAN't has waged a popular education campaign that has raised public awareness/ action (for example, public sharing of various email correspondence with company executives) in attempts to get ALCAN to consider factors outside the calculus of profit/shareholder returns (for example, focused appeals to church-group shareholders in ALCAN or organized yearly protests at company AGMs and commemorations of the martyrdom of the Adivasis killed in a police firing).

Popular awareness raising and associated political pressures have delayed the progress of the project (for example, by demanding that ALCAN make the environmental review public, the company has been visibly stalled in its efforts to justify involvement), while public education has exposed major contradictions in claims being made by ALCAN and the UAIL consortium (for example, countered claims by ALCAN that they have the support of 23/24 leaders in the project-affected area through signatures submitted by the same in opposition to the projects, provision of Adivasi testimo-nies to expose the alleged direct involvement of ALCAN/UAIL employees in harassing movement supporters, etc.). ALCAN't's popular education process has also emphasized the building of coalitions to make strategic use of tactics for flexible scale-up of action at critical junctures in the evolution of the project (for example, through an Urgent Action Alert Network that could potentially stymie company publicity efforts by organizing phone jams).

The use of research and research institutes is also a key element of popular knowledge mobilization around a social concern (for example, QPIRG provides a university-based forum for the exchange of information, analysis, and social-justice related research for campaigns such as ALCAN't; the Polaris Institute supports research interns who are investigating knowledge interests around the campaign, such as research on the ecological impact of such projects; and Mining Watch Canada enhances campaign credibility while providing multiple avenues for mobilizing, raising awareness, and taking action, given its transnational reach).

Finally, the ALCAN't popular campaign is focused around its key demands to ALCAN, which are that the company (a) publicly release the Environmental Impact Assessment of the project or make no claims about the potential environmental impacts of the proposed project, (b) recognize the Kashipur people's title to the land, and (c) follow the example of Norsk Hydro (Norway) and fully divest itself from the joint venture UAIL.

Popular Education in Canadian NGO-Indigenous Movement Praxis in Orissa

In the neighbouring Gajapati district of South Orissa, HELP, a Canadian NGO, has been engaged in the development of an emerging forest-based local movement of Kondh Adivasis and Dalits for close to a decade. Working in conjunction with a partner Adivasi-Dalit community-based NGO, VICALP (which means "alternative" in Oriya), and eight similar community-based NGOs, the partnership has gradually grown from a 10-village mobilization in the mid-1990s to what is now an organized indigenous movement called the Adivasi-Dalit Ekta Parishad (ADEP-unity forum), which includes member organizations spread out across some 600 villages in the region (with a membership of approximately 50,000). In anticipation of development, such as the proposed project in neighbouring Kashipur, the ADEP–VICALP–HELP partnership has always sought to begin a pre-emptive dialogue on the implications of such "development" for Adivasi-Dalit forest/peasant communities with a view to organizing proactively rather than reactively once mining development has been sanctioned.

Popular education (an "indigenized" and constantly reinvented Freire), indigenous historical memory of various ancestral struggles, and contextually relevant contemporary struggles of indigenous and peasant populations in India and elsewhere (as was witnessed through their participation in the recent Mumbai World Social Forum) continue to mould the process of Adivasi politicization in the effort to activate existing constitutional rights and guarantees for indigenous and peasant communities in India.

Numerous and related popular education efforts have helped to shape this growing politicization movement in the region. For instance, VICALP has developed cultural teams to begin dialogical reflection in communities by using popular forums (village gatherings/festivities) and accepted cultural mediums (such as poetry and puppetry). This process in turn has helped with the eventual formation of village, regional, and interregional coalitions and organizational networks along the lines of Adivasi notions of organization and leadership (for example, decision making as a village-up consensual process).

Popular education initiatives also include joint action to address material and cultural survival issues of access/long-term use of forests/land (for example, the popular education process has shaped a systematic approach to alleged encroachment (Kapoor and Prasant, 2002) by using the Directive Principles of State Policy and knowledge of land classification schemes to advance the prospects for land/forest access/control. Along with such long-term efforts, small-scale village-based material interventions to strengthen Adivasi-Dalit subsistence-based economies (for example, strengthening of village grain banks to address times of draught/emergencies) are a crucial element in the popular process because activism alone cannot ensure survival. Subsequently and relatedly, organized action to mobilize state resources in the interests of local well-being, such as small-scale irrigation support (check dams/water catchments), paved roads and small bridges, or access to primary health services, is also undertaken.

Finally, popular education has facilitated coalition building at regional and state levels (formation of ADEP across 600 villages or recent decisions to support/join the Kashipur movement) and with other international NGOs. HELP has facilitated this process to expand the people's process, and two international NGOs have replicated/added to the efforts in the region over the past three years.

Canadian Transnational Collaborations: Popular Education and NGO-SM Praxis in the South

Canadian connections to popular education and NGO-SM praxis in the countries of the South go beyond this context-specific struggle in Orissa. Other NGOs are also actively supporting such local movements in various capacities, including popular education/organizing for social action. Canadian NGO Interpares, with the help of local counterparts such as Nijera Kori in Bangladesh, for instance, has been working with small peasant collectives in South Asia and with organized fisher communities and their coalitions with related struggles in the coastal regions of Bangladesh, India, and Thailand. These initiatives aim to protect community-fishing from Blue revolution TNC aqua-culture, a US$9 billion industry that has had devastating environmental and social consequences on coastal communities (Ahmed, 1997).

Such coalitional support has made it possible for the Save Chilika Lake Movement in coastal Orissa to obstruct World Bank-facilitated (which gave an industry-specific US$425 million loan to the Indian government in the mid-1980s) corporate aqua-culture by pressuring Tatas (Indian industrialists) to abandon the Chilika proposal and to secure an Orissa High Court verdict that prohibits commercial shrimp culture in Chilika Lake. Similarly, organized communities in Bangladesh now declare themselves "shrimp-free zones" and have successfully prevented the shrimp industry from entering these areas with the argument that their priority is to produce food for the coastal communities rather than luxury foods for overseas consumption at the expense of the coastal poor and the environment.

Some "faith-based Canadian NGOs" are also making attempts to support these movements. The Canadian Catholic Organization for Development and Peace (2005), in its "Program of Support for Civil Society in the South," referred to a common strategy for a continental program of 225 partner groups (including unions, peasants, women, and indigenous organizations) in 26 countries that focuses on supporting popular organizations that work for social change by helping to integrate them into networks that will enable them to maximize their impact and influence. The organization runs international seminars on "training for transformation" (Part 1: Overview of the Program, p. 4) methodology, which popular educators from all of the continents attend. It has questioned the "neoliberal economic paradigm of development" and recognized that it "has produced a real crisis for people, communities and the environment" (Part 4: Program of Support for Civil Society in Asia, p. 4). Popular education strives to contribute to the analytical capacity of peasants for economic globalization, the WTO, and the impact on small communities and livelihoods. The Canadian Catholic Organization for Development and Peace is committed to helping indigenous groups "make territorial gains" and "increase access to and control of resources by the poor" (Part 1, pp. 9–10).

STAC Montreal is another Canadian organization that supports indigenous struggles, specifically the Zapatista movement in Chiapas, by, for instance, sending volunteers to participate in the International Education Delegation for Peace in Chiapas, training volunteers to act as international observers in Zapatista communities, and sending students to study Spanish or Tzotzil (local Mayan dialect) in the Zapatista Caracol (cultural and political centre) of Oventik.

Canadian NGOs and campaigns/Northern movements play a significant role in addressing development and economic globalization-related "dislocations" and processes of forced impoverishment generated by the loss of access to necessary resources (land, forests, and water)—resources usurped by state-market-led forces of neoliberalism that are vital for the reproduction of subsistence- and sufficiency-based moral economies. The number of such heralded movements and struggles will continue to proliferate in conjunction with capitalist penetration of the margins. Indigenous, peasant, and rural women's movements and associated transnational advocacy networks have been catapulted onto the contemporary global political map by the likes of the Chipko movement and the Narmada Bachao

Andolan (India); the Sem Terra Landless Workers Movement (Brazil); the Zapatista/EZLN movement (Mexico); Via Campesina, a broad-based transnational network that includes rural women's, peasants', and indigenous organizations; the Greenbelt Movement of organized women (Kenya); the indigenous movement of the Mindanao Islanders (Philippines); the Dayak Indian movement (Kalimantan, Indonesia); and the Coordinadora (Coordination for the Defense of Water and Life, Bolivia) movement against World Bank-initiated water privatization (which created a virtual monopoly for US engineering giant Bechtel, owner of Aguas del Tunari of Bolivia) that forced people to buy permits to collect rainwater from their own roof tanks.

According to the World Commission on Dams, some 80 million people have been displaced by dams alone. Such development-related displacements are the breeding ground for potential mass mobilizations, often with minimal external facilitation by NGOs/transnational advocacy networks. Such engagements will continue to underscore the role for popular education and informal learning in an adult education praxis committed to a radical democratization of material and cultural space. This also creates a concomitant need for adult education research that politicizes knowledge construction in the interests of the margins/grounded struggles within the academe and for research-based knowledge-sharing with these movements to advance movement prospects.

PAR and Research Agendas in the NGO-SM Vortex

PAR provides a political and ontologically compatible (with critical adult education) methodology for understanding the dynamics of a movement and the role of learning/popular education in movements where a researcher engages with the movement as a participant in a collective process of research that is linked to movement aspirations and concerns. Freire's idea of praxis is taken up in PAR, in which knowledge is generated from ordinary persons involved in action and reflection on the ground, who are intimately involved with the social issue under analysis (Hall, 1997)—a process that assumes that the position of knowledge producer/consumer can be transposed in praxis.

In terms of possible research agendas, Foley (1999) pointed to the need for understanding "learning in struggles" and for more "detailed accounts of the complexities and contradictions of emancipatory learning and education in particular situations" (p. 11). Youngman (2000) proposed other research directions in relation to a political economy of adult education that explores the dynamic between state, civil society, and adult education; and Cunningham (2000) suggested that relationships in civil society between social movements and adult education require further investigation to "develop our practical insights into the inequities of power and privilege" (p. 583) while providing "opportunities for contributing to altering conditions of inequity in society" (p. 574).

Concluding Reflections: Critical Adult/Popular Education and Political Praxis in the Margins of the South

Peasant and indigenous assertions in an increasingly invasive capitalist political economy require critical adult educators (with their varied divergent and convergent ethico-political commitments) to continue to expose and challenge conservative attempts to reduce these struggles against neocolonial injustices to charitable cases in need of emergency handouts, modern tutelage, and the management/containment of discontent. Critical reflexivity also calls for critical adult educators to constantly evaluate their own excesses. Many factors prevent critical intellectual political activism, as it relates to the indigenous struggles I've described, from reaching its full potential: a radical left that demands socialist revolution; a democratic reformism and an anesthetized consumer class that patronize peasant/indigenous margins by overlooking self-determination and resorting to truncated notions of cultural pluralism; exaggerated versions of poststructuralism that overextend cogitations about voice, power, and representation; and the need to disembowel colonial rhetoric to the point of displacing material struggles. Meanwhile, despite the various peasant/indigenous assertions, the neoliberal project continues to force these communities out of the forests and off their lands into the swelling ranks of the impoverished multitude awaiting charitable relief and state handouts. This situation is again targeted by a neoliberal agenda that disregards complicity in precipitating such dislocations while simultaneously advocating for the curtailment of the state's ability to provide a modicum of redress in the form of necessary (postdislocation) public services targeted at the dispossessed. Radical democratic critique and a committed CAE/popular praxis must continue to reinvigorate social activism and reflexive collaborations with these struggles, rather than engendering political apathy and obfuscation that conspires with the prevailing hegemonic tendencies of our times.

References

Ahmed, F. (1997). *In defence of land livelihood.* Retrieved August 30, 2005, from http://www.interpares.ca/en/publications/pdf/land_and_livelihood.pdf

Blaser, M., Feit, H., and McRae, G. (Eds.). (2004). *In the way of development: Indigenous peoples, life projects, and globalization.* London: Zed.

Canadian Catholic Organization for Development and Peace. (2005). *Program of Support for Civil Society in the South.* Retrieved August 30, 2005, from http://www.devp.org/testA/overseas.htm

Cunningham, P. (2000). A sociology of adult education. In A. L. Wilson and E. R. Hayes (Eds.), *Handbook of adult and continuing education* (pp. 573–591). San Francisco: Jossey-Bass.

Foley, G. (1999). *Learning in social action: A contribution to understanding informal education.* London: Zed.

Freire, P. (1970). *Pedagogy of the oppressed.* New York: Continuum.

Freire, P. (1994). *Pedagogy of hope: Revisiting pedagogy of the oppressed.* New York: Continuum.

Grande, S. (2004). *Red pedagogy: Native American social and political thought.* Lanham, MD: Rowman & Littlefield.

Hall, B. (1997). Participatory research. In L. Saha (Ed.), *International encyclopedia of education* (pp. 317–323). New York: Elsevier Science.

Hall, B. (2000). Global civil society: Theorizing a changing world. *Convergence, 23*(1/2), 10–32.

Holst, J. (2002). *Social movements, civil society, and radical adult education.* Westport, CT: Bergin & Garvey.

Kamat, S. (2002). *Development hegemony: NGOs and the state in India.* Delhi: Oxford.

Kapoor, D. and Prasant, K. (2002). Popular education and improved material and cultural prospects for Kondh Adivasis in India. *Adult Education and Development, 58*(1), 223–232.

Mayo, P. (1996). Transformative adult education in an age of globalization: A Gramsci-Freirean synthesis and beyond. *Alberta Journal of Educational Research, 42*(2).

Smith, L. (1999). *Decolonizing methodologies: Research and Indigenous peoples.* London: Zed.

Welton, M. (1995). In defense of the lifeworld: A Habermasian approach to adult learning. In M. Welton (Ed.), *In defense of the lifeworld: Critical perspectives on adult learning* (pp. 127–156). Albany: State University of New York Press.

Youngman, F. (2000). The political economy of adult education and development. London: Zed.

21

Environmental Adult Education in Canada

Darlene E. Clover

I n his poetic essay, Cole (1998) asked four provocative questions that form the socio-ecological context for a discussion on environmental adult education (EAE):

- Who is benefiting from cash crop cultures?
- Why is there no talk of Shell oil and Starbucks?
- Where is the collective accountability of commercial enterprise?
- Why should globalization mean poor people in Kenya go without rice because of a war in Iraq? (p. 103)

Although capitalism has brought health and wealth to some, it has contributed disproportionately to social unrest, cultural deterioration, and new forms of injustice, slavery, inequity, and racism. It has also created unprecedented environmental problems. It is now argued that ecological deterioration—a by-product of capitalism's "creative powers over nature" (Bellamy Foster, 1994, p. 41), the insatiable need for natural resources, the destructive methods of extraction, and the inequitable use and ownership of these resources—will soon eclipse ideological conflict as the dominant national security concern throughout the world (Bellamy Foster, 1994; Brown, 1997). Aboriginal peoples across Canada have been forced off their lands to make way for hydroelectric schemes, and their cultures have been destabilized (McCutcheon, 1991). Fresh water, a fundamental source of life, is becoming more polluted and scarce and, worse yet, is being commodified at an alarming rate, which will perpetuate conflict (Clarke and Barlow, 2003). Half of Canada's population lives in cities where for over 20 years studies have linked air pollution to "a rise in morbidity in terms of cancer, bronchitis, emphysema, and other serious illnesses" (Douglas, 1983, p. 167). Every year, as thousands of small and large mammals die, the endangered species list grows and flora diversity is reduced (Bellamy Foster, 1994). There is more, but you already know this.

EAE has emerged as an ecopolitically focused response to contemporary ecological problems. It has arisen as a challenge to the fundamental premises of public environmental education in Canada, which draws from the tenets of environmental education as espoused by UNESCO. These include awareness raising, information sharing, and individual behaviour and attitude change. The focus is on small, individual changes. EAE, on the other hand, aims to provide spaces for dialogue, debate, creativity, and activism. The broad socio-political framework helps adults to uncover the root causes of environmental problems and encourages collective, active citizenship. Drawing on critical adult education, it is premised upon the belief that people have existing ecological knowledges and a variety of human/Earth relationships that must be respected and built upon.

This chapter begins with a brief background of Canada's socio-environmental context, followed by an exploration of five interwoven historical and contemporary capitalist practices—natural resource extraction, production, consumption, marketing, and corporatization—that are at the root of environmental problems. This discussion provides the backdrop to compare and contrast the conceptual frameworks, principles, and theories of public environmental education and EAE. Theory is connected to practice through a description of some past and current EAE activities across the country. Although this article focuses on Canada, environmental problems are global, and the development of the theory and practice of EAE must be recognized as a global effort.

Socio-environmental Context

Canada is rich in natural resources—the cornerstone of the economy. In 1995, when the value of "unused natural resources was included in traditional gauges of industrial output, productivity and other economic activity" (Hessing and Howlett, 1997, p. 5), Canada moved from being the 13th wealthiest country in the world to 2nd place. It is bordered by three oceans teeming with sea life and has lands lush with hard and soft woods. We have approximately 10 times more fresh water than does any other single country, and the country is bursting with mineral, ore, uranium, and petroleum deposits. The prairies grow a diversity of grains and graze everything from cattle to bison. It has a wealth of mammals, birds, reptiles, and insects.

Canada is also very culturally diverse. On a single street in major cities one hears Urdu and Korean spoken and a call to prayer and a Buddhist chant. Canada was built on a tradition of collectivism. Over the years Canadians have worked to establish "the most generous and open-handed benefit provisions to be found anywhere in the world" (Clarke, 1997, p. 17). We created a welfare state that includes everything from a social safety net for employment to a universal health care system, and strong labour laws/unions to accessible public education. We also created public parks for human enjoyment and green spaces, wildlife sanctuaries, and wilderness preservation programs to benefit those who have no voice but do have a right to live on this planet. Together the vast resource base and the benevolent welfare policies should have been able to create and maintain a just and sustainable social, ecological, and cultural environment for all Canadians. But for some this was never the case, and it is no longer the case for many more.

Natural Resources, Global Warming, and Human Rights

There are numerous examples of links between natural resources and human rights abuses. First Nations and Aboriginal peoples have suffered the most. For example, whereas industry-based scientists argue that climate change is either natural or a figment of the left's imagination, (and even the much-touted *Kyoto Protocol* is concerned only that greenhouse gas emissions could cause global warming), a "parcel of studies looking at the oceans and melting Arctic ice leave no room for doubt that it is getting warmer, people are to blame" (Fox, 2005, p. 1), and things are going to get worse. The Arctic Climate Impact Assessment found through a four-year investigation that climate change will render Arctic regions unrecognizable and dramatically disrupt Inuit and other northern Native people's traditional ways of life (FACMM, 2004). In addition, polar bears are becoming thinner and are producing fewer cubs, and with ice going out earlier, their seal-hunting season is shrinking, and they are retreating to land and ransacking garbage dumps (Meadows, 2002). Climate change is also not gender neutral. Women are "more vulnerable to its effects . . . because they represent the world's poor and because they are more than proportionately dependent on natural resources" (Duddy, 2002, p. 1).

Production, Consumption, Marketing, and Corporatization

Production is the creation of saleable goods, including food. Therefore, as von Moltke (1997) argued, "It is not happenstance that the most important environmental threats today (global warming, biodiversity loss, wholesale ecosystem modification and toxic pollution) can be traced directly to production of commodities and commodity manufactures" (p. 38). In precapitalist economies people engaged in production activities as direct reciprocal, personal relations of exchange (Rowe, 1990). Today, producing items is about making profit. Within this, human value and the value of the rest of nature are subordinate to the values of a world market and treated like commodities. There has been an amazing metamorphosis of the term *consumption* from an act of pillage and destruction to an act of virtue and prestige (Rifkin, 1996, p. 19). We now see an unprecedented growth of a consumer society—a term that signifies not just affluence and the expansion of production and markets, but also the increasing penetration of the meaning and images associated with consumption into the culture of everyday life. Consumption is propelled forward by creative and targeted advertising and marketing whose mantra is, The more we consume, the higher our standard of living and, by association, our quality of life. As Montreal advertising executive Duval (Ecodecision, 1995) acknowledged, "It boils down to boosting sales of a product in a particular market, and thus to encouraging consumption; . . . to claim otherwise would be a lie" (p. 59).

Consumerism is gendered. In Canada, as in most societies, women make the primary purchases for the home, which include everything from vegetables to cleaning supplies, sheets to toothpaste. The advertising industry knows this and aggressively targets them to "buy specific products such as those that keep their families 'free from germs'" (Clover, Follen, and Hall, 2000, p. 58). They are often held responsible for the poor consumer choices that harm not only their families, but also the entire planet (Clover et al., 2000; Sandilands, 1993).

Massive, foreign-owned/franchised corporations take over small businesses in Canada and make consumption not only more affordable (child labour), but also more accessible (lots of parking!). Hectares of fertile farmland and small, local shops give way to American-style warehouses. They change the landscape, the economy, the workforce, and the culture. Forming unions is often deeply discouraged, and employment seldom has benefits or security. Health risks such as increased obesity associated with contemporary fast-food diets are rising, and their abattoirs have abysmal work safety records, not to mention inhumane and abusive treatment of animals destined as fodder for this global cannon (Schlosser, 2001). The packaging is used primarily for advertising purposes (Clover et al., 2000), and, along with food and oil waste, is more often sent directly to landfill.

Clarke (1997) argued that 25 years ago there was a great deal more political literacy

> about corporations and the power they wield. Back then, the press and air waves were filled with lively debates about foreign ownership. . . . In more recent years, however, there has been surprisingly little analysis done on the political influence of modern corporations over governments. (p. 5)

Corporations have become educational and lobbying experts. Newspapers and other mainstream media, often monopoly owned and dependent upon advertising, help them to share their ideas and maintain a certain amount of public control and ignorance. Governments are also not blameless as they have pushed for free trade and created tax incentives that sidestep labour and environmental laws (Clarke, 1997).

Environmental Adult Education

Adult education has broadened over the decades to include issues such as welfare, poverty, embodied knowing, gender, sexual orientation, social movements, and race. EAE adds to this critical framework by including a politics of the Earth. It has developed in marked contrast to public environmental education, which focuses on awareness raising and individual behaviour change. EAE sees ecological deterioration as a cultural, political, feminist, economic, race, workplace, youth, global, and local issue. The aim is to acknowledge, respect, and tap into existing ecological knowledges and to explore cultural identities whilst challenging assumptions. As an activist-oriented approach, EAE forges links with social movements and communities and, through imagination, dialogue, and debate, helps people to reconceptualize human/Earth relations and work towards a more just, equitable, and sustainable life on this planet.

Ecological Knowledge and Identity

Beneath the cloak of civilization lies the human who knows the necessity of a rich natural environment. However, there is strength in denying or excluding this knowledge. Public environmental education is premised on the belief that people are unaware of environmental problems and, therefore, the primary activity needs to be awareness raising. However, according to the Global Survey (1997) published in the *Globe and Mail* newspaper during the June 1997 "Mini-Earth Summit" at the United Nations, people's "knowledge of the gravity and scope of environmental problems has greatly expanded" (p. A2) over the past few decades. This has not diminished, and the knowledge often comes from first-hand experience (Clover et al., 2000).

EAE is anchored in an understanding that people have ecological knowledges that can and must be used as the foundation of learning for change. It also recognizes the potential of tapping into spiritual ways of knowing that are linked to the land because this knowledge in inextricably linked to culture (Clover, 2003). The Inuits' cultural and environmental wisdom with regard to the land—about, for example, the migration patterns of animals and the ideal campsites—is being rendered obsolete as the Arctic landscape changes because of global warming (FACMM, 2004). Moreover, culture is both a way of knowing and an identify. It comes from human interaction, but it also comes from the natural world, from a relationship between humans and the Earth. When the land changes irrevocably, culture and knowledge follow (Clover and Harris, 2005).

EAE builds analytically and practically upon the experiential and reflective ecological knowledges that indigenous peoples, fishers, women, and others have within a dialogic interaction of power dynamics and human/cultural/Earth rights. Although it respects and builds upon this knowledge, it also challenges people to test their experiences and assumptions against the collective knowledge of a group and encourages them to make deeper political/power dynamic connections behind existing environmental problems rather than seeing them as purely the inadequacy of individuals. If we are going to create healthy and sustainable communities, we must recognize and respect what people know and how they know it. This does not mean that within this complex milieu of science, politics, development, values, needs, ethnicity, culture, and economics there is not always more to learn and that further information is not valuable and necessary. But to begin with a deficit model, as public environmental education does, means underestimating a fundamentally valuable human/Earth relationship and way of knowing about the natural world as well as how empowering this knowledge and existing relationship can be.

Public environmental education relies heavily on scientific data sharing and expert-driven learning and knowledge. Again, having experts in science-based areas is valuable, but to rely solely on outside experts and to push an overwhelming amount of scientific data onto people reinforces the idea that we can and should attribute different levels of status to knowledge and make one more valuable than the other. This means that professionals "know" and can articulate complex problems, whereas ordinary people, regardless of their experiences, cannot. Second, it camouflages the real need for educational processes based on praxis, conscientization, and active engagement. People may feel fear, apathy, confusion, and an almost total state of paralysis in terms of how to move forward, but people do not *not* know (Clover, 2002).

Political Context and Activism

Public environmental education takes the stance that all humans share an equal responsibility in environmental destruction and, therefore, all individuals must learn to change their attitudes and behaviours. The key is to promote individual actions. One current example of this educational practice is the One-Tonne Challenge. Initiated by the federal government (as so much public environmental education is) around the *Kyoto Protocol* the current One-Tonne Challenge is directed at the general public. The aim is to provide a number of gas-reduction activities that will result in individual behaviour change. Although part of this could be considered legitimate, a deeper analysis shows the fundamental flaws. First, it is difficult to agree that a single mother in Labrador who lives a subsistence lifestyle and relies on public transport has the same impact on the environment as, say, a Bay Street executive who owns two automobiles and a boat. The "equity" assumption inherent in public environmental education is not only ludicrous, but also racist and sexist. EAE is based on the understanding that environmental problems are political and that race, class, and gender injustice and inequities abound. Although individuals can make changes to their lifestyles, focusing on personal behaviour ignores the fundamental cornerstones of capitalism—production and consumption and the tax breaks given to major polluters and corporations such as the chemical industry and factory farms (Clover et al., 2000). And it ignores the impacts of cutbacks to environmental ministries. Public environmental education focuses on asking people to shut off their taps to save water when they brush their teeth while arsenic and other heavy metals leach into groundwater from abandoned mines and large-scale factory-farming pesticides and herbicides contaminate streams. In a particularly poignant case, E. coli bacteria entered the drinking water of a small town in Ontario, Walkerton, causing death and debilitating illness. A judicial ruling in this case highlighted the culpability of funding cuts.

EAE encourages active citizen participation and activism within a framework of ecological justice. Forging links with environmental organisations and other community groups helps to create more workable strategies and achieve mutual goals. The environmental movement has not understood the importance of active and engaged education in bringing about change (Whelan, 2000). It not only has been negligent in recognizing and addressing ecological racism and sexism, but also has perpetuated them. Tan (2004) highlighted the absence of immigrants from the discursive landscape of environmentalism. Many traditional nature-based organisations in Canada marginalize and exclude people of colour. But people of colour "have been actively defining their own ecological struggles despite assertions that immigrants are bereft of ecological traditions. Often this has involved engaging in militant resistance to the imposition of ecologically unsustainable development" (p. 10).

Practices of Environmental Adult Education

The concept of learning in and about place has always been an important element of adult education. EAE broadens this concept of place by using community and the rest of nature. Nothing can stimulate critical debate and dialogue like a trip to Wal-Mart! Workshops in the community and an adult education course at Loyalist College in Belleville, Ontario, used trips to megastores and large grocery chains to discuss connections between waste, packaging, and advertising; gender socialization through toys; the genetic modification of foods; child labour and worker exploitation; and globalization (Clover, 2001). Nature itself is also an excellent teacher and site of learning. It can not only tap into more spiritual and emotional sides of learning, but also help to link issues that at first seem disconnected, to stimulate creativity and imagination, and to tell a story of the community and its problems or strengths. In a small community in northern Ontario, the community identified soil erosion and violence as the two most important environmental problems. At first these appeared to be completely disconnected. However, through a trip to a local park and the collective creation of a collage using natural materials such as plants, worms, water, leaves, and old cigarette butts, a story of an urban–rural power dynamic unfolded. Soil disappeared because it was being removed and bagged so that it could be used for gardens in urban areas, and boys from urban areas came into town and intimidated the young people. We also made links between the diversity of soil and the diversity of people, "and issues of respect and tolerance for difference, and patience with change were addressed 'naturally,' in ways which we could not have predicted" (Hall and Clover, 1997, p. 741).

In 1995 Footprints International at the University of Calgary launched a creative new program. The objectives were to promote the use of popular theatre as a tool to address environmental issues in Canada and the Philippines and create "an entertaining and educational performance about issues of community sustainability that challenged the elite paradigm of sustainable development" (Keough, Carmona, and Grandinetti, 1995, p. 5). The group participated in a skills-building workshop that explored concepts of theatre of the oppressed and "the medium of the mask" and how these could be adapted to environmental issues (p. 7). The slogan of the performance, which aptly fit this gruelling yet exhilarating cross-cultural experience, became "Bigfoot, Littlefoot, stumble, collide and learn to dance" (p. 7).

In 2000 in Toronto a group of environmentalists, artists, and sanitation workers came together to creatively explore the issue of waste. The mediums or canvases chosen were four garbage trucks. Workshops held over a weekend provided the opportunity for the participants to overcome preconceived stereotypes (that environmentalists care only about trees and workers only about jobs) by telling stories and to create a series of images that reflected their concerns about the environment. In particular, the group learned that the people who have the most sophisticated and deepest understanding of waste are not the environmentalists, but rather those who drive the trucks each day to and from landfill sites and recycling plants.

The Environment Centre for New Canadians (ECENECA) in Toronto "views social-economic problems as inherently linked with environmental problems, and strives to address the two as interlocking issues" (Tan, 2004, p. 15). It has recognized that immigrants have a fundamental ecological consciousness and knowledge about the environment that can contribute greatly to Canadian society, but that this has been blocked by a racist and exclusionary culture. ECENECA brings new practices in EAE to African-Canadian and low-income communities that include validating "the social and economic hardships that new immigrants encounter in securing employment, learning a new language, adjusting to a foreign culture, and confronting everyday racism" (p. 15). These practices take on a multidisciplinary approach to developing an ecologically responsible citizenship by offering "community networking, employment skills seminars, computer literacy and writing workshops alongside tree-planting projects, ecosystem restoration, nature exploration, and seminars on transportation, pollution, energy, and other issues" (p. 15).

The University of British Columbia (UBC) and the Polaris Institute in Ottawa have both organized teach-ins and workshops that have brought together activists, students, and NGO workers. The UBC workshops focused on issues ranging from genetically modified foods to the use of art for revolution and direct action to trade and the environment to the military and the corporate complexes. The Polaris Institute's work is designed to enable citizen movements to reskill and retool themselves to fight for democratic social change. Operation 2000 is a project developed to support young adults in developing leadership skills and challenging corporate rule and economic globalization (Clover, 2001).

On Vancouver and Gabriola Islands a group of women developed a creative educational process to involve a community in discussions and protest against a gas-powered plant planned for construction in their community. The issue at hand was that the provincial hydro company would make money from the deal, two US corporations would get the power, and the community would end up with the pollution. The women sent out squares of materials asking people throughout the community to share their ideas and concerns about the plant. Upon their return, the squares created six beautiful "working-protest" Positive Energy Quilts.

The women participated in what they referred to as "quilting in public"to engage people on the streets in further dialogue about the plant. They proudly wore these quilts as they marched on City Hall in protest of the plant. The plant is still on hold (Clover and Markle, 2003).

Conclusion

Do humans (or animals for that matter) have the "right" to a healthy planet? In fact, they do not. The 1992 Rio conference cleverly linked the environment irrevocably to trade, an economic structure, rather than to human rights, a life-sustaining structure. The links between environmental problems and capitalism are profound, and they demand educational opportunities for adults that challenge ecological norms and create new knowledge and actions for socio-environmental change. EAE sees environmental deterioration as a cultural, political, feminist, economic, race, workplace, youth, global, human, and local issue. The aim is to acknowledge, respect, and tap into existing ecological knowledges while at the same time challenging assumptions. Through links to social movements and communities and through imagination, dialogue, and debate, people can reassert their visions and work towards a more just, equitable, and sustainable life on this planet.

References

Bellamy Foster, J. (1994). *The vulnerable planet: A short economic history of the environment.* New York: Monthly Review Press.

Brown, L. (1997). *State of the world.* Washington, DC: World Watch Institute.

Clarke, T. (1997). *Silent coup: Confronting the big business takeover in Canada: Ottawa and Toronto.* Ottawa, ON: Canadian Centre for Policy Alternatives and James Lorimer.

Clarke, T. and Barlow, M. (2003). *Blue gold: The battle against corporate theft of the world's water.* Ottawa, ON: Polaris Institute.

Clover, D. E. (2000). Community arts as environmental adult education and activism: A labour and environment case study. *Convergence, 33*(4), 19–31.

Clover, D. E. (2001). Youth action and learning for sustainable consumption in Canada. In UNESCO/UNEP (Eds.), *Youth, sustainable consumption patterns, and lifestyles* (pp. 73–104). Paris: UNESCO/UNEP.

Clover, D. E. (2002). Environmental adult education. *Adult Learning, 13*(2 and 3), 2–6.

Clover, D. E. (2003). Environmental adult education: Critique and creativity in a globalizing world. In L. H. Hill and D. E. Clover (Eds.), *Environmental adult education: Ecological learning, theory, and practice for socioenvironmental change* (pp. 5–16). San Francisco: Jossey-Bass.

Clover, D. E., Follen, S., and Hall, B. (2000). *The nature of transformation: Environmental adult and popular education* (2nd ed.). Toronto: Transformative Learning Centre, OISE/UT, and International Council for Adult Education.

Clover, D. E. and Harris, C. E. (2005). Agency, isolation, and the coming of new technologies: Exploring "dependency" in costal communities of Newfoundland through participatory research. *Alberta Journal of Educational Research, 51*(1), 18–33.

Clover, D. E. and Markle, G. (2003). Feminist arts practices of popular education: Imagination, counter-narratives, and activism on Vancouver Island and Gabriola Island. *The New Zealand Journal of Adult Learning, 31*(2), 36–52.

Cole, P. (1998). An academic take on Indigenous traditions and ecology. *Canadian Journal of Environmental Education, 3*, 100–115.

Douglas, I. (1983). *The urban environment.* London: Edward Arnold.

Duddy, J. (2002). *Is climate change a gender issue?* Retrieved April 5, 2005, from http://www. awid.org/go

Ecodecision. (1995). Advertising consumption and environment: An interview with Jacques Duval, Chairman of Marketel, McCann Erikson, Canada. *Ecodecision, 16,* 57–59.

FACMM. (2004). *Arctic Climate Impact Assessment policy document: Reykjavik: Fourth Arctic Council ministerial meeting.* Retrieved March 15, 2005, from http://www.acia.uaf.edu/

Fox, M. (2005). *Ocean, Arctic studies show global warming is real.* Retrieved March 15, 2005, from http://www.arcticnet-ulaval.ca/index.php?fa=News.showNews&home=4&menu=55& sub=1&id=41

Global survey. (1997, June). *Globe and Mail,* p. A2.

Hall, B. L. and Clover, D. E. (1997). The future begins today: Nature as teacher and site of learning. *Futures, 29*(8), 737–747.

Hessing, M. and Howlett, M. (1997). *Canadian natural resource and environmental policy: Political economy and public policy.* Vancouver: UBC Press.

Keough, N., Carmona, E., and Grandinetti, L. (1995). Tales from the Sari-Sari: In search of bigfoot. *Convergence, 28*(4), 5–11.

McCutcheon, S. (1991). *Electric rivers: The story of the James Bay Project.* Montreal: Black Rose Books.

Meadows, D. (2002). Polar bears and three-year-olds on thin ice. *System Dynamics Review, 28*(2), 205–206.

Rifkin, J. (1996). *The end of work.* New York: G. P. Putman and Sons.

Rowe, J. S. (1990). *Home place.* Edmonton, AB: NeWest Press.

Sandilands, C. (1993). On 'green' consumerism: Environmental privatization and 'family values.' *Canadian Women Studies, 13*(3), 45–47.

Schlosser, E. (2001). *Fast food nation.* London: Allen Lane, The Penguin Press.

Tan, S. (2004). Anti-racist environmental adult education in a trans-global community: Case studies from Toronto. In D. E. Clover (Ed.), *Global perspectives in environmental adult education,* (pp. 3–22). New York: Peter Lang.

von Moltke, K. (1997). The global trade in commodities: Madonna versus tuna. *Ecodecision, 24,* 37–38.

Whelan, J. (2000). Learning to save the world: Observations of training for effective advocacy in the Australian environmental movement. *Convergence, 33*(3), 62–73.

22

Towards Celebration through Education: Queer Canadian Adult Education

John P. Egan and Anthony J. Flavell

U ntil 1969 consensual homosexual sex between adult males was an indictable offence in Canada, punishable by jail. The concomitant personal costs associated with merely being charged with such offences were, in the long term, worse than the legal consequences: Loss of family, community standing, and career often lead to dire economic and social marginality. It is unsurprising then that few Canadian queers (used here as an inclusive term for lesbian, gay, bisexual, and transgender persons) "chose" to come out prior to the 1970s—which makes the developments over the subsequent 35 years all the more remarkable.

With respect to criminal and civil law, Canada today is one of the most progressive countries in the world regarding homosexuality. And although the current debate over national, legislated equal ("same-sex") marriage is by no means a *fait accompli*, court precedents clearly indicate that eventually all territories and provinces will have to extend civil marriage access regardless of gender, based on the principle of civil marriage as "the lawful union of two persons to the exclusion of all others" (Parliamentary Research Branch, 2005, para 1). The process of getting there continues to unfold.

In most matters of individual civil liberty, queer Canadians share a level of legal entitlement comparable to other "like-minded" social democracies: Sweden, Norway, Denmark, the Netherlands, Belgium, and New Zealand. Homosexual sex between consenting adults (and between consenting minors) is legal; each country also offers explicit protections based on the ground of sexual orientation and gender. Belgium and the Netherlands offer legal marriage, and the rest offer domestic partnerships similar to marriage. However, most Canadian provinces and territories offer same- and opposite-sex couples equal access to joint adoption, whereas nearly all other like-minded nations forbid adoption by queers, single or partnered. Ultimately, it is this area of family law—de facto partnerships, adoption, celebration of civil marriage—that puts Canada slightly ahead among the like-minded group of nations.

These legal entitlements are fantastic! They mean that queer Canadians do not need to worry about the state interfering in their romantic and familial lives. However, there remains a substantial gap between the legal status of queers and the everyday lived experience of many of us. Despite these juridical gains, many of us cannot rely on our neighbours, colleagues, and families of origin to embrace our nascent entitlements. Anti-queer discrimination in matters of housing, employment, and accessing services (including health services) still occurs, despite explicit protection in every provincial, territorial, and federal human rights policy. Anti-gay violence against persons and property remains surprisingly common—even in neighbourhoods such as Montreal's le Village and Vancouver's Commercial Drive, with their strong, visible queer presences.

Thus, while it might be tempting to think that, with most legal issues resolved, we queers can relax a bit, there remains work to be done. Much of this is educational: We need to educate ourselves about our entitlements, about discrimination and prejudice (and how to respond to them), and we need to educate non-queer Canadians about the realities of our lives. With queer-friendly and queer-affirming curricula only now making their way into Canadian public schooling, the onus remains on the community adult education sector to educate both the queer community and Canadian society at large on queer matters.

According to MacDougall (2001), Canadian legal discourses on queer rights have progressed along a continuum, with four main points of demarcation. Over time Canadian queers have moved from condemnation (rejection and vilification), through compassion (tolerance and pity) and condonation (acceptance, if inferior), and, ultimately, to celebration (valued and equal). With the reality of same-sex marriage and joint adoption, we have increasingly integrated queer family rights into our established individual rights and freedoms agenda; being able to marry my partner meant that the state quite literally celebrated our union.

We, along with our activist peers, marvel at how far things have come in the last 15 years, thanks almost entirely to the *Canadian Charter of Rights and Freedoms*. The *Charter* did not list sexual orientation as a ground for seeking redress under the Canadian Human Rights Commission. It did, however, leave room for communities not explicitly listed to have their experiences "read into" the *Charter* and gave (through the courts) a mechanism for queers to seek protected status.

This chapter examines developments in Canadian queer adult education, much of which endeavours to

- improve civil entitlements for Canadian queers;
- mitigate gaps experienced by queers with respect to health, welfare, or security;
- educate mainstream society at large about the inequities experienced by their queer family, friends, and colleagues; and
- foment progressive notions regarding how society makes sense of issues related to human sexuality and notions of gender.

This chapter offers a broad typology of the sorts of themes and issues that have emerged both in the practice of queer adult education and in our literature. Most of the work reflects practice or research conducted in Canada; however, in some instances contributions by persons involved in the queer Canadian diaspora (whose work overseas has been shaped significantly by their experiences in Canada) are also included. Finally, some of the gaps in Canadian queer adult education are discussed.

Overarching Themes: The "4-H" Club

A society that celebrates all persons' consensual, affirming sexual orientations and gender identities would have no ostensive need for queer adult education; Canada is not there yet. Thus, queer adult education remains a primary means of decreasing rancour and building rapport amongst Canadians regardless of their sexuality or gender. And given that (with few exceptions) most queers' families of origin are constructed wholly within a paradigm of heteronormativity—too often in virulently homophobic families and communities—queers themselves also need to unlearn homophobia, heterocentrism, and heteronormativity internalized through lived experience.

Much of Canadian queer adult education, therefore, addresses three social justice themes: *homophobia, heterosexism,* and *heteronormativity*. In terms of theoretical notions and underlying philosophy, all queer Canadian adult education scholarship involves at least one of these themes. However, the topics addressed in the specifics of practice vary widely, with one exception: Matters of queer *health*, particularly HIV/AIDS, predominate. Thus one can characterize the canon of queer adult education as being characterized by a sort of queered 4-H club.

Homophobia

Homophobia, although a term with a great deal of discursive currency, is something of a misnomer. Who among us knows anyone who accedes to being characterized as a homophobe? However, rather than the irrational, intense fear of queers that it is presumed to be, homophobia is the possession of a clear prejudice or dislike for queers. Homophobia is a belief that queers are to be feared, that we present a genuine threat to society at large, and that any degree of tolerance or acceptance of queers is dangerous—to the very fabric of "normal" society. It manifests itself in political organization against civil entitlements for queers, in antagonistic behaviour towards queers (or those perceived to be queer), in the use of anti-queer rhetoric to denigrate queers and allies alike, and, in the extreme, in the use of violence against queers. Homophobes allow for no degree of civic entitlement to queers as individuals or as families. In everyday terms, it argues that queers are unacceptable and are to be isolated or even exterminated.

Heterosexism

Heterosexism allows that queers exist, but that they are inferior to "normal" (with respect to sexual orientation and gender identity) heterosexual people. Heterosexism allows for a modicum of tolerance for queers, but explicitly puts heterosexuality and rigid gender conformity above sexual and gender diversity. It therefore allows for opposite-sex partnerships to be treated better than same-sex ones, though it can allow for some degree of civic entitlement to same-sex families—like civil unions instead of civil marriage. In everyday terms it argues that, although queer is okay, straight is better.

Heteronormativity

Heteronormativity allows for a degree of acceptance of queers, but often misses evidence where queers are marginalized. To a great extent media images of what is "normal" in Canadian society are the strongest evidence of how pervasive heteronormativity is. How often do we encounter matter-of-fact representations of queer individuals and families in our public sphere, on television, in film, in music, or in the press? Cumulatively, the perpetuation of relentless representation of heterosexual Canadian life and of opposite-sex pairings and families conveys the message that queer might be okay, but is not very important. This is a sort of "frequency" argument—that because queer families are a relatively small minority, there is no need to represent them in the public sphere. Would such an argument be tenable in Canada today were the topic multiculturalism or Aboriginal Canadians?

Health

Health, although appearing somewhat extraneous to these other concepts, is, in fact, a direct result of them. For a long time homophobia precluded offering queer-specific health services in Canada. Then such services were offered quietly, but one had to have membership in a specific, closed social network to access them. Today, queer-specific or queer-sensitive services are commonly available in major urban centres, but less so in suburban and rural parts of the country. And much of the funding for "queer health" targets HIV/AIDS prevention and care for queer men as a significant potential liability to Canada's public health infrastructure, an imbalance reflected in the literature reviewed here.

Whether dealing with antagonism, chauvinism, or ignorance, Canadian queer adult education most frequently responds to deficits: in security, understanding, equality, wellness, or local capacity. Integral to much of this work is a critique of rigid, discriminatory notions regarding (homo)sexuality and gender. Many such critiques are informed by *queer theory* (see the following section), but queer theory and Canadian queer adult education are not synonymous.

Queer Theory

A range of theoretical traditions inform the body of queer adult education scholarship in Canada. Without exception, these are critical frameworks that challenge norms, disrupt discourses, and are liberatory in orientation (none argue for the status quo), with queer theory playing an increasingly prominent role. Queer theory, rather than merely prioritizing issues pertinent to lesbians, gays, bisexuals, and transgender persons, challenges—and often rejects—rigid typologies regarding sexual orientation (straight, gay, bisexual, lesbian) and gender (male and female), and the accompanying discourses (Sedgewick, 1993; Seidman, 1994; Warner, 1993). Queer theory positions these (and other) constructs around gender and sexuality as socially situated, historical ways of meaning making that have become reified over time. It rightly connects much of today's language around sexual orientation and gender as a legacy of the medicalization of sexual "deviancy" and the psychological pathologization of anything but matrimonial, opposite-sex, missionary-position, penile-vaginal intercourse. Queer theory therefore rejects essentialized notions about gender and sexuality; thus, relevant psychological and medical discourses are often the target of queer theorists' critiques. Their more compelling critiques include a discursive shift from pathologizing homosexual behaviour to pathologizing gender presentation, as well as focusing on sexual behaviour over one's entire lifetime to categorize one as gay, straight, bisexual, or lesbian.

Queer activists on both sides of the 49th parallel repeatedly return to the 1972 decision of the American Psychological Association (APA) to delist homosexuality as a mental illness as a landmark in the public discourse on homosexuality. However, since 1973 a range of "gender disorders" have effectively made homosexuality acceptable if a male homosexual remains "masculine" or a female homosexual "feminine" (Sedgewick, 1993). In particular, children who resist efforts to make them conform to rigid codes of dress, behaviour, and interest—tomboys and sissies, in the vernacular—are subjected to "therapy" to coerce such conformity. This is not new: Queers have been coerced, even abused, to conform to these rules; what has changed is that psychologists are not supposed to explicitly engage in such practices to change sexual orientation (APA, 2005). The modus operandi remains the same; the goal is allegedly different. And the result—trauma for those whose gender presentation does not fit tidily into rigid ideas about masculinity and femininity—is the same.

A similar problem emerges with respect to what "determines" a person's sexual orientation. Do we assess a person's lifetime sexual expression (in terms of partners and objects) and categorize them accordingly? Or can individuals assert which (if any) of these labels reflects their understanding of their sexuality identity, regardless of whether their lifetime sexual activity does not fit tidily therein? Queer theory rejects that everyone has a determined, concise, tidy sexual orientation. It argues that for many, given a social space in which it is relatively safe to do so, many persons express their sexual and romantic selves across gender and sexual orientation lines. The critique is of both the categorizations and the rigidity of their application. For example, Boshier (1995) "outed" Coolie Verner—a seminal figure in the development of adult education as an academic discipline in Canada and internationally, particularly at the University of British Columbia—as gay, though Verner never addressed issues of sexuality or queer rights (in general or his own) in his work. Whether people's sexual orientation qualifies their work as "queer" when their body of work itself offers no substantive contribution to these areas remains a point of dissent for many.

These critiques are not wholly unproblematic, however. Whereas many queers agree that gender can be tyrannical, many others fairly worship gender in their daily lives—even as they flout the categorizations employed. Butch women and nelly ("effeminate") men assert themselves in terms of their gender play—claiming new categorizations rather than rejecting traditional categorizations out of hand. Other queers strongly link their desire for persons of the same gender to their gender presentation, at least in terms of grooming and dress. With regards to sexual orientation, for many of us the availability of an identity as a gay (and later queer) man offered hope when homophobic, heterosexist, heteronormative society had (and has) worn us down. We draw sustenance from this sense of self, the power of affiliation and community, and the positioning of ourselves in neighbourhoods where queer is normal. We accept many of queer theory's critiques with respect to the rigid application of these categories; we reject, however, any attempt to generalize them to all queers. That seems to replicate and reify, rather than assuage, hegemony and exclusion—they are merely of a different form.

AIDS and Gay Men's Health

For a number of years queer and AIDS were synonymous in adult education—as they were in the Canadian public sphere. At the 31st annual Adult Education Research Conference (AERC), Boshier (1990), reflecting on his experience in animating workshops on HIV prevention for international development workers, found that "horrendous misunderstanding arises from differential interpretations of terms like rear entry, oral sex, penile penetration or sexual orientation" (p. 23) and highlighted the importance of sexual health programs that unpack these sorts of terms. At the Canadian Association for the Study of Adult Education (CASAE) annual meeting a few years later, McKay (1994) examined the evolution of AIDS NGOs in Vancouver and acknowledged the strong ties between queer rights and HIV/AIDS issues because "the more numerous cases [of HIV/AIDS] in the gay population to date have resulted in an organization which has been inextricably tied to gay human rights issues" (p. 269).

Research on HIV/AIDS education for queer men carried out by one of the authors of this chapter (Egan, in press) examined the discourses embedded in HIV prevention materials used in Vancouver over the first two decades of the Canadian HIV/AIDS epidemic. It showed that queer male subjugated knowledges—knowledges that posit male-male desire as a positive and affirming experience that should be discussed openly, candidly, and in everyday language—disrupt traditional, heteronormative, and homophobic public health messages on human sexuality, which establishes a discourse that "continues to transgress the mainstream medical discourse on sexuality" (Egan, 2000, p. 103). Trussler and Marchand (2005), international leaders in the field of community-based research (CBR), contended that AIDS NGOs can "build local knowledge for local action" (p. 44) and allow for enhanced organizational development, community benefit, best-practice improvement, policy development, health promotion, emancipation and empowerment, and rapid assessment. Allan and Leonard's (2005) essay on "positive prevention"—that is, a shift in the current norms and practice of HIV prevention towards the consideration of HIV-positive persons as equal partners in developing educational strategies—was significantly informed by Allan's background in queer and AIDS activism in Canada prior to his migration to Australia.

Grassroots Education

Much of this literature on HIV/AIDS is positioned from the realm of community educators and researchers who work for small and large NGOs. Their community-centric, local, and pragmatic orientation, in addition to substantively contributing to knowledge on HIV/AIDS, also adds to our understanding of grassroots, community adult education. The momentum generated by AIDS activism in the 1980s has had a ripple effect in queer adult education as a whole; in fact, research on HIV/AIDS education by one of the authors of this chapter comes from a preoccupation with grassroots learning—not vice versa. The author's reflection on seeking research training as an activist and endeavouring to acquire skills to facilitate local action (Egan, 2001) was in part inspired by work in queer NGOs.

Mizzi's (2003) work with queer activists in the UN protectorate of Kosovo and as a community health volunteer in Japan has linked the fight for queer justice with the international peace movement. In particular, "identifying queer citizens to build a cycle of empowerment" (p. 76) for themselves as queers and for members of ethnocultural minorities reflects a commitment to transparently link queer justice with broader areas of human rights work. The sorts of challenges that international NGO staff face—in ensuring that locals retain ownership of the programs, for example (p. 79), and integrating critical notions of power and agency—reflect the liberatory discourses found in adult educational foundation works such as Freire's (1983). Moore's (2004) and Butterwick and Selman's (2003) research on feminist action groups emphasized that often the issues that emerge in queer adult education are neither wholly unique nor easily distanced from issues such as sexism, racism, and classism. Identifying and collaborating with allies are necessary to challenge homophobia, heterosexism, and heteronormativity in society at large. Similarly, Low's (2002) proposed culturally appropriate model for sexual health education for Asian youth (queer and not) in British Columbia integrates critiques of racism, sexism and heterosexism—and argues that programs and services that cannot respond to intersections of identity cannot serve diverse communities.

Another important aspect of Canadian queer adult education has been the examination of queer adult educators themselves, including the contexts in which they work, the specifics of their practice, and the theoretical and political stances that inform their work. Much of this work has been conceptualized around the notion of a queer positional pedagogy, which connects "the realms of personal histories, knowledges, dispositions, locations and experiences to education, so that learning might been visioned as a personal and political encounter" (Grace and Gouthro, 2000, p. 13). A queer positional pedagogy means that an educator's queerness should not be divorced from his or her educational practice, particularly in engaging in issues of justice, empowerment, and democracy. In broader terms, positional pedagogies reject the notion that education is ever neutral or objective: Educators of all stripes bring themselves—their lived experiences, their values, their beliefs, their biases—into the classroom (as do learners). Thus it is imperative to deal with the question of positionality upfront to make one's practice more transparent and to create educational spaces where inequity, injustice, and hegemony can be challenged (by students and educators) head on.

Grace (2002) has written extensively on queer positional pedagogies. He often employs autobiographical queer life-narrative research and "investigates the personal and difficult journey to be, become, belong, act, speak, and represent oneself as a queer person, citizen and educator" (p. 100). He has collaborated a number of times with American queer adult education scholar Hill. Grace and Hill (2001) encouraged queer adult educators to develop a "queer praxis [that] contests such privileging of male over female, straight over gay, and private acts over public ones" (p. 147). Theirs is a call for a radical, liberatory queer pedagogy.

Queerying Who's Missing and Where To Next?

Canadian queer adult education scholars have been integral to the increased profile of queer issues in adult education. We have been a driving force in the activities of the AERC/LGBTQ caucus, including the queer preconferences. With the two most recent joint CASAE/AERC events having been held in Canada (Vancouver in 2000, Victoria in 2004), Canadian queer activists have been guest speakers at queer caucus events, including Svend Robinson (Canada's first openly gay MP) in 2000 and James Chamberlain (who fought a banning of queer-friendly children's books from BC public schools) in 2004. And CASAE has proved fertile ground for graduate students interested in queer issues. Two of the first four winners of the CASAE award for best student paper have written about queer issues. And a review of recent dissertations, theses, and graduating papers submitted by students enrolled in graduate adult education programs across Canada shows numerous queer-themed works; what we see at CASAE conferences and in journals is only the tip of the iceberg.

But there are many ways in which Canadian queer adult education remains inadequate. There is a dearth of queer women's voices, both in our literature and at our conferences—despite women often being the driving force behind Canada's more liberatory queer activism. Moreover, the silence on bisexuality has been deafening—for women and men. And although our literature increasingly nominally integrates the issues of transgender persons, there has been no substantive work focused on trans folk and no active representation by out trans persons at our conferences. Queer adult education scholarship in Canada remains largely the domain of gay men.

We can easily take action to mitigate these gaps in our community of scholars, among our undergraduate and graduate students, and at our regional and national conferences. Rather than presume that we've created a welcome space, we need to actively invite queer women and trans folk to participate. Their experiences can only enrich us; their perspective will doubtlessly challenge our work and our biases. These are all good things.

References

Allan, B. and Leonard, W. (2005). Asserting a positive role: HIV-positive people in prevention. *New Directions in Adult and Continuing Education: HIV/AIDS Education for Adults, 2005*(105) 55–64.

American Psychological Association. (2005). *Answers to your questions about homosexuality.* Retrieved April 10, 2005, from http://www.apa.org/pubinfo/answers.html

Boshier, R. (1990). Ideological and epistemological foundations of education about AIDS. In P. Kleiber and L. Tisdell (Eds.), *Proceedings of the 31st Annual Adult Education Research Conference* (pp. 19–24). Athens: University of Georgia.

Boshier, R. (1995). Words from the edge: A postmodern reflection on Coolie Verner and the Black Book. In S. Scott and D. J. Collett (Eds.), *Proceedings of the 36th Annual Adult Education Research Conference* (pp. 19–26). Edmonton: University of Alberta.

Butterwick, S. and Selman, J. (2003). Deep listening in a feminist popular theatre project: Upsetting the position of audience in participatory education. *Adult Education Quarterly, 53*(4), 7–23.

Egan, J. (2000). Interdictions & benedictions: AIDS prevention discourses in Vancouver Canada. In T. J. Sork, V.-L. Chapman, and R. St. Clair (Eds.), *Proceedings of the 41st Annual Adult Education Research Conference* (pp. 101–105). Vancouver, BC: University of British Columbia.

Egan, J. (2001). From grassroots activist to researcher—inside and out. *Convergence, 34*(4), 7–15.

Egan, J. (in press). Interdictions & benedictions: A discursive analysis of AIDS prevention materials in Vancouver Canada. *Canadian Journal for the Study of Adult Education.*

Freire, P. (1983). *Pedagogy of the oppressed* (M. B. Ramos, Trans.). New York: Continuum.

Grace, A. P. (2002). "Transformational ministry" and "reparative therapy": Transformative learning gone awry. In J. M. Pettitt and R. P. Francis (Eds.), *Proceedings of the 43rd Adult Education Research Conference* (pp. 123–128). Raleigh, NC: North State University

Grace, A. P. and Gouthro, P. A. (2000). Using models of feminist pedagogies to think about issues and directions in graduate education for women students. *Studies in Continuing Education, 22*(1), 5–28.

Grace, A. P. and Hill, R. J. (2001). Using queer knowledges to build inclusionary pedagogy in adult education. In R. O. Smith, J. M. Dirkx, P. L. Eddy, P. L. Farrell, and M. Polzin (Eds.),

Proceedings of the 42nd Adult Education Research Conference (pp. 145–150). East Lansing: Michigan State University.

Low, C. (2002). Racy sexy: Sorting through the traffic jam at the intersection of race, culture, ethnicity, and sexuality: A model for intergenerational multicultural sexuality education for parents. In J. M. Pettitt and R. P. Francis (Eds.), *Proceedings of the 43rd Adult Education Research Conference* (pp. 225–230). Raleigh: North State University

MacDougall, B. (2001). The celebration of same-sex marriage. *Ottawa Law Review, 32,* 235–267.

McKay, S. (1994). From umbrella to web: AIDS organizations in Vancouver. In R. Sigaty (Ed.), *Proceedings of the 13th Annual Conference of the Canadian Association for the Study of Adult Education* (pp. 268–273). Vancouver, BC: Simon Fraser University.

Mizzi, R. (2003). In solidarity: Global perspectives on using community health education to build queer peace. In R. J. Hill and A. Grace (Eds.), *Proceedings of the 1ˢᵗ Annual Adult Education Research Conference Lesbian, Gay, Bisexual, Transgender, Queer & Allies Pre-Conference* (pp. 73–78). San Francisco: San Francisco State University.

Moore, M. (2004). Becoming an ally: Power, privilege, and participatory practices in explorations of women's sexual and gender identity. In A. Grace (Ed.), *Proceedings of the 2nd Annual Adult Education Research Conference Lesbian, Gay, Bisexual, Transgender, Queer & Allies Pre-Conference* (pp. 62–64). Victoria, BC: University of Victoria.

Parliamentary Research Branch. (2005). *Civil Marriage Act.* Retrieved June 28, 2005, from http://www.parl.gc.ca/common/Bills_ls.asp?lang=E&Parl=38&Ses=1&ls=C38&source=Bills_ Individuals

Sedgewick, E. K. (1993). How to bring your kids up gay. In M. Warner (Ed.), *Fear of a queer planet: Queer politics and social theory* (pp. 69–81). Minneapolis: University of Minnesota Press.

Seidman, S. (1994). Queer theory/sociology: A dialogue. *Sociological Theory, 12*(2), 166–177.

Trussler, T. and Marchand, R. (2005). HIV/AIDS community-based research. *New Directions in Adult and Continuing Education: HIV/AIDS Education for Adults, 2005*(105), 43–54.

Warner, M. (1993). Introduction. In M. Warner (Ed.), *Fear of a queer planet: Queer politics and social theory* (pp. vii-xxvii). Minneapolis: University of Minnesota Press.

23
Mothers as Popular Educators: Love Lives in Social Action

Dorothy A. Lander

My historical research on women leaders and educators in three social movements supports *eros* (loving relationship) as the (com)passionate life and learning force that animates popular education. *Popular* education, or education "of the people," builds on the writings of adult educator Paulo Freire and his conception of love as foundational to dialogue and praxis (action with reflection) with oppressed groups in Latin America.

This chapter focuses on the loving relationships of three activist women leaders—Lotta Hitschmanova (Unitarian Service Committee of Canada—USC), Letitia Youmans (Dominion Woman's Christian Temperance Union—WCTU), and Mary Arnold (Antigonish Movement and Cooperative League of the USA)—who practiced popular education long before this term entered the lexicon of adult education. An earlier term, *organized mother-love*—used in reference to the WCTU and its "religion of compassionate action" (Garner, 1998, p. 274)—could describe the popular education approach of all three women.

I apply to these three women popular educators Smith-Rosenberg's (1985) term *public mothers*, which described independent women reformers of the nineteenth century—typically not birth mothers—who mobilized and educated to produce subjectivities for social action, deploying the life force of compassionate love (eros), particularly an eros of resistance. I develop the idea of compassionate love as an activating relational force in each of their narratives.

1. Lotta Hitschmanova, Czech immigrant, Holocaust survivor, and executive director of the USC, was very close to her younger sister, Lilly, except for those years of separation in the 1930s and 1940s when Lotta lost contact with Lilly and their parents, who died in the Auschwitz gas chambers (Sanger, 1986).

2. Letitia Youmans, first president of the Dominion (of Canada) WCTU, wrote in her 1893 autobiography of her married life with widower Arthur Youmans, her home-schooling of the younger of eight step-children, and Arthur's support for her temperance activism.

3. Mary Arnold moved from New York to Nova Scotia in 1937 with her lifelong companion, Mabel Reed. Mary was officially a field-worker for the Extension Department of St. Francis Xavier University. Mary and Mabel opened up their home as the centre to build

Tompkinsville, the first cooperative housing community in Nova Scotia associated with the Antigonish Movement of the 1930s.

Popular Education as an Eros of Learning

For Freire (2002), love was the creative force of liberatory movements and critical pedagogies of resistance. Allman (1998) referred to what is perhaps Freire's most important sentence in *Pedagogy of the Oppressed*—his hope that this book might contribute to sustaining the "creation of a world in which it will be easier to love" (Freire, p. 40). She linked Freire's ideas of dialectical thinking to love: "Whenever there are no longer two opposite groups, the possibility emerges of human beings uniting in love, with a commitment to social justice and to care for all of our social and natural world" (p. 10).

The enduring distinctions between public and private that "make us believe that love has no place in the classroom" (hooks, 1994, p. 198) and that the life of a woman teacher in the Victorian era was synonymous with the renunciation of embodied passion (Tamboukou, 2003) also erase eros and the body from popular education. Like hooks, I draw on Sam Keen's (1994) counter-discourse of eros as the relational force that propels every life-form from a state of mere potentiality to one of actuality.

The narrative sources on which I draw highlight loving relationships as the political act of popular education. Critical pedagogies of resistance borne of love, which public mothers such as Lotta, Letitia, and Mary deployed in and for the homeplace as much as in the organizational entity of the social movement (e.g., the Extension Department of St. Francis Xavier University for the Antigonish Movement), offer an alternative model of the relationship between power and knowledge.

Methodologies of Love and Resistance

The memory work involved in representing self and others in the autobiographies and histories of these three public mothers—Lotta, Letitia, and Mary—occupies a hybrid space between the private and the public. Women popular educators as memoirists feature a dialogical and relational "I" akin to Freire's (2002) loving and "authentic (that is, critical) witness" (p. 176). The relational "I" of autobiography encourages critical self-reflection, which is the basis of loving witness and serves to avoid the perils of the us/them mentality that Razack (1993) claimed occurs all too often among popular educators and human rights activists. Razack's experience is a caution against romanticizing these women. I am alert for instances in which they define themselves normatively to the degree that they become overinvested in fashioning the self as the mother–liberator of the oppressed.

My methodology is consistent with genealogy or "history of the present"; that is, the theoretical questions that initiated this study began with this present of ours as women who are popular educators. How do we as women adult educators conceive of ourselves as popular educators within this present? "How have we become what we are and what are the possibilities of becoming 'other'?" (Tamboukou, 2003, pp. 135–136). My genealogical research into the eros of learning in all of its embodied, sensory, pleasure-enhancing relationships, not only sexual, elaborates the relationship of these three public mothers, often with a "great friend"— spouses and sisters, friends and lovers. Eros foregrounds the practices of resistance at the intersection of private and public spaces.

Lotta Hitschmanova

The memories that the name Lotta Hitschmanova (Figure 1) evokes today among Canadians who grew up in the 1950s and 1960s are embodied images—we remember her accented Eastern European voice in the public service announcements for the USC and the famous address, 56 Sparks Street. From the television ads, often on the CBC, we also remember the physically tiny women in a peaked cap and olive-green uniform with rows of medal ribbons (from Lesotho, Korea, India, Greece), and "Canada" firmly pinned on her lapel. Clyde Sanger's (1986) biography of Lotta Hitschmanova—which draws on the memories of Lotta's sister, Lilly Steen, of her life and career before she launched the USC in Canada in 1945—is my principal source.

Figure 1. Lotta Hitschmanova (Courtesy of the National Archives of Canada, PA165329, and the Unitarian Service Committee).

Lotta Hitschmanova articulated her dialogical and loving approach to social action at the chancellor's lecture at Brock University in 1973: "To come as an open-minded friend and good listener when offering help; to say goodbye to a project when it can continue on its own; to serve with a personal touch" (Sather, 2001, p. 5).

Lotta's European accent and the anachronism of wearing a war uniform was a source of mockery that invited characterizations of her as a martinet— an image that endures (Sanger, 1986, p. 156). Lotta explained to reporters that her uniform, modeled on an American army nurse's uniform, proved invaluable because she was instantly recognizable when she arrived in a Canadian city for fund raising or travelled overseas looking for projects (p. 150). Lotta's practice of wearing a uniform qualifies as an erotic pedagogy of resistance on a large scale to patriarchy and war. Her war uniform, which she wore everywhere, acted as a repeated subversive utterance (Butler, 1990) that had the effect of subverting war into peace and poverty into the care and development of the world's children.

Lotta's family history stands out as the deep relational pull that propelled her during her 35 years with the USC to resist the wreckage and child poverty left by wars in Greece, Korea, the Middle East, Vietnam, and Bangladesh. As a refugee in Paris who had escaped the Nazi incursion, Lotta lived on a diet of beetroot and carrots; she made her first contact with the USC when she sought out the American headquarters after fainting in the street from fatigue and hunger in 1942 (Sanger, 1986, p. 25). That same summer she was granted a visa to Canada. In the summer of 1945 Lotta learned of the fate of her parents and their death in the Auschwitz gas chambers; by this time she had been organizing the USC full-time for nearly three months, and her sister Lilly, an architect, was underemployed as a dressmaker in Palestine. In an evocation of eros as coupling and uncoupling, Lotta wrote to a woman friend in Europe:

> If I tell you that nobody is waiting for me any longer, that I have lost the beings who are the most dear to me, you will measure my despair, for you have the same sorrow. There's only one thing: to work, so that their sacrifice may not be in vain. (p. 38)

Lotta's Central European authoritarianism as a public mother in the context of the institutional address (56 Sparks Street) and the heavy annual turnover of staff for many years, according to Sanger (1986), gave rise to deserving comments such as, "The only thing lacking was the general's insignia on the shoulders" (p. 137). Even when she was absent from Ottawa, she insisted on receiving a letter twice a week when abroad, three times a week when touring Canada, from each of the "desks" (Canadian, Publicity, and Foster Parents; p. 153). She graded the scripts for radio spots and news releases as "Excellent, Very Good, Good, and so on down" (p. 154).

Smith-Rosenberg's (1985) comparison of Jane Addams and other settlement-house women as public mothers who "felt the same devotion for their 'children' that biological mothers did" (p. 263) served to justify new roles for women outside the family. As a public mother, Lotta's homely slogans such as Bread for Greece and the March of Diapers, and the familiar image of her "bending over some scrap of a child, ladling out milk, 'white gold from Canada,' . . . into a tin mug" (Sanger, 1986, p. 10) highlighted her readiness to invoke maternal images of her subjectivity at the interstices of public and private spheres. Lilly's immigration to Canada in 1948 coincided with Lotta's efforts through USC Canada to organize shipments of food and clothing to children's refugee camps in Czechoslovakia and her cross-Canada tour to set up the foster parent scheme for "adopting" a Czechoslovak child for three months for $45 (p. 55).

Letitia Creighton Youmans

The eros of learning intersects the private and public in Letitia Youmans's (1893) autobiography. In 1849 Letitia Creighton accepted the position of assistant teacher at Picton Ladies' Academy and continued there until receiving an offer of marriage from widower Arthur Youmans. She married Arthur in 1850 when she was 23 years old, taking on a family of eight—"some of them not much my junior in age, others of them helpless children" (p. 68)—and the new roles of mother and farm wife. When Arthur decided to dispose of the farm and flour mills and they moved into the town of Picton, Letitia's work as a temperance educator began in earnest. With the Band of Hope (a generic term for children's temperance organizations), she introduced total-abstinence pledges into Bible class and Sunday school. A subscriber to Sabbath-school periodicals, she learned of an assembly to be held at Lake Chautauqua in 1874, and she and Arthur journeyed there by train and steamer. When the assembly was drawing to a close, the temperance women met to take steps towards forming a Woman's National Temperance Association, arranging themselves in groups according to the states they represented. In the first of many instances, Letitia acknowledged Arthur's strategic support:

> I alone was left out in the cold being the only Canadian woman. My husband standing very near the enclosure or tent, addressed the lady presiding, "Mrs Willing, could you take in Canada?" She responded smilingly, "Certainly, we will make it international." (pp. 103–104)

In the same year, Letitia organized a WCTU chapter in her hometown of Picton.

Letitia received requests for her platform oratory that would take her all across Canada and the US, as well as England, Scotland, and Ireland. Among the requests that began to come in for her assistance in organizing WCTU chapters in many towns and villages in Ontario, she received an invitation to speak at a convention in Cobourg (where she grew up) for the purpose of uniting two orders of Templars. As Letitia stood to speak, she experienced a "choking sensation" (Youmans, 1893, p. 128), but the impediment removed, and she managed to present her position, which she was to repeat in her speeches throughout her career:

I assured the audience that I had not come there to advocate women's rights, but that I had come to remonstrate against women's and children's wrongs. But there is one form of woman's rights in which I firmly believe, and that is, the right of every woman to have a comfortable home, of every wife to have a sober husband, of every mother to have sober sons. (p. 128)

Letitia travelled the length of southern Ontario to form WCTU chapters, canvassing in the interest of the "local option" Dunkin Bill and speaking in "little country churches full to overflowing" (Youmans, 1893, p. 161). As a public speaker, Letitia was happy to speak to an audience with mothers and their crying babies. She "considered that some of those mothers could never get out unless they took the infant with them, and they had rights as well as others" (p. 162). She recalled one instance when the "little tot . . . mounted the pulpit behind me, and with open music book, . . . commenced to sing something she knew . . . very loudly, 'Shoo fly, don't bodder me'" (p. 162).

Letitia chose her words strategically: "The term prohibition, when applied to the liquor traffic, was obnoxious, so much so that I would announce my subject as 'home protection'" (Youmans, 1893, p. 207). However, when she encountered anti-prohibition forces, she did not hold back anger, a pedagogy of resistance not usually associated with the good mother of maternal feminism. Cartoonist and prohibitionist John Bengough (1887), on the cover page of his political satire magazine *Grip* (Figure 2) showed Ontario WCTU President Letitia Youmans giving cabinet minister the Honourable George Foster an "exemplary trouncing" (p. 1). Professor Foster, as "noble knight of prohibition," came up from Ottawa to address the WCTU convention, and "his speech was the exasperating platitudes about the country not being 'ripe,' the wisdom of high license for the present etc. etc." (p. 1). Invariably visual and textual references to Letitia Youmans associated her considerable girth with her social action. According to prohibitionist Bengough, "Metaphorically laying him [George Foster] over her ample knee, she gave him the most effective castigation that any public man in Canada has ever received" (p. 2). Anger is not a typical attribute of the feminine or the private sphere; however, Bengough normalized this emotion—perhaps reorganized woman's anger for a largely male readership—by representing Letitia Youmans in the maternal act of spanking a boy who was behaving badly.

Arthur had been Letitia's travelling companion for the first several years of her temperance work, and initially his death on November 1, 1882, "a marked era in [Letitia's] life history" (Youmans, 1893, p. 238), suggested to her with "overwhelming force, I can never go out alone, my journeying must cease" (p. 240). The life force of eros emerges as pure sensation at the moment of death. Letitia went on with her life work, "missing, oh, how sadly, the strong arm on which I had leaned" (p. 241). She accepted as her husband's dying message the letter he had sent her a few days before: "Do all you can, your reward will come in the great future. Your affectionate husband" (p. 240). Letitia saw her *"duty was quite plain"* (p. 207) in 1885

Figure 2. Front cover of Grip, October, 1887 (Courtesy of National Library of Canada).

when the Ontario government gave unmarried women the municipal vote: "to vote myself and urge my sisters to do the same. It did seem a dear price to pay for a vote when my husband was taken away" (p. 207). In an early example of dialectical thinking and autobiography as a pedagogy of resistance, Letitia spoke her mind: "An old-fashioned maxim declares, 'It is a poor rule that won't work both ways.' . . . If only widows and spinsters are allowed to vote, then surely bachelors and widowers should be the only men eligible to the same privilege" (p. 207).

Mary Ellicott Arnold

Mary Ellicott Arnold (1876–1968) was the operational and educational force behind the cooperative housing project, Tompkinsville (near Reserve Mines, Cape Breton)—11 single dwelling houses were built in one year, 1937. Arnold's association with her lifelong companion, Mabel Reed, and Mabel's role in the housing project are an untold story of the Antigonish Movement (see Neal, 1999). Arnold's (1940) participation in *The Story of Tompkinsville* was submerged by the voices of the Roman Catholic priests and academics, Moses Coady and Jimmy Tompkins, and the miners who built the houses. Eros is erased from *The Story of Tompkinsville*, and thus the opportunity for Arnold to fashion a relational self is excised. In contrast, eros *embodies* Mary and Mabel's account of living, teaching, and learning with

Figure 3. Mary Arnold and the Tompkinsville Housing Study Club
(Courtesy of the St. Francis Xavier University Archives, #89-977-1067).

the Karok Indians in California in 1908–1909 (Arnold and Reed, 1957). *In the Land of the Grasshopper Song* features pictures of both Mary and Mabel, on horseback and in the company of their Indian friends—men, women, and children. *The Story of Tompkinsville* includes only pictures of Mary with the miners. However, I presume that some of the folksy comments and imagined dialogue in Mary's comprehensive outline of a suggested course of study for a study club (Figure 3) on how to build houses must have arisen in conversations with Mabel.

Delaney (1985) recorded that the home of Mary Arnold and her companion, "Mabel Read [*sic*]," was the centre of education for the men working on the technical and business details of the housing project but also for the women's meetings: "They made curtains and quilts and pored over house plans" (p. 142).

Neal (1999) agreed with historian Anne Alexander that women leaders in the Antigonish Movement are largely represented in "supporting roles" in conformity with the "larger ideological boundaries of the Antigonish movement's gender construction—Catholic wife, sister, mother and helpmate" (p. 59). Mary Arnold did not conform with these stereotypes.

Mary Arnold's correspondence with Moses Coady reveals their mutual affection. In her letters she extended "warm personal greetings" from "miss and myself" (as cited in Neal, 1999, p. 62), and Coady in turn acknowledged the relationship. In the introduction to *The Story of Tompkinsville,* Coady (1940) reported that in the summer of 1937 "Miss Mary Arnold and Miss Mabel Reed, of New York, came down to acquaint themselves with our Adult Education Program. Miss Arnold was a dyed-in-the-wool cooperator" (p. 3).

Mary Arnold was in conflict with A. B. MacDonald, the administrator of the Extension Department, who, in her view, was more supportive of credit unions than of her housing initiatives; and in a letter to Coady she sought to clarify her position and authority in the organization. Again, she acknowledged Mabel Reed and their joint experience in the Extension Department and wrote to Coady that, however the issue was resolved, "Miss Reed and I have learned" (Neal, 1999, p. 65).

Implications for Present-Day Popular Educators

Genealogy responds to a question/issue asked in "our present." Eros leads the practices of resistance that public mothers and popular educators take up in contexts mostly beyond the entity-like organization with a fixed address and regulated time. These three women in three social movements at three different historical moments assumed different subjectivities in the field and in the office. The field experiences of Lotta, Letitia, and Mary are exemplary of deriving theory of social action and popular education from the eros of everyday life. The private relationships in concert with the public oratory and/or autobiographical writing of these three public mothers operate as critical pedagogies of resistance that popular educators deploy to transgress oppressive cultural norms. Letitia Youmans self-identified as a temperance crusader against the status quo of the liquor traffic and, in an instance of loving witness, consistently represented the norms, values, and beliefs of the liquor sellers who actively resisted change as deviant and as "the principal contradiction of society" (Freire, 2002, p. 176). The three public mothers in my study exercised erotic pedagogies of resistance, but, when situated in a traditional organizational structure, they often manifested the masculinist-coded managerial practices of organizational control. Lotta's management practices at 53 Sparks Street versus those in far-flung war zones stood as a principal contradiction in her life and in society, but there is no evidence that she engaged in critical self-reflection (Razack, 1993), in dialectic thinking focused on the tension between control and resistance, in fashioning a relational self.

These three public mothers often illustrated the eros of informal education. In her argument for using the language of "home protection" rather than "prohibition," Letitia Youmans did not abandon her moral authority as mother–educator. Similarly, Lotta Hitschmanova's use of maternal imagery in fashioning her self and her advertising copy for the March of Diapers demonstrated the eros of informal learning that produces power relations (exercising both power and resistance to power).

The three case studies support Trask's (1986) argument for feminist eros: Women's erotic forms of social practice are closer to the sources of the pleasure principle and less subjugated by the performance principle. This enhances the potential for collapsing "their *work* into their *life*, forcing them to mediate a false division while also supporting it" (p. 90). Popular education engages public mothers as loving witnesses, which expands Freire's (2002) dialectical ideas of love as "the foundation of dialogue and dialogue itself" (p. 89).

The intolerable contradictions of women's experience of "timelessness" set against the dominant masculinist and capitalist regulation of time (Tamboukou, 2003, pp. 56–57; Trask, 1986, p. 91) appeared in the diverse sites of Lotta's work world: As the Diaper Lady she cared for the refugee children in Greece and contributed productively to the conversational space; as an office manager at headquarters in Ottawa she was oppressed and oppressed others in her demands for time-organized "performance" from the "desks" (Sanger, 1986, p. 153). In the cooperative housing project the boundaries between Mary Arnold's home with Mabel Reed—the first model home built in Tompkinsville—and the construction sites were blurred, whereas she sought clarification of her position and authority within the Extension Department at the university vis-à-vis the Extension Department administrator's capitalist priorities of time and other resources. These three case studies raise the possibilities of becoming "other" (Tamboukou, 2003, pp. 135–136) for today's popular educators; we must take account of the ways that linear time and entity-like organization impede pedagogies of resistance and the eros of learning and thus the opportunities for popular education and cultural change. The sustaining of two opposite groups or two opposite worldviews of time and space impedes the possibility of human beings' uniting in love and committing to the cause of liberation (Allman, 1998). These three public mothers spoke to today's popular educators and the continuity of the abstract construct of *woman* "confined to the private; but *women* as concrete historical beings, cross borders into the public—although in restrained conditions—subverting any attempt to establish fixed boundaries" (Hernández, 1997, p. 44).

A genealogical approach helps in understanding the possibilities for disrupting the enduring distinctions between public and private that erase the body and eros from social movements and popular education. Eros, especially the loving relationships of life partners associated with the homeplace, leads the trajectory of public mothers as popular educators. Eros leads the critically reflective process of questioning assumptions and imagining alternatives. This comparative study of Lotta Hitschmanova, Letitia Youmans, and Mary Arnold invites practitioners and academics to enact loving witness in popular education situations. An eros of learning in everyday life holds potential for fashioning a relational self that refuses existing power/knowledge formations and begins to create a world in which it will be easier to love.

References

Allman, P. (with Mayo, P., Cavanagh, C., Heng, C. L., and Haddad, S.). (1998). ". . . The creation of a world in which it will be easier to love." *Convergence* [Tribute to Paulo Freire], *31*(1/2), 9–16.

Arnold, M. E. (1940). *The story of Tompkinsville*. New York: The Cooperative League.

Arnold, M. E. and Reed, M. (1957). *In the land of the grasshopper song*. New York: Vantage Press.

Bengough, J. (1887, October 29). Mrs. Youmans dresses down Foster [Cartoon] *Grip*, p. 1.

Butler, J. (1990). *Gender trouble: Feminism and the subversion of identity*. New York: Routledge.

Coady, M. M. (1940). Introduction. In M. E. Arnold, *The story of Tompkinsville* (pp. 1–6). New York: The Cooperative League.

Delaney, I. (1985). *By their own hands: A fieldworker's account of the Antigonish Movement*. Hantsport, NS: Lancelot Press.

Freire, P. (2002). *Pedagogy of the oppressed* (30th anniversary ed.). New York: Continuum. (Original work published 1972)

Garner, N. G. (1998). The Woman's Christian Temperance Union: A woman's branch of American Protestantism. In D. Jacobsen and W. V. Trollinger (Eds.), *Reforming the center: American Protestantism, 1900 to present* (pp. 271–283). Grand Rapids, MI: William B. Eerdmans.

Hernández, A. (1997). *Pedagogy, democracy, and feminism: Rethinking the public sphere*. Albany: State University of New York Press.

hooks, b. (1994). Eros, eroticism, and pedagogy. In b. hooks (Ed.), *Teaching to transgress: Education as the practice of freedom* (pp. 191-200). New York: Routledge.

Keen, S. (1994). *The passionate life: Stages of loving*. San Francisco: HarperCollins.

Neal, R. (1999). Mary Arnold (and Mabel Reed): Co-operative women in Nova Scotia, 1937–1939. *Acadiensis, 38*(2), 58-70.

Razack, S. (1993). Story-telling for social change. *Gender and Education, 5*(1), 55–70.

Sanger, C. (1986) *Lotta and the Unitarian Service Committee story*. Toronto, ON: Stoddart.

Sather, K. S. (2001). *Dr. Lotta Hitschmanova and the USC.* Retrieved September 7, 2003, from the Canadian Unitarian Council Web site: http://www.cuc.ca/worship_celebration/hitschmanova.htm

Smith-Rosenberg, C. (1985). The new woman as androgyne: Social disorder and gender crisis, 1870–1936. In C. Smith-Rosenberg (Ed.), *Disorderly conduct: Visions of gender in Victorian America* (pp. 245–349). Oxford. Oxford University Press.

Tamboukou, M. (2003). *Women, education, and the self: A Foucauldian perspective*. London: Palgrave Macmillan.

Trask, H. K. (1986). *Eros and power: The promise of feminist theory*. Philadelphia: University of Pennsylvania Press.

Youmans, L. (1893). Campaign echoes: The autobiography of Mrs. Letitia Youmans. Toronto, ON: William Briggs.

24

Adult Education and the Arts

Shauna Butterwick and Jane Dawson

Jan: I turned my body away, wrapped in the red cloth, yet twisted my head and neck back to center, toward the speakers. The flight instinct was intense! Yet so was the desire to stick with the scene, the dangerous moment.

Shauna: As I looked around the circle at what others had done with the cloth, what shape of body sculpture they had assumed, where they were located, I was amazed to see the diversity. I found myself deeply curious as to the meanings of these shapes.

The above comments, which emerged from a community-based popular-theatre project (Butterwick and Selman, 2003, p. 11), speak to the transformative learning potential of arts-based processes such as theatre. In this chapter we consider the relationship between the arts and adult education, taking note of the aesthetic sensibilities of knowing and being that open up in working with various art forms. We direct attention to some historical and current examples of arts-based adult education initiatives to illustrate the strong links between arts and adult education. In this limited discussion, we cannot do justice to the variety of historical and contemporary adult education activities where the arts are central. Our goal, rather, is to support the growing interest and recognition of the powerful relationship that exists between the arts and adult learning. Each author comes to this discussion as an adult educator now teaching and researching in academia. We are not artists, but have made conscious efforts to bring an arts orientation to our teaching and research. We join other adult educators who recognize and seek to understand the power and contribution that arts-based approaches bring to pedagogy, research, policy, and theorizing.

As Roby Kidd and Gordon Selman (1978) noted:

It is hardly surprising that programs of adult education are responsive to economic need. But man [*sic*] hungers for beauty as well as for bread, for meaning and self-understanding as well as survival. The arts and adult education are old and familiar partners. (p. 270)

The place of the arts in adult education spans a range of political perspectives from high culture to radical social protest. In this discussion the term *arts* refers to all manner of creative expression, including theatre, visual arts, poetry, music, and dance, to name a few.

The Contribution of the Arts

The relationship between the arts and adult education can be considered on two dimensions: art as process (the act of making) and art as product (the resulting work). To some extent, as David Jones (1999) argued, "The different spaces in which these activities take place embody different value systems" (p. 8). There is great value in both aspects, particularly in relation to the rich possibilities for learning and understanding that take place through creative activity. Through the arts, as process *and* product, a more holistic approach to learning and inquiry can occur, drawing on an aesthetic, non-instrumentalist orientation where the heart, mind, spirit, and body are engaged.

Elliot Eisner (2004) contended that contemporary education has been overtaken by a technically rationalized industrial culture that values the measurement and predictability of outcomes. Although the focus of Eisner's comments is on formal schooling, this industrial culture, "whose values are brittle and whose conception of what's important [is] narrow" (p. 3), also dominates the contemporary policy and funding context of adult education. The arts, Eisner posited, offer a counter to this narrow perspective, where the goal of education should be *the preparation of artistic forms of thinking*:

> These forms of thinking . . . encourage students and teachers to be flexibly purposive, they recognize the unity of form and content, they require one to think within the affordances and constraints of the medium one elects to use and they emphasize the importance of aesthetic satisfactions as motives for work. (p. 10)

The flexible and integrative forms of thinking that the arts can foster are needed now more than ever with the proliferation of misinformation that requires critical discernment.

Maxine Greene (1995) offered a similar perspective on the need for creativity and imagination in addressing urgent issues of contemporary society. For Greene, through critical, reflective, and imaginative encounters with the arts, new and sometimes unexpected patterns of meaning are woven, which invite new possibilities for understanding:

> The extent to which we grasp another's world depends on our existing ability to make poetic use of our imagination, to bring the "as if" worlds created by writers, painters, sculptors, filmmakers, choreographers and composers, and to be in some manner a participant in artists' worlds reaching far back and ahead in time. (p. 4)

Audre Lorde (1984), speaking particularly about the poetic imagination, asserted that poetry, as with other art forms, is not simply a cultural frill: "Poetry is not a luxury. It is a vital necessity of our existence. It forms the quality of light within which we predicate our hopes and dreams towards survival and change" (p. 37). The arts, as Clover, Stalker, and McGauley (2004) argued, can tap into our unconscious biases and offer creative solutions to problems. Arts can also provoke, generate outrage, challenge biases, and show us things that we might not want to see:

> This . . . is important precisely because it cultivates the capacity to reflect on issues that open a vision of human possibility so that together, we might begin to challenge the morality of many social, economic, political and military priorities. (p. ii)

Using the term *the arts* can suggest that we are referring to only some agreed-upon (Western) canon. However, it is important to avoid reproducing Eurocentric and patriarchal views of what counts as art and beauty and to draw attention to how power is operating in what gets defined as art and/or creative expression. Art as a product is all too easily conscripted into hegemonic and elitist aesthetic conventions. Art as a process is similarly neither an immune nor an innocent set of practices that stand outside class, gender, and race struggles that locate White, male, and European/Western as the norm to which "others" are compared and often rendered inferior or invisible. "Arts education practices that reinscribe cultural orthodoxy must be revisioned if we are to serve students in new and more meaningful ways" (Sanders, 2005, p. 199).

Other challenges to the biases that shape our understanding of the arts are raised by activists who seek to include indigenous creative processes as part of the larger lexicon of artistic expression and by those who see access and freedom to engage in artistic expression not as a preserve of elites, but as a matter of social justice. As Rajdeep Gill (2004) argued, "Creativity, both human and non-human, is present everywhere, challenging the art world and its discursive arenas to open up to its vitality, criticality and sacredness; no one body can hoard creativity, nor can it be contained" (p. 79).

Historical Cases

There are some prominent historical examples of the long association between adult education and the arts in Canada, including the Banff School of Fine Arts, now known as the Banff Centre, and the National Film Board (NFB). The Banff Centre is nowadays not often part of the conversation about adult education in Canada, but in its early years it was an important landmark in the emergence of the field. The original version of what was to become the Banff School was launched in 1933 under the auspices of the University of Alberta's Department of Extension, which focused much of its activities on encouraging the arts in isolated communities. It was first established as a School of Drama, offering a single three-week summer drama class to provide leadership for the many theatre groups that had arisen in the rural communities of the region. At that time the head of Extension, E. A. (Ned) Corbett, a noted pioneer in the history of Canadian adult education, was a key player in starting the school (with a Carnegie Foundation grant). Corbett had a vision of how the Banff school could help "people find keener enjoyment in art, music, philosophy, literature, and nature" (Harris, 1998, p. 57). The summer drama schools quickly became popular, and within a few years the Banff School broadened its mandate to include other arts such as painting and music, and eventually added other programs such as creative writing, pottery, textiles, and photography. Following Corbett's departure, Donald Cameron became director and remained so for 33 years. Cameron's leadership was informed by his tour of Danish folk high schools, where the arts were central to their vision of social justice. The school grew and prospered, becoming an internationally acclaimed artistic institution with a reputation as a centre of innovation and a catalyst for creativity.

Another well-known Canadian arts-based initiative was the NFB, established in 1938 by John Grierson with a mandate to produce films that would inform Canadians about their country. Grierson saw film as a creative medium to explore and express aspects of modern life, to "bring alive" essential but taken-for-granted dimensions of the modern experience. He believed that documentary film, in shunning repression and mystification, could play the role of "honest broker" between the power of the state and ordinary people, with the capacity to startle people into new ways of seeing. As he frequently put it, "Art is not a mirror, but a hammer" (Selman and Dampier, 1991, p. 49).

Within the NFB, another significant development was the establishment of Studio D, a filmmaking unit devoted to films by women about women's lives. Kathleen Shannon, who served as Executive Director from 1974 to 1986, was instrumental in its establishment. Studio D started out in a basement storeroom and became one of the most celebrated units of the NFB, being the only women's filmmaking unit of its kind in the world that provided not only funding, but also training and mentoring for women in production roles. Shannon brought a fierce commitment to using film to tackle discrimination:

> Racist and sexist prejudices and stereotypes flourish only in people's ignorance of each other's true selves. That's why it's urgent that our media start to reflect the real diversity of our population, and give access to the stories and perspectives of Canadians of all backgrounds and, in particular, the women. (National Film Board of Canada, 2005, ¶ 1)

Over 80 films were created under the direction of Kathleen Shannon. Studio D continued until 1996, when it was closed down following massive federal budget cuts.

In both of the above-mentioned cases, apart from the first few years when the drama classes at the Banff School were directed towards amateur rural community participants, the artist is seen primarily as a professional or a person with distinct talents, either in training (as in the Banff School) or working at his or her craft (as with the filmmakers supported by the NFB). However, the relationship between adult education and the arts has never been a matter of simply providing training or distributing opportunities for working artists, but also using the arts with ordinary people to foster individual learning for their own personal growth and development or with a broader goal of community development and social change.

An example of this can be seen in the community arts movement in rural Nova Scotia in the 1940s under the leadership of Guy Henson and Betty Murray (Harris, 1998). The aim in community arts at that time was to use the arts, in partnership with other learning activities, to help foster a greater sense of individual and community pride. The Depression and war years had taken a serious toll on rural Nova Scotia, and many communities were struggling economically and socially. In common spirit with the better-known activities of Moses Coady and the extension workers of the Antigonish Movement in northeastern Nova Scotia, Henson and Murray were committed to adult education for community renewal in other parts of the province. For these community educators, both (as with Donald Cameron of the Banff School) inspired by the Danish model, political awareness and cultural development always went hand in hand.

From Past to Present

The link between adult education and the arts continues, and many of the dimensions reflected in these three historical examplars of adult education and the arts in Canada are mirrored and extended in more contemporary examples. The Banff Centre retains a high profile as an arts training facility, and although the role of the NFB has vastly diminished since John Grierson's and even Kathleen Shannon's day, there are still instances of documentary film as a vehicle for adult education in the form of ideology critique, identify formation, and community building (Riecken, 2003). Many of the initiatives with which Betty Murray was involved have changed or petered out in the less arts-friendly political climate of Nova Scotia (and, indeed, all of Canada), but the idea of the arts as a forum for community development lives on in a number of different arts-based initiatives.

There are numerous adult learning projects in contemporary Canada in which the arts figure prominently. Evidence of this activity can be found in the proceedings of the last few years of the Canadian Association for the Study of Adult Education's (CASAE) annual conference. In addition to the research reports, it has been a tradition to include an arts-space evening at the annual CASAE conferences where members read poetry, sing songs, play music, and share through different art genres their adult education passions and experiences. At more recent conferences, arts-based approaches such as readers' theatre and other performative approaches have been used to present research findings. Outlined below are a few examples of some contemporary arts-based adult education projects from British Columbia, Alberta, Ontario, and Nova Scotia.

In Vancouver, arts became an important component of a literacy project for sex-trade workers in the Downtown Eastside, a poor inner-city area that is struggling with issues of poverty, racism, violence, and addiction.

The WISH (Women's Information Safe House) Drop-In Centre Society, a non-profit agency that began in 1987, offers a drop-in centre for high-risk, street-involved women sex-trade workers. In 2000 an innovative literacy project was launched. Given these women's needs and circumstances, the staff realized that setting up a traditional learning centre would not be effective; and, as a result, a number of nonthreatening "in-the-door" activities were offered. Many involved arts-based and craft activities such as creating panels and wall hangings, knitting, and making candles. Not only did these arts-based activities contribute to a renewed interest in learning, but they were also linked to harm reduction as the women began to experiment with reducing their drug use as they got involved with the various activities at the centre. "Their eagerness to be learning and our courage to 'try anything' resulted in a vibrant Learning Centre" (Alderson and Twiss, 2003, p. 24).

Another adult education project in BC that began in 1999 used popular-theatre techniques to explore feminist coalition and organizing politics. Women from a variety of grassroots feminist organizations in Vancouver came together in 1999 and again in 2000, meeting every Saturday for four months of intensive workshop activities. The focus of the theatre project was to explore the participants' experiences of feminist organizing, noting in particular that many feminist groups struggle to create inclusive practices that honour women's differences in age, race, class, culture, and sexuality. Conflict is a not surprising outcome of failed efforts to create social justice within feminist organizations, and in this project, theatre's potential to work creatively with conflict was explored. "We chose to use theatre as we pursued questions about coalition and community in women's action movements because it allows us to express and integrate our history, passions, insights, knowledge, and ideas" (Butterwick and Selman, 2003, p. 4).

The politics of difference was also a central concern in an Edmonton-based project. André Grace and Kristopher Wells (2005) have been working with a group of gay, lesbian, bisexual, and transgendered youth in using arts as a form for storytelling and critical analysis. In one particular project, youth painted and decorated old school lockers, the results of which were part of an installation at the Edmonton Public Library during Gay Pride Week in 2004. The outside of the lockers reflected the external, often stereotypical gaze of teachers, classmates, parents, and community. The inside of the lockers reflected the inner self of these youth, what was often kept hidden from the outside world.

> The juxtaposition of the outer and often misrepresented self with the inner and often more secret self helped to create a profoundly textured and performative display that served to emphasize how homophobia and heterosexism constantly circulate to police and enforce normative subjectivities. (p. 114)

Echoes of the cultural programs offered by the Banff School of Fine Arts can be found in the development of numerous "Clemente" humanities programs in Canadian cities such as Calgary (see Groen, 2005) and Vancouver, as well as other parts of the world. These programs are based on the ideas of Earl Shorris, who was instrumental in running the first of these programs at the Roberto Clemente centre in lower Manhattan. The idea of these programs is to offer university courses in arts, philosophy, literature, and so on to the economically disenfranchised. Shorris (1997) believed that "the humanities are a foundation for getting along in the world, for thinking, for learning to reflect on the world instead of just reacting to whatever force is turned against you" (p. 6). These programs recognize the barriers that many people who live in poverty face and thus provide on-site meals and financial support to cover the costs of transportation and child care, as well as mentoring and tutor support.

Another project that illustrates how arts-based approaches can both inform research and provide a powerful learning experience is the work of Susan Walsh and Susan Brigham (2005), who are undertaking a project with women teachers in Halifax who have immigrated to Canada. All of the women were teachers in their home countries who now face barriers to finding similar work in Canada. These researchers and adult educators used arts-informed practices to problematize these women's experience as well as their own. "Visual arts, spontaneous writing and conversation provide alternative ways of symbolizing-resymbolizing—how these professional women immigrating to Canada interpret their experiences" (p. 3). Using play dough, Lego, paint, and spontaneous writing, the 11 participants in their projects quickly came together as a group, eager to share their experiences. The project "demonstrate[s] how one person's experience can become more porous through art, writing, and talk" (p. 6).

Similar to earlier community arts programs in Nova Scotia and elsewhere, a variety of crafts and arts-based activities including quilts, murals, theatre, and performance art were part of the Myths and Mirrors Community Arts project that began in 1996 as a feminist community development initiative in Sudbury, Ontario (Clover et al, 2004). The vision was to "engender a sense of community identity, to challenge the manufacture of consent, and to provide a public forum for the voices of the marginalised" (p. 91). Two low-income downtown neighbourhoods were involved in examining, through the arts, preventing development on the sole green space in a community, designing a local community centre, and making women's voices part of the public discussion.

Conclusion

The above-mentioned historic and contemporary examples of arts and adult education illustrate the powerful learning outcomes that occur when adults and their communities are offered opportunities to engage in various artistic genres. Whereas earlier instances of arts-oriented programming often tended to offer an unproblematized link between the arts and personal and social growth, many current practices take a more explicitly critical stance. Renewing communities, breaking silence, naming injustices, and imagining and creating alternative worlds are some of the outcomes towards which they work. It is important to understand the arts in the widest possible way, not just through acquiring "high culture," but also through awakening personal creativity and provoking radical ways of re-seeing and being in the world. As adult educators, we need to expand our own learning by exposing ourselves to the arts and using various art forms in our own searching and communication about what we know. Creating a strong bond between adult education and the arts offers an antidote to the instrumental values and assumptions driving our competitive society. As Eisner (2004) noted, the process is neither about tinkering towards utopia, nor about mounting a revolution. "What we can do is generate other visions of education, other values to guide its realization, other assumptions on which a more generous conception of the practice of schooling can be built" (p. 4). We close with a poem by Jane:

Sing

They told us not to

look, they said seeing

is not—after all—believingbelieving is closing:

Eyes,

lips,

"ora cordis"—ear of the heart.

Not aloud.

Not allowed.

Someone else said,

Wait. Listen

to the sharp instruction

of crows at dawn—

awe, awe, awe.

The necessary lexicon

of our strangled yearning

starts with two words:

open

sing

Acknowledgment

We want to thank Jackie Quigley, MA student in adult education at UBC, for her library search of articles and documents for this chapter.

References

Alderson, L. and Twiss, D. (2003). *Literacy for women on the streets: The British Columbia Adult Literacy Cost-Shared Program*. Vancouver, BC: Capilano College.

Butterwick, S. and Selman, J. (2003). Deep listening in a feminist popular theatre project: Upsetting the position of audience in participatory education. *Adult Education Quarterly, 53*(4), 7–23.

Clover, D., Stalker, J., and McGauley, L. (2004). Feminist popular education and community arts/crafts: The case for new directions. In D. Clover (Ed.), *Proceedings of the joint international conference of the Adult Education Research Conference (AERC) and the Canadian Association for the Study of Adult Education (CASAE)* (pp. 89–94). Victoria, BC: University of Victoria.

Eisner, E. W. (2004). What can education learn from the arts about the practice of education? *International Journal of Education and the Arts, 5*(4), 1–12.

Gill, R. S. (2004). Notes on planetarity and curatorial practice. *Yishu: Journal of Contemporary Chinese Art, 3*(3), 73–80.

Grace, A. and Wells, K. (2005). Out is in: An arts-informed, community-based approach to social and cultural learning by and for queer young adults. In S. Mojab and H. Nosheen (Eds.), *Proceedings of the 24th annual conference of the Canadian Association for the Study of Adult Education (CASAE)* (pp. 112–118). London, ON: University of Western Ontario.

Greene, M. (1995). *Releasing the imagination: Essays on education, the arts, and social change*. San Francisco: Jossey-Bass.

Groen, J. (2005). Storefront 101: Intuitive connections to the tradition and practices of adult education: Theorizing from the literature. In S. Mojab and H. Nosheen (Eds.), *Proceedings of the 24th annual conference of the Canadian Association for the Study of Adult Education (CASAE)* (pp. 119–123). London, ON: University of Western Ontario.

Harris, C. (1998). *A sense of themselves: Elizabeth Murray's leadership in school and community*. Halifax, NS: Fernwood.

Jones, D. (1999, July). *Different theatres, different audiences: The arts and the education of adults*. Paper presented at the 29th annual SCUTREA conference, University of Warwick. Retrieved April 25, 2005, from http://www.leeds.ac.uk.educol/documents

Kidd, J. R. and Selman, G. (1978). *Coming of age: Canadian adult education in the 1960s*. Toronto, ON: CAAE.

Lorde, A. (1984). Poetry is not a luxury. In A. Lorde (Ed.), *Sister outsider: Essays and speeches* (pp. 36–39). Trumansburg, NY: Crossing Press.

National Film Board of Canada. (2005). *Kathleen Shannon*. Retrieved April 15, 2005, from http://www.nfb.ca/portraits/fiche.php?id=267&v=h&lg=en

Riecken, T. (2003, November). *The traditional pathways to health project: Film making as community based health promotion*. Paper presented at the Learning and the World We Want conference, Victoria, BC.

Sanders, J. (2005). Rethinking practices in community-based arts education. In M. C. Powell and V. M. Speiser (Eds.), *The arts, education, and social change: Little signs of hope* (pp. 199–215). New York: Peter Lang.

Selman, G. and Dampier, P. (1991). *The foundations of adult education in Canada*. Toronto, ON: Thompson Educational.

Shorris, E. (1997) *New American blues: A journey through poverty to democracy*. New York: W.W. Norton.

Walsh, S. and Brigham, S. (2005). *The messiness of experience: Immigrant women and an arts-based research process*. Paper presented at the 24th annual conference of the Canadian Association for the Study of Adult Education (CASAE), University of Western Ontario, London, ON.

Part 5

CONTEXTS OF PRACTICE

25

Training of Adult Educators in Quebec

Mohamed Hrimech and Nicole A. Tremblay

The aim of this chapter is to outline adult educator training in Quebec to examine some past and present trends, as well as to identify the explanatory elements of the current situation. First, we will provide a brief history of adult education in the province. Next, we will trace the evolution of basic and advanced educator training and offer an overview of the current adult educator training situation. Then we will look at new trends and discuss future challenges in adult educator training.

Adult Education in Quebec

The 1960s and 1970s were, in a way, the golden age of adult educator training in Quebec: Hopes ran high, and the need for training was great. Nowadays the situation is slightly different. Some programs underwent a transformation, others had to merge with related fields of study to survive, and still others simply disappeared. What was Quebec's position on the various developments related to adult educator training? It could be considered a middle-of-the road position: a mix that was neither totally American nor totally French, because in Quebec the East-European conception of *andragogy* and the French discourse of lifelong learning have had as much influence as the theoretical approach suggested by North American leaders. Even though French, European, and American influence could have been "bearers of wealth," somehow they ended up being a source of misunderstanding and even division among the founders, who in the 1970s were trying to establish adult educator training in departments of continuing education and lifelong learning.

The Training of Adult Education Specialists in Quebec

In Quebec, a province with a distinct social evolution in North America, the training of adult educators was the natural consequence of a long tradition at the crossroads of both the English and the French legacies. The beginning of the nineteenth century witnessed the creation of adult education-oriented institutions, the Mechanics' Institutes based on the British and Scottish models. From 1840 onwards, those establishments offered evening education for the working class. During the same period the *Institut Canadien de Montreal* (Canadian Institute of Montreal) was established, a mass-oriented bilingual educational institution. Moreover, McGill University had been offering adult education since 1827, the Agricultural Society of Lower Canada had opened farm schools for farmers, and many parochial and professional libraries were opening their doors. In the mid-1800s a group of organizations that were geared towards adult education in the fields of agriculture and industry was formed, in both English and French. Yet there was no formal training for adult educators.

Stemming from the *Report of the Royal Commission of Inquiry on Education in the Province of Quebec* (Government of Quebec, 1964), recommendations on remedial education were the starting point for an in-depth study of adult education. Because adult education was not in the mandate of that particular commission, a new committee (Comité d'étude sur l'éducation des adultes, 1964) was created that emphasized the urgency to carry on research on adult education and pedagogy. It made the universities responsible for conducting research on adult education and set a framework for the advanced training of adult education specialists.

The report brought about the reform of remedial education in adult education oriented institutions, which were required by politicians to formalize their activities. It was the first to call for an advanced training program for experts in adult education. The newborn Ministry of Education of Quebec responded to the recommendation by creating the Directorate of Continuing Education. For adult education, these were years of great work: Three major projects were launched that had a substantial impact on the development of adult education and educator training:

- "Project départ," to determine the educational needs of the area of Montreal
- "Project Sésame," to draw the outlines of adult-oriented high school programs and train competent educators.
- "Project TEVEQ," to create an experimental educational television channel for isolated communities

These educational projects were witnesses to the social recognition that adult education gained as a specific field of study and can be considered the initiation of programs created to further the training of adult education specialists.

Université de Montréal: The First Program in Quebec.

The *Université de Montréal* developed the first university curriculum for the advanced training of adult educators in Quebec. The model developed in Montreal has been an inspiration to other programs in Quebec. It has three main components: (a) foundations of adult education or andragogy (i.e., sociology, philosophy, and psychology), (b) practical tools for action (i.e., curriculum development, learning and teaching methodologies, working with groups), and (c) personalized professional activities according to a student's own needs (i.e., internships, reading projects). The training was planned to take into account the fundamental sciences on which it depends: sociology, philosophy, and psychology. Other courses also provided students with appropriate tools by focusing on actual professional practices—programming, intervention, and stimulation methods—which maximized the heterogeneous audiences through exchange seminars, research, and documentation activities in which personalized, professional profiles were defined.

Development of Adult Education in Quebec.

At the beginning of the 1980s a commission inquired into adult education, took into consideration the different roles that adult educators play in society, and examined recommendations from world agencies (such as UNESCO and the European Council on training policies) that were in line with the realities of the intervention fields: cross-disciplinary training, tailor-made to fit Quebec adult educators' needs (Commission d'études sur la formation des adultes, 1982). The universities were expected to offer training for quality research in andragogy. Regarding the professionaliza-tion of adult educators, the commission made it clear that it was impossible to create a legal status for a group so diverse and whose members often had a precarious status as consultants or pay-per-lesson educators. In fact, 98 percent of adult educators were considered to be in a precarious situation. The commission carried out investigations, and this was the first time that figures were collected on the situation of adult educators in Quebec.

The academic training of adult educators and specialists is a 30-year tradition. In 2001, at least 16 programs at the three university levels in nine different universities were operating in Quebec. These programs have reached out to a good part of the adult educators' population. More than 4,000 educators have graduated from them, their competency certified by their diplomas. Branches of the *Université du Québec* (University of Quebec) in Hull, Rimouski, and Chicoutimi have helped, as was their vocation, to reach out to the educators of the regions. As for the Université de Montréal, it has appealed to students from other Canadian provinces, French Europe, South America, and Africa, therefore contributing to the development of adult educator training in other universities at the provincial, national, and international levels.

The Training of Adult Educators and the Professional World.

Since the 1960s, universities have played an active role in training adult educators. However, since the beginning of the 1990s, because of the change in the paradigm of the workplace, which has become a learning organization, an increased use of new technologies, mainly of the Internet, and new forms of advanced training have emerged.

The shift of adult education from the academic to the professional world in the mid-1990s is a trend that has been heavily documented by current research and practice. Law 90 (investment of 1 percent of salaries in training), adopted by the government of Quebec, has just caused the phenomenon to accelerate. A poll that Doray, Bagaoui, and Ricard (1994) conducted reveals that the amount invested in training in Quebec's companies is $1 billion. However, of Canada's provinces, Quebec does not invest the most in training per capita at an estimated $642 per person, which is less than Ontario ($897) and Western Canada ($974). These figures, although they allow financial comparisons with the rest of Canada, are not an accurate reflection of the reality of the continuous education of company personnel.

From 1960 to 1970 the Quebec government held a position that was highly favourable to the legal status of adult educators and created a general direction that was dependent on the Ministry of Education. Today, there is no longer a specific agency since adult and youth education merged, and even the minister asks specialists in youth education for advice, as was the case in the report of a sketch of policy recommendations (Inchauspé, 2000). Obviously, adult educator training has fled the world of education and migrated to other locations where government recommendations and customary academic approaches have almost no influence.

The New Trends in the Profession.

Professional recognition of adult educators has not gained much ground since the 1990s. There have been serious losses in Quebec, first in community training, where the tradition has almost disappeared because of budget cuts. Second, the academic adult educators were forced to agree to share their already small allotment with regular teachers, thus weakening their chances of gaining recognition. Moreover, these educators have had to struggle with increasingly younger students (16 to 25 years) in remedial-school projects, which are constantly being filled by teenagers who drop out of the regular school system. The context obviously has an influence over the very definition of the position and has created new training needs for educators to which the existing programs were not always respond-ing.

In addition to the changes observed in community and academic training, there have been changes in the workplace. We have witnessed the birth of the learning organization and the information society and have seen how important training is. These new requirements have helped to change the customary roles of adult educators, at least in the way that they were shaped by the training programs of the 1960s and 1970s.

What is expected today of adult educators when adult instruction is seen as one dimension of human-resource management? We are now chal-lenged to provide training to an educator who must be multiskilled and be able to animate and teach, design and apply, and think management and training. In that respect, Allouche-Benayoun and Pariat (2000) believed that the training of adult educators should provide, along with traditional training on animation and teaching, qualifications for dealing with the management of other co-workers, identifying organizational problems in relation to the political and financial constraints of the training, assuming the responsibilities of department manager or regional manager for training operations, and so forth. These authors cautioned that this goes beyond the strict model of training that was thought to be the answer to the new corporate expectations.

As far as we know, this new job of providing training that prevailed in the 1990s has not translated into new programs. The most noticeable efforts have been made in programs essentially based on what is called *training engineering* or *training management*. It might actually be time for in-depth program revision and the creation of new programs. One might wish, in that respect, to see systematic proceedings similar to those implemented by US researchers in the 1960s and 1970s regarding the practice of adult educators in North America. One hopes that we will maintain a critical mind to prevent us from abiding by the "management/training" motto that has recently been in fashion and remember that there are still educators who work in a more discreet manner and with more financial limitations in academic and community environments.

Conclusion

What does the future hold for the training of adult educators in Quebec? First of all, we are evolving along the same lines as the rest of Canada, Europe, and elsewhere. The seminar leader of the postwar period became the remedial education specialist in the wave that hit Quebec in the 1970s and 1980s. Nowadays the educator has become a training consultant or a work-training mediator, in the words of Wittorski (1997). In the 1990s, the field of adult education was undergoing changes in work organization in which training shifted from a social development tool to a productivity gain, which directly challenges our purpose and social mission.

The right to education for all has yet to be recognized for adults, and the means to implement it are scarce. The fight for this right is far from being on the agenda in today's social and economic context. Cruikshank (1998) suggested that adult educators who still believe in education in terms of social justice must be alert to the dangers of this new reality of corporate training. Today's globalization, combined with the development of distance education and an increasingly present virtual world, brings its share of upheavals to the customary training of adult educators. How relevant are our lengthy graduate programs with all their academic and time constraints when the clientele is increasingly made of learner–consumers who are used to quick changes, on the lookout for tailor-made, small, and fast courses. One wonders whether our universities have responded quickly enough compared to private training services for adult educators. Competition is great from private consultation companies, internal training departments, and professional colleges that provide their own continuing education to their members and training to instructors. Consider the many catalogues of seminars and workshops published by private training organizations. Moreover, their training is often offered on very appealing and fairly informal premises. Training activities also obey the principle of scale economies. Major US universities such as Princeton,

Yale, and Stanford have formed a consortium and made available online training in several languages. The Quebec and French-speaking Canadian populations are often bilingual; therefore, the US distance-training market is accessible to them. Finally, there is an urgent need to assess Quebec's adult educators and their training to better organize and structure the field and to clarify their training needs. From that perspective, France's creation in 1996 of the National Association for Adult Vocational Training of the National Institute for Training Professions is an incentive for us.

References

Allouche-Benayoun, J. and Pariat, M. (2000). *La Fonction de formateur: Identités professionnelles, méthodes pédagogiques et pratiques de Formation.* Paris: Duodi.

Comité d'étude sur l'éducation des adultes. (1964). Rapport du comité présidé par Claude Ryan. Ville de Québec, PQ: Gouvernement du Québec, Ministère de la jeunesse.

Commission d'études sur la formation des adultes. (1982). Apprendre: Une action volontaire et responsable: *Amorce d'une politique globale de l'éducation des adultes dans une perspective d'éducation permanente.* Ville de Québec, PQ : Gouvernement du Québec, Ministère des communications.

Cruikshank, J. (1998) Are we aiding the enemy? Adult education in the global economy. *Canadian Journal of University Continuing Education, 24*(1), 101–113.

Doray, P., Bagaoui, R., and Ricard, D. (1994). *La formation dans les entreprises québécoises: Études de cas auprès de 15 entreprises performantes.* Montréal, PQ: Centre interuniversitaire de recherche sur la science et la technologie et Conseil de la science et de la technologie du Québec.

Inchauspé, P. (2000). *Pour une politique de l'éducation des adultes dans une perspective de formation continue: Avis aux ministres.* Ville de Québec, PQ: Gouvernement du Québec, Ministère de l'éducation.

Government of Quebec. (1964). *Report of the Royal Commission of Inquiry on Education in the Province of Quebec.* Quebec City, PQ: Queen's Printer.

Wittorski, R. (1997). Évolution de la formation et transformation des compétences des formateurs. *Éducation permanente, 132,* 59–72.

26

Not Waving but Drowning: Canadian University Extension for Social Change Revisited

Denis J. Haughey

This chapter updates and extends my argument in *Learning for Life* (Haughey, 1998), where I critiqued the decline of Canadian university extension work for social change. Then, I not only recounted what I considered to be significant issues with the university extension movement, but I also pointed the way to some possible remedies. The chief issues were (a) the importance of engaging new sites of practice, (b) the intellectual passivity of professional university extension educators and the necessity to engage new theory, and (c) cultivating new intra- and extramural partnerships. I want to return to those issues to see how we have fared in the past seven years and to extend the discussion.

Introduction

What is meant by university extension work for social change, and should we still concern ourselves about it as Canadian university adult educators? I see the focus as being similar to that advanced by Plumb and Welton (2001), who acknowledged the tradition of critical thinking in various strands of the overall adult education tradition, not the least of which is our own distinctive Canadian one. They grounded the characteristic critical thinking approach inherent in university extension work for social change in the Habermasian concept of the *critical paradigm*, which is oriented towards the elimination of oppressive social relationships through the promotion of critical thinking and reflection, leading to transformative action. As I outlined in *Learning for Life* (Haughey, 1998), Canadian university extension has made a distinguished contribution here, and it would be sad to see it wholly abandoned by contemporary practitioners. Similarly, Bagnall (2000), in describing the democratic progressive tradition, stated, "The purpose of education is to inform social action for the development of a more humane, tolerant, just and egalitarian society of liberated, empowered, individuals, acting collegially in the public good" (p. 26). Relatedly, Tobias (2000), in looking at both institutional and community contexts, referred to "adult education programmes for active citizenship, i.e. programmes explicitly intended to promote, inform, analyse, critique, challenge, or raise public consciousness about public policies and issues" (p. 418).

However, Welton (2003) saw problems in enacting this ideal because in his view, at least regarding the issue of adult education and world terrorism, adult educators confront a world of power and ruthlessness that completely rejects the ideals of deliberative democracy that underpin their traditional approaches to this kind of programming. Ironically, Bagnall (2000) noted that, although informed cultural critique is probably more pervasive than it has ever been, its impact has been largely negated because of the prevalence of a dominant discourse oriented towards economic determinism. This means that "contemporary educational change is largely and ultimately driven, framed or determined by considerations of cost and benefit as measured through the economy" (p. 21).

A currently pervasive theme in international critical commentary (Barr, 2002; Field, 2001; Foley, 2001; Martin, 2003) is the subversion of the concept of lifelong learning to an economic agenda. Martin reminded us that in the UK in particular, and in other parts of Europe, despite the flourishing of lifelong learning, the dominant framing discourse is a political rather than educational one. There exists a clash of philosophies, with government's "modernizing" agenda being "about the radical restructuring of the welfare state and the hitching up of social and educational policy to the imperatives of economic policy" (p. 567). Martin further contended that in countering this policy distortion and in advancing the central issue of progress towards a more equitable distribution of material and cultural resources among citizens, it is

> the task of critical adult education, as distinct from economistic models of lifelong learning, to raise such questions as urgent issues for democratic deliberation and debate, and to expand our notions of what it means to be active citizens in a democratic society. (p. 566)

Adult education for social change and characterized by a tradition of dissent must resist being co-opted by government in particular and, under the guise of lifelong learning, as Martin put it, being marketed as a political ideology and instrument of social policy. This is an issue for Canadian adult educators as well as their colleagues throughout the developed world.

Barr (2002) discussed the difficulties confronting universities and university teachers in contributing to the creation of a more just society. Advancing ideas from political economy, critical social science, and feminism as a theory and practice of social transformation, she strongly advocated the repositioning of adult and higher education to counter the prevalence of global processes of economic, cultural, and workplace restructuring; the myopic and restrictive perspective of the postmodernists; and the tendency to restructure the role of university personnel "precisely to *exclude* wider, social, political and cultural understandings and engagements, as well as imaginings" (p. 323). In particular, she reinforced the legitimacy and necessity of the university's involvement with its community, notably through dialogue and inclusive knowledge practices.

Pointedly, Barr (2002) noted the diversity that constitutes the contemporary university community and the challenge and necessity of understanding the complexity of the links between community and campus, since community demands for equality, recognition, and material entitlement have still to be satisfied. Given the multicultural context of Canada and the emergence and legitimation of more diverse "voices" in the past decade, university extension personnel in particular need to pay close attention to the implications of diversity as they conceptualize and enact their core responsibilities to contemporary Canadian society.

Canadian Implications

Although still contested (see Field, 2001) with regard to its more radical roots and manifestations, lifelong learning or lifelong education, it seems to me, represents the ideal to which many progressive and socially conscious adult educators aspired in terms of a learning society. Furthermore, it has customarily been seen by Canadian university extension adult educators as comfortably accommodating more radical streams of work, including that strand oriented towards profound social change. Thus the current conflation of lifelong learning with skills development and personal economic advancement, particularly by government, industry, the private sector, and, not infrequently, universities in Canada, is evidence of a shifting and potentially restrictive discourse here too. I believe that because of the rise of neoliberal governments in Canada in the past decade, chiefly in Alberta and Ontario, and the subsequent fiscal and ideological pressures on universities, there is substantial evidence that this kind of thinking has infiltrated extension operations and considerably blunted the critical social approaches with which we were previously more comfortable and adept.

Plumb and Welton (2001) contrasted the *critical paradigm*, which poses basic questions about the inherent value base of adult educators' actions and decisions, with the *technical paradigm*, which sees them acting in a neutral and technically transmissive manner. Although noting that it is currently under attack from all sides, chiefly because of the rise of cyber-capitalism and the global economy, Plumb and Welton affirmed that its influence in adult education has nevertheless been profound. Optimistically, they contend:

> To this day, the critical paradigm continues to both irritate and animate. New critical voices—lesbian, gay, feminist, ecological, aboriginal—continue to appear challenging us to realize that it is not time to hibernate until the sun goes down on globalization. While conservative adult educators continue to expend considerable and careful effort in suppressing the transformative effects of critical inquiry, it seems very difficult for them to inhibit critique in a society that is changing as rapidly as our own. (p. 74)

This last assertion contains a troubling, but in my view valid, criticism that may be levelled at much of contemporary university extension work in Canada, though there are some notable exceptions. I will be less harsh, however, in arguing that what I see as the regrettable loss of most reputable social purpose work in Canadian university extension spheres is more by default than design. Furthermore, it is not so much that this kind of work is not occurring elsewhere, as that university extension's longstanding and formerly imaginative leadership in the area has withered. I want to examine this criticism by revisiting those points that I formerly made in critiquing Canadian university extension work for social change (Haughey, 1998).

Gains or Losses? 1998 to 2005

In attempting to assess the current state of the Canadian university extension movement against these markers, I examined Canadian research, especially the *Journal of the Canadian Association for University Continuing Education (CAUCE)*. Here I expected to find the leading thinking about the condition and evolution of Canadian university extension programs of all kinds. For an alternative perspective I looked internationally, notably, but by no means exclusively, at the *International Journal of Lifelong Education*. So regarding my former points of criticism and using both Canadian and international professional research commentary as a guide, how has Canadian practice responded in the past seven years?

The Importance of Engaging New Sites of Practice

I argued (Haughey, 1998) that the university extension movement was responding unimaginatively to new sites of practice by failing to break out of the campus confines, especially intellectually, and to open itself up to dialogue and partnership with creative and courageous community groups. With few exceptions, I see little progress in this area. Simon Fraser University in Vancouver has done valuable and creative work through its Community Education Programs, especially around poverty and human rights issues with Aboriginal, inner-city, and immigrant groups, by using imaginative campus and community-based partnerships. The University of Saskatchewan has a longstanding and distinguished commitment to rural community development, though even that is now on a tight fiscal diet. However, I see virtually no evidence from my reading of the Canadian research in the past seven years that Canadian university extension in general is even thinking seriously about this issue, let alone responding.

The international adult education community, including the university extension sector, is also struggling with the overall problem of the support of social purpose work, but at least the discussion around it is lively, informed, and provocative. Johnston (1999), in examining the question of the reconstruction of the social purpose tradition, notably education for citizenship, commented, in fact, that adult learning is flourishing; it is just that a lot of it is now situated outside the formal confines of the university and we need to recognize and respond to that. Foley (2001) looked at radical adult education and learning and observed that the terrain shifts and the spaces for radical education and learning change.

In response, I find much of the same, tired old instrumentalist thinking in the writing of Canadian university extension practitioners. For example, a survey of the professional development needs and interests of CAUCE members (Thompson and Archer, 2003) revealed that expertise in the area of online learning *was* the most frequently identified skill sought. Additionally, a group of the organization's deans and directors stated that, besides the largely technical skills identified by the respondents, "some broader, more outward-looking skills were needed, such as environmental scanning, striving for a culture of excellence, change management, effective lobbying, leadership, transference of learning, and building teams to implement change" (p. 80).

Percival (2001) attributed the current prominence of a more business-like approach rather than a social-change perspective, in the main, to inadequate financing and associated issues such as internal mission and role, program issues, finances, teaching, and technology. These issues, she conceded, are not new. I agree, because in my view they have been a tired and overworked staple of the discontent in Canadian university extension circles for the past few decades, at least! But, by 2005, the field had moved on elsewhere, and thus both the CAUCE survey and this commentary strike me as pretty staid. I still find the internal professional discourse in Canadian circles such as the CAUCE membership to be quite parochial and uninspired. Finally, though there is evidence of modest change in certain institutions campus-wide, I find little convincing evidence of progress overall on the new sites of practice issue.

The Intellectual Passivity of University Extension Practitioners and the Necessity to Engage New Theory

In *Learning for Life* (Haughey, 1998) I was critical of what I considered to be the failure of many in university extension to "reinvent" themselves, to reconstruct their work more as an intellectual pursuit in order to deal with what Johnston-Riordan (1994) then referred to as the necessity to mount a challenge to "the traditional frameworks of adult education pedagogy and research both from the existing, traditional social science perspectives and these newer perspectives" (p. 210). I also noted Tett's (1996) call for university adult education's engagement with "alternative discourses" (p. 211) and her contention that traditional adult education fails to do this. Further, I contended that "even when committed adult educators do engage in social action programs, many operate from relatively obsolete models of practice infused more with the fervor of tradition than informed by the intellectual and socio-political realities of today" (p. 211). I was never challenged on this assertion.

There are glimmers of hope here, but it is still problematic. Some possible reasons follow. Plumb and Welton (2001) observed that adult education is dominated by an "action" ethos and all too often far more emphasis is placed on "doing" adult education than on thinking about what is done or why. Similarly Tobias (2003), in looking at the provision of continuing professional education (CPE), reported that educators working in this field are poorly served by the lack of adequate social theory. He also pointed out what he termed the limitations inherent in technicist and instrumentalist theories and various forms of liberal functionalist theory of professionalization and CPE, moving on to propose the beginnings of an alternative critical social theory that may inform thinking about professionalization and CPE.

I still believe, since I found little convincing evidence to the contrary, that many Canadian practitioners continue to operate from uncritical and functionalist models of practice. However, McLean (1996), a Canadian university extension educator, in a more theoretical and for that reason still relatively rare study of the changing role of socially activist university continuing education programs in the postmodern context, noted that we need to think differently about such concepts as oppression, power, and resistance in trying to understand and resist emerging patterns of domination in Canada. To do so, he employed an analysis drawn from Foucault, pointing out in the process that it will be difficult, but crucial, for contemporary university extension educators to change themselves to adapt to radically new forms of activist practice not currently treated in the literature. As an example, he cited the regulating and disciplining of identities, part of a transformed process of oppression and different from the sites of economic and political oppression against which Canadian universities have traditionally struggled. In his view, "if we lose touch with how oppression is being accomplished, we risk losing relevance as social activists and becoming complicit actors in the subjection of ourselves and our learners" (p. 15).

To return to Bagnall (2000), he too urged engagement with contemporary theory as a way of framing and grappling with a particularly limiting construction of lifelong learning:

> It is suggested that if the prevailing lifelong learning discourse is to be made more culturally progressive—in both its educational activities and its learning outcomes—it cannot be through a return to traditional progressive ideologies. Rather, it must accept prevailing epistemology in refocusing that discourse. (p. 20)

In the university extension and wider Canadian adult education sectors I see glimmers that professionals who support or devise university extension programs—programs oriented towards the kinds of social purpose that has been discussed so far—are beginning to conceptualize issues in a way that, at least partially, responds to the imperatives I have just discussed. In the process, this forces them to accept and endure the often painful struggle involved in moving outside their own personal intellectual comfort zone. It involves risk and considerable daring, but currently it is the indisputable price of remaining credible and relevant in both the professional and public spheres.

Cultivating New Intra- and Extramural Alliances

Highlighting the shift in focus from the local to the global, I called, in *Learning for Life* (Haughey, 1998), for the reinvention of the role of the university extension professional involved in programs for social change to encompass a more outreach function. I emphasized competence in politics and cultural theory, and internal and external alliance building to match new sites of practice. Edwards and Miller (2000), in looking at issues in contemporary adult education and lifelong learning, also reinforced the crucial point that in lifelong learning greater emphasis is placed upon learner control and what goes on outside the educational institution; thus, placing boundaries around that learning and creating spaces for learning in the face of other demands becomes problematic. Learning can be adopted as part of lifestyle rather than arising from a need for enlightenment. Foley (2001) pointed out that extremely vital and comprehensive learning and teaching for social purposes is taking place not only in educational institutions, but in the workplace, families, communities, the mass media, and social movements. Increasingly, the new terrain is outside of the formal university setting and requires a new understanding of the role of the adult educator. Notably, the person working in the radical tradition will still need to be critical and emancipatory, but more strategic. Johnston (1999) corroborated the need for more flexible partnerships and negotiated role change.

However, when I look at the Albertan response to some of the most pressing issues confronting its citizens in the last decade—the restructuring of health care and education, the imposition of highly centralized government control and power, urban poverty, Aboriginal alienation and neglect, the decline of rural life—I do not see the leading reactions coming from university extension units. Instead, the most incisive and provocative critique is coming either from academics in other sectors of the university or, more frequently, from individuals, organized pressure groups, think tanks that span the ideological spectrum, and online discussion forums.

Good examples of this include the writing of the Edmonton journalist and political commentator Mark Lisac (1996, 2004), whose two books on Alberta politics, *The Klein Revolution* and *Alberta Politics Uncovered: Taking Back Our Province*, constitute a major contribution to informed public debate around the democratic trade-offs involved in accepting the economic policies of the current provincial government. Publications by the University of Alberta–based Parkland Institute, an Alberta research network situated within the Faculty of Arts, have critiqued not only the "reforms" in education and for-profit health care, but also the negative impact of globalization and trade agreements in transforming rural communities in Western Canada. Notably, Epp, in a book on issues affecting rural communities, *Writing Off the Rural West* (Epp and Whitson, 2001), observed that redressing key problems caused by the closure of rural schools and the contamination of ground water by oil and gas operations will require the rebirth of political activism outside party politics. The articulate and politically astute group Friends of Medicare has defended public health care interests in Alberta and probably represents the kind of learning force of well-educated Canadians that constitutes our greying population. Such groups have as much to teach university adult educators as educators have to learn from them, and it is here that I feel that university extension in pursuit of social justice needs, but has largely failed, to connect. The university has intellectual capital to offer, but it needs to be in genuinely equal and open partnerships if connections occur at all. Consequently, extension personnel need to strive harder to cement these links. Besides, those institutions that have not already done so need to be more creative in consolidating intramural links with committed colleagues. This is where we need effective, not effete, decanal leadership and imagination.

Revealingly, the University of Alberta's Faculty of Arts (2005) is currently marketing itself as being dedicated to building bridges into the community as well as offering innovative classes in citizenship. It also offers a Community Service Learning program designated as a mutual exchange, in which the needs of the community and academic learning are considered and served. I believe that we are seeing here an emergence and broadening of the university's conception of community involvement primarily at the undergraduate level, but also touching areas of social need, and to which concerned mainstream faculty members are paying increased attention. This cannot help but focus increased attention on some of the kinds of social development work formerly in the almost exclusive domain of Faculties of Extension. However, if Canadian university extension's presence is to remain prominent in this, it needs to recognize that its future lies in sensitive coalitions on and off campus. Even so, there is a strong risk that extension may be eclipsed if its intellectual contribution internally is not rated on par with colleagues. In some cases, I believe that this has already happened and that these units, lacking clear policy and committed and courageous leadership, are now seen as largely redundant.

I acknowledge the committed extension professionals who struggle valiantly to keep a social-change emphasis alive, frequently without internal support. However, I contend that university extension in Canada has come through a phase of often courageous and creative commitment to programs for social change that was strained, in the past decade, with the overall retrenchment in universities and exacerbated pressures to balance social responsibility with fiscal rectitude. Yet this is not the real reason for the continuing decline in extension's involvement in this kind of work. I believe the key reason is poignantly ironic: With few exceptions, the movement has largely failed in positioning itself to anticipate the shifts in society that now situate the learning agenda and the intellectual capital to pursue it, mainly outside as opposed to inside the university. Society, learning environments, and even universities overall have evolved, and this is both inevitable and desirable. Unfortunately, the university extension movement appears to have been unable or unwilling to change itself fast enough to keep pace—to paraphrase poet Stevie Smith (2002), perhaps a case of having been much too far out all its life and now not waving but drowning.

References

Bagnall, R. G. (2000). Lifelong learning and the limitations of economic determinism. *International Journal of Lifelong Education, 19*(1), 20–35.

Barr, J. (2002). Universities after postmodernism. *International Journal of Lifelong Education, 21*(4), 321–333.

Edwards, R. and Miller, N. (2000). Go your own way: Lifelong learning and reflexive autobiographies in postmodernity. *International Journal of Lifelong Education, 19*(2), 126–140.

Epp, R. and Whitson, D. (Eds.). (2001). *Writing off the rural west: Globalization, governments, and the transformation of rural communities.* Edmonton, AB: University of Alberta Press.

Faculty of Arts. (2005). *Community outreach.* Retrieved April 19, 2005, from http://www.uofaweb.ualberta.ca/arts/outreach.cfm

Field, J. (2001). Lifelong education. *International Journal of Lifelong Education, 20*(1/2), 3–15.

Foley, G. (2001). Radical adult education and learning. *International Journal of Lifelong Education, 20*(1/2), 71–88.

Haughey, D. J. (1998). From passion to passivity: The decline of university extension for social change. In S. M. Scott., B. Spencer, and A.M. Thomas (Eds.), *Learning for life: Canadian readings in adult education* (pp. 200–212). Toronto, ON: Thompson Educational.

Johnson-Riordan, L. (1994). In and against the grain of "new times": Discourses of adult education and the challenge of contemporary cultural theory. *Australian Journal of Adult and Community Education, 34*(1), 10–17.

Johnston, R. (1999). Adult learning for citizenship: Towards a reconstruction of the social purpose tradition. *International Journal of Lifelong Education, 18*(3), 175–190.

Lisac, M. (1996). *The Klein revolution.* Edmonton, AB: NeWest Press.

Lisac, M. (2004). *Alberta politics uncovered: Taking back our province.* Edmonton, AB: NeWest Press.

Martin, I. (2003). Adult education, lifelong learning, and citizenship: Some ifs and buts. *International Journal of Lifelong Education, 22*(6), 566–579.

McLean, S. (1996). Continuing education and the postmodern arts of power. *Canadian Journal of University Continuing Education, 22*(2), 7–26.

Percival, A. (2001). University continuing education: Traditions and transitions. In D. Poonwassie and A. Poonwassie, (Eds.), *Fundamentals of adult education: Issues and practices for lifelong learning* (pp. 133–146). Toronto, ON: Thompson Educational.

Plumb, D. and Welton, M. (2001). *Theory building in adult education.* In D. Poonwassie and A. Poonwassie, (Eds.), *Fundamentals of adult education: Issues and practices for lifelong learning* (pp. 63–75). Toronto, ON: Thompson Educational.

Smith, S. (2002). *Selected poems.* London, UK: Penguin.

Tett, L. (1996). Community education: The "underclass" and the discourse of derision. *International Journal of Lifelong Education, 15*(2), 19–31.

Thompson, G. and Archer, W. (2003). A survey of the professional development needs and interests of CAUCE members. *Canadian Journal of University Continuing Education, 29*(2), 73–84.

Tobias, R. (2000). The boundaries of adult education for active citizenship: Institutional and community contexts. *International Journal of Lifelong Education, 19*(5), 418–429.

Tobias, R. (2003). Continuing professional education and professionalization: Travelling without a map or compass? *International Journal of Lifelong Education, 22*(5), 445–456.

Welton, M. (2003). "No escape from the hard things of the world": Learning the lessons of empire. *International Journal of Lifelong Education, 22*(6), 635–651.

27

Distance Education Online: A Forum Adult Education?

Dianne Conrad and Bruce Spencer

A t the end of online learning's first decade of widespread institutional use, do adult educators have at their fingertips an easily accessible vehicle to teach adults effectively and to promote socially relevant and purposeful adult education and learning?

In this chapter the authors support the argument that online learning can be used to promote *adult education*, which is broadly defined and as it was understood by Lindeman (1947): "True adult education is social education" (p. 55). A brief overview of distance education and the move to online learning, including an understanding of degrees of "online-ness" and the potential of the "virtual classroom," will precede a discussion of the characteristics of adult education and the capability of online learning to be a forum for adult education.

Distance Education and the Move to Online Learning

Distance education includes a variety of delivery methods and media whereby the instructor and student do not meet in the same physical space "face to face." In recent years, however, the term *distance education* has become synonymous with *online learning*, or *e-learning*. These terms are used interchangeably with, and at times in place of, many others: *technology-mediated learning, computer-mediated conferencing, online collaborative learning, computer-supported collaborative learning, tele-learning, virtual learning, Net-based learning,* and *Web-based learning*. That this type of distance learning has become the dominant form of distance education discourse in the West is clearly apparent in the literature, which has all but abandoned discussions of other, older forms of distance education such as correspondence education, audio- and video-teleconferencing, radio, film, and television.

Defining distance education is itself a lengthy discussion that elicits argument. Garrison (1989) supported the view that "distance education is a species of education characterised by one structural characteristic—the non-contiguity of teacher and student" (p. 8). *Distance education, distance learning, open learning, flexible learning, virtual learning, hybrid* or *blended learning,* and *distributed learning* are all terms that refer to teaching and learning interactions that entail full or partial physical separation of learner and instructor.

Keegan (1980) described the "separation of teacher and student" (p. 4) as the first of six elements present in defining distance education, the others being the influence of an educational organization, especially in planning and preparing learning materials; the uses of technical media; the provision of two-way communication; the possibility of occasional seminars; and participation in the most industrialized form of education. (See Spencer, 1998, in *Learning for Life* for a discussion and references.) Keegan's list demonstrated the field's early fascination with distance education as a "content delivery" issue. However, as Shale (2003) questioned in a discussion of defining distance education: "Is the delivery of content to spatially isolated learners really the heart of the issue—or is there a deeper effect that results when students are removed from easy and ready access to a teacher and/or their fellow students?" (p. 397). In answering his own question, Shale echoed others who have shifted the focus of study to the ability of "Internet technologies [to] facilitate the educative experience" (p. 397). When considered in this light, the discussion of online learning becomes one of knowledge construction, communication, participation, language, and community. The study of the practice of distance education as exercised online, therefore, reflects the same learning concerns that are shared by adult educators everywhere, regardless of delivery format.

Although some current distance education literature has focused on learning, learners, and theory, it must be recognized that the evolution of online learning has been paced by developments in technology. Early distance education, print based and at times delivered as correspondence courses, is often termed *first-generation* distance education. As distance technologies have evolved, the labelling of successive generations has varied. Currently, although commentators dispute whether online learning with *virtual classrooms* (usually a discussion board with students posting messages week by week) falls into third-, fourth-, or fifth-generation iterations of distance education, it is agreed that learning in this way is characterized by an increased degree of learner control and flexibility, interactive communication, and group-oriented processes.

The Introduction of the Virtual Classroom

The introduction of online learning and electronic classrooms has raised questions around the teaching–learning exchange and its underpinning theory. Some distance educators, in fact, question the validity of older theory that explained distance education in industrialized terms— referring to the production and delivery processes of print-based courses. (Some practitioners, however, have noted increased roles for instructional designers and various technicians in the preparation of online courses, which has resulted in an increased distancing of subject specialists from the final online technological versions of their courses—a renewed "industrialism.") However, the new questions raised in distance education of interest to adult educators are often critical, social, and epistemological in nature. Does online learning enable open, critical, liberal adult education? Does the online venue permit authentic dialogue? Does it encourage the blending of learners' experience with other knowledge? Does it encourage, facilitate, or permit the pursuit of social educational aims, such as the promotion of participatory democracy and citizenship?

Online learning is used in many ways in post-secondary education; there are degrees of "online-ness." Institutions that are dedicated in their mandate to distance education may conduct much of their activity virtually; traditional institutions are more likely to add a virtual component to their face-to-face delivery formats to create a *blended learning* delivery model. The addition of an online component to an existing face-to-face course (or to an individualized print-based distance education course) does not necessarily move that course to a group learning experience. Such an online component in a course may provide little more than access to Internet resources and the opportunity for emailed assignments. It may include an online instructional lesson or online quizzes, but it does not necessarily use computer-mediated technology (beyond email) to link students to the instructor or connect a student to other students online. Many traditional classroom-based courses, although technologically enhanced through learners' and instructors' use of Internet resources, remain primarily didactic, nondiscursive, and information-delivering in nature. Additionally, the interaction possible in paced online courses (in which students start and finish at the same time as a cohort group) is qualitatively different from that possible in unpaced courses (in which students enrol throughout the year and move at their own pace) in that students are working at different points in the same course. Although student-to-student-to-tutor/ instructor interaction is possible in both, the intensity of student discussions and the possibilities for group work in paced courses are generally much greater than what is achievable in the unpaced courses.

Traditional classroom teachers may see the use of online formats as vehicles for moving learners *away* from face-to-face classroom exchanges and dialogical education as online discussions using computer conferences replace traditional classroom courses with virtual classrooms. However, for distance educators who have relied on individualized, print-based formats and/or telephone tutoring, or for students engaged in face-to-face mass lectures, online virtual classrooms can move students *towards* increased dialogue. Interactive virtual classrooms can reduce the isolation of individualized study that characterized earlier generations of distance education where there was little, or only occasional, contact with the course tutor.

Although there are differences between participatory virtual classrooms and traditional face-to-face small or seminar classrooms (of up 30 students or so), there are no significant differences in students' educational achievements (Bernard et. al., 2004). Technical expertise is generally no longer an issue for students either. Most online programs give students ready access to a computing services helpdesk, although connectivity can still be a problem in some rural areas or for students with limited means. Generally speaking, the technologies used for online learning are relatively simple and stable.

The virtual classroom can then, at its best, epitomize a constructive, collaborative, communicative learning environment. Adherents of social learning theory recognize that the communal or social aspects of online learning are the glue that bonds learners together and encourages sustained interaction in meaningful ways, often even extending learners' relationships with each other to venues outside the virtual classroom. (For references and supporting arguments, see Conrad, 2005.)

Distance education's recent shift to online learning raises other issues that challenge our understanding of traditional forms of communication. For example, do the new technologies replicate small or seminar classrooms? In most cases, the systems of computer conferencing that support online learning reflect a written/textual practice rather than an oral practice. The fact that the many qualities of oral communication and the dynamics of traditional face-to-face seminars are not present makes the "best of both worlds" thesis, claimed by some distance education enthusiasts, not sustainable. However, the virtual classroom that allows for student-to-student-to-tutor/instructor interaction does represent a shift towards the small or seminar face-to-face classroom. Therefore, the virtual classroom—although *different* from the traditional classroom, but with its own strengths and weaknesses—can also be a place of social learning. (For a discussion of the strengths and weaknesses of virtual classrooms and for references, see Spencer, 1998, *Learning for Life*; or Spencer, 2004.)

The most common difference between virtual classrooms and traditional face-to-face classroom learning is described in terms of "seeing" the other learners and/or the instructor. Visual proximity to other group members is a physical comfort factor to which learners have been accustomed in traditional classroom formats. Although it has therefore formed a part of learners' social expectations, visual proximity is *not* the key issue in understanding learning or in distinguishing online learning as a forum for good pedagogy. To understand this point, we might ask ourselves, Do I continue to learn if I am absent from my (bricks-and-mortar) classroom for a month because of my broken leg? Can I learn if I am vision impaired?

Some also believe that the absence of visual and verbal clues in the virtual classroom obstructs good learning. Although it is more awkward and less intuitive to replicate these gestures in the virtual classroom, it is not impossible. Creative distance learners and teachers make use of punctuation and emoticons (although hopefully with restraint) to indicate affective responses. Words must be carefully chosen; the rhythm and pacing of expression can go a long way towards indicating excitement, disbelief, agreement, and even humour. Capital letters, although generally frowned upon in email correspondence as "shouting," can be used cautiously and discreetly to "shout" out exuberance responses.

On the matter of teachers' reading visual clues from their learners, an instructor learning to teach online offered this reflection:

You can't see them and their faces. I think that's a good thing. The interested people you'll hear from. What I found from the feedback [in face-to-face courses] is that some of the people who looked like they were dying thought it was the best course they ever took. So you can't really tell from their faces. (Conrad, 2004, p. 36)

The issues of asynchronicity (with students posting messages at different times), immediacy, and cognition in online learning are more valid concerns that truly reflect the online culture. Similarly, issues of interaction, participation, and models of learning are validly raised by distance educators when they discuss the impact of virtual classrooms. Research, however, has made it clear that online delivery models need not compromise the quality of learning that can exist with the use of communication technologies (Bernath and Rubin, 2003). Numerous studies of practices of online educators have shown that critical, socially relevant education is possible online. It may be different from face-to-face, with its own strengths and weaknesses, but it is no less effective. (For example, when an important question is raised towards the end of a face-to-face class, it may get some brief attention with a promise to return to it next week; but online the question can be explored in depth throughout the week, unlimited by time constraints.) The importance of the connection of community, learning, and social process is also reflected in research that investigates the phenomenon of online learners' attempts to adapt to new roles and identities as fully engaged online contributors and thinkers.

Online Learning and Socially Relevant Adult Education

Can distance education in its current online form serve the social purposes of adult education that demand authenticity, openness, critical thinking, purposeful and respectful reflection, and the promotion of participatory democracy and citizenship? With the advent of collaborative online learning, distance education has moved from individualized and often isolated study to dynamic, interactive exchanges that, properly facilitated, encourage knowledge building, teamwork, and communication skills. The groundwork has been laid for social purpose educational practices and outcomes.

Current distance education theory emphasizes social, communication-based, and constructivist learning (Garrison, 2000; Wenger, 1998). At the heart of this understanding of online learning, supported by a sound body of literature and based on empirical studies, are social learning theory and the notion of community. The creation of community simulates for online learners the comforts of home and provides a safe climate, an atmosphere of trust and respect, an invitation for intellectual exchange, and a gathering place for like-minded individuals who are sharing a journey that includes similar activities, purpose, and goals. Social learning theories hold that the interrelationships of the learning process are mediated by complex webs of factors both within and outside of learners' immediate learning domains. Formats that promote the centrality of a community of learning link learners through social processes to social purpose as an integral part of the online teaching–learning dynamic. Such a linkage can promote socially responsive adult education as described by Lindeman (1947). (For references and supporting arguments, see Conrad, 2005.)

Outside of formal learning opportunities, communication technologies that connect social actors over space and time, that allow them to share experience and learning, can contribute to the potential for social change. For example, the World Social Forum relies on electronic communication to build a "horizontal community." In another example, a website named WhoLivesNearYou.com allows big-city residents to virtually meet their neighbours and thus develop the small-town feel of community. Some of this informal learning that occurs via Web logs (blogs), listserves, and non-institutional Internet sites can also spill out from nonformal or formal distance learning. How, and if, this learning connects to social purposes depends on the students' connection to social movements and social change agents. Taylor (2002) provided an example of a successful online union course that was designed to achieve social actions and was possible because of the course members' union connections—their existing social movements.

Earlier chapters in this edited collection describe the characteristics of adult education that historically have made its classrooms a rich environment for adult learning and in some cases important social actions. Some of these characteristics as they relate to distance education are highlighted in the upcoming sections.

Pedagogy, Critical Thinking, and Critical Theory

Early distance education reflected a fascination with its technologies; however, some research and practice has always demonstrated that distance technology is a tool whose purpose is to serve the teaching and learning function. Good distance education does employ good pedagogy; Web-based technologies can promote sound pedagogy and critical thinking beyond what was possible in previous distance education formats.

Trying to get students to move beyond critical thinking to an understanding of the role of critical thought has always been a challenge within traditional forms of distance education (and face-to-face education), but the discursive possibility of the virtual classroom expands the openings for this kind of knowledge. Knowledge exploration is linked to the distinction between *critical thinking skills* and *critical thought* (as promoted in critical theory). Critical thought begins by questioning belief systems and by asking who benefits from dominant ideas: Its project is educational *and* emancipatory (Burbules and Berk, 1999).

Collaboration and Experience

Philosophically, it is generally accepted that adult education rests on the humanistic approach that recognizes the importance of life experience and promotes students' autonomous and self-directed learning. Adult-education instructors traditionally practice collaborative, interactive, and group learning strategies that permit adults to participate experientially and at levels appropriate to them. Well-facilitated and -designed online learning can also promote collaborative and group learning activities because group discussion in online asynchronous course conferences may continue through a week or longer; it is not bounded by the face-to-face class meeting times. Many adult online learners report high levels of productive group learning and its resultant benefits.

Distance education institutions can also collaborate with community colleges and other institutions and groups to help deliver educational opportunities to learners that would not otherwise be available to them locally.

Community

A sense of community is closely connected to a group's collaborative efforts. *Community*, defined as "a general sense of connection, belonging, and comfort that develops, over time, among members of a group who share purpose or commitment to a common goal" (Conrad, 2005, p. 5), both contributes to and flows from a group's collaborative pedagogical and social energies. Face-to-face classrooms produce community in different and more intuitive ways than do online learning experiences because learners can see and enjoy each other in natural, social ways, such as sharing coffee at breaks. The energy that results from group exchanges fuels adults' appreciation for sharing ideas and learning tasks. As with other aspects of online delivery, a robust sense of community can emerge from online experiences (online classrooms, virtual "coffee rooms," and chat rooms), and its presence can work to sustain high levels of commitment to the learning task at hand.

Working within disadvantaged communities is often more difficult for distance institutions than it is for traditional, locally-based, face-to-face organizations; but online classrooms can help to link different geographic communities and sustain links for disadvantaged groups across time zones and space.

Citizenship, Responsibility, and Respect

Two foundational notions that underlie adult education classrooms, responsibility and respect, are just as necessary and present in well-facilitated online teaching as they are in face-to-face teaching. The success of online courses requires that learners participate, individually and often in groups and teams. Turn-taking and other rudimentary functions of the traditional classroom are not as intuitive online, and learners must work harder at defining themselves and understanding the results of their actions.

Online learning in adult education settings not only provides avenues to discuss the role of participatory democracy at work and in society, but also permits learners to explore, through practice, what it means to be knowledge-sharing, active citizens in the twenty-first century.

Access and Openness

Distance education has always been closely associated with opening up access to educational opportunities, as is indicated by the name of the British Open University and Athabasca University's claim to be "Canada's Open University." Although some institutional efforts towards openness have resulted in, for example, greater access for women, for people with disabilities, and for those without traditional university entry requirements than have previously been achieved by many traditional face-to-face institutions, achieving openness for all disadvantaged groups remains an ongoing struggle. Online courses do require that students have access to the necessary equipment, but once that is achieved, students can participate in virtual classroom discussions at times of their choosing. This flexibility opens up access to many and varied adult students who are limited by time available for study or by location.

Conclusions

It is clear from the discussion above that interactive and collaborative online learning can score highly on a matrix of key indicators of good adult education provision. The learning experience is different for online students than it is in face-to-face situations, but the differences are not necessarily negative; the strengths and weaknesses of both formats should be considered separately.

Traditional liberal adult education, including community-based social purpose education, has been in decline in the Western world for some time now. (For a discussion and references, see the Haughey, 1998, chapter in *Learning for Life*.) Online education has been developed primarily to enhance adult learners' ability to earn credentials and advance vocationally, and in that regard it parallels the current emphasis of mainstream adult education provision. However, the online learning environment can also support socially relevant adult learning when informed adult educators use its strengths to assist learners in building community and knowledge and sharing their local community-based connections with other learners in different "places and spaces." In this way, online distance education can support learning for social purpose and continue to work towards Lindeman's (1947) vision of "true adult education" (p. 13).

References

Bernard, R. M., Abrami, P. C., Lou, Y., Borokhovski, E., Wade, A., Wozney, L., et al. (2004). How does distance education compare with classroom instruction? A meta-analysis of the empirical literature. *Review of Educational Research, 74*(3), 379–439.

Bernath, U. and Rubin, E. (2003). (Eds.) *Reflections on teaching and learning in an online master program: A case study.* Oldenburg, Germany: Bibliotheks-und Informationssystem der Carl von Ossietzky Universität.

Burbules, N. and Berk, R. (1999).Critical thinking and critical pedagogy: Relations, differences, and limits. In T. Popkewitz and L. Fendler (Eds.), *critical theories in education: Changing terrains of knowledge and politics* (pp. 45–65). New York: Routledge.

Conrad, D. (2004). University instructors' reflections on their first online teaching experiences. *Journal of Asynchronous Learning Networks, 8*(2). Retrieved November 27, 2004, from http://www.aln.org/publications/jaln/v8n2/v8n2_conrad.asp

Conrad, D. (2005). Building and maintaining community in cohort-based online learning. *Journal of Distance Education, 20*(1), 1–21.

Garrison, D. R. (1989). *Understanding distance education.* London: Routledge.

Garrison, D. R. (2000). Theoretical challenges for distance education in the 21st century: A shift from structural to transactional issues. *International Review of Research in Open and Distance Learning, 1*(1). Retrieved November 27, 2004, from http://www.irrodl.org/content/v1.1/randy.html

Haughey, D. J. (1998). From passion to passivity: The decline of university extension for social change. In S. M. Scott, B. Spencer and A. M. Thomas (Eds.), *Learning for life: Canadian readings in adult education* (pp. 200–212). Toronto, ON: Thompson Educational.

Keegan, D. J. (1980). On defining distance education. *Distance Education 1*(1). 13–36.

Lindeman, E. C. (1947). Methods of democratic adult education. In S. Brookfield (Ed), *Learning democracy: Eduard Lindeman on adult education and social change* (pp. 53–59). London: Croom Helm, 1987.

Shale, D. (2003). Does "distance education" really say it all—or does it say enough? A commentary on the article by Kanuka and Conrad. *Quarterly Review of Distance Education, 4*(4), 395–399.

Spencer, B. (1998). Distance education and the virtual classroom. In S. M. Scott, B. Spencer, & A. Thomas (Eds.), *Learning for life: Canadian readings in adult education* (pp. 243–253). Toronto, ON: Thompson Educational.

Spencer, B. (2004). On-line adult learning. In G. Foley (Ed.), *Dimensions of adult learning: Adult education and training in a global era* (pp. 189–200). New South Wales, Australia: Allen & Unwin.

Taylor, J. (2002). Union e-learning in Canada. In B. Spencer (Ed.), *Unions and learning in a global economy: International and comparative perspectives* (pp. 149–157). Toronto, ON: Thompson Educational.

Wenger, E. (1998). *Communities of practice: Learning, meaning, and identity.* New York: Cambridge University Press.

28

Coming to Terms with Prior Learning Assessment

Geoff Peruniak and Rick Powell

Prior learning assessment (PLA) is a relatively new phenomenon in higher education. PLA measures experiential learning toward formal educational credit. Several forces have converged to place PLA on the agendas of universities in Canada—often to their discomfort. After all, life and informal learning experiences do not shape themselves for the convenience of educators. In this chapter, we will first identify some of the forces that shape PLA in higher education and then examine definitions. We will then discuss PLA from the standpoint of the Canadian university community as well as from an adult student perspective. We conclude with a summary of key concerns for the university community's coming to terms with PLA.

Socio-economic and Political Environments of PLA

The recognition of experiential learning at a university level has a short history, beginning in the 1980s (Bélanger and Mount, 1998). It came somewhat to the fore only in the early 1990s in Canada. The impetus toward accepting PLA as "legitimate" did not stem from the university community but from underlying demographic, economic, and political forces. The demographic impetus was the aging of the labour force. With low birth rates, the labour force could not renew itself from traditional students; because of rapid technological change, increased occupational mobility, and restructured workplace organization, the existing labour force must be retrofitted for the "knowledge economy" and the "global economy" (Conference Board of Canada, 1995).

Governments and state-supported research agencies began to take notice of PLA as an element of national economies in the mid-1990s in Canada. For example, the Conference Board of Canada (1995), Industry Canada (2001), and Human Resources Development Canada (2002) all called for PLA credentialing in one form or another to meet demographic and economic workforce challenges. PLA seems to be a financial shortcut for the individuals involved and for employers and governments in their quest for accreditation. Why reteach people subject matters that they already know?

PLA and Credentialism

PLA is, by definition, concerned with credentialing. The definition of *credentialism* seems always to be cast in negative terms. Buon (1998) cited three definitions:

> the empty pursuit of . . . credentials that are not necessarily related to intellectual or educational achievement; . . . entry qualifications for an occupation [that] are up-graded but there is no commensurate change in the knowledge or skill requirements of the job, [and] . . . unproductive use of credentials as a means of screening people for the job. (p. 1)

Nonetheless, governments and many economists see the credentialing of knowledge as evidence of building human capital. In their view, educational credentials enhance the competitiveness of a country's labour force by increasing worker productivity and labour force mobility. Workplace learning acknowledged at one place of work or in one industry might not be acknowledged elsewhere without some form of external credentialing. However, the "human capital" argument—that credentials issued equate to higher labour force productivity—has remained contentious. Critics of credentialism dispute the equation of educational credentials attained with increased labour-force competence and productivity—or even as a valid selection device used by employers. Also, far from democratizing employment opportunities, insistence on formal educational qualifications discriminates against the poor and marginalized sectors of society (Buon, 1998; Davis, 1981).

Our approach to credentialism is pragmatic. However contentious the drive toward credentialism is, it is nonetheless a fact. PLA by itself does not accentuate the negative aspects of credentialism but can mitigate the downsides of the phenomenon. Furthermore, we do see the positive educational outcomes of PLA, often unanticipated by petitioners, as important quite apart from the credentials issued.

Terminology

So far we have largely skirted the matter of defining exactly what we mean by PLA and how it applies. Since the early 1970s the Council for Adult and Experiential Learning (CAEL)—first called the Cooperative Assessment of Experiential Learning and then the Council for the Advancement of Experiential Learning—has been using the term *PLA*. However, the terminology associated with the accreditation of informal learning has changed over time and across borders. In Australia it is known as the *recognition of prior learning* (RPL), in Britain as *assessment of prior learning* (APL), and lately in Canada as *prior learning assessment and recognition* (PLAR).

The term PLA and its sister acronyms encompass a wide area and mean different things. For example, the Conference Board of Canada's (1995) understanding of the term extended to the recognition of out-of-country and even out-of-province credentials not acknowledged by professional licensing bodies. PLA also comprises both occupational (i.e., trades and professional designations) and educational (i.e., technical school, college, and university) credentialing. At a more theoretical level, definitional ambiguity is to be expected when common words such as *learning* and *experience* begin to take on technical meanings (Hamilton, 1994). The terminology surrounding PLA will take time to settle down. As a result, commentators, theorists, and researchers have to make clear their understanding of PLA. The following is our understanding of PLA.

PLA concerns informal learning; that is, learning not formerly attested to by an accredited educational institution. PLA is a means by which informal and nonformal learning can be recognized by accredited programs of study. We offer the following definition of PLA from Sargent (1999):

> PLA is an assessment process and a variety of tools that assist adults in reflecting upon, articulating, and demonstrating learning for the purpose of having it measured, compared to some standard, and in some way acknowledged by a credentialing body. (p. 27)

Evaluative procedures include course challenge or departmental examinations, evaluations of "in-house" training programs, and individual portfolio assessments that may include interviews and demonstrations. Note that PLA accredits *learning* that results from experience rather than the *experience* per se (Willingham, 1977). Credit is granted for what was actually learned from an experience, not for having had an experience. Also, note that assessment procedures vary widely, and some may well be discomfiting for the academics charged with attesting to the validity of prior knowledge in awarding credits at a university level. We will limit ourselves to portfolio-based PLA. In this form of PLA, students are required to reflect on their past learning as it relates to university subject matters and to demonstrate that this learning has been achieved through both a written submission and external references from qualified persons such as employers and suitably qualified supervisors.

PLA: A University Perspective

According to government and government-sponsored agencies, Canadian universities will face two pressures in the near future: a demographic decline in their traditional (under 25 years of age) candidate populations and an increased demand by employers, employees, and governments to address the needs of adult part-time students. As we write, these pressures have not been felt, but demographic trends tend to be inexorable.

Given such circumstances, the attractiveness of PLA seems obvious. PLA shortens the timeline towards earning credentials and is much cheaper than forcing students who already know the material to jump through academic hoops. Moreover, universities face the prospect of declining enrolments from their traditional constituencies. However, the Canadian university community continues to be reluctant to embrace PLA as an integral component of its educational provision.

Canadian universities have long recognized informal learning as legitimate in special cases. These practices have ranged from setting challenge examinations, to waiving prerequisites to grant entry to programs and courses, to using reading courses that capitalize on a student's previous learning. However, such arrangements have generally been exceptions to normal accreditation practice.

PLA has been a marginal practice in the Canadian university system for at least one reason. Universities have always been primarily focused on traditional students under the age of 25. After all, most people under the age of 25 have not had the time to acquire informal university-level learning. By acknowledging the legitimacy of informal learning, we are looking at organizing and standardizing such practices at a system level. This task is difficult especially given long-standing university traditions and practices (Thomas and Klaiman, 1992).

Attitudinal Barriers

There is certainly a constituency within the Canadian academic community that is fundamentally opposed to PLA. They have argued that university-level learning can take place only in a classroom and when taught by an academic. Although this school of thought is undoubtedly a barrier to the acceptance of PLA, it is probably not critical because a number of respected Canadian universities have formally acknowledged PLA as legitimate—at least in principle. A much more serious barrier is the challenge of PLA to academics' notions of their educational role—even those who might accept PLA in principle.

Academics have traditionally viewed their educational roles of teaching and student assessment as an organic whole. The acceptance of PLA as an integral practice rather than a marginal practice means unpacking these educational functions. The discomfort of academics is understandable. A necessary but usually tiresome and unrewarding aspect of their university role now comes to the forefront. Moreover, one must attest to what one has not taught.

In a conventional university setting, *formal* course learning objectives and expectations are not usually needed. They are implied by the course syllabi and reinforced through the process of classroom instruction. Indeed, academics' take on course objectives may undergo change as a result of the classroom experience. Formalizing course objectives and learning expectations has not traditionally been emphasized. Also, some forms of PLA (e.g., portfolio-based) are assessed by panels: Collective assessment is a foreign experience to most academics. When PLA becomes an integral, rather than a marginal, practice for assessment and attestation, it extends beyond the comfort zone of even the most sympathetic of academics.

Legitimacy Barriers

To date, some forms of PLA have been accepted by the university community as legitimate. This has been, in large part, because they have been treated as exceptions to the rule. Nonetheless, the legitimacy of PLA-accorded credit is certainly open to question when its role expands and the scope of PLA measurement practices increases.

The validity of PLA-issued credit is both an internal (to the academic community) and an external issue. Internally, PLA-awarded credit is suspect—particularly when it extends beyond academics' confidence in attesting to student learning. Beyond so-called "objective testing"—that is, though multiple response questions (itself a hotly debated issue)—assessment has always had a subjective component. This subjectivity has been constrained by accepted practices for marking and academics' precise knowledge of what was taught within the confines of their courses. The issue of subjectivity expands greatly in PLA. Inevitably, there are those who would be generous in their assessment of informal learning and those who would be strict. But the accustomed rules of the game no longer apply. What are the standards for responsible assessment and attestation to prior learning?

There are also concerns about the validity of PLA-assisted credit in terms of external validity. Irresponsibly accredited PLA can do serious harm to a university's reputation and credentialing authority. The notion of becoming a "degree mill" haunts the university community—and rightly so.

Practical Barriers

Basically, universities are not set up for PLA. Even if professors like the idea of PLA, they do not know how to do it responsibly because it is outside of their training. There are also registry concerns. How will universities record PLA credit on student transcripts? There are financial issues. To do PLA in a credible way costs money: Assessors have to be paid in one way or another. New policies need to be developed (such as the guiding principles of PLA), existing policies revisited, and registry procedures overhauled, along with the training of assessors, student advisors, and students themselves. All of these factors have contributed to notable foot dragging by universities that accept PLA (Bélanger and Mount, 1998; Learning From Experience Trust, 2000; Taylor and Clemans, 2000).

PLA: Adult Student Perspective

Theoretical examinations and opinion papers have dominated the academic literature on PLA. Empirical studies have been mainly confined to surveys of institutional approaches to PLA and the success of PLA-assisted students compared with "conventional" students. The students' point of view—why students undertake PLA, how they view the process, and what they get out of it—has rarely been discussed.

Peruniak and Powell (2004) investigated PLA from a student perspective at Athabasca University (AU). AU introduced portfolio-based PLA in 1997, and then only on a tentative basis. The candidate population was small—198. Nonetheless, an examination of student records revealed that AU students who had received portfolio-based credit were markedly more successful than "normal" AU students in terms of both persistence and course pass rates.

The study was qualitative in design and based on teleconferenced group interviews. The sample was stratified to include program graduates as well as students who had dropped out, students well along in their programs, students who had taken a few AU courses, and students currently enrolled in a portfolio development course, but who had not undergone assessment. The total sample was 32. The relevant background characteristics of the study population were the following:

- The age of students at the time of portfolio assessment clustered closely around 39 years;
- Two-thirds were female;
- About 90 percent were employed in the public sector; and
- Three-quarters of the students were enrolled in applied programs, such as the Bachelor of Administration program.

These characteristics suggest something about PLA applicants. They are in mid-career; they want certification in applied programs of study, wherein prior learning may be more readily accredited; and most are women, which suggests that women need credentials more than men do to advance in their careers. Also, there is a definite bias towards public-sector employment, which implies that the public sector is willing to take the lead toward the acceptance of PLA. Finally, PLA students were not typical of AU program students as a whole, at least in terms of their choice of program and age.

A finding of note is that the five sub-samples were much alike in their background characteristics and motivations for undertaking portfolio-based PLA. The sample design was predicated on identifying differences, but the results showed a basic commonality in terms of motivations, experience, and satisfaction with PLA.

Five themes predominate among portfolio-assessed students. First, these were highly motivated and self-directed mid-career students with a clear idea of their educational goals. They were not aimlessly wandering and hoping to "find themselves." A good number of them received substantial employer support, including paid time off and fee subsidy for study.

Second, and related to the foregoing, these students were particularly successful compared with the university's regular program students. PLA-assessed students completed more courses than regular students did, had higher grades, and had a higher rate of program completion.

Third, their primary motivations were instrumental or "extrinsic": They needed to earn a parchment to advance their careers or even, in one case, to keep a job. Portfolio assessment was a means to reduce their course-taking requirements. A couple of examples of extrinsic motivations might illustrate these characteristics.

> I knew a number of people who went this route, and I knew it was going to be advantageous for me to start here. I'm a psychiatric nurse and want to get my degree. . . . I know that if I don't have a degree, my advancement is severely limited.

> I was actually getting a lot of pressure from work to have a degree. I work for Alberta Learning and, of course, Learning [the government department] is into degrees and so on. . . . My effort was to see if I could get some credit toward it [the degree] as [otherwise] it was going to be a long haul.

Several participants cited prior *employer* recognition of PLA-assisted degrees as important. The following comment illustrates this: "I had an interview for a job last week. . . . If I didn't have the degree, I couldn't have even applied for the job. They checked my educational record and my PLA, and there didn't seem to be any problem."

Several students mentioned the importance of external credibility for PLA even though employers for this sample of students were largely supportive of PLA:

> In our organization [police] there was a big push on for education. We're doing PLA for U.S. colleges down in the States. Then this opportunity came up with AU, and what we found was that your university [AU] was a lot more credible than the ones they were using.

Fourth, apart from the credit-earning potential of PLA, almost all respondents reported unexpected dividends from the process of developing their learning portfolios:

> I think I had never realized what I had done in so much of my life and the accomplishments. So yes, it was for the credits, but it was really nice to learn that you've accomplished so much in your career. And also, it gave me a little boost in my confidence.

> It was a welcome experience to look at my life and where I had been. . . . I was able to take the PLA . . . skills that I gained and actually utilize it very quickly afterwards. I was working with a youth group in the high school, . . . where they were talking about starting to build a portfolio . . . so they would have a portfolio when they went into the workforce. . . .

> And . . . the other thing that I gained was the opportunity to . . . encourage the health care system, sitting in senior position, toward higher learning or experiential learning assessment tools in some of the classifications where we now have bigger requirements with respect to legislation and association membership for the people who are working in health care.

> Putting it together gave all of a sudden a nice neat picture. It helped me really see that I had a definite direction, . . . with all of my experiences pointing in that direction [degree]. It helped me even as I was doing it to show that I was going in the right direction and how to apply everything I had learned toward this career.

Then once it was completed and they had notified me of my credits, they also made recommendations on which courses to take and which ones not to take.

These unanticipated outcomes from PLA were educational, both for the students and for others. Reflection on one's past learning, whether in school or out of school, is a part of lifelong learning. Self-affirmation is another part. The application of the portfolio later for preparing resumes or helping students and the recognition of PLA in participants' workplaces were added bonuses. Finally, PLA assessment for students can help them plan their formal programs of study: "The course [PLA] helped me to understand more about my degree and what I was heading into. It gave me some focus on what was in there and what I was up against going forward."

The fifth theme that arose from the results was that the compilation of a portfolio of prior learning is not a trivial matter. One has to demonstrate learned experience rather than the experience itself in order to be responsibly accredited. Most participants commented on the amount of time required to produce their portfolios. Students who had undergone the process, almost to a person, thought it worthwhile and rewarding. Some in the sub-sample of students currently registered in AU's portfolio development course who had not yet gone through the entire process were not so sure: "I did find the portfolio exercise difficult. It was very time consuming"; "I agree that it has been very time consuming. I have done a number of other courses from AU, and the amount of time I've spent on this course, I could have completed two or three others"; and "I've taken a number of AU courses. . . . The number of hours it's taken to do this course [AU's course on portfolio development] . . . has already superseded several other AU three-credit courses." These quotations underline the gulf between students' initial expectations of the process and the potential benefits—although it should be noted that they earn credit for taking the portfolio course, and the portfolio produced is then submitted for additional credit.

Coming to Terms with PLA

We have outlined the demographic, economic, and political pressures that will affect the university community as well as the community's reluctance to shoulder the responsibility for assessment and attestation of knowledge not taught in a classroom. It seems clear that PLA is not a passing fad. But PLA implies assessment methods that have to accommodate self-directed adult learners who bring informal learning to the academy for recognition. Nonetheless, the sensibilities of Canada's academic community are real, considered, and need to be acknowledged. These primarily relate to the external recognition of PLA-assisted program credentials.

Academics and registrars turn their eyes to other universities for confirmation of the respectability of their programs. Recognition of PLA-assisted degrees in the university community is unlikely to come quickly, particularly when students apply for graduate-level studies or to transfer PLA-based credit elsewhere. However, employer recognition of PLA is important, particularly for students who see a bachelor-level degree as a terminal qualification. In Canada it appears that some employers, to date mostly in the public sector, not only have little problem with the legitimacy of PLA-attested credit, but also encourage the process. Whatever the external agent of recognition is, the credibility of assessment procedures remains at the forefront. Nobody wants PLA to be turned into a "degree mill." Not only must PLA be credible, but it must also appear credible. PLA decisions need to be open, transparent, and readily reviewable by others. The credibility of PLA is, in the first instance, an internal matter for universities. Externally, PLA may be given a "free pass" for now by (primarily) public-sector employers, but this may well change if the validity of PLA-assisted credit comes under question.

Although we do see PLA becoming a permanent fixture in Canada's university system, it will not be a panacea for the parties involved. The evidence to date suggests that PLA can work and work well for a selected group of adult students. However, PLA's efficacy seems to be related to its role as both a selection device and a motivator. By definition, successful PLA petitioners must have had credit-worthy experiential learning. Also, portfolio development is an arduous and time-consuming project. It appeals to adults who are already confident learners who are highly self-directed and educationally motivated. Expanding the use of PLA beyond this group of adult learners will not likely be of any benefit.

Responsibly attested PLA benefits students, employers, and governments—and potentially the university system itself. The trick is not only to do it responsibly, but also to be seen to be doing so.

References

Bélanger, C. and Mount, J. (1998). Prior learning assessment and recognition (PLA) in Canadian universities. *Canadian Journal of Higher Education, 28*(2, 3), 99–120.

Buon, T. (1998). *The use of educational credentials for employee selection.* Retrieved February 3, 2005, from http://www.genbuchat.org.uk.docs.credential.htm

Conference Board of Canada. (1995). *Brain gain: The economic benefits of recognizing learning and learning credentials in Canada.* Ottawa, ON: Author.

Davis, D. J. (1981). Back to the beginnings: Credentialism, productivity, and Adam Smith's division of labour. *Higher Education, 10*(6), 647–661.

Hamilton, R. J. (1994). Semantic and conceptual ambiguities in prior learning assessment. *Journal of the National Institute on the Assessment of Experiential Learning, 1,* 5–12.

Human Resources Development Canada. (2002). *Knowledge matters: Skills and learning for Canadians.* Ottawa, ON: Author.

Industry Canada. (2001). *Achieving excellence: Investing in people, knowledge, and opportunity.* Ottawa, ON: Government of Canada.

Learning From Experience Trust. (2000). *Mapping APEL: Accreditation of prior experiential learning in English high education institutions.* Retrieved December 5, 2004, from http://www.dfes.gov.uk/dfee/heqe/let_final.htm

Peruniak, G. and Powell, R. (2004). *An investigation of students receiving prior learning assessment credit by portfolio at Athabasca University.* Athabasca, AB: Athabasca University.

Sargent, B. (1999). *An examination of the relationship between completion of a prior learning assessment program and subsequent degree program participation, persistence, and attainment.* Sarasota, FL: University of Sarasota.

Taylor, T. and Clemans, A. (2000). Avoiding the hoops: A study of recognition of prior learning processes in Australian faculties of education. *Asia-Pacific Journal of Teacher Education, 28*(3), 263–280.

Thomas, A. M., and Klaiman, R. (1992). The utilization of prior learning assessment in Canada. *Canadian Journal of University Continuing Education, 18*(1), 7–26.

Willingham, W. W. A. (1977). *The CAEL validation report.* Columbia, MD: CAEL.

29

Towards a Canadian Research Culture in Adult Literacy Learning

Maurice Taylor and Adrian Blunt

In today's knowledge age, adult literacy is a complex and multidimensional issue that involves many voices and many perspectives. With the recent attention and call for a concerted national literacy agenda, the role of research in advancing adult literacy in Canada can evoke much discussion (Canadian Education Association, 2004; House of Commons Standing Committee on Human Resources Development and the Status of Persons with Disabilities, 2003; Movement for Canadian Literacy, 2002). The understanding of literacy and its definition for policy and programming have shifted over time as the perceived value of literacy to society has shifted from humanistic and citizenship frames to an economic one. Today literacy is very broadly conceived as the capacities required by persons to function effectively in the social spheres of work, community, culture, and recreation, including reading, writing, numeracy, and the essential skills required for employment, such as computer use, document use, and working with others (Human Resources and Skills Development Canada [HRSDC], 2003). The purpose of this chapter is to provide an account of current Canadian efforts to expand and strengthen adult literacy research capacity and to critically comment on the newly emergent research culture in adult literacy learning. First, we highlight the major domestic factors that currently influence Canadian adult literacy research efforts; second, we review significant and potentially influential research developments in the UK and the US; third, we look at current trends in Canadian literacy research publication; and, finally, we discuss the factors likely to influence the culture of English Canada literacy research in the near future.

Tracing the Major Events and Influences in the Canadian Research Landscape

An understanding of the Canadian adult literacy research culture begins with the questions, Who has funded adult literacy research? and How has this influenced the creation of the current knowledge base? Central in this landscape is a government agency, the National Literacy Secretariat (NLS), HRSDC. Recognized and admired in both the national and the international community for its leadership in literacy work, the NLS has been pivotal in funding adult literacy research in Canada. For over 17 years the NLS has supported research projects that have a direct application to literacy programs, address literacy training for specific parts of the population or economy, and seek ways to help prevent literacy problems and improve adult literacy. Some of the NLS-commissioned large-scale surveys included the Literacy Skills Used in Daily Activities (LSUDA), the International Adult Literacy Survey (IALS), and the Adult Literacy and Life Skills Survey (ALLS). All of these works have been fundamental in creating awareness of the Canadian situation among service providers, the business and labour sectors, provincial governments and territories, researchers, and policy analysts.

As a means of renewal, the NLS conducts regular program reviews through a wide-ranging consultative process. In 1998 this resulted in the development of a five-year framework, "Enhancing Literacy Research in Canada," aimed at building a research capacity and a knowledge base for improving practice and informing public policy. A recent examination of this national research program for the period of 1998 to 2003 revealed that over 400 research projects have been funded, including such areas as program model research, needs assessment, and teaching strategies (R. St. Clair, personal communication, October 22, 2004). Both this program review and a key national consultation with research experts and stakeholders have led to a new research framework launched in 2005 called "Research Partners Projects." This initiative identifies priorities to be supported over the next five years with themes that include exploring accountability and effectiveness in literacy education, developing Aboriginal adult literacy research, developing francophone literacy research, and supporting research in practice.

Another key event occurred in 1999 at the national level with the launch of the program *Valuing Literacy in Canada*, a joint initiative between the Social Sciences Humanities Research Council and the NLS. This program was aimed at funding strategic research in adult literacy issues from a variety of social, cultural, and economic perspectives. It encouraged cooperation between researchers and adult literacy practitioners and stimulated collaboration among researchers from different disciplines. The program also encouraged the training of future researchers in the field of adult literacy. In total, there were 8 partnership development grants, 14 research grants, 8 doctoral supplements, and 2 postdoctoral supplements. The final year of the program saw a Virtual Scholar-in-Residence whose primary task was to review the NLS research track and contribute to a future statement of priorities and a research agenda for the agency (L. LeBrun, personal communication, April 14, 2005).

According to Campbell (2003), among the 13 jurisdictions, Ontario has taken a lead role in establishing and supporting a research culture. For example, in 2000 the Ministry of Training, Colleges, and Universities initiated a strategy to promote research to inform adult literacy practice and policy in Ontario. At the national level there are seven literacy organizations: Movement for Canadian Literacy, La Fédération canadienne pour l'alphabétisation en français, National Indigenous Literacy Association, National Adult Literacy Database, ABC Canada Foundation, Frontier College, and Laubauch Literacy of Canada. These organizations have been collaborating on a results-based national plan with a number of research projects that inform a blueprint for action. For example, ABC Canada Foundation, whose main goal is to raise awareness about literacy in the private sector, has conducted a number of national studies as a means of directing their public awareness campaigns by looking at questions of participation and nonparticipation in literacy and upgrading programs.

Also situated in this research culture are three major initiatives that are focused on literacy across the lifespan, early literacy development, and lifelong learning. In 1999 the Centre for Research on Literacy was created at the University of Alberta. This centre conducts research on literacy across the continuum from emergent to third-age literacy. It also sponsors the Directory of Canadian Adult Literacy Research in English, which is an online database that contains close to 250 Canadian research studies conducted by academics and practitioners over the past 10 years. In 2001 a National Centre for Excellence on early and emergent literacy development was funded through the three major federal granting councils. This Canadian Language and Literacy Research Network has conducted a number of studies that include both children and adults. Funding for the Centre has now been extended for an additional term.

Another recent event was the establishment of the Canadian Council on Learning (CCL), which came about as a tangible result of the federal government's Innovation Strategy, which underlines lifelong learning as a core component. Created through an agreement with HRSDC in 2003–2004, the CCL is a national, independent, and non-profit corporation that is committed to improving learning across the country and across all walks of life by providing a skills and learning architecture. It is organized around five Knowledge Centres located in a specific geographic area. These include Work and Learning, Early Childhood Learning, Adult Learning, Aboriginal Learning, and Health and Learning and Structured (formal) Learning. Through these centres the Council intends to promote and disseminate research, report on progress on learning outcomes, and provide the national infrastructure for exchanging information, analysis, and practices (CCL, 2004). At the time of writing, proposals have been requested for the "State of the Field Review" from each Knowledge Centre, with a focus on elementary, secondary, and post-secondary education, and five cross-cutting themes of gender, culture, French as a minority language, e-learning, and literacy. Of interest to this research landscape is that projects conducted in the theme area of adult literacy may generate generalizations from the empirical evidence, major gaps in knowledge, and future lines of inquiry.

Much of the previous information has chronicled research activities that are usually considered under the rubric of academic. However, practitioners have also been engaged in research. As a result of three national literacy consultations on workplace, research, and technologies hosted by the NLS in 1996 and 1997, practitioners identified a need to recognize, link, and support adult literacy research in practice. Although literacy educators have been engaged in research as the field has evolved, there has been little systematic effort to encourage and support, as Quigley and Norton (2002) called it, "literacy research in practice" (p. 1). They used the term to refer to literacy research conducted by or with people directly engaged in adult literacy teaching and learning. Following a popular participatory model used in other countries, the province of Alberta initiated the Research and Practice in Adult Literacy Network in 2000. The term *network* is used here to refer to organized and coordinated ways in which literacy practitioners are helped and supported to conduct research or inquiry into their own practices. As a result, practitioners from the field are now forming research teams. In one such case, this group of researchers developed two axes of inquiry by focusing on the essential question of how adults with little formal education learn, and how literacy practitioners actually engage in collaborative research (Niks, Allen, Davies, McRae, and Nonesuch, 2003).

Since the inception of research into adult literacy learning, provinces such as Alberta, British Columbia, and Ontario have developed practitioner-driven research initiatives such as the Research Circles Project, Research in Practice Institutes, and graduate courses in adult literacy learning offered through the Festivals of Literacy at the Ontario Institute for Studies in Education, University of Toronto. The journal *Literacies: Researching Practice, Practicing Research* is the main forum through which people can share ideas and experiences about how research and practice connect and how each can inform the other. As Murray (2003) pointed out, a clear message has been given that literacy workers, learners, researchers, tutors, and administrators from all provinces and territories must have a voice in developing literacy research priorities within a pan-Canadian literacy agenda. Although progress has been made towards this goal, some countries have already established an adult literacy research enterprise.

Significant Research Developments in the UK and the US

Two countries that have influenced Canadian literacy research in the past, the United Kingdom and the United States, have developed national development research centres that have significantly increased awareness of adult literacy as a key social and economic factor, as well as of the importance of setting research priorities. An examination of both the National Centre for Research and Development (NCRD) for Adult Literacy and Numeracy in the UK and the National Centre for the Study of Adult Learning and Literacy (NCSALL) in the US suggests that there are a number of common elements between the two organizations. Both initiatives are funded through their respective Departments of Education and were established in response to national reports that highlighted the concerns about the high number of adults with basic literacy needs (NCSALL, 2003; NCRD for Adult Literacy and Numeracy, 2003).

Both centres are sites of expert and experienced consortia of partners and stakeholders. In the UK some of the key partners include the Institute of

Education, University of London; the Literacy Research Centre, Lancaster University; the School of Continuing Education, University of Nottingham; the School of Education, University of Sheffield; and the Basic Skills Agency. The NCSALL consortium involves Harvard Graduate School of Education; World Education, the Centre for Literacy Studies, University of Tennessee; and the lab-site partners of Portland State University and the Graduate School of Education, Rutgers University. What is common in both consortia is the development of an interdisciplinary research team and culture that create a strong evidence base for making decisions. Although purposes and strategic aims differ between the two centres, each has a similar focus on improving practice in the field and informing policy. Each centre also works towards increasing knowledge by examining critical issues that affect adult literacy learning and developing a strong professional identity with providers through communication strategies and expertise networks.

As a means of ensuring that research is both methodologically rigorous and grounded in the needs of learners, practitioners, and employers, the NCRD has adopted a model called the research and developmental cycle. This has resulted in five interconnected programs of research underpinned by key national priorities that include economic development and social inclusion, participation, effective teaching and learning, professional development, and the content and infrastructure of the Skills for Life. Similarly, the NCSALL identified a national plan for research and development through wide consultation and highlighted five interrelated themes: adult learning, recruitment, and persistence; teaching and instruction; learner assessment and evaluation; staff development; and policy structure. It seems in both examples given here that through setting research priorities, the results have had a stronger probability of impacting practice and policy. However, in Canada this argument has been difficult to make. As Campbell (2004) pointed out, in a recent national consultation entitled "Setting Priorities for Literacy Research," some participants clearly expressed the need for identifying specific research themes, whereas others did not.

Recent Research Publication Patterns

The *Directory of Canadian Adult Literacy Research in English* (2005) is an online database that currently lists over 270 reports of studies completed between 1994 and early 2005. Submissions to the *Directory* are publicly invited from known literacy researchers and organizations. Because the *Directory* relies largely on authors' submissions, it likely excludes studies completed by those who do not strongly self-identify as members of the national and provincial literacy research communities. However, the *Directory* is a unique national, English-language research repository that, overall, reflects the breadth of mainstream research activity and the "state of the art" in Anglophone Canada.

Campbell (2003) examined the *Directory's* (2005) first 228 studies completed prior to 2003 and identified 10 broad research themes, each consisting of between 6 and 17 reports. The 10 themes are: access and retention, educators and students, family literacy, health, learning, literacy and the labour market, programs, reading and writing strategies, technology, and workplace education. However, because one of Campbell's criteria for the naming of a research theme was that there be five or more reports on a topic (Campbell, 2003, p. 5), only half (113: 50.4%) of the *Directory's* research reports were categorized within the 10 themes. Since 2003, federal funding provided by the NLS, SSHRC, and HRSDC for best practices and essential skills-focused research will likely have resulted in a sufficient number of reports to expand Campbell's list to include new themes such as evaluation and Aboriginal literacy. Campbell's 10 themes, therefore, are best regarded as a historical, incomplete, and simplified snapshot of mainstream literacy's research landscape for the period 1994 to 2002. It is not a goal of this chapter to present a meta-analysis of the *Directory's* research findings, although one is needed; rather, our intent is to deduce from the *Directory's* listings, contributors, and the original publishers of the research reports some understandings of Canada's current Anglophone research community and culture.

Only 53 (19.2%) of the 276 reports currently listed in the *Directory* (2005) are reports published in academic and practitioner journals. Among the more than 30 journals that have published reports listed in the *Directory* are *Adult Basic Education* (11), *Canadian Social Trends* (4), *Alberta Journal of Educational Research* (3), *International Journal of Lifelong Education*, and *Perspectives on Labour and Income*. If the *Directory* includes the majority of research articles published in journals, it would appear that many journals have published only one Canadian literacy article over the eight-year period from 1994 to 2002. Universities and colleges published the largest number of reports (73: 26.4%). Approximately 60 (21.7%) reports were published as books, chapters in books, or monographs that had been assigned International Standard Book Numbers (ISBNs). Publishers of these reports included provincial literacy organizations and commercial publishers. A further 35 (12.7%) reports were published in-house by community organizations, and 10 were conference proceedings of adult education organizations such as the Canadian Association for the Study of Adult Education and the Adult Education Research Conference. Government departments and agencies published 38 (13.8%) reports, and 13 (4.7%) *Directory* listings had no publisher's information.

When the contribution of sponsoring agencies is considered, the pattern of research production offers another interesting perspective. Of the 270 completed reports listed in the *Directory* (2005), 145 (53.7%) were university sponsored, including the majority of journal articles (37), book chapters, and monographs with an ISBN (51); and 48 were in-house reports without an ISBN. The second largest sponsor of published literacy research was the government, with 46 (17.0%); and community organizations contributed 27 reports (10.4%), 10 of which had an ISBN and 17 did not. Only one community organization-sponsored study resulted in a published journal article. Similarly, provincial organizations sponsored 23 (8.5%) studies that resulted in 13 book chapters with an ISBN, 5 of which were in one anthology. National literacy organizations sponsored 13 studies, 5 of which were published as books or chapters in books with an ISBN; and 8 reports were self-published monographs. Surprisingly, given their engagement in the delivery of programs, colleges sponsored only 14 (5.2%) publications, only 4 of which had an ISBN. "Other" sponsors published 4 (1.5%) reports, the private sector published 3 (1.1%), and non-profit organizations such as anti-poverty groups sponsored no studies that resulted in published reports. Community organizations such as the YWCA and recreation centres, common sites of literacy learning, are no more likely to engage in publishing research than are the non-profit groups such as immigrant women societies and faith-based organizations that are common advocates for literacy education.

The *Directory's* (2005) data on publishers confirm that only a small proportion (19.2%) of Canadian English-language literacy research reports are submitted to the rigorous canons of scholarly peer review and that literacy articles in social science and professional development journals are relatively rare. However, with a further 26.4% of reports being self-published by researchers affiliated with universities and colleges, academe is the dominant site of literacy research publication and print dissemination. Whether or not a text has an ISBN may serve as a valid indicator of a publisher's commitment to the quality and value of a text and to its dissemination through libraries and bookstores. The combined numbers of journal articles and reports assigned ISBNs reveal that only 40% of the *Directory's* current listings meet the basic criteria for the identification of "professional" publications. Although government departments and agencies such as Statistics Canada and HRSDC maintain high research standards, critical studies that challenge traditional thinking and methodologies may be produced less frequently within these agencies than is purely descriptive and normative reporting. Similarly, community agencies and provincial organizations dependent upon government grants may in some cases lack the resources and independence necessary to report research findings as rigorously as academe's social scientists would expect. The *Directory* likely provides a service to the field by making accessible a large number of research reports; however, a *Directory* listing may not be an indicator of a study's rigour, validity, and veracity.

From this limited perspective on the *Directory's* (2005) contents, a picture emerges of the current research scene that confirms an increase over the previous decade in the numbers of adult literacy research projects being undertaken and published. Comparative data are not available, but it appears that the numbers of persons publishing research have increased, with more university-based academic researchers and program-based practitioners working collegially and in teams and community and national organization partners working on externally (government) funded projects. Few authors, most of them likely practitioner–researchers, have contributed more than one publication to the *Directory*. Although many literacy practitioners have completed research projects and theses while earning graduate degrees, remarkably few have contributed to the field's research base through subsequent publications, which suggests that research and writing are seen as academic hurdles to be leaped over rather than essential professional competencies to be acquired.

The large number of research topics beyond those captured in Campbell's (2003) 10 themes indicates that researchers' personal choices and interests determine the problems to be investigated and that practitioner – researchers' interests, in particular, emanate from problems that they encounter in their daily work. Similarly, the interests and priorities of engaged organizations including provincial professional organizations, government agencies, and universities differ depending on their organizational goals and priorities.

Research Culture: Challenges and Prospects

Two dialogical problems persist to shape and define the culture and common spaces occupied by literacy researchers. *Dialogism*, according to Bakhtin (1981), is the occurrence of opposing positions among social actors, positions that are permanently irresolvable; they are foundational positions that are self-affirming and sustain resistance to the positions of others. The first dialogical problem is the difference in priorities between practitioner–researchers in the field and researchers in academe. Typically, practitioners value most highly research that focuses directly on the problems that they encounter in their daily work. They tend to seek concrete solutions to improve practice; that is, strategies to enhance the effectiveness of instruction and the achievement of community program and individual learners' goals. Although academic researchers may espouse similar pragmatic outcomes for their research, as social scientists they must also use abstractions of reality to develop theory, seek conceptual understandings that will allow research findings to be extended beyond micro-level local concerns, and seek understandings and findings to inform policy and program development at the macro-societal level.

The second sphere of dialogism is apparent in discourses on the purposes and valuing of adult literacy education in society. On one hand, literacy is highly valued and resources are provided for *homo economicus*, "an actor whose salient criterion is an economic calculus, and who is educated for productive roles in the commercial world" (Blunt, 2001, p. 103). On the other hand, resources are withheld and literacy education is not provided for *homo literatus*, "an actor who thinks as a person-in-the-community, . . . [with] multiple roles in society, [who values] person-within-the-community relations, and . . . [who acts] to meet valid labour market demands" (p. 103).

The sub-fields of literacy work sustain the proliferation of research topics, which makes it difficult to bring coherence to the body of work completed and an integration of findings at the meta level. Further, it is likely impossible to establish a broad commitment among researchers to a national agenda for research when there is a failure to agree on the national purposes and priorities for adult literacy education. Both dialogisms demonstrate how social practices in literacy work are linked to ideological positions, which in turn are linked to social sites and communities. The metaphor of a mosaic to describe the culture of literacy research is as valid and problematic for the field as it is a national metaphor to describe and construct Canadian national identity and social cohesion.

The NLS and its parent department HRSDC recently entered this fractured field with new programs to promote the identification of a research agenda and to maximize the return on public investments in literacy research. As previously mentioned, *Valuing Literacy in Canada* was introduced to promote multidisciplinary research on literacy, build alliances between academic disciplines and policy makers, assess the state of literacy research, identify new avenues for future work, and promote innovative literacy research. In 2004 a second SSHRC joint initiative project, the Essential Skills program, was introduced to support multidisciplinary research on the application and utility of generic literacy and related skills in the workplace and community.

These programs demonstrate the federal government's commitment to improving the nation's—in particular, the labour force's—functional literacy skills. At the same time, the Canadian Education Association has contributed to strengthening relationships among researchers, promoting new partnerships, and sharing research experience through its Literacy, Research Policy, and Practice project to map the literacy research field (Canadian Education Association, 2004). Collectively, these and similar local initiatives have impacted the culture and practices of the research community in a number of direct and indirect ways. They encourage literacy researchers to seek partners from other disciplines, establish community–campus partnerships, increase their research productivity, examine their own priorities, and engage more directly in both policy- and practice-related discourses.

Through the synergy created by the injection of new research funds and the social, career, and disciplinary forces, the two underlying dialogisms of the Canadian literacy research culture and field are for periods of time, in particular research sites, suspended or diminished, which allows innovative and responsive research projects to emerge. While balancing the twin goals of promoting literacy for economic and social development and simultaneously requiring funded research to be conducted across disciplines and within community partnerships, the federal and, to a lesser extent, provincial governments are stimulating more research on their own agendas. By expanding the numbers and capacities of engaged researchers from both academe and the field of practice, it is likely that more modestly funded projects with high local relevance will also be initiated. Opportunities for researchers to focus more attentively on special, frequently neglected populations may also result, for example, on literacy work with groups such as the differently abled, the incarcerated, and highly transient workers. Challenges facing researchers in the near future include the issues of research rigor, quality, policy relevance, and dissemination. Through expanded multidisciplinary networks and closer working relations between academe and the field of practice, combined with greater engagement in wider discourses, the culture of Canada's literacy research community will become more inclusive and more learner and community responsive.

References

Bakhtin, M. M. (1981). *The dialogical imagination* (C. Emerson and M. Holquist, Trans.). Austin, TX: University of Texas Press.

Blunt, A. (2001). Workplace literacy: The contested terrains of policy and practice. In M. C. Taylor (Ed.), *Adult literacy now* (pp. 89–108). Toronto, ON: Irwin.

Campbell, P. (2003). *From coast to coast: A thematic survey of Canadian adult literacy research.* Retrieved February 20, 2005, from http://www.nald.ca

Campbell, P. (2004). Research review: Setting research priorities. *Literacies, 3,* 42–44.

Canadian Council on Learning. (2004). *Knowledge centres.* Retrieved April 14, 2005, from http://www.ccl-cca.ca

Canadian Education Association. (2004). *The promise and problem of literacy for Canada: An agenda for action.* Retrieved March 15, 2005, from http://www.cea-ace.ca/media/en/Lit_PBrief_Eng.pdf

Directory of Canadian Adult Literacy Research in English. (2005). Retrieved April 2, 2005, from http://www.nald.ca/crd

House of Commons Standing Committee on Human Resources Development and the Status of Persons with Disabilities. (2003). *Raising adult literacy skills: The need for a pan-Canadian response.* Ottawa, ON: Communication Canada.

Human Resources and Skills Development Canada. (2003). *Essential skills research project.* Ottawa, ON: Author.

Movement for Canadian Literacy. (2002). *A National literacy action agenda.* Retrieved February 6, 2005, from http://www.literacy.ca

Murray, F. (2003). The field speaks on Literacy research. *Literacies, 2,* 26–27.

National Centre for Research and Development for Adult Literacy and Numeracy. (2003). *Strategy 2003-2007: Generating knowledge and transforming it into practice.* London, UK: Author.

National Centre for the Study of Adult Learning and Literacy. (2003). *Connecting research and practice.* Cambridge, MA: Author.

Niks, M., Allen, D., Davies, P., McRae, D., and Nonesuch, K. (2003*). Dancing in the dark: How do adults with little formal education learn? How do practitioners do collaborative research?* Nanaimo, BC: Malaspina University College.

Quigley, B. A. and Norton, M. (2002). *It simply makes us better: Learning from literacy research in practice networks in the UK, Australia, and the United States.* Edmonton, AB: RiPal Network.

30

What Does It Mean to Be a "Professional"? The Challenges of Professionalization for Adult Literacy and Basic Education

B. Allan Quigley

The fundamental basis of knowledge is agreement. (Babbie, 1992, p. 17)

Demand is building for the field of adult literacy and basic education to professionalize. There is mounting controversy in the United States, but professionalization issues are emerging in the literacy discourse in the United Kingdom, Australia, and Canada as well. In the US, as Sabatini, Ginsburg, and Russell (2002) explained, "Factors have converged over the past decade to steadily accelerate the drive for professionalization in the literacy field" (p. 203). The converging factors to which Sabatini et al. referred are not unique to American literacy education. Added to funding sponsors' ever-increasing requirements for funding and outcomes accountability in most industrialized nations is a new set of expectations in the US that has evidently been precipitated by the current Republican administration. Now, calls for *evidence-based* instruction, planning, and program outcomes in literacy and adult basic education (ABE) are appearing in the American literacy literature (Comings, Beder, Bingman, Reder, and Smith, 2003). This term and its new accountability expectations are also being seen in some of Canada's policy statements; therefore, in addition to other programmatic accountabilities, we are seeing *practice accountability* being added. Questions of practitioners' qualifications, certification, professional development approaches, and even licensure have all appeared in the adult literacy discourse lately (Smith and Hofer, 2003).

Although Canadian practitioners are not yet fully caught up in this debate, the "drive to professionalize" in the US is providing a roadmap for the anticipated journey ahead. This chapter asks readers to consider the implications of this debate before our field in Canada is asked—perhaps forced—to drive down the same road.

"No Certificate? Sorry. You're Not Qualified to Teach Literacy"

Much is at stake in this debate. Adult literacy and basic education is a field largely comprised of volunteer tutors and part-time teachers—a teaching workforce that is both our greatest strength and possibly our greatest weakness in this context. Seen as "unqualified," these practitioners could be required to become credentialed to practice, as is the case in the schooling system. As of 2002, in fact, 12 American states had decided that literacy teachers would be required to obtain an adult teaching certificate or credential, and another 12 were reported to be requiring either a state elementary or a secondary certificate to be employed in adult literacy (no matter that this means being required to know how to teach children in order to teach adults).

There are major fundamental questions at issue here, including, "What does 'professionalism' mean anyway?" and "Of what should literacy professionalism consist?" Because the current discourse typically begins with a "glass-half-empty," deficit perspective, at no point does one see the possibility that literacy practitioners may be acting professionally now, because few have clarified what professionalism is.

Some are turning to other established professions in search of a "better professional model" for literacy. Some in the US have suggested that adult literacy needs to look to the schooling system. Foster (1990) bluntly claimed, "Literacy programs are a bastard of the educational system" (p. 81). She insisted that until adult literacy implements consistent standards, literacy practitioners will not be acting professionally and will not know how to "improve accountability" (p. 80). Others have argued that the field needs to find its models in the workplace and business professions. Chisman & Associates (1990) contended that standardization is necessary if the field is to build the workforce. Still others believed that literacy should turn to social services, health agencies, and, increasingly, faith-based organizations for models and directions. No matter what the purpose or direction, the logic used seems to tell us there is a formula to be followed; namely, Standardization + Certification + Accountability = Professionalism. Is it really this simple?

Seeing Professionalism from the Other End of the Telescope

In this chapter I suggest that we should not begin with deficit assumptions, but rather with consideration of individual and collective practice, beliefs, skills, and knowledge—the narrow end of the telescope. By focusing on who we are, what we do, and where we have come from, we can begin with practice questions. We can place ownership for the debate with those to be most affected—the practitioners. Second, I suggest that we untangle the language being used.

Informed by the work of Collins (1991) and Dawson (2005), *professionalizing* a field assumes that *external criteria* are introduced into collective practice. But *professionalism* or *acting professionally* involves an attempt to improve practice in ways that are *self-identified*. It is the difference between turning to absolute *external criteria* for direction and seeking to be more professional through personal aspiration, agency, and *self-discipline* (Foucault, 1980). Our field may ultimately *choose* externally developed codes, guidelines, and even regulated requirements; but it is to be hoped that this choice will be made from within the field informed by the culture, strengths, and unique mission of adult literacy—from the "inside out."

However, to advocate this course is to advocate that researchers, practitioners, policy makers, and learners consider more of the things we do *right* in this field more often. It means advocating a stronger collective sense of professional self and professional pride. It means a better fieldwide sense of our many successes. To this end I want to offer a strength-based model that I will call *praxis professionalism*. This proposed model will actually be a familiar one. The analogy I use is to imagine yourself entering a literacy or ABE classroom. If you believe that one should begin, not with "perceived deficits" or "perceived failures," but with learner strengths, then professionalism should also begin with strengths.

Framing a Strengths-Based Approach to Praxis Professionalism

To achieve praxis professionalism, we need to build greater knowledge and pride in who we are and become better at learning from past successes on a far wider scale. Unfortunately, because our past is typically undervalued and undocumented, not only is it difficult to make wide-scale advances in literacy practice, but literacy policies are also often amazingly repetitive of past political efforts (Quigley, 1997). Without a common past, the lessons of local and landmark successes that have changed the destiny of individuals, regions, and entire nations simply are not part of the field's legacy or growth. Even among literacy practitioners, few can name a single major figure in the history of Canadian literacy. Without a common past or known legacy of our accomplishments, little wonder that we are open to being thought of as a "bastard" of the K–12 system.

Nothing could be further from the truth. Adult literacy practice predates Confederation and the established schooling systems in Canada (Quigley, in press). Among Canada's "earliest experiments in adult education" (Ross, 1951, p. 26)—as early as 1859—courses in "reading, spelling, and grammar" (p. 26) were being taught at the YMCA in Kingston, Ontario. Those YMCA courses echoed the design and purposes of the very first adult literacy program in documented history, in Bristol, England. In 1812 William Smith—described as an "unlettered" Methodist church doorman—began an organized adult Sunday school so that adults in the poorer sections of Bristol could learn to read the Scriptures (Verner, 1816/1967). This volunteer-based movement spread throughout the British colonies and, by 1815, had arrived in Philadelphia and New York (p. 15). The historical linkages between English language literacy and religion are consistent from England to New England, from London to Upper Canada. Although the purposes may be different, the passion and commitment seen then can still be found in adult literacy today.

Among the first organized programs in the US was Port Royal, South Carolina. In 1863 the Union navy found freed slaves abandoned on plantations, standing in rags. Free to starve. William Richardson and his Gideonite brethren from the northern states worked to help the freed slaves become literate and self-reliant. Thousands of northern adult literacy teachers joined this remarkable movement in one of America's least known literacy stories. In 1911 the Moonlight Schools of Kentucky became what is called "the official beginning" (Cook, 1977, p. 13) of literacy education in America. Cora Wilson Stewart opened the doors of the local Rowan County school houses, hoping that perhaps 200 adults might come to learn to read and write. Moonlight was the signal for the adults to come down from the hills to the small, white schoolhouses below. In fact, thousands came forward. The Kentucky night school model swept state after state in a matter of a decade (Cook, 1977).

Meanwhile, in Canada, Frontier College was not waiting for students to come to them. From 1899 to today, labourer–teachers have taken literacy education to some of Canada's remotest regions. Likewise, from the 1920s through the 1950s, the Antigonish Movement revolutionized the economy of the Maritime provinces, with cooperatives and credit unions using literacy as one of its tools for economic change (Quigley, in press).

Far from being a "bastard" of the schooling system—or any other system—ours has a proud history based on sacrifice and heroism—attributes still carried forward in Canadian communities today. Is this legacy to be thought of as "unprofessional"?

But Are We Qualified?

The current deficit-discourse typically assumes that literacy practitioners are "unqualified." The starting point seems to be to compare our field with others and find literacy wanting. In fact, research from the US (Smith and Hofer, 2003) has indicated that 40 percent of full-time and 33 percent of part-time instructors have masters' degrees and higher (unfortunately, there are no equivalent Canadian data). Most will argue that more professional education is both desirable and necessary, but it is a fallacy that part-time and volunteer teachers are, by definition, unqualified and therefore acting unprofessionally. In fact, graduates of our literacy programs often make superb teachers with little or no further university training. A pig does not become fatter by merely weighing it; a good teacher does not *necessarily* become more professional by adding credentials.

But beyond degrees, in Canada, England, the US, and Australia, among other nations, practitioners have initiated their own research through research-in-practice. They seem to be sufficiently "qualified" to be contributing original research to the academic literacy knowledge base (Quigley and Norton, 2002). Finally, although few will say that it is sufficient, hundreds of professional development events are conducted in Canada every year. Literacy practitioners come forward knowing that there will be no "career advancement" and no salary bonus due to their efforts because most receive no salary, and rarely is there a "career" in this field. Yet they come forward, and do so for the best of reasons. So what do we mean by *professional?*

What Does *Professionalism* Mean?

The origins of *professional* do not derive from paradigms calling for standardization or certification. In *The Shorter Oxford English Dictionary*, Onions (1970) explained that, as early as 1560, to *profess* meant to "affirm one's faith in or allegiance to (a religion, principle; God, a saint, etc.)" and that in the Middle Ages, "the act or fact of professing" meant "the declaration, promise, or vow made on entering a religious order; . . . the fact of being professed in a religious order" (p. 1593). This earliest definition was about giving and dedication. According to Collins (1991), professionalism should be "unencumbered with a high concern for exclusive self-interests . . . [and] is very much in line with the practice of a vocation" (p. 87). Likewise, Dawson (2005) concluded that "the common idea underpinning [vocation] is the concern for meaningfulness of action as the hallmark of purposeful individual and social existence" (p. 646).

Although practitioners enter the field for many reasons (Smith and Hofer, 2003), most in our field are "givers" who have seen how enhanced reading, writing, and numeracy skills can make a profound, transformative difference. Is this all to be considered "unprofessional conduct"? I argue that we should not wait to become a "recognized profession" by external criteria. With a stronger sense of professional identity and pride in who we are and where we have come from, we need to advocate for professionalism enhancement on the basis of the strengths we have brought to Canadian society.

Towards a Professionalism of Pluralism: What Can We Learn from the Literature?

We may face questions such as, "What does it mean to be a professional?" "Will volunteers 'qualify' for their own work?" "Will part-time practitioners be 'acceptable' for hiring?" "Would standardization across testing, reporting, and curricula actually benefit learners?" "Can certification 'guarantee' professionalism?" and "What will the ongoing sacrifice of thousands of practitioners 'count for' when assessed by a regulatory body?" and it will help to be cognizant of the literature on such topics. During the 1970s and 1980s the mainstream adult education literature—that is, the wider body of adult education literature beyond literacy— was caught up with a number of hotly contested controversies, including, "Should Professional Certification Be Developed for Adult Educators?" (Kreitlow & Associates, 1981, pp. 71–96); "Should Government-Funded Adult Education Programs Meet Established Standards of Performance?" (pp. 97–124); and "Should Adult Education be Competency-Based?" (pp. 125-150). More recently, Sork and Welock (1992) expanded the discourse to include the question of whether adult education should have a common code of ethics. Space does not allow for a full review of these topics, but following is an overview of the professionalism debate.

Learning from the Adult Education Literature

Most of the research literature and discourse written on this topic in adult education through the past two decades has assumed that there are essentially three components of the professionalism construct: (a) knowledge, (b) skills, and (c) values. These three are shown in Figure 1.

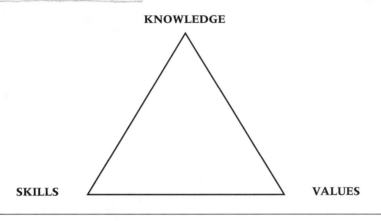

Figure 1. Components of the professionalism construct.

Although they can be nicely balanced in a diagram, they are rarely in balance in the literature. Rather, one of the three typically dominates the others in the three-way triangle.

Professionalism from the Functionalist Viewpoint

When asked, "What makes a professional?" most will turn to the longstanding view of functionalism for an answer because, according to Cervero (1988), it is the most widely known view of professionalism. Also termed the "static approach" (p. 5), in this paradigm professionalism can be assessed with a "checklist" of skills and knowledge. This paradigm comes out of a long history. As early as 1915 Abraham Flexner suggested that to decide "whether an occupation is or is not a profession" (p. 23), we should first look at *how well things function*. His test for a profession was simple. An occupation must (a) involve intellectual operations, (b) derive material from science, (c) involve definite and practical ends, (d) possess an educational communicable technique, (e) tend to self-organization, and (f) be altruistic.

As time went by, this checklist of six items became longer and longer. As Cervero (1988) found, "The major problem with this approach [was] the persistent lack of consensus about the criteria that should be used to define professions" (p. 6). This is essentially what happened in adult literacy during the adult performance level (APL) movement of the 1970s. At that time, teaching learners "measurable competencies" was the bandwagon for literacy curricula and testing in the US, with concurrent influences in Canada. But, because the functionalist approach requires consensus, lists of required competencies for learners, as well as lists of competencies for literacy and basic education teachers, were getting longer. By 1974 Mocker had identified and ranked no fewer than 291 competencies that he considered absolutely essential for ABE teachers.

The theoretical framework behind competencies, and the functionalist approach, proved to be too simplistic (Cervero, 1988). *Functional literacy* was a highly popular term in the 1970s and 1980s, but the APL movement ultimately failed, and reference to functional literacy has largely disappeared. Nevertheless, this paradigm appears to be rising again in the professionalization debate.

But is there an alternative to the functionalist view? A highly debated countermovement occurred in the discourse in the late 1980s and 1990s that was called the *conflict viewpoint* (Cervero, 1988).

Professionalism from the Conflict Viewpoint

Behind any argument for consistencies lies the unspoken issue of power. From the conflict viewpoint that arose in the professionalism literature, self-declared professions were not necessarily accepted as "professions" simply because they claimed that all members had fulfilled their skills and knowledge "checklists." In fact, their practice conduct often proved otherwise. Those in the critical paradigm said that they had often just "secured a monopoly for their services in the market-place" (Cervero, 1988, p. 26) and had built an "aura of mystery about professional work and [promoted] myths about . . . the relative difficulty [of their work]" (p. 26). Illich (1977) put it this way: Simply having "the power to prescribe" (p. 17) has come to mean the power to be a profession. From the conflict perspective, functionalism requires limited alternatives and creativity, few avenues for recourse or appeal for practitioners regulated by an internal elite body, and a limited voice for constructive critique from inside or outside the insular walls of a self-proclaimed profession. The conflict viewpoint rejects the professionalization mystique.

Whether one agrees with the conflict view or not, it can be agreed that understandings of professionalization and professionalism within the functionalist paradigm are a long way from the sixteenth century origins of "to profess."

Building Responsible Practice

The power to deny someone the ability to make a living is no small thing. According to those in the conflict school, the job of today's professional is to return to earlier, truer values. It is to question the social-structural hierarchies of professional organizations and their hegemonies to restore self-responsibility and honour to the original meaning of *profession* (Cervero, 1988; Dawson, 2005).

This view has made its presence felt in the adult education literature, which has largely turned from issues of "acquisition"—acquisition of technical skills, authorized knowledge, and professional jargon. Whereas *altruism* appeared *last* in Flexner's (1915) checklist, as seen earlier, it is considered far more significant for practice today. Now, *responsible planning, ethical decision making,* and *morals in practice* are part of the mainstream discourse. The adult education research has shifted to deeper questions of "why" and away from many of the "how-to-dos."

However, the move towards more responsible practice has brought with it higher expectations for practitioners—on clarity of purpose, on reflectivity in practice, and on increased concern for the ways that practitioners can learn from their own work and share their learning with others. The move has been away from functionalist professionalization to more pluralist professionalism in the adult education mainstream.

For adult literacy and basic education, this points us towards a need to learn from the current literacy debate and past adult education discourse. It points to a need for a fuller discussion of possibilities in literacy professionalism. And, as I will propose, I believe that it means that a new door is opening for the field of adult literacy.

Towards Balance through a Professional Praxis Model

As the discussion grows around us, I believe that we have a chance in adult literacy to draw from the best of both worlds. Canadian literacy practitioners are especially well poised to make well-informed decisions in this discussion. Provincial and territorial governments have not (yet) locked the field into the functionalist approach, although there is pressure from federal government agencies along these lines. We are not (yet) in the position of advocating the conflict viewpoint as a result of external or imposed criteria.

Yet, as we look at the two viewpoints thus far, one does want to ask, "Where is the learner?" Are we not also supposed to be concerned with the needs of the learner, not only the needs of practitioners and the health of our fields? As we look for a way forward, I believe that we should ask, "Can we explore approaches to professionalism that bring the best qualities of the functionalist viewpoint and the conflict viewpoint together around the needs of learners?"

Building on the literature and the perspectives discussed, I propose that literacy practitioners, researchers, and policy makers consider a three-part framework—(a) skills, (b) knowledge, and (c) values—arising from our own field. How can this be implemented? Schön (1983) found that the world's top professionals were not necessarily those with the most prestigious certificates, but that the best-of-the-best had truly mastered ways to learn from all aspects of practice. They could critically reflect on what they had learned through their own experience, from the literature, and from others; and they could internalize both theory and practice into their current work. Schön argued for practitioner critical reflection. No external list of requirements will force striving for excellence; no standardization will force professionalism. The energy for literacy professionalism needs to be placed in enhancing what we do well now. This can be seen as a *praxis approach* and is suggested as a way forward.

Praxis Professionalism as a State of Mind

According to the *International Dictionary of Adult and Continuing Education* (Jarvis, 1990), *praxis* is "a term . . . referring to the congruence between individual reflection and the action that results from it" (p. 272). Action and reflection working in harmony is a way of conduct and growth for professionals. Here, professional development through praxis can mean the enhanced ability to reflect critically and take creative action. The onus is on the individual, not on a regulatory board, to make meaning of events, to build on the past, and to share and learn with others across this field. It is a three-way, more balanced approach to professionalism than what has been seen so far.

As shown in Figure 2, from a praxis viewpoint, professionalism can derive from within and will be successful in the context of practice through collaborative sharing and comparing with others. The praxis approach can be observed, experienced, and, in many ways, measured.

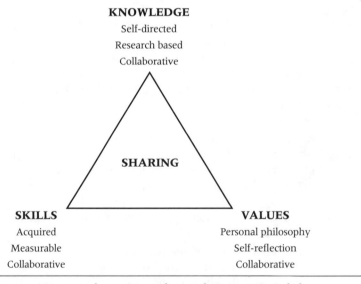

Figure 2. A praxis approach: putting professional components in balance.

Praxis Professionalism: Choosing Our Alternatives

In closing, I will reiterate that the challenge for adult literacy is to enhance skills, enhance knowledge, clarify and challenge values, and build upon all three through shared reflective practice. We can balance the three components of a skills-knowledge-values framework, I believe, if we keep all three as goals in the professionalism debate. Once again, this is familiar territory. Practitioners seek to help learners to see options; they seek to enable learners to gain skills, knowledge, and values clarification; they work to help learners to become more critically reflective. Why not do the same for ourselves, but in ways that are more systematic and fieldwide?

Is praxis professionalism realistic in literacy education? Are there really alternatives like this for us? I believe that there are. As Jonathon Dale (1996), a Quaker who spent much of his life working in the depressed inner cities of England, wrote, "First we must dream. Nothing is harder, . . . [because] dreaming has to break through the constantly reinforced assumption that 'There is no alternative'" (p. 1).

We have alternatives in literacy in Canada. Let's talk about them.

References

Babbie, E. (1992). *The practice of social research* (6th ed.) Belmont, CA: Wadsworth.

Cervero, R. (1988). *Effective continuing education for professionals*. San Francisco: Jossey Bass.

Chisman, F. P. & Associates (1990). *Leadership for literacy*. San Francisco: Jossey-Bass.

Collins, M. (1991). *Adult education as vocation: A critical role for the adult educator*. New York: Routledge.

Comings, J. P. (2003). *Establishing an evidence-based adult education system*. Cambridge, MA: National Center for the Study of Adult Learning and Literacy.

Cook, W. D. (1977). *Adult literacy in the United States*. Newark, DE: International Reading Association.

Dale, J. (1996). *Beyond the spirit of the age*. London: Quaker Home Service.

Dawson, J. (2005). Vocation. In L. English (Ed.), *International encyclopedia of adult education* (pp. 643–646). London: Palgrave Macmillan.

Flexner, A. (1915). Is social work a profession? *School and Society, 1*, 901–911.

Foster, S. E. (1990). Upgrading the skills of literacy professionals: The profession matures. In F. P. Chisman & Associates (Eds.), *Leadership for literacy: The agenda for the 1990s* (pp. 73–94). San Francisco: Jossey-Bass.

Foucault, M. (1980). *Power/knowledge: Selected interviews and other writings, 1972-1977*. New York: Pantheon.

Illich, I. (1977). *Disabling professions*. London: Martin Boyers.

Jarvis, P. (1990). *An international dictionary of adult and continuing education*. New York: Routledge.

Kreitlow, B. & Associates (1981). *Examining controversies in adult education*. San Francisco: Jossey Bass.

Mocker, D. W. (1974). *A report on the identification, classification, and ranking of competencies appropriate for adult basic education in teachers*. Unpublished doctoral dissertation, University of Missouri, Kansas City.

Onions, C. T. (Ed.). (1970). *The shorter Oxford English dictionary* (3rd ed.). Oxford, UK: Clarendon Press.

Quigley, B. A. (1997). *Rethinking adult education: The critical need for practice-based change.* San Francisco: Jossey-Bass.

Quigley, B. A. and Norton, M. (2002). *It simply makes us better: Learning from literacy research in practice networks in the UK, Australia, and the United States.* Edmonton, AB: RiPal Network.

Quigley, B. A. (in press). *Building professional pride in literacy: A dialogical guide for staff development in adult literacy and basic education.* Malabar, FL: Krieger.

Ross, M. G. (1951). *The Y.M.C.A. in Canada.* Toronto, ON: The Ryerson Press.

Sabatini, J., Ginsburg, L., and Russell, M. (2002). Professionalization and certification for teachers in adult basic education. In J. Comings, B. Garner, and C. Smith (Eds), *Annual review of adult learning and literacy* (Vol. 3, pp. 243–247). San Francisco: Jossey-Bass.

Schön, D. A. (1983). *The reflective practitioner: How professionals think in action.* New York: Basic Books.

Smith, C. and Hofer, J. (2003). *The characteristics and concerns of adult basic education teachers* (NCSALL Report #26). Boston: Harvard Graduate School of Education, National Center for the Study of Adult Literacy and Learning.

Sork, T. and Welock, B. A. (1992). Adult and continuing education needs a code of ethics. In M. Galbraith and B. Sisco (Eds.), *Confronting controversies in challenging times: A call for action* (pp. 115–122). San Francisco: Jossey Bass.

Verner, C. (1967). *Pole's history of adult schools.* Washington, DC: Adult Education Associates of the USA. (Original work published 1816)

31
Adult Education Without Borders

Shahrzad Mojab

A ny collection of readings about such a diverse endeavour as adult education is, inevitably, partial, limited, and idiosyncratic. With that in mind, a comprehensive synthesis in this concluding chapter is neither possible nor, I would argue, necessary. In a chapter such as this I can only hope to highlight the key aspects of adult education practice, identify some parallels between its different areas, and point out the major trends and developments that the earlier sections and chapters raise. However, I can also step outside the confines of what is presented and help to identify some broader influences on Canadian adult education, its links with civil society, and its involvement with social movements and social groups. I can also raise some questions about the contexts of adult education, the spaces between them, and the broad practice of adult education in general.

In this chapter I am replicating Chandra Talpade Mohanty's (2003) ingenious title, *Feminism Without Borders,* to recall, as she does, Doctors Without Borders and similar groups who offer alternatives to the strictly bordered world that has evolved in the last two centuries. Also, much like her, I have developed awareness of the ways in which colonialism and imperialism have turned bordered divisions such as nations into prisons for women and other oppressed groups. It is in this political, cultural, and historical context that I would like to think through some of the challenges to adult education as we have practiced it. Although I have no claim to formulate all the challenges and offer answers, I try to historicize adult education in rather unusual ways. We live in a very troubled world: The conditions that sustain life, both human and non-human, are seriously deteriorating; human beings, or rather small sections of them, have created conditions that disrupt the ability of living beings on the planet to reproduce the conditions of their (co)existence. The modern institutions of the market and nation together with institutions such as patriarchy, state, and religion are at work in creating these conditions. The ever-growing rule of the capitalist market—globalization—destroys borders but creates new boundaries that sharply divide the world's haves and have-nots. If this characterization of our world is accurate, the most urgent question for us would be the role of adult education. If we indeed witness a serious turn in the history of the world, how do we envisage adult education?

Adult Education and Knowledge Production in the Era of War and Imperialism

We have witnessed in the last few decades explosions of knowledge in many areas and in many countries. We also know that these quantitative leaps take place under conditions of extreme inequality in the production, dissemination, and utilization of knowledge—issues alluded to in many of the previous chapters. However, my concern here is not about extreme inequalities in the production of knowledge or access to it. I am concerned not with the quantity of knowledge production, but rather its quality. Even here I am concerned only with the relationship between knowledge and power. The claim to the neutrality of academic knowledge has been seriously challenged. Marxists have for a long time emphasized the class nature of consciousness. Feminists have demonstrated the gendered nature of all knowledge. Today, we know that knowledge is also shaped by race, ethnicity, nationality, sexuality, and other social and historical formations.

Based on my experience of teaching in the last two decades, I have reached the conclusion that much of the current critical knowledge is not critical enough to be of use for pedagogical projects interested in offering an alternative to the status quo. To be more specific, there is a considerable amount of knowledge that is critical of globalization, patriarchy, war, poverty, ecocide, and other contemporary problems. And this is the knowledge produced not only by academia, but also by popular culture, human rights groups, and social movements.

Academia also produces useful critiques of the status quo. There is, for instance, a vast literature on neoliberalism and its agenda for ensuring the domination of the world by the market. In the field of education, for example, Henry Giroux (1999, 2004) has shown that American neoliberalism aims at turning the market into the organizing principle of not only the economic system, but also society, culture, and politics. He has shown that neoliberalism violates the rules of the game that were laid down by free-competition or laissez-faire capitalism. Promoting a culture of fear and uncertainty, the state advocates the welfare of the market and ties it to the defence of the nation. National security and the security of markets become one and the same. This leads to increasing militarization of both the state and the market, especially in the United States, where, for example, the number of security guards in public spaces including schools is increasing and more prisons and prison guards are provided (Sudbury, 2005) while prisons themselves go through privatization.

Giroux revealed the ties that bind the political to the economic. He noted that the war against terrorism is used as an excuse for a neoliberal war on liberal democracy and against demands for equality and justice. Much of Giroux's critique of American neoliberalism applies to Australia, Britain, Canada, and New Zealand, to name just a few countries known as liberal democracies. Although this type of critical study is useful for engaging in radical pedagogy, it fails to provide a pedagogy and practice of alternative possibilities.

Much of the current literature of pedagogy is limited by conceptual and theoretical frameworks that do not go beyond the old liberal range of debate. For instance, studies of globalization often tend to ignore capitalism as its engine, its *raison d'être*, and its requirement. Globalization is generally reduced to its cultural or technological dimensions, as if technological development can occur outside or independent of the socioeconomic system. Equally problematic is the rejection of concepts such as *imperialism* as a stage or era in the development of capitalism; it seems that we still live in the age of "free competition," in which the "invisible hand of the market" is thought to smoothly regulate the national economy. The separation of globalization from capitalism often leads to explanations and activism that do not target capitalism as the source of globalization (Mojab, 2004a). This type of knowledge about globalization and resistance against it lead to localist and nationalist defence of capitalism. Nationalism is a product of capitalist development, and it would be impossible to prevent or constrain globalization through nationalist politics. Although some nationalists oppose globalization, many support it in order to enhance the global status of their nation. This is the case because, as Lenin emphasized, capitalism embraces two apparently contradictory tendencies: One is the creation of national borders, and the other is the violation of these borders.

The conceptual and theoretical repertoire of much of the current critical knowledge, from which adult education borrows extensively, is inadequate for understanding a major contradiction of our time: Human beings, equipped with today's knowledge, are able to produce enough food, clothing, and shelter to sustain the population of the planet without destroying the environment and the conditions that reproduce living beings. Why, then, is there more poverty, disease, homelessness, child labour, tens of millions of street kids, and millions of young girls and women trafficked and sold every day? Why have world arms sales reached the level of $1 trillion annually and why are there more wars and genocides in the post-Cold War period? Why is ecocide threatening the planet and Africa being depopulated by AIDS, malaria, and poverty? How can we explain the contradiction between our capacity to live peacefully and prosperously and our inability to do so?

This major contradiction between potential prosperity and actual poverty cannot be explained through the currently fashionable theoretical positions that reduce human relations to questions of *identity, difference,* and *othering.* Our ability to think critically has been seriously limited by the psychologization of social theory. One hundred and ten years ago, Emile Durkheim (1895/1982) warned that "every time a social phenomenon is directly explained by a psychological phenomenon, we may rest assured that the explanation is false" (p. 129). If the reduction of the social to the psychological is problematic, it is in full accord with the politics of liberalism and individualism. Psychologization blames the individual and lets power structures off the hook. Cultural studies have not done better. They have, in fact, discarded many crucial concepts needed for a critical and radical approach to capitalism, globalization, and the struggle against it.

Cultural studies have created a vast body of knowledge that undoubtedly has provided us with a more refined understanding of social relations. However, cultural studies and poststructuralist literature have done what liberal knowledge had failed to achieve. Liberal knowledge and pedagogy have always resented Marxist and feminist theorizations of social relations in terms of exploitation, oppression, alienation, domination, ideology, emancipation, liberation, socialism, and revolution. However, if liberalism had a difficult moment in discrediting or discarding these conceptualizations, poststructuralism does so in the guise of a critical framework that rejects liberalism too. Let me be more specific and share with you a pedagogical moment.

I included David Harvey's (2000) Marxist text *Spaces of Hope* in the reading list of a doctoral-level course on the political economy of adult education in global perspectives and in an independent Critical Adult Education Reading Group in 2000 when the book had just appeared (for a discussion of this point, see my review of the book, Mojab, 2004b). It was awhile ago that I was looking for a text to introduce to my politically eager graduate students to foster a more adequate understanding of the social relations of capital—the understanding of capital not as a thing, but as a regime of social relations; the understanding of capitalism as a social and economic formation and not reduced to "modernity," as it is done in poststructuralism and cultural studies. In my initial perusal of the book, some of its promises captured my attention. First was the historicization of our era and its contextualization within the spread and growth of global capitalism. In the current intellectual environment, many, including students, even those at the graduate level, do not gaze historically. Interconnecting social, political, and economic events, especially on the world scale, is a rare intellectual exercise that will be readily branded as *totalization, grand narrative*, and the like. The history of social movements of the 1960s, from anticolonial uprisings in most of the "developing world," to student movements, to labour struggles, antiwar movements, civil rights, and women's movements in the West, has not anchored in the consciousness of this generation.

Second was the book's critical interrogation of the notion of *alternative*, a populist political-social idiom within the field of adult education. Being "alternative" and "transformative," in and of itself, is considered a political act, even resistance or subversion. What is not clear is what is being subverted. One may ask, Alternative to what, whom, where, and why?

Finally, the book also presented a well-articulated critique of poststructuralist and postmodernist positions, another rarity in the current book-publishing industry. Graduate students are either fascinated with or disillusioned by this body of theorization. Harvey's (2000) contextualization of poststructuralist and postmodernist theorization in capitalist relations of domination and unequal divisions of power has considerably demystified the project of privileging multiplicity, contingency, identity, or positionality as the building blocks of the social universe. Critical adult educators easily identify with some of the spaces of hope for change that Harvey suggested. Indeed, his reference to Raymond Williams's and Antonio Gramsci's writings resonates with revolutionary pedagogy (p. 17). Harvey began the book with a personal pedagogical experience with reading and teaching Marx and raised a question: Marx's Capital "was much sought after and studied in radical circles at a time when it had little direct relationship to daily life. But now, when the text is so pertinent, scarcely anyone cares to consider it. Why?" (p. 8). This is my question too.

It is clear that *Spaces of Hope* (Harvey, 2000) is not a typical adult education text. Nonetheless, there is a rich debate taking place among radical educators (e.g., Allman, 1999, 2000; Apple, 2000; Giroux, 1999; McLaren, 2000; Rikowski, 2001) who have proposed, albeit in variations, Marxist theorizations of learning, training, education, and social change under capitalism. This body of literature, again in varying degrees and intensity, has focused on theorization of labour power, alienation, and consciousness. They, much like Harvey, intended to advance an agenda of social change through education. *Spaces of Hope* was, therefore, not quite a stranger in the theoretical and epistemological imagination of some class participants. However, uncertainty about the possibility of change, together with the confusion in understanding capitalism that graduate students have expressed in reading Harvey, is symptomatic of the current ideological and theoretical struggles within Marxism, Marxist feminism, and adult education. I will refer to only two of these symptoms. One is the interpretation of *capital* in the age of imperialism, euphemistically called *globalization*. The second is the tendency of academic Marxists to flatten out Marx's dialectical analysis of capital and its internal contradictions to an acceptable sociological approach, which, incidentally, dovetails with the ancient philosophical idealism.

Today, the tendency is to reduce the complex world of education/labour/ capital to language games, discursive constructions, culture, identity, and modernity. If in the past economic determinists were quite good in reducing the world to economic categories that shared little with Marx's "capital as social relations," contemporary poststructuralist theorists and advocates of linguistic, cultural, and discursive determinism say farewell to capitalism, exploitation, and alienation. Paula Allman's (1999, 2000) theorizing is distinguished from both types of reductionism by her dialectical approach to the exercise of power by capitalism and the possibility of challenging it through conscious intervention.

The fear of *essentialism* and its contagious power has pushed some feminists to positions that liberal patriarchs could only envy. Now that extensive violence is perpetrated on women throughout the world and antifeminism is rampant in North America, it is inappropriate in poststructuralist circles to use concepts such as *woman, patriarchy,* or *oppression*. This retreat from feminist politics is so debilitating that Spivak (1997), who has played a prominent role in this intellectual game, has had to retract and accept a form of essentialism that she calls *strategic essentialism*.

Some of the critical concepts used by social movements (*capitalism, exploitation, oppression, alienation, domination, imperialism, ideology, emancipation, liberation, socialism,* and *revolution*) are replaced by the less harmful concepts of *modernity, globalization, margin/centre, space, difference, discourse, resistance,* and *negotiation*. These replacements aim at reducing the scope and depth of class, gender, and ideological and political struggles against capitalism and patriarchy. The concept of negotiation in cultural studies gives the illusion of equal footing in the highly unequal divisions of power in our world.

Adult Education Without Borders: Pedagogy and Practice of Crossing and Hope

Since the publication of the United Nations Human Settlements Programme (UN-Habit) in 2003, entitled *The Challenge of the Slums*; Mike Davis's (2004) subsequent article, "Planet of Slums: Urban Involution and the Informal Proletariat"; and Donovan Plumb's (2005) more recent piece, *The Learning City in the Planet of Slums*, there has been renewed interest in exposing the relations of capitalism, urbanization, unemployment, poverty, violence, war, and notions such as *knowledge economy, lifelong learning, learning cities,* or *learning society*. Davis suggested the notion of *surplus humanity* to argue the decline of formal economy and formal proletariat and the rise of informal economy and informal proletariat:

> Overall, according to Slums, informal workers are about two-fifths of the economically active population of the developing world. According to researchers at the Inter-American Development Bank, the informal economy currently employees 57 percent of the Latin American workforce and supplies one of five new 'jobs.' Other sources claim that more than half of urban Indonesians and 65 percent of residents of Dhaka subsist in the informal sector. . . . Informal economic activity accounts for 33 to 40 percent of urban employment in Asia, 60 to 75 percent in Central America and 60 percent in Africa. (pp. 23–25)

Thus, it is in the context of surplus humanity that we must consider the dominant notions of the field of adult education such as learning, training, and skilling and try to understand and explain the ways that they have been deployed within capitalist relations of production. I have written elsewhere that (Mojab, in press):

> the current theorization of lifelong learning, underpinned by critics of human capital theory, point out that if the life experiences and learning of marginalized workers were recognized, they could attain equality through a better paid job. This critique leaves the organization's ownership of workers' learning unchallenged. However, if we understand relations of work in the context of capitalism, the worker cannot be confused with the idea of capital. To understand the relationship between the worker and capital, we must recognize that labour power is a commodity in the capitalist mode of production. As a commodity, labour power is subject to the law of supply and demand, and workers are in direct competition

with one another to sell their labour. In this configuration, knowledge and skill acquisition can become part of the competition. The more the concept of 'lifelong learning' becomes synonymous with market requirements, the more it becomes commodified, and alienated from the learner.

Much of what I have said may not be new. However, who can reasonably argue that we are not experiencing a systematic and speedy deterioration of the quality of life and the inability of adult education to respond to it? Where do we, adult educators, stand? In my assessment, education in general and adult education in particular have inadvertently and sometimes faithfully served the building of this militarized empire of the state and market. This empire thrives only if we follow its dictates: to acquire skills, to get jobs, to have income, to consume, and to live and die as consumers/clients. In an always changing and unpredictable market, we must get lifelong education (e-learning, e-governance, or e-commerce). Adults can no longer choose a career or a profession that they prefer to sustain throughout their life. Only two or three decades ago, young people could dream of becoming teachers, nurses, carpenters, doctors, hairdressers, or pilots. These dreams cannot be realized in the anarchy of the market, in which "all that is solid melts into air" (Marx's words as title of a book by Berman, 1982). Stability, to the extent that it existed, has given way to almost absolute instability and unpredictability. *Lifelong learning* is the educational response to the new market order. I have no doubt that the theorization of lifelong learning is a response to the increasing melting of the solidity of capitalism and its tendency to melt into air. My objections aim at being self-critical and locating our work in the social and historical contexts in which we live. If we are indeed moving fast towards a human and ecological disaster, what kind of education do we provide so that we do not contribute to its mission, but reverse its march, when possible? The main obstacle to resistance is the mission of formal education under conditions of capitalism. People usually want to acquire skills to make a living. The current dynamics of deskilling and reskilling are usually imposed by the anarchy of production. In precapitalist societies, jobs or professions were usually hereditary, and skilling was more often informal. The deadening stability of precapitalism is replaced by the destructive instability of the market. Under capitalism, formal education has itself turned into a commodity. Increasingly, people pay to acquire a skill. How can we then turn education, especially adult education, away from the dictates of the market? How can we treat our students or trainees as citizens rather than consumers or clients?

It is rather clear to me that this is not an either-or situation. We cannot expect citizens to get an education that does not help them to earn their livelihood. We can, however, provide education for jobs and at the same time provide skills to resist the trend of destruction. We can learn from social movements, in which adult education has roots. Let me make my point clearer by going back in time to 500 years ago, to Thomas More in England. More lived at a delicate period in history—during the decline of feudalism and the rise of capitalism. He saw the rapid destruction of the peasantry and the rise of a new regime of mercantile capitalism. In this evolving social and economic order, he saw

> a conspiracy of the rich to advance their own interests under the pretext of orga-
> nizing society. They think up all sorts of tricks and dodges, first for keeping their
> ill-gotten gains, and then for exploiting the poor by buying their labour as cheaply
> as possible. Once the rich have decided that these tricks and dodges shall be offi-
> cially recognized by society—which includes the poor as well as the rich—they
> acquire the force of law. Thus an unscrupulous minority is led by its insatiable
> greed to monopolize what would have been enough to supply the needs of the
> whole population. (as cited in Harvey, 2000, p. 279)

More not only criticized the oppressions of British society, but also proposed alternatives. In his *Utopia*, he wrote:

> With the simultaneous abolition of money and the passion for money, how many
> other problems have been solved, how many crimes eradicated! For obviously
> the end of money means the end of all those types of criminal behaviour. . . .
> And the moment money goes, you can say good-bye to fear, tension, anxiety,
> overwork and sleepless nights. Why, even poverty itself, the one problem that
> has always seemed to need money for its solution, would promptly disappear if
> money ceased to exist. (p. 279)

More condemned poverty and cruel laws against the poor. He was among the first to describe a just social system of the future, though he had no idea about how to achieve such a system. We may have failed in our academic endeavour, but it is clear that citizens have not given up their resistance to the status quo. The young and old adults who resist global-ization, militarism, and war have taught the market and the state a good lesson. However, I do not expect the market/state bloc of power to listen to protest movements, much less to respond positively. Adult educators, though, should be able to listen, learn, and respond constructively.

I think the challenge for our field is to catch up with critical thinkers of the past and present, some of whom I have named and quoted so far, and with young and old adults marching and chanting for peace and justice in the cities around the world. For two decades the state and the media have promoted the slogan "All Power to the Market!" It may not be an accident of history that during these decades social theory has replaced the concept of *dominance* with *difference* and the very idea of hierarchical and conflic-tual organization of power with notions of margin and centre, in which the two can more easily transform into each other. My own assessment of the literature of the last two decades is one of despair, disillusionment, and abandonment of the idea of education as a project of liberation.

I, like David Harvey (2000), believe that "in this moment in our history we have something of great import to accomplish by exercising an optimism of the intellect in order to open up ways of thinking that have for too long remained foreclosed" (p. 17). Paula Allman (2000) suggested that we engage, intellectually and politically, in a dialectical reading of Freire. She wrote:

> Freire stresses that both humanization and dehumanization are real possibilities, but only the former is the vocation of the human species. To exist humanly, or to engage in the process of humanization, we need not wait for a revolution. Even in the most limiting situations we can begin to perceive those limits, our reality, critically and engage in the struggle to transform our societies. (pp. 92–93)

To be thoroughly, humanly "with the world" means that people would have developed a critical perception and would have taken collectively their environmental, social, political, and economic destiny into their own hands. To begin that struggle is to begin with the world.

The claim that borders and nation-states are eroding fast is, I have tried to argue, rather mythical. Although under capitalism everything solid, including national borders, may collapse, new solidities including new borders emerge. Under conditions of fragmentation of human beings by wide gulfs such as class, gender, race, and religion, new dividing lines continue to emerge. Indeed, the rather old borders of nations and nation-states continue to solidify themselves. Even when borders indeed collapse as in the European Union, they regroup as "fortress Europe." However, if it is not easy to evade the boundaries of power in the realm of economy and politics, we should be able to erode old borders in the domain of intellect. The vision of *adult education without borders* challenges ideas such lifelong learning. I see in a borderless adult education the possibility of crossing the network of boundaries that liberal theory has set up since the eighteenth century. Our field continues to work within these bounded intellectuals' homes long after the very idea of liberal democracy and liberal economics has suffered serious setbacks under the offensive of monopoly capitalism and its unceasing globalizing roller coaster.

It is within these broader contexts that we continue to struggle—in Canada at least—for an adult education without borders. In the concluding paragraph of *Learning for Life*, Michael Welton (1998) challenged Canadian adult educators to respond to the question, "How can civil society be secured, sustained and invigorated in our time?" (p. 372). Clearly, the question is still as pertinent as ever, but, thanks in part to the authors of these readings, our answers are that much richer.

References

Allman, P. (1999). *Revolutionary social transformation: Democratic hopes, political possibilities and critical education*. Westport, CT: Bergin & Garvey.

Allman, P. (2000). *Critical education against global capitalism: Karl Marx and revolutionary critical education*. London: Bergin & Garvey.

Apple, M. (2000). *Official knowledge: Democratic knowledge in a conservative age*. New York: Routledge.

Berman, M. (1982). *All that is solid melts into air: The experience of modernity*. London: Verso.

Davis, M. (2004). Planet of slums: Urban involution and the informal proletariat." *New Left Review, 26*, 5–34.

Durkheim, E. (1982). *The rules of sociological method* (W. D. Halls, Trans.). New York: The Free Press. (Original work published 1895)

Giroux, H. (1999)."ethinking cultural politics and radical pedagogy in the work of Antonio Gramsci. *Educational Theory, 49*(1), 1–19.

Giroux, H. (2004). *The terror of neoliberalism: Authoritarianism and the eclipse of democracy.* Boulder, CO: Paradigm Press.

Harvey, D. (2000). *Spaces of hope.* Berkeley, CA: University of California Press.

McLaren, P. (2000). *Che Guevara, Paulo Freire, and the pedagogy of revolution.* Boston: Rowman and Littlefield.

Mohanty, C. T. (2003). Feminism without borders: Decolonizing theory, practising solidarity. Durham, NC: Duke University Press.

Mojab, S. (2004a). From the "Wall of Shame" to September 11: Wither adult education? In P. Kell, M. Singh and S. Shore (Eds.), *Adult education at 21ˢᵗ century* (pp. 3–19). New York: Peter Lang.

Mojab, S. (2004b). *Spaces of hope* [Review of the book *Spaces of hope*]. *Globalization, Societies, and Education, 2*(2), 302–306.

Mojab, S. (in press). Gender, nation, and diaspora: Kurdish women in feminist transnational struggles. In B. Francis and C. Leathwood (Eds.), *Gender and lifelong learning: Critical feminist engagements.* London: Routledge.

Plumb, D. (2005). The learning city in a planet of slums. *2005 National Conference On-Line Proceedings* [24th annual conference, Canadian Association for the Study of Adult Education]. London, ON: University of Western Ontario.

Rikowski, G. (2001). *The battle in Seattle: Its significance for education.* London: Tufnell Press.

Spivak, G. (1997). In a word [Interview with Ellen Rooney]. In L. Nicholson (Ed.), *The second wave: A reader in feminist theory* (pp. 356–378). New York: Routledge.

Sudbury, J. (2005). *Global lockdown; Gender, race, and the rise of the prison industrial complex.* New York: Routledge.

United Nations Human Settlements Programme. (2003). *The challenge of slums: Global report on human settlements.* London: Earthscan.

Welton, M. (1998). Educating for a deliberative democracy. In S. M. Scott, B. Spencer, and A. M. Thomas (Eds.), *Learning for life: Canadian readings in adult education* (pp. 365–372). Toronto, ON: Thompson Educational.

Name Index

A

Abdi, A.A., 203
Abrami, P., 314
Agger, B., 122
Ahmed, F., 245
Alderson, L., 286
Allan, B ., 266
Allen, D., 329
Allman, P., 101, 133, 136–137, 236, 271, 279, 351, 354
Allouche-Benayoun, J., 295
Alvesson, M., 87
Anderson, B., 50
Apple, M., 351
Archer, W., 302
Arnold, M, 270, 276–279
Aronowitz, S., 131
Asun, J., 234
Azoulay, K., 54

B

Babbie, E., 336
Bagaoui, R., 294
Bagnall, R., 298–299, 303
Baker, C., 159
Baker, D., 220
Bakhtin, M., 234, 333
Ball, S., 175
Barlow, M., 250
Barnow, B.S., 164
Barr, J., 299, 300
Basran, G., 200, 201
Bastow, S., 173, 175
Bateson, G., 145
Battiste, M., 106, 112
Bauman, Z., 49, 106, 109, 114
Becker, G.S., 165–167
Beckett, D., 188, 192
Bélanger, C., 316, 320
Bélanger, P., 182
Bellah, R., 103
Bellamy Foster, J., 250
Bengough, J., 275
Benigeri, M., 221
Berk, R., 312
Berman, M., 353
Bernard, R., 309
Bernath, U., 311
Billett, S., 191, 192
Blaser, M., 239
Bloch, E., 125

Blunt, A., 22, 326, 333
Borokhovski, E., 314
Boshier, R.W., 204, 264, 265
Bottomore, T., 124
Bouchard, P., 19, 164
Bourdieu, P., 167
Boyd, R., 154
Boyer, L., 234
Bratton, J., 189
Breen, M.J., 221
Brigham, S., 18, 81, 287
Briton, D., 102, 106, 108, 113, 150
Britzman, D., 192
Brodie, J., 178, 180
Brookfield, S., 107, 108, 111, 113–114, 128–129, 144
Brown, L., 250
Buon, T., 317
Burbules, N., 312
Burke, 215
Burstow, B., 58, 66
Burton, W., 18, 36
Butler, J., 273
Butterwick, S., 21, 58, 62, 107, 141, 191, 266, 281, 286

C

Cameron, J., 73
Campbell, P., 222, 225, 327, 330–331, 333
Carmona, E., 256
Carriere, E., 107, 109
Carroll, W.K., 180
Cavanagh, C., 280
Cervero, R., 341–342, 343
Chapman, V., 106–107, 109, 111, 114–115
Chisman, F., 337
Chovanec, D., 20, 157, 218, 236
Church, K., 191
Clark, M., 106–107
Clarke, T., 250, 251, 253
Clemans, A., 320
Clement, W., 173, 177
Clover, D., 20, 58, 63–64, 141, 231, 236–237, 250, 253–258, 282, 287
Coady, M., 25–27, 34, 58, 69, 72, 74, 141, 236, 276–278, 285
Cohen, J.L., 233
Cohen, M.G., 190
Cole, P., 250
Collins, M., 19, 118–120, 122–123, 133, 135, 136, 147, 337, 340

Collins, P., 61–62
Coloma-Moya, N., 191
Comings, J., 336
Conrad, D., 21, 307, 310–313
Conway, A., 126
Cook, W., 339
Cooke, M., 66, 80
Corbett, E., 27, 58, 119, 141, 283, 284
Couton, P., 200
Covell, K., 71
Coyne, A., 178, 180
Cruikshank, J., 296
Cunningham, P., 204, 206, 247

D

Dale, J., 345
Dampier, P., 141, 284
Dave, R.H., 174
Davies, P., 329
Davin, N., 43
Davis, B., 193
Davis, D., 317
Davis, M., 352
Dawson, J., 21, 281, 337, 340, 343
Dei, G.J.S., 203, 204, 205
Delaney, I., 277
Derwing, T., 73, 200
Desjardins, R., 183
Dewey, J., 71, 94, 97, 148
De Zoysa, R., 175
Diani, M, 231, 233
Dickason, O., 36
Dirkx, J. M., 154, 161
DiStefano, C., 113
Doray, P., 294
Douglas, I., 250
Draper, J., 39, 47
Dreyfus, H., 106, 109
Duddy, J., 252
Durkheim, E., 349

E

Eagleton, T., 123
Edwards, P, 93
Edwards, R, 304
Egan, J., 21, 260, 265–266
Eisner, E., 282, 288
Elias, J., 93, 95–97
Elliott, J., 203
Ellsworth, E., 101
Engeström, Y., 147–148
English, L., 14, 19, 63, 105–109, 111–112, 236, 330
Epp, R., 304
Eyerman, R., 232–234

F

Fanon, F., 119
Faris, R., 232
Farrell, L., 191
Favreau, L., 165, 170
Feit, H., 239
Fenwick, T., 20, 59, 146, 150, 187, 194
Field, J., 175, 299–300
Finger, M., 234
Fitzpatrick, A., 25, 27, 72
Flannery, D., 61, 64
Flavell, A., 21, 260
Fleras, A., 203
Flexner, A., 341, 343
Foley, G., 146, 232, 234–235, 247, 299, 301, 304
Fontan, J.M., 191
Fordjor, P., 83
Foss, K., 20, 218
Foster, S., 250, 337
Foucault, M., 102, 109–110, 123–124, 149–150, 204, 303, 337
Fox, M., 252
Freeman, R., 167
Freire, P., 101, 111, 113, 119, 121, 124, 129, 133, 154, 206, 220–221, 233, 239, 244, 247, 266, 270–271, 278–279, 354–355
Freud, A., 100, 144–146

G

Gannage, C., 202
Garcia, R., 144
Garner, N., 270
Garrick, J., 195
Garrison, D., 307, 311
Gereluk, W., 215
Geronimo, B., 215
Ghosh, R., 203
Giddens, A., 131, 175–176, 178, 180
Gill, R., 283
Gill, S., 177
Gillen, M., 108
Gillis, D.E., 220
Gilroy, P., 49–50, 57
Ginsburg, L., 336
Giroux, H., 128–129, 131–133, 136, 348, 351
Glesne, C., 87–88
Gorman, R., 63, 194
Goulart, M., 234
Goulding, A., 82
Gouthro, P., 18, 58–59, 64, 81, 107, 114, 141, 267
Grace, A., 19, 107, 128–129, 135–138, 141, 150, 230, 267, 286
Gramsci, A., 113, 124, 235, 351

Grande, S., 240
Grandinetti, L., 256
Grant, W., 25
Graveline, F., 84
Greenberg, D., 219, 221
Greene, M., 282
Greer, D.S., 219
Groen, J., 287
Gruber, H., 143
Gustavsson, B., 173

H

Habermas, J., 121, 131–132, 150, 233, 240
Haddad, S., 280
Hager, P., 188, 192
Haig-Brown, C., 39
Hall, B., 20, 49–50, 54, 141, 230–231, 236,
    240, 247, 253, 256
Hall, P.A., 178
Hamilton, R., 212–213, 318
Hardy, N., 141
Harris, C., 254, 283, 285
Harvey, D., 350–351, 354
Haughey, D., 21, 298, 301–302, 304, 314
Hawthorn, H., 44
Hayes, E., 58, 60–61, 64–65
Hegel, G., 121
Heidegger, M., 122–123
Helms Mills, J., 189
Hemphill, D., 105–106
Henderson, L., 82
Heng, C., 280
Henry, F., 200, 204, 205
Henson, G., 24–25, 32–34, 285
Herdman, E., 223
Herman, L., 78
Hernández, A., 279
Hessing, M., 251
Hill, R., 135–137, 230, 267
Hirst, P., 29
Hofer, J., 336, 339, 340
Hohn, M.D., 221
Holford, J., 232
Holst, J., 235, 240
hooks, B., 55, 271
Howe, B., 71
Howlett, M., 251
Hrimech, M., 21, 292
Hughes, A., 71
Hurl, C., 118
Hwang, S.W., 234

I

Illeris, K., 143–147, 149–151
Illich, I., 342
Inchauspé, P., 295

J

Jackson, N., 190
James, P., 83
Jamieson, K., 73
Jamison, A., 232–234
Jarvis, P., 144, 344
Jenkins, R., 72
Johnson, C., 137
Johnson-Bailey, J., 90
Johnson-Riordan, L, 306
Johnston, R., 301–302, 304
Jones, D., 282
Joshee, R., 73
Jung, C., 153, 158, 159

K

Kamat, S., 240
Kanpol, B., 71
Kant, I., 93–94, 102
Kapoor, D., 20, 239, 245
Kee, Y., 90
Keefer, T., 126
Keegan, D., 307–308
Keen, S., 271
Kelly, J., 18, 44, 49–51, 55
Keough, N., 256
Kerans, M., 231
Kerka, S., 223
Khan, S., 106, 112, 126
Kidd, J., 58, 119, 141, 281
Kincheloe, J., 145, 194–195
Kindig, D.A., 220
Klaiman, R., 319
Klein, N., 126
Knight, G., 92–95
Knowles, M., 121, 145, 199
Kohlberg, L., 71
Kohn, A., 71
Kolb, D., 144–145
Kotoh, A., 90
Krahn, H., 200–202, 205
Kreitlow, B., 340
Kunz, J.L., 180
Kwamefio, A., 90

L

Labonte, R., 223, 225
Lander, D., 21, 112, 270
Lange, E., 19, 92, 156–157
Lankshear, C., 130–131
Lather, P., 223
Lee, M.Y., 90
Lee, S., 234
Lee, Y.J., 234
Lengrand, P, 174
Leonard, W., 266
Leslie, J., 39–44

Lévesque, B., 165, 170
Lewis, A., 126
Lewis, J., 137
Li, P., 200–202, 204
Lindeman, E., 307, 312, 314
Lisac, M., 304
Livingstone, D.W., 187, 190
Lorde, A., 282
Lotz, J., 232, 236
Low, C., 266
Lucas, C., 93–94
Lyon, D., 131–132
Lyotard, J., 109

M

MacDougall, B., 137, 261
MacIsaac, A., 220
MacKinnon, D., 84
MacLean, H., 48
Madsen, R., 103
Maguire, R., 39–44
Manathunga, C., 84
Manicom, L., 235
Marchand, R., 266
Marginson, S., 174
Marker, M., 107
Marshall, T., 68
Martin, D., 215, 231
Martin, I., 175, 299
Martin, J., 173, 175
Martin, P., 87–88, 173
Martinez, A., 63
Marx, K., 119, 121, 129, 144, 146,
    235–236, 351, 353
Mathieu, S., 52
Mattis, 200
Mayo, P., 106, 111, 239
McBride, S., 177, 178
McCutcheon, S., 250
McGauley, L., 282
McIlroy, 49, 215
McIlroy, J., 49, 215
McIntyre, J., 195
McKay, S., 73, 265
McKeen, W., 177
McLaren, 71, 131, 133, 134, 204, 351
McLaren, P., 71, 131, 133–134, 204, 351
McLaughlin, D., 71
McLean, S., 303
McRae, D., 329
McRae, G., 239
Meadows, D., 252
Melucci, A., 233
Menzies, H., 156
Merriam, S., 89, 93, 95–97
Mezirow, J., 132, 144–145, 147, 154,
    156–158

Miles, A., 141, 147
Millard, E., 45
Miller, J., 43
Miller, N., 304
Mirchandani, K., 191
Mizzi, R., 266
Mocker, D., 342
Mohanty, C., 347
Mojab, S., 22, 63, 113, 141, 150, 194, 200,
    202, 347, 349–350, 352
Moore, M., 126, 266
Morrison, J.H., 232
Mount, J., 316, 320
Muhamad, M., 90
Mulder, 200
Munro, M., 73
Murphy, K.M., 166
Murray, F., 329
Murray, M., 225
Myers, J. G., 154

N

Nah, Y., 84, 89
Neal, R., 276–278
Neatby, H., 97
Nesbit, T., 13, 235
Newman, M., 215
Newman, O., 175
Ng, R., 191, 202
Nielsen-Bohlman, L., 220, 221
Niks, M., 329
Nonesuch, K., 329
Norton, M., 222, 225, 329, 339
Ntseane, G., 90
Nurss, J., 220
Nutbeam, D., 222, 223

O

Olssen, M., 130–131
Onions, C., 340
Osborne, K., 71
Owusu, E., 90

P

Panzer, A.M., 220
Pariat, M., 295
Parker, R., 220
Pateman, C., 75
Paterson, R., 93, 96
Percival, A., 302
Perrin, B., 219, 220, 221
Peruniak, G., 21, 316, 321
Peters, M., 130–131
Piaget, J., 143–145
Piercy, M., 230
Pleasant, A., 219

Plumb, D., 106–107, 109, 111, 113, 150, 298, 300, 302, 352
Pluye, P., 221
Point, G., 18, 36
Poonwassie, D., 38
Porter, A., 177
Powell, R., 21, 316, 321
Prentice, S., 59–60, 65
Prichard, C., 112
Pyrch, T., 189

Q

Quigley, B. Allan, 22, 220, 329, 336, 338, 339

R

Rabinow, P., 106, 109
Raphael, D., 223
Rawlings, T., 191
Ray, A., 36–38
Razack, S., 114, 271, 278
Rebick, J., 58, 62
Reed, M., 270, 276–279
Rees, T., 200
Reich, R., 174, 184
Reinke, L., 83
Reitz, J., 200, 202, 203, 205
Ricard, D., 294
Riecken, T., 285
Rifkin, J., 252
Rikowski, G., 351
Rootman, I., 218, 222
Ross, M., 338
Roter, D.L., 220
Roth, W.-M., 234
Rowe, J.S., 252
Rubenson, K., 107, 113–114, 173–175, 182–183
Rubin, E., 311
Rudd, R.E., 218, 219, 220, 222
Russell, M., 39, 336

S

Sabariego, M., 71
Sabatini, J., 336
Sanders, J., 283
Sandilands, C., 253
Sanger, C., 270, 272–274, 279
Sangha, J., 191
Sargent, B., 318
Sather, K., 273
Saul, J., 103
Sawchuk, P., 19, 140, 146, 187, 189–190, 193
Schlosser, E., 253
Schön, D., 144–145, 343–344
Schott, T., 83

Schugurensky, D., 18, 68
Schultz, T.W., 166, 167
Scott, J., 49
Scott, S., 13, 19, 43, 50, 107, 120, 123, 141, 153, 157, 160
Scown, A., 82–83
Sears, A., 71
Sedgewick, E.K., 264
Seidman, S., 264
Selman, G., 118–120, 141, 284
Selman, J., 266, 281, 286
Selman, M., 118–120
Sen, A., 169, 183
Shah, S., 88
Shale, D., 308
Sheared, V., 135
Shohet, l., 220, 221
Shor, I., 101
Shorris, E., 287
Shragge, E., 191
Sim, S., 107–108
Simpson, D., 104
Simpson, J., 94
Singleton, K., 219
Sissel, P., 135
Sköldberg, K., 87
Smith, C., 164, 336, 339, 340
Smith, D., 59, 61, 231
Smith, L., 240
Smith, S., 306
Smith-Rosenberg, C., 270, 273
Snow, D.A., 230, 232
Somerville, M., 191
Sork, T., 341
Sousa Santos, B., 77
Spacey, R., 82
Sparks, B., 86–87
Spencer, B., 13, 20, 21, 107, 120, 141, 147, 208–209, 216, 231, 307–308, 310
Spivak, G., 114, 352
Stalker, J., 59–60, 65, 282
Stanage, S., 135
Steele, T., 49
Steer, S., 25
Stein, M., 158
Steinberg, S., 145
Stonebanks, R., 26
Strong-Boag, V., 70
Sudbury, J., 348
Sullivan, W., 103
Sumara, D., 193
Sumner, J., 236
Swidler, A., 103
Symes, C., 195

T

Taber, N., 58, 60

Tamboukou, M., 271–272, 279
Tan, S., 256, 257
Tator, C., 200
Taylor, C., 103
Taylor, G., 26
Taylor, J., 20, 195, 208, 210, 231, 312
Taylor, M., 22, 326
Taylor, T., 320
Tett, L., 302
Thomas, A., 13, 107, 119–120, 141, 147, 149, 319
Thomas, B., 215
Thompson, G., 302
Thomson, W., 25, 28–32, 34
Thwaites, R., 36
Tilford, S., 220, 222, 223
Tipton, S., 103
Tisdell, E., 65, 108
Tobias, J., 39
Tobias, R., 298, 303
Tompkins, J., 25–27, 236, 276
Tones, K., 220, 222, 223
Tong, R., 63–64
Trask, H., 278–279
Tremblay, N., 21, 292
Trussler, T., 266
Turcotte, E., 63
Twiss, D., 286

V

Valdivieso, S., 182
Van Moltke, 252
Verner, C., 141, 264–265, 338
Vonèche, J., 143
Vosko, L., 173, 177
Vygotsky, L., 148–150

W

Wade, A., 314
Walcott, R., 49, 54
Walker, James, 53
Walker, Judith, 19, 173
Wall, C., 215
Wallis, J., 101
Walsh, S., 287
Walters, S., 232, 235
Wanner, 201
Warner, M., 264
Washburn, M., 154, 159
Watkins, M., 177
Weiler, K., 133
Welch, F., 166
Wells, K., 138, 286
Welock, B., 341
Welton, M., 18, 24, 26–27, 31, 36, 74, 121, 132–134, 142, 150, 187, 206, 232, 235–236, 240, 298–300, 302, 355

Wenger, E., 57, 144, 311
Westheimer, J., 69
Westwood, S., 49
Whelan, J., 255
Whitaker, 199
Whitson, D., 304
Wilbur, K., 153
Wilkinson, 200
Williams, M., 220
Williams, R., 49, 140, 143
Willingham, W., 318
Winks, R., 50
Wittorski, R., 296
Woodman, M., 159
Wozney, L., 314

Y

Yoon, E.-S., 183
Youmans, L., 270, 274–275, 278–279
Young, T.R., 204–205
Youngman, F., 236, 240, 247

Z

Zarcadoolas, C., 219, 221
Ziguras, 82
Zong, L., 200, 201

Subject Index

ABC Canada Literacy Foundation, 327-328

Aboriginal adult education in Canada, 36-48, 73, 81-82, 84, 154, 183, 230, 250, 252, 301, 304, 327-328, 331
   acculturation, aboriginal people and, 42
   colonization, 37ff
   Indian control of Indian education, 44-47

accreditation, 200, 316-317, 319

activity theory, cultural-historical, 142, 147, 193

Adult Basic Education (ABE), 45-46, 336

adult education
   aboriginal peoples and, 36-48
   adult citizenship and, 68-80
   adult learning, theories of, 140-151
   arts and, 281-290
   Black communities and, 49-57
   contexts of, 15-22
   critical legacy and, 118-127
   cross-cultural teaching and research and, 81-90
   distance education online and, 307-315
   environmental, 250-259
   health and, 218-228
   immigration and, 198-207
   just learning society and, 24-35
   labour education and, 208-217
   political economy of, 173-186
   philosophy and, 92-104
   prior learning assessment and, 316-325
   professionalization of, 336-346
   queer Canadian communities and, 260-269
   schools of thought (philosophical approaches), 94-103
   theories of adult learning, 140-151
   training and (Quebec), 292-297
   transformations for a new century and, 153-162
   without borders, 347-356
   women and, 58-76
   work, learning and, 187-197
   university extension and, 298-306

adult learning, theories of, 140-151

adult literacy learning, 326-235

African-Canadian community in Alberta, history of, 50ff

agency, concept of, 68-69, 72-74, 76, 78, 101, 121-122, 124, 130-131, 156, 172, 187, 189, 191, 266, 337

andragogy, 84, 95, 108-110, 292-294

Antigonish Movement, the, 25, 32, 58, 74, 119, 232, 236, 270-271, 276-277, 285, 339

Arnold, Mary Ellicott, 276-279

arts, adult education and the, 281-290

assessment of prior learning (APL), use of term, 317
   see also prior learning assessment

assessment, 81, 84, 200, 203-206
   see also prior learning assessment

Atlantic Region Labour Education Centre (ARLEC), 212

auto-ethnography, 60

Banff Centre, as an historical example of relationship of the arts to adult education, 282-83

Blacks in Canada, building identity and community, 49-57
   African Canadian community in Alberta, history of, 50ff
   Living History Group, the (LHG), 55

blended learning delivery model, notion of, 309

Canada Council on Learning, 328

Canadian Charter of Rights and Freedoms, sexual orientation and the, 261

Canadian Labour Congress, labour education and the, 211

Canadian way, adult learning and the, 181-184
   see also political economy, adult education and the

Capilano College (labour education program), 212-213

certification, teaching adult literacy and, 336-337

Citizens' Forum, 28, 74

citizenship, 68-80
   adult citizenship education, 72-75
   concept of, 68-69
   international agenda for, 75
   main orientations, 70-72
   towards an integrated program, 76-78

civil society, 24, 27, 30, 32-34, 75-76, 174-175, 182, 235, 240, 246-247, 347

Coady International Institute, 27

cognition, 143, 145, 148, 151, 188, 233, 311

colonization, aboriginal peoples and, 7ff

commodification, 121, 123, 130, 134

communicative rationality, 132

communities of practice, 49, 54, 57, 193, 195

community development, 44, 72, 285, 287, 301

community, perspectives on adult education, 49-50

compassionate love, as an active relational force, 270
    see also mothers as popular educators

competency-based education, 114, 340

constructivism, 95

cooperatives, the, 126, 171, 216, 339

credentialism, 317

credentials assessment, 200
    see also immigration, changing context of, and work, learning and adult education in Canada

critical adult education
    critical legacy, the, 118-127
    critical pedagogy and, 133-134
    frameworks for a synthesis, 140-152
    mothers as popular educators, 271
    NGO-SM praxis, and 240
    overview, 130-132
    critical praxis, 136-138
    transformation for a new century, 155-157
    university extension revisited, 298-306

cross-cultural teaching and research in adult education, 81-90
    assessment and, 84
    curriculum and, 83-84
    Jamaican example of, 85-86
    research, issues in, 87-89
    technology and, 82

deskilling, 198, 201- 202, 216, 352
    see also immigration, changing context of, and work, learning and adult education in Canada

dialogic, 129, 254

distance education online, 307-315
    socially relevant adult education, and 311-312

ecological knowledge and identity, 254
    see also environmental adult education

economics and social responsibility, 168-170

empowerment, concept of, 78, 101, 133, 191, 194, 218, 221-223, 266-267

environmental adult education, 250-259

epistemology (feminist), 61, 94

essentialism, 49, 54-55, 65, 95, 115, 351-352

ethnography, 60

Eurocentrism, 111

experiential learning, 100, 108, 145, 188, 316-317, 322, 324
    see also prior learning assessment

Farm Forum, 52, 119

feminism, 59, 61-67, 106-107, 113, 131, 275, 299, 347, 351

First Nations, *see* Aboriginal adult education in Canada

Frankfurt School, the, 130-131, 146

Freireian pedagogy, 114, 119

Frontier College, 72, 119, 219-212, 225, 232, 327, 339

gender, 59-67, 157, 232, 235, 255-256

geneology, methodology of, 271-272, 278-279

globalization, 63, 81, 118, 120, 131, 164, 173, 178, 189, 216-217, 239-40, 246, 250, 256-257, 296, 300, 304, 347, 352, 354
    changing workplace, and, 189-196
    adult education and, 348-352

Hamburg Declaration on Adult Education, 75

health, adult education and, 218-228
    critical look at health literacy, 222
    responding to concerns, 220-222

hegemony, 77, 105, 129, 132, 203, 240, 265, 267

heteronormativity, 262

heterosexism, 262

Hitschmanova, Lotta, 272-274

HIV/AIDS, 230, 262-263, 265-266, 268, 349
    grassroots education and, 266

homophobia, 137-138, 262

human capital, 19-20, 164-172, 174-175, 177, 184, 200, 317, 352
    economics and social responsibility, 168-170
    human capital, concept of, 165-166
    knowledge economy and, 164-172
    work and employment, 170-172

human resource management (HRM), 295

human rights, 52, 75-76, 114, 193, 239, 252, 258, 261, 265-266, 271, 301, 348

humanism, 99-101

hybridity, 112, 141, 151

immigration, changing context of, 198-207
see also work, learning and adult education in Canada

imperialism, adult education in the era of, 348-350

inclusivity/inclusion, 16, 18, 58, 60, 68, 70, 77, 84, 114, 137-138, 171-172, 182-183, 234, 330

India, Canadian engagements with indigenous social movements in, 241

indigenous knowledge, 111-112

informal learning, 146, 191-192, 234, 247, 278, 312, 316-320, 323
see also practice-based learning, prior learning assessment

International Monetary Fund (IMF), 120, 170

just learning society, intimations of a, 24-35

knowledge, value of, 167-168

Labour College of Canada, 211

labour education, past and present, 208-217
Atlantic Region Labour Education Centre (ARLEC) and, 212
Canadian Labour Congress, and the, 211
Capilano College (labour education program) and, 212-213
core and other, 214-216
Labour College of Canada and, 211
Niagara College (labour education program) and, 211-213
Workers Educational Association (WEA) and, 209-211

labour movement
see labour education

learning organization, 24, 63, 194, 294-295

learning society, 24-34, 300, 352

LGBTQ (Lesbian, gay, bisexual, trans-identified, queer), 128, 136-138, 267

lifelong learning, 15-16, 20, 24, 36-37, 58-59, 64, 173-176, 181-182, 184, 190, 292, 299, 300, 303-304, 323, 328, 352-353, 355

lifeworld, concept of, 33, 113-114, 122-123, 132-33, 240

Living History Group (LHG), 55

Marx and Marxism, 10, 63, 102, 112-113, 119-126, 144, 146, 149-150, 157, 193, 235-236, 348, 350-351, 353

Mechanics' Institutes, 39, 119

metanarrative, 102, 106

mothers as popular educators, 281-291

movements, social
see social movements, adult education and

National Film Board, as a historical example of relationship of the arts to adult education, 282-83

National Literacy Secretariat, 326

NGO-SM activism, 239-248

Niagara College (labour education program), 211-213

non-governmental organizations (NGOs), 175, 182, 216, 239-240, 243-247, 265-266

North American Free Trade Organization [NAFTA], 177

old social movements and new social movements, 208

online learning
see distance education online

orientations in adult education
see schools of thought in adult education

participatory action research (PAR), 329

philosophy, adult education and, 92-104
schools of thought, 94-103
transformations for a new century, 153-162

political dimension of adult education in Canada, 118-120

political economy, adult education and the, 173-186
political economy of Canada, 177-180

popular education
engagements with social movement in the South, 239-249
mothers as popular educators, 281-291
PAR, popular education and, 247
transnational collaboration, popular education and, 245
see also, social movements, adult education and

positionality, 18, 59, 61, 81, 86-88, 90, 267, 351

postfoundationlism, adult education and 105-117
concept of, 105
examples and specifics, 108-115
contribution to the field, 113-115

poverty, the fight against, 349-350

practice-based learning, 192-193, 195

praxis, definition of, 344

prior learning and recognition (PLAR), use of term, 317
  see also prior learning assessment

prior learning assessment (PLA), 316-325
  student perspective on, 320
  university perspective on, 318
  use of terms, 318-319

professionalism, meaning of, 340
professionalization of adult education, challenges for literacy and basic education, 336-346

program planning, 82, 115, 171

Provincial Support for Adult Education in Nova Scotia (Henson Plan, 1946), 32-34

public mothers, concept of, 270

publication patterns in the field of adult education, 330

qualitative and quantitative research, 59-61

Quebec, training of adult educators, 292-297

queer Canadian adult education, 260-269
  queer theory, 263-265
  see also social movements, adult education and

racism, 50-52, 62-63, 190, 202, 204, 214, 230, 250, 255, 257, 266, 285

recognition of prior learning (RPL), use of term, 317
  see also prior learning assessment

reflexivity, 89, 109, 114, 248

Report of the Royal Commission of Inquiry on Education in the Province of Quebec (1964), 293

research culture, in adult literacy learning, 326-335

schools of thought in adult education (philosophical approaches), 94-103
  liberal orientation, 95
  progressive orientation, 96
  behavioural orientation, 98
  humanist orientation, 99
  radical/critical orientation, 100-101
  postmodern orientation, 102-103

self-directed learning, 84, 108, 110, 121, 145, 149, 313

social movement learning, 231
  theorists of, 233-235
  Canadian contributions to, 235-236

social movements, adult education and, 230-238
  environmental adult education and, 250-259

popular education and, 239-249
queer adult education, 260-269
  see also labour education

socially relevant adult education, online learning and, 311-312

socio-environmental context, adult education and the, 251

story-telling, 117, 280

study circles, 210

synthesis of the field, frameworks for a, 140-152

technical rationality, 121, 123, 135

technology, 81-83, 189-190
  see also distance education online

theory, *see* critical adult education; philosophy, adult education and

Third Way, the (Anthony Giddens), 175-180

trade union movement and adult education, the, *see* labour education

training adult educators (Quebec), 292-297

transformation for a new century, adult education and the, 153-162

university extension revisited, 298-306

virtual classroom, the, 308-311

visible minorities, 56, 198

voluntary organizations, 72, 239

women and adult education in Canada, 58-67
  research on, 58-61
  feminist adult education theories, 61-64
  implications for practice, 64-66

work, learning and adult education in Canada, 187-197
  definitions and contexts, 188-189
  themes, 189
  implications for practice, 195
  see also distance education online, labour education, practice-based learning

Workers' Educational Association (WEA), 26, 32, 49, 209-211, 214

workplace learning, 187-197, 209, 216
  theoretical orientations, 188
  practice-based learning, 192
  see also work, learning and adult education in Canada, labour education

World Social Forum, 244, 312

World Trade Organization (WTO), 177, 246

Youmans, Letitia Creighton, 274-276